BUSINESS CYCLES

BUSINESS CYCLES

DURATIONS, DYNAMICS, AND FORECASTING

Francis X. Diebold and Glenn D. Rudebusch

PRINCETON UNIVERSITY PRESS   PRINCETON, NEW JERSEY

Copyright © 1999 by Princeton University Press
Published by Princeton University Press, 41 William Street,
Princeton, New Jersey 08540
In the United Kingdom: Princeton University Press,
Chichester, West Sussex

Library of Congress Cataloging-in-Publication Data
Diebold, Francis X., 1959–
    Business cycles: durations, dynamics, and
forecasting / Francis X. Diebold and Glenn D.
Rudebusch.
        p. cm.
    Includes bibliographical references and index.
    ISBN 0-691-01218-0 (alk. paper)
    1. Business cycles—Statistical methods.
    2. Business forecasting—Statistical methods.
    I. Rudebusch, Glenn D., 1959– . II. Title.
    HB3711.D54   1999
    338.5'42'0151—dc21   98-34877
                                                                    CIP

This book has been composed in Times Roman.

The paper used in this publication meets the minimum
requirements of ANSI/NISO
Z39.48-1992 (R1997) (*Permanence of Paper*)
http://pup.princeton.edu
Printed in the United States of America
10 9 8 7 6 5 4 3 2 1

To

Susan, Hannah, and Frankie
and
Pat, Katherine, and Jane

Contents

Preface

THIS BOOK brings together much of our joint research on business cycles. Although we were graduate students together at the University of Pennsylvania, our collaboration did not begin in earnest until we arrived at the Federal Reserve Board in 1986. We found the Federal Reserve Board to be a vibrant research arena, with many bright, technically adept colleagues who shared a strong practical interest in understanding the dynamics of the macroeconomy. This heady mix of technical prowess and practical concerns helped fuel our economic investigations. Indeed, the research included in this book is characterized by the application of modern econometric techniques to the classic problems of business cycle analysis. We confront questions of business cycle measurement, modeling, and forecasting with modern methods, including nonparametric analysis, fractional integration, and regime-switching models.

This book, and particularly the first chapter, is an attempt to uncover threads that run through our own work as well as to place recent empirical business cycle research in perspective. In writing academic research papers that have been published with various lags and in disparate places, we have had little opportunity to survey the underlying themes and questions of recent business cycle analyses. The collection of research in this book facilitates such a survey. We have grouped our work into three broad categories. The first of these concentrates on business cycle durations, that is, the lengths of expansions and contractions. The second examines business cycle dynamics more formally in the context of linear models. The final section treats a variety of issues related to forecasting business cycles.

Our debts to others are large. Many colleagues in the Federal Reserve System and in academe have provided guidance and expertise, and this is especially true for the various co-authors for several of the chapters in this book. Above all, however, our families have always provided inspiration and support.

Acknowledgments _____

MUCH OF THIS book was initially published elsewhere. We acknowledge permission to reprint the following articles.

Chapter 2: "Have Postwar Economic Fluctuations Been Stabilized?" by Francis X. Diebold and Glenn D. Rudebusch. Originally published in *American Economic Review*, 82 (1992), 993–1005. Reprinted courtesy of the American Economic Association.

Chapter 3: "Shorter Recessions and Longer Expansions," by Francis X. Diebold and Glenn D. Rudebusch. Originally published in *Business Review*, Federal Reserve Bank of Philadelphia, November–December 1991, 13–20. Reprinted courtesy of Federal Reserve Bank of Philadelphia.

Chapter 4: "A Nonparametric Investigation of Duration Dependence in the American Business Cycle," by Francis X. Diebold and Glenn D. Rudebusch. Originally published in the *Journal of Political Economy*, 98:3 (June 1990), 596–616. © 1990 by The University of Chicago. All rights reserved.

Chapter 5: "Further Evidence on Business-Cycle Duration Dependence," by Francis X. Diebold, Glenn D. Rudebusch, and Daniel E. Sichel. Originally published in *Business Cycles, Indicators, and Forecasting*, ed. J. H. Stock and M. W. Watson, 1993, University of Chicago Press for the NBER, 255–280. © 1993 by the National Bureau of Economic Research. All rights reserved.

Chapter 6: "Measuring Business Cycles: A Modern Perspective," by Francis X. Diebold and Glenn D. Rudebusch. Originally published in *The Review of Economics and Statistics*, 78:1 (February 1996), 67–77. © 1996 by the President and Fellows of Harvard College and the Massachusetts Institute of Technology.

Chapter 7: "Regime Switching with Time-Varying Transition Probabilities," by Francis X. Diebold, Joon-Haeng Lee, and Gretchen C. Weinbach. Originally published in *Nonstationary Time Series Analysis and Cointegration*, ed. C. Hargreaves, 1994, Oxford University Press, 283–302. Reprinted by permission of Oxford University Press.

Chapter 8: "Trends and Random Walks in Macroeconomic Time Series: A Reexamination," by Glenn D. Rudebusch. Originally published in *International Economic Review*, 33 (1992), 661–680. Reprinted courtesy International Economic Review.

Chapter 9: "The Uncertain Unit Root in Real GNP," by Glenn D. Rudebusch. Originally published in *American Economic Review*, 83 (1993), 264–272. Reprinted courtesy of the American Economic Association.

Chapter 10: "The Uncertain Unit Root in Real GNP: Comment," by Francis X. Diebold and Abdelhak S. Senhadji. Originally published in *American Economic Review*, 86, 1996, 1291–1298. Reprinted courtesy of the American Economic Association.

Chapter 11: "Long Memory and Persistence in Aggregate Output," by Francis X. Diebold and Glenn D. Rudebusch. Reprinted from *Journal of Monetary Economics*, 24 (1989), 189–209, with kind permission of Elsevier Science–NL, Sara Burgerhartstraat 25, 1055 KV Amsterdam, The Netherlands.

Chapter 12: "Is Consumption Too Smooth? Long Memory and the Deaton Paradox," by Francis X. Diebold and Glenn D. Rudebusch. Originally published in *The Review of Economics and Statistics*, 73:1 (February 1991), 1–9. © 1991 by the President and Fellows of Harvard College.

Chapter 13: "On the Power of Dickey-Fuller Tests against Fractional Alternatives," by Francis X. Diebold and Glenn D. Rudebusch. Reprinted from *Economics Letters*, 35 (1991) 155–160, with kind permission from Elsevier Science S. A., P. O. Box 564, 1001 Lausanne, Switzerland.

Chapter 14: "The Past, Present, and Future of Macroeconomic Forecasting," by Francis X. Diebold. Originally published in *The Journal of Economic Perspectives*, 2: 2 (Spring 1998), 175–192. Reprinted courtesy of the American Economic Association.

Chapter 15: "Scoring the Leading Indicators," by Francis X. Diebold and Glenn D. Rudebusch. Originally published in *Journal of Business*, 62:3 (July 1989), 369–391. © 1989 by The University of Chicago. All rights reserved.

Chapter 16: "Turning Point Prediction with the Composite Leading Index: A Real-Time Analysis," by Francis X. Diebold and Glenn D. Rudebusch. Originally published in *Leading Economic Indicators: New Approaches and Forecasting Records*, ed. Kajal Lahiri and Geoffrey H. Moore, 1991, Cambridge University Press, 231–256. Reprinted with the permission of Cambridge University Press.

Chapter 17: "Forecasting Output with the Composite Leading Index: An Ex Ante Analysis," by Francis X. Diebold and Glenn D. Rudebusch. Originally published in the *Journal of the American Statistical Association*, 86 (1991) 603–610. Reprinted with permission from the *Journal of the American Statistical Association*. Copyright 1991 by the American Statistical Association. All rights reserved.

Chapter 19: "Comparing Predictive Accuracy," by Francis X. Diebold and Roberto S. Mariano. Originally published in the *Journal of Business and Economic Statistics*, 13 (1995) 253–265. Reprinted with permission from the *Journal of Business and Economic Statistics*. Copyright 1995 by the American Statistical Association. All rights reserved.

BUSINESS CYCLES

Part I _____

INTRODUCTION

Chapter 1 focuses on a few fundamental questions about the empirical nature of business cycles. The answers given to these questions are based on the subsequent chapters of this book and on the research of others. Thus, besides providing an overview of the rest of the book, chapter 1 also places the subsequent chapters in context—both in relation to one another and to the rest of the literature.

1

Questions about Business Cycles

FRANCIS X. DIEBOLD AND GLENN D. RUDEBUSCH

THIS CHAPTER examines five questions about business cycles. They are difficult questions, and we do not provide definitive answers. Instead, we focus on the range of relevant evidence and discussion provided in recent research. These are the five questions we consider:

1. Have business cycles moderated recently? The possible postwar stabilization of the economy has been the subject of much controversy. After reviewing the evidence, our tentative conclusion is that the economy has undergone somewhat shorter and shallower recessions in the postwar period.

2. Do expansions (or contractions) die of old age? We consider whether business cycle regimes are more likely to end as they get longer. Contrary to popular wisdom, we find little supporting evidence in the postwar period for the notion that expansions become more fragile as they age.

3. What are the defining characteristics of the business cycle? We focus our discussion on two issues. The first is how economic variables move together, or co-vary, over the cycle, or, roughly speaking, how broadly business cycles are spread throughout the economy. The notion of co-movement—and particularly accelerated and delayed co-movement —leads naturally to notions of coincident, leading, and lagging business cycle indicators. Second, we consider the timing of the slow alternation between expansions and contractions. In particular, we examine the persistence of business cycle regimes using both linear and nonlinear models.

4. How can secular growth be distinguished from cyclical fluctuations? Understanding the difference between the economy's trend and its cycle is crucial for business cycle analysis. A long debate has raged on the appropriate separation of trend and cycle; we summarize recent elements in this debate and sift the relevant evidence. In the end, a great deal of uncertainty remains; however, it appears to us that some traditional trend/cycle decompositions with quite steady trend growth are not bad approximations in practice.

5. How can business cycles be forecast? We consider a variety of issues associated with the problem of business cycle forecasting, including both forecast methodology and forecast evaluation. We pay special attention to the problem of forecasting business cycle turning points instead of merely predicting the level of future economic activity. We find the index of leading indicators to be a very weak predictor especially when evaluated in a real-time setting.

Question 1: Have Business Cycles Moderated Recently?

It would not be too surprising if the empirical characteristics of business cycles varied secularly over time. There have been important changes in the economy in the postwar era, including, for example, changes in the composition of production and of the labor force, changes in the technology of inventory management, and changes in the importance and behavior of government. All these developments might plausibly affect the nature of economic fluctuations, and in the 1960s and 1970s, the common wisdom was that the U.S. economy had become more stable in the postwar period than before. Indeed, this conclusion fairly leapt from the data: Conventional measures of prewar real output have a variance around trend that is about 70 percent higher than in the postwar period (Baily, 1978). However, the other side of the debate on volatility stabilization was taken by Romer (1986), who argued that the diminished volatility displayed by macroeconomic aggregates spuriously reflected changes in the methods used to construct those aggregates in the postwar period rather than an actual stabilization of the economy.

The course of this debate on stabilization is described in chapters 2 and 3. However, these chapters also introduce a new element, namely a business cycle duration perspective. Whereas the earlier debate focused only on the relative volatility of the economy in the prewar and postwar periods, our analysis in these chapters considers the relative duration of expansions and contractions in the two periods. Specifically, duration stabilization would be reflected by longer expansions and shorter contractions in the postwar period. This new perspective shifts the focus from the relative amplitude of recessions and economic fluctuations to their relative frequency.

In providing evidence for duration stabilization, chapters 2 and 3 employ a different type of data than examined in the previous volatility stabilization literature. We look directly at durations of expansions and contractions obtained from the National Bureau of Economic Research (NBER) chronology of business cycle turning points. This business cycle chronology is constructed from examining the concordance of a large number of business indicators—a much greater variety of series than those included, for example, in the components of real aggregate output. Thus, besides adding a new dimension on which to evaluate postwar stabilization, we also implicitly bring new information to this debate.

To test for duration stabilization, chapters 2 and 3 examine whether the distributions of expansions and contractions have shifted from the prewar period to the postwar period. The null hypothesis is that there has been no change in these distributions, that is, no postwar stabilization. The alternative hypothesis of stabilization states that there have been location shifts in the distributions toward shorter contractions and longer expansions in the postwar period. If the distributions of expansion and contraction durations were normal, then a simple *t*-test of shift in location would suffice. Because these distributions are distinctly nonnormal, we use a distribution-free analog of the *t*-test known as the Wilcoxon test, which uses the ranks of the observations rather than the values of the observations themselves.[1]

Our empirical results are striking. There is a clear rejection of the null hypothesis of no postwar duration stabilization. Expansions have been significantly longer and contractions significantly shorter since World War II.

A crucial issue, of course, given the earlier debate on volatility stabilization, is the historical comparability of prewar and postwar turning point dates in the NBER chronology. For our results to be valid, it is important that a recessionary episode in the prewar period be dated in the same manner as it is in the postwar period. Chapter 3 discusses this topic in some detail. In order to ensure the robustness of our results, we explored numerous variations to the basic chronology that excluded various dubious episodes, and our results remained valid.

Our work on duration stabilization has been directly followed by several careful reexaminations of the evidence that focus on the comparability of the prewar and postwar business cycle dates. Romer (1994) provides a comprehensive historical analysis of the prewar and postwar business cycle chronologies. Following the theme of her work on volatil-

---

[1] The key insight underlying the Wilcoxon test is that, despite the nature of the duration distribution, under the null of no stabilization, the average rank of prewar and postwar durations should be the same. Because exact finite-sample critical values are available for the test, we are assured of correct test size, even in the small samples that are available. In addition, it has been shown that the test has very good power properties.

ity stabilization, she attempts to construct a consistent chronology of turning points over the two periods.[2] She finds much less—but still some—evidence for postwar duration stabilization.[3] Her results suggest that the average lengths of prewar and postwar contractions are roughly equal but that prewar expansions are shorter than postwar expansions. Thus, her results may weaken but do not destroy the evidence for duration stabilization.

Watson (1994) takes a somewhat different approach to the same issue. In a review of the underlying source data, Watson finds little evidence of duration stabilization in the postwar period relative to the period before the Great Depression. For example, he dates turning points in a series on "plans for new buildings" from 1869 through 1929 and in the "building permits" series from 1947 through 1990. As for the many other series he examines, Watson finds little change in average contraction and expansion length across these two series. Of course, there are questions about the dating procedures for individual series and about finding comparable variables in the prewar and postwar periods, especially at a monthly frequency. Still, it is surprising that so little duration stabilization is apparent in individual series given the aggregate evidence. Watson also finds little evidence that duration stabilization could reflect changes in the composition of aggregate output (say, a shift toward a service economy), assuming no duration stabilization in individual sectors. Overall, Watson provides a further cautionary note with regard to the adequacy of the NBER prewar business cycle chronology.

How do we summarize the debate on both postwar volatility and duration stabilization? Although the evidence is not nearly as strong as it seems at first glance, it does appear to us that there has been some moderation in economic fluctuations in the postwar period.[4] The evidence has held up surprisingly well for volatility stabilization (although volatility has not perhaps fallen as much as previously believed). Even Romer's reconstructed measures of aggregate output, which were not uncontrovertible improvements, display a volatility stabilization of about 20 to 30 percent. Watson too finds considerable evidence of reduced variances in the postwar era. For duration stabilization, the evidence is probably just as strong, especially when the joint hypothesis of both

---

[2] Much of Romer's criticism of the NBER's chronology focuses on inconsistent treatment of the trend in dating turning points. Romer's new business cycle chronology is not without critics. For example, Watson (1994) suggests that her procedure may have biases.

[3] Formal tests of duration stabilization using the Romer chronology are conducted by Parker and Rothman (1996).

[4] This is also the conclusion of Zarnowitz's (1992a) comprehensive review of the issue.

longer expansions and shorter contractions is considered. That is, it appears that the *proportion* of time that the economy spends in recession has clearly diminished.[5] This evidence would be further reinforced by the addition of the most recent observations: the short (8-month-long) 1990–91 recession and the very long subsequent expansion.

Several issues regarding macroeconomic stabilization deserve further scrutiny. An obvious but important step for further research would be a careful reconstruction of the prewar business cycle chronology, building on the analyses of Romer and Watson.[6] There are also other dimensions along which macroeconomic performance should be compared in the prewar and postwar eras. For example, the average severity of recessions (as in Romer 1994) and the variability of their duration are interesting objects for study. Finally, of course, understanding the causes of the moderation of business cycles remains a crucial issue. Chapters 2 and 3 provide some discussion of this issue. Zarnowitz (1992a) catalogs fifteen different hypotheses on why the postwar period may have become more stable, and Watson provides some evidence on a few of these. Still, much more analysis is required.

Question 2: Do Expansions (or Contractions) Die of Old Age?

As an ongoing business cycle expansion endures, questions inevitably arise as to when it will end. The general issue of business cycle turning point prediction is examined in question 5 below, but here we deal with a distinct, though related, question: Are long business expansions (or long contractions) more likely than short ones to end soon simply because they are long? In the popular press, it is usually assumed that longer expansions do indeed have a higher mortality rate. For example, in the *Wall Street Journal*, Malabre (1988) cautioned that the ongoing expansion

> endures on a very large amount of borrowed time. Six years old this month, it already has gone on 39 months longer than the average for the previous 30 business-cycle upswings.... Business-cycle experience suggests, in brief, that the present expansion has become exceedingly long in the tooth.... Moreover, there's a broad consensus that the current upswing, regardless of the next recession's arrival date, is at long last manifesting its considerable age in ways bound to complicate economic policy making.

[5] This is particularly true if one includes the Great Depression in the prewar period (unlike Watson, for example). It would seem that avoidance of Great Depressions is one of the manifestations of postwar macroeconomic stabilization.

[6] Boldin (1994) provides a useful review of some methods for dating peaks and troughs of the business cycle.

The exact rationale for such pronouncements of caution is rarely stated, but the analogy to human mortality is straightforward. As the expansion ages, the accumulation of assorted stresses and strains engenders a macroeconomic fragility; thus, the economy is susceptible to and can be jeopardized by ever smaller shocks.

The notion of the increasing fragility of an aging expansion had wide currency among business cycle theorists in the prewar period. Gottfried Haberler's (1937) classic synthesis of prewar business cycle theory devotes an entire section to this topic with the title "Why the Economic System Becomes Less and Less Capable of Withstanding Deflationary Shocks After an Expansion Has Progressed beyond a Certain Point." Additionally, there is a section entitled "Why the Economic System Becomes More and More Responsive to Expansionary Stimuli After the Contraction Has Progressed beyond a Certain Point." In both sections, Haberler finds the reasoning, which is based on the inelasticity of the supply of money and of the factors of production, compelling. Indeed, the fact that an economic expansion or contraction gave rise to "maladjustments in the economic system (counterforces) which tend to check and reverse" itself was usually accepted by early writers as "dogma, at least so far as the expansion is concerned."[7]

Chapters 4 and 5 provide empirical evidence on whether expansions and contractions sow the seeds of their own demise and become progressively more fragile with age. This evidence is obtained from the same duration perspective used in chapters 2 and 3, which searched for potential postwar shifts in the distributions of expansion and contraction durations. Chapters 4 and 5, however, focus on the *shape* of the duration distributions with novel techniques drawn from the literature on hazard and survival analysis. These techniques had been most prominently employed in the analyses of individual mortality rates in medical trials and analyses of failure and reliability rates in engineering problems, although they had been employed in certain microeconomic contexts, including, for example, examinations of the lengths of individual unemployment spells.[8]

As noted in chapter 4, the techniques of survival (or duration or reliability) analysis are extremely well-suited to an investigation of question 2. Question 2 essentially asks whether the conditional probability that an expansion will end given that it has lasted x months

---

[7] In the 1939 revised edition (but not in the original), Haberler does admit to "the possibility of a more or less stationary state with unemployment and fairly stable prices as envisaged by Mr. Keynes and his followers"; that is, an enduring contraction.

[8] See Kiefer (1988) for an excellent introduction to econometric duration analysis. Hazard analysis is also used in a macroeconomic setting in Rudebusch (1995) to model the durations between changes in the monetary policy instrument.

changes as the expansion endures, that is, as x gets larger. If it does not change, then a thirty-month-old expansion has the same chance of ending, or *hazard rate*, as a sixty-month-old expansion. In contrast, an expansion that exhibits a hazard rate with (positive) *duration dependence* will be more likely to end in any given month as it grows older. The crucial insight of survival analysis is that it allows inference about unobservable hazard rates to be made on the basis of the observed distribution of the actual durations (i.e., the unconditional distribution). In the same way, for example, a demographer can calculate the mortality rates at various ages by examining the age distribution of all deaths.

Chapters 4 and 5 take nonparametric and parametric approaches, respectively, to investigating business cycle duration dependence. In the parametric approach, a statistical model of business cycle durations is postulated, parameters are estimated using the available duration data, and inference is conducted about the shape of the distribution of durations and equivalently the presence or absence of duration dependence. The nonparametric approach eschews a particular parametric specification and instead provides a very general test of the shape of the distribution and of the extent of duration dependence. Each approach has certain advantages under specific circumstances.

Reassuringly, both the parametric and the nonparametric approaches give very similar answers.[9] The evidence indicates somewhat different results for the prewar and postwar samples. In the period before World War I, it appears that business expansions were more likely to end as they grew longer (positive duration dependence) but that long contractions were no more likely to end than short ones (no duration dependence). This is true for the United States as well as for France, Germany, and Great Britain (as shown in chapter 5).[10] For the postwar period in the United States (the only country for which consistent data are available), the results are different. The evidence indicates that expansions show no effects of aging or duration dependence, whereas contractions are increasingly likely to end with age. Thus, while prewar business cycle analysts were perhaps accurate in their assessment of expansion duration dependence, postwar commentators are not justified in suggesting that a business cycle peak is more likely to occur as an expansion ages.

Accordingly, chapters 4 and 5 provide evidence for a postwar structural change in the process governing business cycle durations. As noted

---

[9] Largely consistent results are also obtained with an alternative nonparametric procedure in the appendix to chapter 16 and with an alternative parametric approach in Sichel (1991).

[10] See Mudambi and Taylor (1995) for confirming prewar British results with yet another nonparametric methodology.

above, all of these chapters leave open many questions regarding the source of this change. One obvious candidate hypothesis is that the pattern of duration dependence has been altered by the greater influence of the federal government.[11] The highly significant duration dependence of postwar contractions may reflect the commitment of the government to end recessions decisively once they have started (after some recognition lag). Much work, however, remains in understanding the pattern and source of structural change. Hansen (1993) provides a useful step in this direction by applying formal tests of structural stability to the parametric model in chapter 5. He confirms our finding of structural change but does stress that the source of this change is unknown.

Much other recent work has explored the question of duration dependence with a regime-switching model of the type pioneered by Hamilton (1989). We will consider this model in some detail in question 4 below, and chapter 7 essentially presents a variant of this model that allows for variable hazard rates. Important work that builds on ours includes Durland and McCurdy (1994), who modify Hamilton's basic model of the business cycle to allow for duration dependence (in a fashion partly inspired by the work in chapter 7). They calculate hazard rates that are broadly similar to those in chapter 5—significant duration dependence for contractions and very little for expansions. Kim and Nelson (1998a) also confirm our results with a multivariate regime-switching model. In contrast, Lahiri and Wang (1994), who use a Markov-switching model for the leading index, find no evidence of duration dependence.

It should be noted that much of the earlier literature (including chapters 4 and 5) examined whether the hazard rates depended on duration alone without taking into account variation in other factors, such as inventories, balance sheets, and asset prices, which may be important for determining hazard rates.[12] The amount of duration dependence in hazard rates after conditioning on other information is unknown, and further research on this issue remains to be done. The scanty available evidence is from studies that attempt to forecast cyclical turning points, an issue we discuss in question 5 below. For example, one careful study is Stock and Watson (1993), which finds some evidence that, even after conditioning on other variables, the

---

[11] Zarnowitz (1992b) provides some discussion of this issue.

[12] Another possibility is methodological problems, and Hansen's (1993) caution of possible deep identification problems with this approach should be noted.

duration of the current regime is helpful in forecasting the next turning point. We conjecture that their results reflect the strong duration dependence of postwar contractions.

Finally, although the discussion thus far has been in terms of the duration dependence of either expansions or contractions, chapters 4 and 5 also investigate the closely related question of the duration dependence of whole cycles—measured either from peak to peak or from trough to trough. As discussed in chapter 4, the question of whole-cycle duration dependence is one way of asking whether business cycles are periodic. Business cycle periodicity often refers to a regularity in time intervals between similar phases of the business cycle.[13] The existence of such periodicity has long been debated. Mitchell (1927) was an early skeptic, arguing that the term "periodicity" should not be used "with reference to business cycles, or with reference to crises. For the time intervals between crises are far from regular" (p. 378). On the other hand, certain political business cycle theorists (e.g., Klein 1996) and others (e.g., Britton 1986) have argued that periodicity is an important consideration.

Chapter 4 provides some much-needed structure to this debate and, along with chapter 5, offers some empirical evidence on the existence of business cycle periodicity. The key insight is recognizing the equivalence between positive cyclical duration dependence and the clustering of business cycle durations around a specific length. If business cycles are regularly close to four years in length, then cycles that are longer than four years are more likely to end immediately than cycles that are shorter than four years; that is, the cycle must have positive duration dependence. Thus, chapters 4 and 5 apply the nonparametric and parametric techniques described above to peak-to-peak and trough-to-trough business cycle durations. Overall, these investigations find little consistent evidence for even weak business cycle periodicity, a result that has been confirmed and amplified by Mudambi and Taylor (1991).

Question 3: What Are the Defining Characteristics of the Business Cycle?

In the discussion of question 2 (on whether expansions and contractions die of old age), we argued that there is little evidence for periodicity or regularity in the timing of the business cycle. Instead, there are two widely acknowledged key characteristics of the cycle. First, a large

---

[13] This refers to the *weak* periodicity of chapter 4. It differs from the *strong* periodicity that would be evident in spectral analyses as in, for example, Howrey (1971).

number of macroeconomic variables appear to move together; we speak of the *co-movement* of economic series over the cycle. Second, fluctuations in economic activity exhibit *persistence*; deviations from the average or trend level of activity are maintained for considerable lengths of time, as alternations between expansion and recession are fairly slow and broadly diffused throughout the economy.

The prewar literature focused on the first characteristic, co-movement among macroeconomic variables, as the defining attribute of the business cycle; the work of Burns and Mitchell (1946) remains a classic distillation. Chapter 6 provides a modern interpretation of the Burns and Mitchell focus, drawing heavily on the idea that some shocks are sector-specific, whereas others are common, and that the common shocks naturally produce co-movement. Formal models in that vein are said to display factor structure. Dynamic factor models have strong intuitive appeal for business cycle analysis: We observe hundreds of business cycle indicators, each of which fluctuates in part because of dependence on a latent common macroeconomic factor, which represents aggregate macroeconomic shocks, and in part for idiosyncratic reasons.

Static factor models have a long history in multivariate statistical analysis, but dynamic factor models are a more recent construct. Dynamic factor models trace to Sargent and Sims (1977) and Geweke (1977) and underlie a variety of recent and ongoing developments in business cycle analysis, such as the construction of business conditions indicators, as in Stock and Watson (1989, 1997), and the analysis of macroeconomic panel datasets, including cross-country, cross-region, and cross-state business cycle data, as in Quah and Sargent (1993) and Gregory, Head, and Raynauld (1997).

Co-movement is much but certainly not all of the story of business cycles. There are also important considerations regarding the persistence of macroeconomic fluctuations over the cycle. In the response to question 2, we considered the importance of duration in regulating the transition between expansions and contractions. As we consider the second defining characteristic of the business cycle—persistence—we provide a more complete discussion of empirical analyses of business cycle dynamics.

As we also discuss in chapter 6, there is a clear contrast between postwar and prewar conceptions of business cycle persistence. Most of the postwar literature focuses on cyclical models composed of single or multiple linear stochastic difference equations. In contrast, the prewar literature, again well represented by Burns and Mitchell (1946), often focused on the separation of expansions from contractions and the associated idea of turning points. Following the postwar and prewar literatures, we segment our discussion of business cycle persistence into, first, an examination of the dynamic aspects of linear models, and second, an examination of the nonlinear regime-switching perspective.

The postwar linear perspective on business cycle persistence emphasizes linear models of aggregate output and its components. The ideas trace at least to the 1920s, when Slutsky (1927) and Yule (1921) recognized that simple linear stochastic difference equations, or autoregressive processes, converted serially uncorrelated shocks into persistent outputs whose dynamics closely resembled those of many business cycle economic indicators. Frisch (1933) put the Slutsky-Yule framework to work in formulating the idea of impulse and propagation mechanisms in economic dynamics. The idea remains very much alive in modern macroeconomic analyses, whether univariate as in Nelson and Plosser (1982) or multivariate as in the vector-autoregressive tradition initiated by Sims (1980).

The prewar perspective on business cycle dynamics and persistence, in contrast, has a nonlinear flavor associated with emphasis on regime switching between successive periods of expansion and contraction. The idea is also manifest in the great interest in the popular press, for example, in identifying and predicting turning points in economic activity, because it is only within a regime-switching framework that the concept of a turning point has intrinsic meaning.[14] Hamilton (1989) provides an elegant and modern interpretation of the old idea of regime switching. In Hamilton's model, the dynamics of the economy differ in expansions and contractions, with transitions governed by a first-order Markov process. Hence the name "Markov-switching" models.

Many chapters of this book contribute to the study and characterization of persistence in economic time series. On the linear side, we make three main contributions. First, we sound a warning regarding difficulties associated with attempts based on "unit root tests" to determine whether macroeconomic shocks have a permanent component. In chapters 8 and 9, we show that, at least for some key macroeconomic series, the data are simply not informative regarding the existence of a permanent component. At the same time, the analysis of chapter 10 makes clear that uncritical repetition of the "we don't know" mantra is just as scientifically irresponsible as blind adoption of the view that "no macroeconomic series have a permanent component," or the view that "all macroeconomic series have a permanent component." Taken to-

---

[14] In linear frameworks, by way of contrast, there are no turning points, or switch times, in probabilistic structure. One can, of course, define turning points in terms of features of sample paths, but such definitions are fundamentally ad hoc.

gether, chapters 8, 9, and 10 promote more careful use and interpretation of tests for macroeconomic unit roots.

Second, we emphasize that the *importance* of permanent components
in macroeconomic series is a question distinct from the *existence* of
permanent components, and we propose a refined measure of persistence. The essence of the refinement is to measure the effects of shocks
to macroeconomic series not in the infinite future, as in the important
earlier work of Campbell and Mankiw (1987) on which we build, but
rather at the horizons of economic interest, which might be from one to
one hundred years into the future. Chapter 11 implements the ideas for
aggregate output, and chapter 12 focuses on more specialized issues in
the analysis of consumption.

Finally, running throughout chapters 11 through 13 is the idea that
long-memory models, which display fractional integration, provide a rich
and flexible framework for the analysis of macroeconomic persistence.
Since we wrote, there has been an explosion of theoretical and applied
work on long-memory dynamics. Baillie (1996) provides a fine survey of
recent theory, as well as applications to both macroeconomics and
finance; Michelacci and Zaffaroni (1997) provide an interesting recent
macroeconomic contribution.

We also make a number of contributions to the analysis of persistence from the nonlinear regime-switching perspective. Our work in
chapters 4 and 5 on business cycle duration dependence can be viewed
from the vantage point of regime-switching models; it effectively
amounts to inquiring as to whether the transition probabilities are
constant. Our finding of strong duration dependence in postwar U.S.
contractions made us wary of regime-switching models that exclude
from the outset the possibility of time-varying transition probabilities;
hence, in chapter 7, we propose formal models of regime switching that
relax the constant transition probability constraint. Contemporaneous
and independent work of Filardo (1994) pursues similar goals. Subsequent to our and Filardo's work, the literature on allowing for time-
varying transition probabilities in regime-switching models has grown. It
is a dominant theme, for example, in the 1994 *Journal of Business and
Economic Statistics* symposium on Markov-switching models (e.g., Durland and McCurdy, 1994) and is featured prominently in a number of
powerful recent developments, such as Kim and Nelson (1998a,b).

We have discussed our view that dynamic factor structure provides a
useful framework for thinking about business cycle co-movement,
and we have similarly discussed our contributions to linear and nonlinear analysis of persistence. We hasten to add that the dynamic factor
framework facilitates combination of those ideas. In particular, in
chapter 6, we suggest interpreting business cycles, and the history of

business cycle analysis, through the lens of a dynamic factor model with a Markov-switching factor, possibly with time-varying transition probabilities. The factor structure incorporates linear dynamics and co-movement in the usual way, and it also incorporates nonlinearity via the Markov-switching factor, resulting in a multivariate dynamic regime-switching model with commonality in the timing of turning points across business cycle indicators.

Since we wrote, a number of authors have provided what we only suggested: rigorous econometric fitting of the model to business cycle data. Kim (1994) provides the key filtering theory for a very general class of state space models, which includes ours as a special case, and shows how to obtain approximate maximum-likelihood estimates. Kim and Yoo (1995) and Chauvet (1998) use the Kim algorithm to obtain approximate maximum-likelihood estimates of the dynamic factor/Markov-switching business cycle model; they extract estimates of the factor (the "coincident index"), using both quarterly and monthly data and a variety of detrending procedures.

Most recently, a number of authors, including Filardo and Gordon (1996) and Kim and Nelson (1998a,b), have exploited recent advances in Markov Chain Monte Carlo to perform Bayesian analyses of the Diebold-Rudebusch model and comparisons to other models. Kim and Nelson (1998a,b), in particular, use a multi-move Gibbs sampler to estimate the Diebold-Rudebusch model, allowing for time-varying transition probabilities. They find that both co-movement and regime switching are empirically relevant features of the cycle, and moreover, they confirm in a multivariate framework the univariate Diebold-Rudebusch finding that U.S. contractions display clear positive duration dependence, whereas expansions do not. Finally, they extract an estimate of the latent factor from the model, which is effectively a composite index of coincident indicators, and find that its turning points coincide remarkably closely with those designated by the NBER.

Question 4: How Can Secular Growth Be Distinguished from Cyclical Fluctuations?

Macroeconomic analysis and research has generally maintained an important distinction between the trend and cyclical components of macroeconomic time series. The former described the long-run growth path of the economy, whereas the latter represented the short-run fluctuations about this trend. Indeed, theories of economic growth, stressing real human and physical capital accumulation and productivity, and theories of business fluctuations, often emphasizing nominal rigidities, were typically constructed without reference to one another. In empirical work, a similar dichotomy was assumed in that detrended data were often employed for business cycle analysis.[15]

If indeed there is little interaction between the trend growth of the economy and its short-run fluctuations, then analysts are justified in removing the trend from the data in order to bring the business cycle into better focus. However, even assuming that the trend and cycle are largely independent of one another, instability in the trend component can complicate the separation of trend from cycle. If the economy is fluctuating around a steady growth path, it is relatively easy to discern its cyclical deviations. In fact, in the 1960s and 1970s, a common practice among almost all economists was to assume that the long-run growth of the economy followed a simple linear deterministic trend. Although perhaps a useful approximation, the assumption of a constant deterministic trend seems somewhat implausible over long historical periods where there were likely structural changes in the economy as well as varying rates of factor accumulation and technical progress. Thus, it is plausible to entertain the notion of shifts or breaks in the trend or even period-by-period random or *stochastic* trends. Such variability in the trend complicates its separation from the cycle.

These twin issues—the exogeneity and the variability of the economy's trend—have been the subject of heated debate in macroeconomics over the past two decades. This debate was initiated by Nelson and Plosser (1982), who argued that macroeconomic time series such as real output and employment were better represented as stochastic processes that have no tendency to return to a deterministic linear trend (so-called difference stationary or DS processes) than as processes that do have such a tendency (that is, trend stationary or TS processes). In essence, Nelson and Plosser argued that the trends in many macroeconomic series were stochastic, and they supported their position with the results of a "unit root" statistical test for each time series. These test results could find no evidence for variables such as real output and employment that disagreed with a DS representation. This suggestion of a stochastic rather than a deterministic trend had a profound influence on macroeconomic theory and empirical work. Many embraced Nelson and Plosser's results as confirmation of a stochastic trends view of macroeconomic dynamics. Notably, Campbell and Mankiw (1987) argued that postwar real output followed a DS process; therefore, a shock to the level of output in any period shifted the entire future path of output. In this way, the effects of a shock were not eliminated through reversion to

---

[15] The use of such detrended data is exactly analogous to the use of seasonally adjusted data, which is done on the assumption that the seasonal cycle is independent of business fluctuations (see, e.g., Miron and Beaulieu 1996).

trend but persisted indefinitely. This stochastic or variable trend view of the world began to predominate among researchers (e.g., Stock and Watson, 1988).

Chapters 8 through 13, in large part, take issue with this stochastic trends consensus. These chapters argue that at the very least there is considerable uncertainty regarding the nature of the trend in many macroeconomic time series, and that, in particular, assuming a fairly stable trend growth path for real output—perhaps even a linear deterministic trend—may not be a bad approximation.

Chapter 8 confronts the Nelson and Plosser evidence directly. It uses precisely their data set but employs a different methodology for conducting inference about unit roots. This methodology focuses on two issues. First, by using the small-sample distributions of the test statistics, the precise amount of evidence that is contained in the relatively short data samples available can be determined. Second, by investigating the distributions of the test statistic under *both* the DS and TS models, the evidence regarding the validity of each of these models can be considered. Both of these issues turn out to be crucial. Chapter 8 shows that the Nelson and Plosser data sample does not support the proposition that unit roots or stochastic trends are a pervasive element in real macroeconomic time series. Indeed, the Nelson and Plosser data do not appear to be able to differentiate between plausible DS and TS representations for many series.

Chapters 9 and 10 apply this small-sample testing methodology to other real output data series and again find little decisive evidence for the DS model.[16] Chapter 9 examines postwar quarterly real GNP, and, again, the unit root tests say little about the relative likelihood of plausible DS and TS models of the data even though these models display distinctly different dynamics at cyclical horizons (of, say, less than five years). Thus, typical point estimates of dynamic persistence using this data set, say, in Campbell and Mankiw (1987), are misleading because they ignore the large uncertainty regarding the estimates. Chapter 10 considers several annual U.S. output series that stretch over a hundred years to 1875. With this long span of data, the TS model is distinctly favored over the DS model; that is, the deterministic trend model appears to fit the past century of data fairly well.[17]

---

[16] Also see Cheung and Chinn (1997).

[17] Although using such a long span of data, even at an annual frequency, holds the potential for illuminating the importance of a unit root (Perron 1989), some caveats should be noted. The U.S. prewar real output data are of distinctly lower quality than the postwar data, which may be cause for some concern (though Cheung and Chinn [1997] argue not). In particular, Murray and Nelson (1998) argue that spurious data outliers will prejudice the evidence against DS models. In addition, studies of countries (e.g., Kormendi and Meguire 1990), some of which have better long-span data than the United States, generally favor DS specifications over TS ones.

Chapters 11, 12, and 13 provide a different perspective on the trend-cycle decomposition and the persistence of macroeconomic shocks. These chapters introduce and explore a general statistical model of *fractional integration* (introduced as the ARFIMA model) that nests the DS and TS models as special cases. Here, too, the conclusion is that, for many real-time series, there is a great deal of uncertainty with regard to any estimate of macroeconomic persistence and the decomposition of trend and cycle.[18]

What can we conclude then about the nature of trend and cycle decompositions? As a blanket statement, painfully little. The safest recommendation is to approach each time series with an open mind and consider the sensitivity of the results to a variety of assumptions about the variability of the trend. For U.S. real output, it appears that a trend representation that is very smooth, even if not exactly linear, is a viable candidate.[19]

Question 5: How Can Business Cycles Be Forecast?

Almost all the chapters in this book implicitly touch on, and are relevant for, macroeconomic forecasting. Our earlier discussions of the moderation of the postwar business cycle, duration dependence in expansions and contractions, business cycle co-movement and persistence, and the separation of secular from cyclical fluctuations, all have clear implications for forecasting.

As contained in Part IV, however, some of our work is even more intimately and explicitly linked to business cycle forecasting. In particular, chapter 14 is an assessment of the past, present, and future of macroeconomic forecasting. The discussion—which is both descriptive and prescriptive—argues that, broadly defined, macroeconomic forecasting is alive and well. Nonstructural forecasting, which is based largely on reduced-form correlations, has always been well and continues to improve. Structural forecasting, which aligns itself with economic theory and hence rises and falls with theory, receded following the decline of Keynesian theory in the 1970s but is poised for possible

[18] These conclusions are supported in further work by Sowell (1992) and Hassler and Wolters (1994).

[19] There is also other work in the same spirit that attempts to explore some middle ground between the TS and DS models. Notably, some models allow for limited flexibility in trend through trend shifts and trend breaks (Perron 1989, 1997; Balke and Fomby 1991; Bradley and Jansen 1995; Cogley 1997). These allow for discrete breaks in the trend but only rarely and not in every period as in the DS model.

resurgence in the wake of the powerful new dynamic stochastic general equilibrium theory developed subsequently.

Still, even if the new structural models are off to a good start, they nevertheless have a long way to go if they are to be truly useful for macroeconomic forecasting. Workable estimation strategies, for example, are still in their infancy and need further development.[20] Moreover, the models will have to be fleshed out with richer impulse and propagation dynamics, and the possibility of parameter non-constancy will have to be taken seriously, because for a number of reasons discussed subsequently, the allegedly "deep structural parameters" of the new models may not be immune to the Lucas (1976) critique.

Following the discussion of broad issues in chapter 14, we delve into two key themes in greater detail: The first is the meaning, use, and forecasting ability of leading economic indicators, and the second is the evaluation and comparison of forecasters and forecasting models, often on a real-time basis, rather than on the usual ex post basis with the full sample of final revised data.

Forecasting with a Composite Leading Index

Much, although not all, of our work on business cycle forecasting proceeds from the nonlinear business cycle perspective discussed above in our answer to question 3. By the time we began working in the area in 1986, a nonlinear perspective was starting a modern resurgence, as evidenced, for example, by the contemporaneous and independent work of Hamilton (1989). Without doubt, however, we owe a great debt to Neftci's (1982) pioneering work, which helped us recognize that turning points are most naturally defined in nonlinear models of regime switching, shaped our views on probabilistic characterizations of business cycle dynamics involving regime switching, and piqued our curiosity regarding business cycle duration dependence.

Our first research on the leading indicators (chap. 15) viewed turning points as times of regime switches. We generated business cycle turning point forecasts using nonlinear methods for assessing the regime of the composite index of leading economic indicators. As the evidence mounts for a turning point in the composite index, the probabilistic assessment of an imminent turning point in the business cycle (within the next six months, say) rises. The turning point forecasts are then evaluated using

---

[20] In particular, as noted in chapter 18, the popular Generalized Method of Moments (GMM) strategy for estimating deep parameters may exhibit poor finite-sample performance.

variants of a scoring rule originally proposed by Brier (1950).[21] Perhaps surprisingly, we judge the performance of U.S. turning point forecasts produced using the composite leading index to be quite poor.

The poor performance of the composite leading index in turning point prediction is a sobering finding, particularly when one considers that the poor predictive performance obtains even though the final revised leading index used in the exercise of chapter 15 contains a wealth of information not available in real time. One would expect the turning point forecasting ability of the leading index actually available in real time to be no better, and potentially much worse, because the index is subject to extensive revisions. We confirm that conjecture in the real-time U.S. turning point forecasting analysis of chapter 16.

Given the potential insights to be gained from ex ante or real-time forecast evaluations, as opposed to the conventional ex post evaluations, in chapter 17 we continue our inquiry into prediction with the composite leading index in real time, this time in a standard linear framework. Our analysis is motivated by Auerbach (1982), who performs a standard Granger-Sims causality test using the revised leading index and concludes that it has strong predictive power. Again, the extensive revisions to which the leading index is subject and our negative findings in chapter 16 regarding turning point prediction in real time make us similarly doubtful about the real-time predictive ability of the leading index using linear methods. Hence, we study the ability of the composite leading index to predict industrial production in a linear model, taking care to use only the leading index data that were actually available in real time. We effectively do a real-time Granger-Sims causality test, by comparing the forecasting ability of two models: In the first, industrial production is regressed only on lags of itself, and in the second, industrial production is regressed on lags of the composite leading index in addition to lags of itself. As it turns out, our real-time analysis produces a dramatic reversal of Auerbach's results: In real time, including lags of the leading index in an autoregression fails to improve forecasting performance.

Taken as a whole, our work casts doubt on the effectiveness of what was often called "the government's primary forecasting tool" and leads one to question what, if anything, the leading index leads. Others, for example, Koenig and Emery (1991, 1994), have subsequently confirmed our results for the U.S. business cycle. In fact, since we delivered our pessimistic assessment of the track record of the composite index of

---

[21] The use of econometric probability forecasts and associated scoring rules has increased recently. For interesting recent contributions, see Lopez (1996) and Estrella and Mishkin (1995); for a recent survey, see Diebold and Lopez (1996).

leading economic indicators, the U.S. government has gotten out of the business, having transferred the rights to the Conference Board in the mid-1990s.

In much of the contemporaneous and subsequent work on the construction and use of composite indexes of economic indicators, including that of the Conference Board as well as Stock and Watson (1989, 1993, 1997), greater care is taken to implement statistically rigorous and replicable methods of leading index construction, with reduced emphasis on the periodic reweighting or redefining of the index that can make its predictive ability appear much better ex post than in real time.

In other countries, similarly poor performance of indexes of leading indicators has been documented recently. For example, Artis et al. (1995a) examine the performance of the U.K. Central Statistical Office's indexes of leading indicators for predicting turning points in the United Kingdom's growth cycle. They examine two indexes, one designed to have a short lead time and one designed to have a longer lead time. Even though Artis et al. use ex post values of the leading indexes (real-time values are not available), the short index performs poorly, and the long index performs only a little better.

At the same time, others have occasionally found more encouraging results in the United States using different methods. Lahiri and Wang (1994), for example, use an alternative nonlinear procedure: They model regime switching in the composite leading index using Hamilton's Markov-switching framework, and they find good forecasting performance even with the real time or ex ante data. Lahiri and Wang note, however, that their analysis differs in several important ways from ours, and they issue some strong caveats regarding their optimistic results.

In an interesting development, Hamilton and Perez-Quiros (1996) use an alternative *linear* procedure and also obtain encouraging results for the United States. They find that the composite leading index is useful for forecasting gross national product (GNP), both in sample and in an out-of-sample real-time exercise. They begin with a nonlinear specification in which cyclical shifts in the composite leading index precede those in GNP, but they find that better forecasts are provided by a simple linear relation between current GNP growth and lagged growth in the composite leading index, along with an error-correction term corresponding to the lagged logarithmic difference between GNP and the composite leading index.

Finally, we look forward to new analyses making use of more novel and focused indicators. For example, following Stock and Watson (1989), Estrella and Mishkin (1995) have some success in forecasting U.S. turning points using financial variables, in particular, the term structure "tilt" and the spread of corporate over treasury bonds. Reinhart and

Reinhart (1996) examine the ability of similar financial variables for forecasting Canadian turning points and find that they perform well, even though the Canadian composite leading index does poorly. The good performance of financial variables in forecasting many U.S. and Canadian recessions, however, should be tempered by their miserable performance in forecasting the most recent U.S. recession of 1990. As for the key issue of whether the recent poor predictive performance of the term structure was merely a bad draw, or whether a structural break occurred, only time will tell.

We also look forward to more applications that forecast variables other than the traditional NBER reference cycle. Artis et al. (1995b), for example, use leading indicators to forecast turning points in U.K. inflation and obtain good results. Kaminsky et al. (1997) take a leading indicator approach to forecasting currency crises, with good results, and their analysis could be extended in a variety of ways. For example, they use single indicators rather than combining them either via an index or by running a regression.

Evaluating Forecasters and Forecasting Models

The second key theme running through our work is concern with evaluating and comparing business cycle forecasts and forecasting models. One manifestation of that theme is our use of forecast accuracy comparisons to help separate true predictive value from the spurious effects of data mining, as illustrated in the evaluations of turning point forecasts in chapters 15 and 16. A number of subsequent authors followed our lead; one prominent example is Mark's (1995) study of foreign exchange rate fluctuations, in which he argues that economic "fundamentals" affect the determination of exchange rates, by showing that the current deviation of an exchange rate from its fundamental value has predictive content for its long-term evolution.

In chapter 18, we examine the forecasting accuracy of older (e.g., accelerator) and newer (Euler equation) models of a key macroeconomic variable: business fixed investment. Many would regard the allegedly "deep structural" specification of the Euler equation model as likely to produce superior forecasts, but the forecasting competition indicates otherwise: The new models fare much worse than the old.

Chapter 18 has important implications for the empirical significance of the Lucas critique and has stimulated research in that direction. For example, in light of the poor predictive performance of Euler equation investment models, Oliner et al. (1996) assess the structural stability of the new models and find that they are no more stable than the older models, even though the new models were designed to be immune to the Lucas critique. Perhaps the structural instability of the new models is due to their reliance on the representative agent paradigm, which would be consistent with the work of Geweke (1985), Kirman (1992), and Altissimo (1997), who show that "the representative agent" can change when policy changes.

We also have developed formal statistical tests for assessing the significance of apparent accuracy differences across forecasters. Given the obvious desirability of a formal statistical procedure for forecast accuracy comparisons, one is struck by the casual manner in which such comparisons are typically carried out. The literature contains literally thousands of forecast accuracy comparisons; almost without exception, point estimates of forecast accuracy are examined, with no attempt to assess their sampling uncertainty. Our work owes a great debt to Granger and Newbold (1986), who make creative use of an orthogonalizing transformation pioneered by Morgan (1939–40) in developing a forecast accuracy comparison test. Their test, however, depends on a number of restrictive assumptions, which we begin to relax in the context of assessing the results of the forecasting horse race of chapter 17 and fully relax in chapter 19. Our forecast accuracy comparison methods have been refined and extended by West (1996), West and McCracken (1998), and Harvey, Leyborne, and Newbold (1997, 1998).

Conclusion

As should be evident, although much has been done, many questions about business cycles remain unanswered. Indeed, it should be stressed that our investigations thus far have been limited in scope and that we are disappointed about not yet investigating several other important business cycle questions.

For example, there is the basic question of, What are the causes of business cycles? Can we formulate an explanatory model of economic fluctuations, instead of just a statistical or forecasting description of business cycles? In our judgment, there has been very little success in the literature in forging a consensus about the nature of such an explanatory model. For example, it is instructive, although dismaying, to examine the analyses of Blanchard (1993), Hall (1993), Hansen and Prescott (1993), and Walsh (1993), which try to determine the causes for one particular contractionary episode, the recession of 1990–91. In these papers, a long list of explanations is considered and various models are estimated, but no clear causal driving force is uncovered. In the end, the leading causal candidates vary substantially across papers and include: (1) a spontaneous decline in consumer confidence (i.e., animal spirits); (2) a jump in oil prices; (3) a deliberate disinflation by the central bank; (4) a negative technology shock, perhaps through a change to the legal and regulatory system. Indeed, Hall (1993, p. 278) candidly summarizes his analysis with: "I conclude that established models are unhelpful in understanding this recession, and probably most of its predecessors." This broad sentiment is shared by Blanchard and Fisher (1989, p. 277) who state that "there is little agreement as to the main sources of [business cycle] disturbances—monetary or real, and if real from changes in tastes or in technology, from the private sector, or from the government."

We also have not given any detailed treatment of international considerations. For example, an interesting question for future research is, What are the similarities in business cycles across different countries? The existing literature, although not extensive, suggests that there is a commonality in the cyclical behavior of real quantities across countries (e.g., Backus and Kehoe, 1992). Thus, it seems that one could usefully pool cross-country evidence to ascertain business cycle characteristics, as, for example, in chapter 5. A related international business cycle question is, What are the linkages across business cycles in different countries? The extent and nature of a "world" business cycle is largely unknown. There are clearly some global business cycle shocks, such as the oil price increases of the 1970s, as well as international propagation mechanisms acting through foreign trade and capital flows. Canova and Dellas (1993), Gregory, Head, and Raynauld (1997), and Artis et al. (1997) provide useful introductions to some of these issues and make some progress toward exploration of business cycle synchronization across countries.

A final question is, What is the appropriate role for countercyclical government policy? Especially since the Great Depression and the Keynesian Revolution, debate has raged about the proper role for monetary and fiscal policy in smoothing the business cycle. The Employment Act of 1946 legislated a government responsibility to promote full employment and production, and many policymakers and economists have continued to believe in the importance of active stabilization policy. For example, Yellen (1996) argues that monetary policy "is needed, and has succeeded, in smoothing the ups and downs of the business cycle." Other economists have been persuaded by old arguments about the long and variable lags of policy or new arguments about the Lucas critique and time inconsistency, and they doubt the effectiveness, and perhaps even the influence, of any active stabilization policy.

In this book, we discuss closely related issues many times. Of course, the whole point of chapters 2 and 3 is to describe and quantify the postwar stabilization of the business cycle, which government policy may have played a major role in achieving. At a deeper level, however, as discussed in chapter 11, the whole notion of countercyclical policy may need to be rethought in a world with stochastic trends. Regarding the narrower operational question of the appropriate conduct of policy, as noted above, any increasing fragility of aging business expansions, or duration dependence—chapters 4 and 5—complicates countercyclical policy. More generally, given the lags in the effects of policy on the economy, the issue of forecasting the business cycle is crucial to making good policy (see Rudebusch and Svensson 1998). This last fact provided the main motivation for much of our research contained in the final set of chapters on forecasting the business cycle and, in particular, for the real-time analyses with leading indicators in chapters 16 and 17. Still, many questions regarding policy and business cycles, which are arguably among the most important to be considered, remain unanswered.

References

Altissimo, Fillipo (1997), "Essays in Macroeconometrics," Ph.D. dissertation, University of Pennsylvania.

Artis, Michael J., Robin C. Bladen-Hovell, Denise R. Osborn, Graham W. Smith, and Wenda Zhang (1995a), "Turning Point Prediction for the U.K. Using CSO Leading Indicators," *Oxford Economic Papers*, 47, 397–417.

—— (1995b), "Predicting Turning Points in the U.K. Inflation Cycle," *Economic Journal*, 105, 1145–64.

Artis, Michael J., Zenon G. Kontolemis, and Denise R. Osborn (1997), "Business Cycles of G7 and European Countries," *Journal of Business*, 70, 249–79.

Auerbach, Alan J. (1982), "The Index of Leading Indicators: 'Measurement without Theory' Thirty-Five Years Later," *Review of Economics and Statistics*, 64, 589–95.

Backus, David K., and Patrick J. Kehoe (1992), "International Evidence on the Historical Properties of Business Cycles," *American Economic Review*, 82, 864–900.

Baillie, Richard T. (1996), "Long Memory Processes and Fractional Integration in Econometrics," *Journal of Econometrics*, 73, 5–59.

Baily, Martin Neil (1978), "Stabilization Policy and Private Economic Behavior," *Brookings Papers on Economic Activity*, (1), 11–60.

Balke, Nathan S., and Thomas B. Fomby (1991), "Shifting Trends, Segmented Trends, and Infrequent Permanent Shocks," *Journal of Monetary Economics*, 28, 61–85.

Blanchard, Olivier (1993), "Consumption and the Recession of 1990–1991," *American Economic Review, Papers and Proceedings*, 83, 270–74.

Blanchard, Olivier Jean, and Stanley Fisher (1989), *Lectures on Macroeconomics.* Boston: MIT Press.

Boldin, Michael (1994), "Dating Turning Points in the Business Cycle," *Journal of Business*, 67, 97–131.

Bradley, Michael D., and Dennis W. Jansen (1995), "Unit Roots and Infrequent Large Shocks: New International Evidence on Output Growth," *Journal of Money Credit and Banking*, 27, 876–93.

Brier, G. W. (1950), "Verification of Forecasts Expressed in Terms of Probability," *Monthly Weather Review*, 75, 1–3.

Britton, Andrew (1986), *The Trade Cycle in Britain, 1958–1982.* Cambridge: Cambridge University Press.

Burns, Arthur F., and Wesley C. Mitchell (1946), *Measuring Business Cycles.* New York: National Bureau of Economic Research.

Campbell, John Y., and N. Gregory Mankiw (1987), "Are Output Fluctuations Transitory?" *Quarterly Journal of Economists*, 102, 857–80.

Canova, Fabio, and Harris Dellas (1993), "Trade Interdependence and the International Business Cycle," *Journal of International Economics*, 34, 23–47.

Chauvet, Marcelle (1998), "An Econometric Characterization of Business Cycle Dynamics with Factor Structure and Regime Switching," *International Economic Review*, 39, 969–96.

Cheung, Yin-Wong, and Menziw D. Chinn (1997), "Further Investigation of the Uncertain Unit Root in GNP," *Journal of Business and Economic Statistics*, 15, 68–73.

Cogley, Timothy (1997), "Evaluating Non-Structural Measures of the Business Cycle," *Economic Review*, No. 3, Federal Reserve Bank of San Francisco, 3–21.

Diebold, Francis X., and Jose A. Lopez (1996), "Forecast Evaluation and Combination," in G. S. Maddala and C. R. Rao (eds.), *Handbook of Statistics*, Amsterdam: North-Holland, 241–68.

Durland, J. Michael, and Thomas H. McCurdy (1994), "Duration-Dependent Transitions in a Markov Model of U.S. GNP Growth," *Journal of Business and Economic Statistics*, 12, 279–88.

Estrella, Arturo, and Frederic S. Mishkin (1995), "Prediction U.S. Recessions: Financial Variables as Leading Indicators," NBER Working Paper No. 5379, Cambridge, Mass.

Filardo, Andrew J. (1994), "Business-Cycle Phases and Their Transitional Dynamics," *Journal of Business and Economic Statistics*, 12, 299–308.

Filardo, Andrew J., and Stephen F. Gordon (1996), "Business Cycle Turning Points: Two Empirical Business Cycle Model Approaches," Manuscript, Research Department, Federal Reserve Bank of Kansas City.

Frisch, Ragnar (1933), "Propagation Problems and Impulse Problems in Dynamic Economics," in *Economic Essays in Honor of Gustav Cassel.* London: Allen and Unwin.

Geweke, John (1977), "The Dynamic Factor Analysis of Economic Time-Series Models," in D. J. Aigner and A. S. Goldberger (eds.), *Latent Variables in Socioeconomic Models.* Amsterdam: North-Holland, 365–83.

—— (1985), "Macroeconomic Modeling and the Theory of the Representative Agent," *American Economic Review*, 75 (May), 206–10.

Granger, Clive W. J., and Paul Newbold (1986), *Forecasting Economic Time Series*, 2d ed. Orlando, Fla.: Academic Press.

Gregory, Alan W., Allen C. Head, and Jacques Raynauld (1997), "Measuring World Business Cycles," *International Economic Review*, 38, 677–701.

Haberler, Gottfried (1937), *Prosperity and Depression: A Theoretical Analysis of Cyclical Movements*. Geneva: League of Nations.

—— (1939), *Prosperity and Depression: A Theoretical Analysis of Cyclical Movements*, rev ed. Geneva: League of Nations.

Hall, Robert E. (1993), "Macro Theory and the Recession of 1990–91," *American Economic Review, Papers and Proceedings*, 83, 275–79.

Hamilton, James D. (1989), "A New Approach to the Economic Analysis of Nonstationary Time Series and the Business Cycle," *Econometrica*, 57, 357–84.

Hamilton, James D., and Gabriel Perez-Quiros (1996), "What Do the Leading Indicators Lead?" *Journal of Business*, 69, 27–49.

Hansen, Bruce E. (1993), "Further Evidence on Business-Cycle Duration Dependence: Comment," in J. H. Stock and M. W. Watson (eds.), *Business Cycles, Indicators, and Forecasting*. Chicago: University of Chicago Press for the NBER, 280–84.

Hansen, Gary D., and Edward C. Prescott (1993), "Did Technology Shocks Cause the 1990–1991 Recession?" *American Economic Review, Papers and Proceedings*, 83, 280–86.

Harvey, David I., Stephen J. Leybourne, and Paul Newbold (1997), "Testing the Equality of Prediction Mean Squared Errors," *International Journal of Forecasting*, 13, 281–91.

—— (1998), "Tests for Forecast Encompassing," *Journal of Business and Economic Statistics*, 16, 254–59.

Hassler, Uwe, and Jurgen Wolters (1994), "On the Power of Unit Root Tests Against Fractional Alternatives," *Economics Letters*, 45, 1–5.

Howrey, E. Philip (1971), "Stochastic Properties of the Klein-Goldberger Model," *Econometrica*, 39, 73–87.

Kaminsky, Graciela, Saul Lizondo, and Carmen M. Reinhart (1997), "Leading Indicators of Currency Crises," Working Paper, International Monetary Fund.

Kiefer, Nicholas M. (1988), "Economic Duration Data and Hazard Functions," *Journal of Economic Literature*, 26, 646–79.

Kim, Chang-Jin (1994), "Dynamic Linear Models with Markov-Switching," *Journal of Econometrics*, 60, 1–22.

Kim, Chang-Jin, and Charles R. Nelson (1998a), "Business Cycle Turning Points, A New Coincident Index, and Tests of Duration Dependence Based on A Dynamic Factor Model with Regime-Switching," *Review of Economics and Statistics*, 80, 188–201.

—— (1998b), *Dynamic Time Series Models and Markov Switching: Classical and Gibbs Sampling Approaches with Applications*. Manuscript, Department of Economics, University of Washington.

Kim, Myung-Jig, and Ji-Sung Yoo (1995), "New Index of Coincident Indicators: A Multivariate Markov Switching Factor Model Approach," *Journal of Monetary Economics*, 36, 607–30.

Kirman, Alan (1992), "Whom or What Does the Representative Agent Represent?" *Journal of Economic Perspectives*, 6, 117–36.

Klein, Michael W. (1996), "Timing Is All: Elections and the Duration of United States Business Cycles," *Journal of Money, Credit, and Banking*, 28, 84–101.

Koenig, Evan F., and Kenneth M. Emery (1991), "Misleading Indicators? Using the Composite Leading Indicators to Predict Cyclical Turning Points," *Economic Review*, Federal Reserve Bank of Dallas, July, 1–14.

—— (1994), "Why the Composite Index of Leading Indicators Does Not Lead," *Contemporary Economic Policy*, 12, 52–66.

Kormendi, Roger C., and Philip A. Meguire (1990), "A Multicountry Characterization of the Nonstationarity of Aggregate Output," *Journal of Money, Credit and Banking*, 22, 77–93.

Lahiri, Kajal, and Jiazhuo G. Wang (1994), "Predicting Cyclical Turning Points with a Leading Index in a Markov Switching Model," *Journal of Forecasting*, 13, 245–63.

Lopez, Jose A. (1996), "Regulatory Evaluation of Value-at-Risk Models," Manuscript, Research and Market Analysis Group, Federal Reserve Bank of New York.

Lucas, Robert E. (1976), "Econometric Policy Evaluation: A Critique," in K. Brunner and A. Meltzer (eds.), *The Phillips Curve and the Labor Market* (Carnegie-Rochester Conference Series, Vol. 1). Amsterdam: North-Holland, 19–46.

Malabre, Alfred L. (1988), "An Aging Expansion Complicates Policy," *Wall Street Journal*, November 14, A1.

Mark, Nelson (1995), "Exchange Rates and Fundamentals: Evidence on Long-Horizon Predictability," *American Economic Review*, 85, 201–18.

Michelacci, Claudio, and Paolo Zaffaroni (1997), "(Fractional) Beta Convergence," Manuscript, London School of Economics.

Miron, Jeffrey, and Joeseph Beaulieu (1996), "What Have Macroeconomists Learned about Business Cycles from the Study of Seasonal Cycles?" *Review of Economics and Statistics*, 78, 54–66.

Mitchell, Wesley C. (1927), *Business Cycles: The Problem and Its Setting*. New York: NBER.

Morgan, W. A. (1939–1940), "A Test for the Significance of the Difference between the Two Variances in a Sample from a Normal Bivariate Population," *Biometrika*, 31, 13–19.

Mudambi, Ram, and Larry W. Taylor (1991), "A Nonparametric Investigation of Duration Dependence in the American Business Cycle: A Note," *Journal of Political Economy*, 99, 654–56.

—— (1995), "Some Non-Parametric Tests for Duration Dependence: An Application to U.K. Business Cycle Data," *Journal of Applied Statistics*, 22, 163–77.

Murray, Christian J., and Charles R. Nelson (1998), "The Uncertain Trend in Real GNP," manuscript, University of Washington.

Neftci, Salih N. (1982), "Optimal Prediction of Cyclical Downturns," *Journal of Economic Dynamics and Control*, 4, 225–41.

Nelson, Charles R., and Charles I. Plosser (1982), "Trends and Random Walks in Macroeconomic Time Series: Some Evidence and Implications," *Journal of Monetary Economics*, 10, 139–62.

Oliner, Stephen, Glenn D. Rudebusch, and Daniel E. Sichel (1996), "The Lucas Critique Revisted: Assessing the Stability of Empirical Euler Equations for Investment," *Journal of Econometrics*, 70, 291–316.

Parker, Randall E., and Philip Rothman (1996), "Further Evidence on the Stabilization of Postwar Economic Fluctuations," *Journal of Macroeconomics*, 18, 289–98.

Perron, Pierre (1989), "The Great Crash, the Oil Price Shock, and the Unit Root Hypothesis," *Econometrica*, 57, 1361–1401.

—— (1997), "Further Evidence on Breaking Trend Functions in Macroeconomic Variables," *Journal of Econometrics*, 80, 355–85.

Quah, Danny T., and Thomas J. Sargent (1993), "A Dynamic Index Model for Large Cross Sections," in J. H. Stock and M. W. Watson (eds.), *Business Cycles, Indicators and Forecasting.* Chicago: University of Chicago Press for NBER, 285–310.

Reinhart, Carmen, and Vincent Reinhart (1996), "Forecasting Turning Points in Canada," manuscript, Federal Reserve Board.

Romer, Christina D. (1986), "Is the Stabilization of the Postwar Economy a Figment of the Data?" *American Economic Review*, 76, 314–34.

—— (1994), "Remeasuring Business Cycles," *Journal of Economic History*, 54, 573–609.

Rudebusch, Glenn D. (1995), "Federal Reserve Interest Rate Targeting, Rational Expectations, and the Term Structure," *Journal of Monetary Economics*, 24, 245–74.

Rudebusch, Glenn D., and Lars E. O. Svensson (1998), "Policy Rules for Inflation Targeting," NBER working paper #6512.

Sargent, Thomas J., and Christopher A. Sims (1977), "Business Cycle Modeling without Pretending to Have Too Much a Priori Theory," in C. Sims (ed.), *New Methods of Business Cycle Research.* Minneapolis: Federal Reserve Bank of Minneapolis, 45–110.

Sichel, Daniel E. (1991), "Business Cycle Duration Dependence: A Parametric Approach," *Review of Economics and Statistics*, 73, 254–60.

Sims, Christopher A. (1980), "Macroeconomics and Reality," *Econometrica*, 48, 1–48.

Slutsky, Eugen (1927), "The Summation of Random Causes as the Source of Cyclic Processes," *Econometrica*, 5, 105–146.

Sowell, Fallaw B. (1992), "Modeling Long-Run Behavior with the Fractional ARIMA Model," *Journal of Monetary Economics*, 29, 277–302.

Stock, J. H., and M. W. Watson (1988), "Variable Trends in Economic Time Series," *Journal of Economic Perspectives*, 2, 147–74.

—— (1989), "New Indexes of Coincident and Leading Economic Indicators," in O. Blanchard and S. Fischer (eds.), *NBER Macroeconomics Annual.* Cambridge, Mass.: MIT Press, 351–94.

—— (1993), "A Procedure for Predicting Recessions with Leading Indicators: Econometric Issues and Recent Experience," in J. H. Stock and M. W. Watson (eds.), *Business Cycles, Indicators and Forecasting.* Chicago: University of Chicago Press for NBER, 255–84.

—— (1997), "Adaptive Diffusion Indexes," Manuscript, Kennedy School, Harvard University, and Woodrow Wilson School, Princeton University.

Walsh, Carl E. (1993), "What Caused the 1990–1991 Recession?" *Economic Review*, Federal Reserve Bank of San Francisco, (2), 33–48.

Watson, Mark W. (1994), "Business Cycle Durations and Postwar Stabilization of the U.S. Economy," *American Economic Review*, 84, 24–46.

West, Kenneth D. (1996), "Asymptotic Inference About Predictive Ability," *Econometrica*, 64, 1067–84.

West, Kenneth D., and Michael W. McCracken (1998), "Regression-Based Tests of Predictive Ability," *International Economic Review*, 39, 817–40.

Yellen, Janet L. (1996), "Monetary Policy: Goals and Strategy," *Business Economics*, 31, 40–44.

Yule, G. U. (1921), "On the Time-Correlation Problem, with Special Reference to the Variate-Difference Correlation Method," *Journal of the Royal Statistical Society*, 84, 497–526.

Zarnowitz, Victor (1992a), "Facts and Factors in the Modern Evolution of U.S. Economic Fluctuations," in V. Zarnowitz (ed.), *Business Cycles: Theory, History, Indicators, and Forecasting.* Chicago: University of Chicago Press for NBER, 77–124.

——(1992b), "What is a Business Cycle?" in M. T. Belongia and M. R. Garfinkel (eds.), *The Business Cycle: Theories and Evidence.* Boston: Kluwer Academic Publishers, 3–72.

Part II

The chapters in this section assume that recessions and expansions are distinct, separate regimes that are useful objects to study in themselves. For example, chapters 2 and 3 provide evidence that periods of expansion have become longer and that periods of contraction have become shorter in the postwar period. Chapters 4 and 5 provide evidence on whether expansions or contractions are more likely to end as they endure. Chapter 6 surveys recent theoretical and empirical research on two key attributes of the business cycle: the co-movement of many individual macroeconomic series, and the different behavior of the economy during expansions and contractions. It also suggests an empirical synthesis—a dynamic factor model with regime switching—that incorporates both features. Finally, chapter 7 provides a further contribution to the regime-switching model, in part, by incorporating the insights of chapters 4 and 5.

2

Have Postwar Economic Fluctuations Been Stabilized?

FRANCIS X. DIEBOLD AND GLENN D. RUDEBUSCH*

ARTHUR F. BURNS (1960 p. 2) was one of the first to assert that business cycles in the postwar era had changed in character:

> Between the end of the Second World War and the present, we have experienced four recessions, but each was a relatively mild setback. Since 1937 we have had five recessions, the longest of which lasted only thirteen months. There is no parallel for such a sequence of mild—or such a sequence of brief—contractions, at least during the past hundred years in our own country.

The steady growth of the 1960's produced a general acceptance of the view that the U.S. economy was more stable in the years after World War II than in the prewar period. This consensus was reinforced by formal examinations of postwar stabilization, notably by Martin N. Baily (1978) and J. Bradford De Long and Lawrence H. Summers (1986). Such examinations focused on the changing *volatility* of business fluctuations, and they uniformly concluded that the variability of various macroeconomic aggregates about trend had diminished during the postwar period.

The consensus on the postwar volatility stabilization of macroeconomic aggregates was seriously challenged by Christina D. Romer (1986a–c, 1988, 1989). She argued that the apparent higher volatility displayed by prewar aggregates (whether real gross national product [GNP], industrial production, or the unemployment rate) reflected differences in the methods used to construct prewar and postwar data; when similar methods are employed for both periods, she argued, the

* We thank Jeff Miron, Andy Rose, Mark Watson, David Wilcox, and two anonymous referees for comments. We gratefully acknowledge financial support from the National Science Foundation (grant SES 89-21715), the University of Pennsylvania Research Foundation (grant 3-71441), and the Institute for Empirical Macroeconomics. Joon-Haeng Lee, Tom Brennan, and Ralph Bradley provided research assistance.

difference between prewar and postwar volatility is greatly lessened. In Romer's interpretation, the apparent postwar moderation of the business cycle was simply an artifact of inconsistent data.

Romer's contention has itself been challenged. Some authors have constructed still more alternative versions of prewar aggregates and have reached traditional conclusions about prewar versus postwar macroeconomic volatility (David R. Weir, 1986; Nathan S. Balke and Robert J. Gordon, 1989). Others, such as Stanley Lebergott (1986), have argued that Romer's reconstructed aggregates, like the original series, depend importantly on unverifiable assumptions and therefore are not unambiguously better than the original series. Our reading of the literature on volatility stabilization is that the paucity of source data makes it very difficult to construct incontrovertible aggregate measures of the prewar U.S. economy, even at the annual frequency. Moreover, because the quantitative size of fluctuations in these constructed macroeconomic aggregates will be crucial for the resolution of the volatility debate, the inadequacy of aggregate measures of the prewar economy undermines any comparison of prewar and postwar volatility.

Hence, we address the issue of stabilization, but we do not join the debate on volatility. Instead, we provide new evidence on the stability of the postwar economy by investigating a different aspect of stabilization and by employing a different type of data. Drawing upon the perspective of Diebold and Rudebusch (1990), we approach the question of stabilization in terms of the relative duration, rather than the relative volatility, of prewar and postwar business cycles. Duration is clearly one aspect of the postwar stabilization that Burns had in mind when he noted the unusual brevity, as well as mildness, of postwar contractions.[1] In modern terminology, the duration perspective considers the frequency of business cycles, while the volatility debate has focused only on their amplitude.

To examine durations, we employ a chronology of business-cycle turning points. By eschewing examination of the amplitude of business fluctuations, we avoid relying on estimates of the quantitative movements of a prewar macroeconomic aggregate, which are critical to conclusions about volatility. Compared with an aggregate measure of economic activity, a business-cycle chronology contains *less* information

---

[1] Duration stabilization has largely been ignored by researchers: exceptions include De Long and Summers (1988), Victor Zarnowitz (1989), and Daniel E. Sichel (1991), who address similar issues with other techniques.

because the chronology is only qualitative, not quantitative, and *more* information because the chronology can incorporate a greater variety and number of sources of cyclical information. The former attribute is obvious: designating turning points largely requires only a qualitative sense of the direction of general business activity. Thus, for example, concluding that the second quarter of 1894 was a cyclical peak is much easier than determining that real GNP rose x percent in the second quarter and fell y percent in the third quarter of that year.

At the same time, because only qualitative information is required, a business-cycle chronology can be constructed from a greater number of indicators of business activity than just the components of an aggregate measure such as real GNP or industrial production. For example, the business-cycle chronology of the National Bureau of Economic Research (NBER), which we use below, incorporates a wide variety of sources of cyclical information, including the price movements of stocks and other assets, as well as descriptive accounts of economic activity from historical business annals. Sources such as these have necessarily been ignored in the volatility-stabilization debate, which has focused on aggregate measures: thus, our use of the NBER business-cycle chronology implicitly brings new information to the debate about the changing nature of business fluctuations.[2]

In our analysis, however, we do not accept the NBER chronology unquestioningly. One clear truth in U.S. economic history is that the quantity and quality of economic data have increased markedly over the last century. The relative scarcity and poor quality of earlier data may affect the comparability of prewar and postwar turning-point dates. Such data considerations may be important for judging changes in cyclical duration, just as similar data problems were crucial for the volatility debate. Accordingly, we take care to assess the robustness of our results to variations in the prewar chronology.

The paper proceeds as follows. In Section 1 we discuss the NBER business-cycle dating procedures and the historical consistency of the NBER turning-point dates. In Section 2, we describe a test of the null hypothesis of no duration stabilization, that is, that the distributions of

---

[2] The ability of the NBER to construct its chronology at a monthly frequency demonstrates the richness of the chronology's information set. Previous volatility studies have been able to construct the requisite aggregates at only an annual frequency, which is quite crude for assessing business cycles. Consideration of broader information sets in volatility comparisons also motivates the analyses of Matthew D. Shapiro (1988), who uses stock prices, and Steven M. Sheffrin (1988), who uses international data.

prewar and postwar durations are identical. We provide empirical results in Section 3 and offer a summary and interpretation in Section 4.

1. The NBER Business-Cycle Chronology

The dates of U.S. business-cycle peaks and troughs designated by the NBER are shown in Table 2.1, along with the associated durations of expansions, contractions, and whole cycles (measured from peak to peak and from trough to trough). As noted above, the earlier volatility debate has hinged on the issue of the comparability of prewar and postwar data, and we focus the discussion in this section on an analogous issue: the historical consistency of the prewar and postwar NBER turning-point dates and the comparability of the associated cyclical durations.

A brief review of the NBER dating procedure is in order. An early description of this method is Burns and Wesley C. Mitchell (1946 pp. 76–7).[3]

> Our first step toward identifying business cycles was to identify the turns of general business activity indicated by [descriptive business] annals. Next, the evidence of the annals was checked against indexes of business conditions and other series of broad coverage. In most cases these varied records pointed clearly to some one year as the time when a cyclical turn occurred. When there was conflict of evidence, additional statistical series were examined and historical accounts of business conditions consulted, until we felt it safe to write down an interval within which a cyclical turn in general business probably occurred. We then proceeded to refine the approximate dates by arraying the cyclical turns in the more important monthly or quarterly series we had for the time and country.

The last step is the most important, because it focuses directly on the amount of cyclical comovement or coherence among economic variables. For Burns and Mitchell, this comovement is the prime definitional characteristic of the business cycle: "... a cycle consists of expansions occurring at about the same time in many economic activities, followed by similarly general recessions ... " (Burns and Mitchell, 1946 p. 3). Thus, in determining the monthly dates of business-cycle turning points, Burns and Mitchell considered hundreds of individual series, including those measuring commodity output, income, prices, interest rates, banking transactions, and transportation services. The turning points of these individual series are not randomly distributed; rather,

---

[3] A more recent description is Geoffrey H. Moore and Zarnowitz (1986), which provides an excellent overview of the NBER cyclical dating method and related issues.

TABLE 2.1
NBER Business-Cycle Dates and Durations

Trough	Peak	Contractions	Expansions	Trough to Trough	Peak to Peak
December 1854	June 1857	—	30	—	—
December 1858	October 1860	18	22	48	40
June 1861	April 1865	8	46	30	54
December 1867	June 1869	32	18	78	50
December 1870	October 1873	18	34	36	52
March 1879	March 1882	65	36	99	101
May 1885	March 1887	38	22	74	60
April 1888	July 1890	13	27	35	40
May 1891	January 1893	10	20	37	30
June 1894	December 1895	17	18	37	35
June 1897	June 1899	18	24	36	42
December 1900	September 1902	18	21	42	39
August 1904	May 1907	23	33	44	56
June 1908	January 1910	13	19	46	32
January 1912	January 1913	24	12	43	36
December 1914	August 1918	23	44	35	67
March 1919	January 1920	7	10	51	17
July 1921	May 1923	18	22	28	40
July 1924	October 1926	14	27	36	41
November 1927	August 1929	13	21	40	34
March 1933	May 1937	43	50	64	93
June 1938	February 1945	13	80	63	93
October 1945	November 1948	8	37	88	45
October 1949	July 1953	11	45	48	56
May 1954	August 1957	10	39	55	49
April 1958	April 1960	8	24	47	32
February 1961	December 1969	10	106	34	116
November 1970	November 1973	11	36	117	47
March 1975	January 1980	16	58	52	74
July 1980	July 1981	6	12	64	18
November 1982	July 1990	16	92	28	108

Note: Durations are given in months. Wartime expansions and whole cycles are underlined.

they form clusters of peaks and troughs. The monthly dates of the central tendencies of such clusters are designated as the turning points of the general business cycle. For the period from 1854 through 1938, these dates are listed by Burns and Mitchell (1946 p. 105). Dates in the postwar period have been designated by successive NBER researchers who have closely adhered to the Burns and Mitchell methodology (see Moore and Zarnowitz, 1986).[4] Note that, contrary to popular folklore, NBER researchers have never used two consecutive quarterly declines in real GNP as the criterion for dating downturns.

The historical consistency of the procedures used by NBER researchers to designate turning points supports the use of these dates in prewar–postwar comparisons. Nevertheless, although the general dating procedures have not changed, both the number and quality of the underlying individual series examined have greatly increased over time. For example, in Burns and Mitchell's (1946 p. 82) analysis, only 19 individual monthly or quarterly series were available for dating in the 1860's, while 199 were available for the dates after 1890, and 665 were available after 1920. The increase in the number of underlying individual series, which was also accompanied by an increase in the quality of most series, is presumably associated with increased reliability of the NBER dates. Clusters of individual turning points are quite narrow in the postwar period; in contrast, inadequate data result in much more uncertainty about some of the prewar NBER dates. The changes in the reliability of the dates, as certain individual series necessarily assume more importance in the absence of others in the prewar period, could affect the validity of a prewar–postwar comparison of NBER cyclical durations. The rest of this section addresses this issue and describes some of the variations of the canonical NBER chronology that we consider in order to ensure the robustness of our results.

All of the researchers who have designated NBER turning points have cautioned that there is some uncertainty about the precise timing of the general turns in business activity. One indication of the uncertainty associated with the official dates is the discrepancy between these dates and a number of alternative dates that have been suggested by NBER researchers and by independent observers.[5] Let us first consider the reliability of the postwar dates. The NBER turning-point dates during the early part of the postwar period were the subject of some controversy, with several alternative chronologies hotly debated (Moore,

---

[4] Two detailed illustrations of the postwar application of the NBER dating methodology are Zarnowitz and Moore (1977) for the 1973–1975 recession and Zarnowitz and Moore (1983) for the 1980 recession.

[5] Indeed, this is one of the procedures used by Burns and Mitchell (1946 p. 108) to examine the dependability of their dates.

1961; Lorman C. Trueblood, 1961; George W. Cloos, 1963a,b; Zarnowitz, 1963a,b). The differences between the proposed alternatives and the official postwar chronology are minor; of the eight dates examined by Cloos, for example, his suggested changes would shift one peak back by one month, another forward by two months, and one trough back by three months. Given the striking nature of our subsequent results, these differences are insignificant.

The choice of more recent dates in the postwar period (since 1960), and indeed the entire NBER turning-point methodology, has gained additional support from research by James H. Stock and Mark W. Watson (1989).[6] They have attempted to formalize the notion that the business cycle is defined by the comovements of many macroeconomic time series by specifying a dynamic factor model that identifies the unobserved common component in the movements of many coincident variables. The cyclical peaks and troughs of the extracted common component coincide with the NBER chronology, except in 1969, when the NBER-dated peak is two months later.

As suggested above by the large changes in the number of time series employed by Burns and Mitchell (1946), the prewar dates are of varying quality. The dates in the interwar period (1918–1938) appear to be little more questionable than those in the postwar period. Of the original 12 turning points in this period specified by Burns and Mitchell (1946), careful reevaluations by the NBER staff led to three changes of one month and two shifts of two months (Moore and Zarnowitz, 1986). These revisions are broadly indicative of the small amount of uncertainty in the interwar dates.

The turning-point dates before World War I are more questionable. Again, we can compare alternative business-cycle chronologies for this period, such as those of Joseph Kitchin (1923), Warren M. Persons (1931), and Leonard Ayres (1939), in order to gauge the uncertainty associated with the NBER's choices. From this perspective, the NBER dates appear to be reasonable choices, with no clear bias; however, the range in variation among the alternatives is fairly large, with an average shift of about four months. Careful examinations of the early NBER dates, notably Rendigs Fels (1959) and Zarnowitz (1981), place the greatest uncertainty on the timing of the dates before 1885. Very few comprehensive statistics are available at a monthly frequency before the mid-1880's; consequently, the clusters of individual series available for Burns and Mitchell (1946) are rather sparse and diffuse. In our empiri-

---

[6] The postwar NBER chronology is also broadly confirmed by James Hamilton (1989), who posits an underlying nonlinear regime-switching model and uses optimal-signal-extraction techniques to estimate turning-point dates.

cal analysis, we shall examine the robustness of our results when the pre-1885 turning points are excluded.

Although the early NBER dates appear to provide a reasonably unbiased delineation of good times from bad, there is a remaining question about whether some of the designated recessions represent true cyclical contractions or rather are simply periods of very slow growth (i.e., growth recessions). This distinction is more difficult to make for recessions in the pre-World War I period because several data series are only available on a trend-adjusted basis, making actual declines in real economic activity difficult to judge. In the period after 1885, the 1887–1888 recession is the most dubious, although the 1899–1900 recession was also very mild (Kitchin, 1923; A. Ross Eckler, 1933; Fels, 1959; Zarnowitz, 1981). Although we remain undecided on the classification of these episodes, we examine the consequences of treating 1887–1888 and 1899–1900 as growth slowdowns rather than as business-cycle contractions.

In light of the above concerns about the historical consistency of the NBER dates, we consider two variations on the official chronology in order to assess the robustness of our results: (i) exclusion of the pre-1885 turning-point dates in order to avoid potentially unreliable dates in the very early period and (ii) elimination of the 1887 and 1899 recessions[7] in order to account for the possibility that these were merely growth recessions. As a further sensitivity test, we consider three different terminal dates for the prewar period (June 1938, August 1929, and December 1914), thus excluding from consideration the Great Depression and other interwar recessions, which may be atypical observations. Finally, we also consider the exclusion of wartime expansions and cycles in order to avoid possible spuriously long observations. A complete listing of all of the various duration samples used in our analysis is given in Table 2.2, along with the associated mnemonics. (The A, B, and C samples are all loosely termed "prewar" samples.)

2. A Test of Duration Stabilization

Consider the two samples of prewar and postwar durations of size n_x and n_y, $\{X_1, \ldots, X_n\}$ and $\{Y_1, \ldots, Y_n\}$. Denote the corresponding population prewar and postwar duration distribution functions by F and G. The null hypothesis of no postwar duration stabilization implies that these distributions are identical ($F = G$). Depending on the situation, we shall subsequently be interested in both one-sided and two-sided

---

[7] The "elimination" of a recession means that we replace that contraction and its immediate preceding and succeeding expansions by one long expansion.

TABLE 2.2
Listing of Duration Samples

A. Pre-World War II (December 1854–June 1938):
  A1:   All observations
  A2:   Excluding observations before May 1885
  A3:   A2, eliminating 1887 and 1899 contractions
  A1*:   A1, excluding wartime observations
  A2*:   A2, excluding wartime observations
  A3*:   A3, excluding wartime observations

B. Pre-Great Depression (December 1854–August 1929):
  B1:   All observations
  B2:   Excluding observations before May 1885
  B3:   B2, eliminating 1887 and 1899 contractions
  B1*:   B1, excluding wartime observations
  B2*:   B2, excluding wartime observations
  B3*:   B3, excluding wartime observations

C. Pre-World War I (December 1854–December 1914):
  C1:   All observations
  C2:   Excluding observations before May 1885
  C3:   C2, eliminating 1887 and 1899 contractions
  C1*:   C1, excluding wartime observations
  C2*:   C2, excluding wartime observations
  C3*:   C3, excluding wartime observations

D. Post-World War II (February 1945–July 1990):
  Z: All observations
  Z*:   Z, excluding wartime observations

---

alternatives. The interpretation of the one-sided alternative that Y is stochastically larger than X is that (i) $F \neq G$ and (ii) $G(k) \leq F(k)$ for all k [or equivalently, $P(Y > k) \geq P(X > k)$ for all k]. The inequalities are reversed for the one-sided alternative that X is stochastically larger than Y. The two-sided alternative, $F \neq G$, has the obvious interpretation.

We shall test the null hypothesis of no postwar stabilization using the Wilcoxon, or rank-sum, test. Replace the observations $\{X_1, \ldots, X_{n_x}, Y_1, \ldots, Y_{n_y}\}$ by their ranks. $\{R_1, \ldots, R_n\}$, where $n = n_x + n_y$.[8] Then the Wilcoxon test statistic is formed as the sum of the ranks in the second

---

[8] In the case of a tie, the relevant ranks are replaced by the average of the ranks of the tied observations.

sample:

$$W = \sum_{i=n_x+1}^{n} R_i. \tag{1}$$

The intuition of this statistic is obvious: under the null hypothesis that $F = G$, the average rank of an observation in the prewar sample should equal the average rank of an observation in the postwar sample, and W is a sufficient statistic for this comparison. Furthermore, the distribution of W under the null hypothesis that $F = G$ is invariant to the underlying distribution of durations. This invariance follows from the fact that the null distribution of the ranks (assuming the independence of observations) is simply given by

$$P(R_1 = r_1, \ldots, R_n = r_n) = 1/n! \tag{2}$$

for all permutations $(r_1, \ldots, r_n)$ of $(1, \ldots, n)$. Because W is a function of the ranks, the distribution of W is also invariant to the underlying distribution of durations. Indeed, equation (2) enables computation of exact finite-sample p values of W, which are calculated numerically using the algorithm of Diebold et al. (1992).[9]

The Wilcoxon test is a nonparametric test designed to have particularly high power against alternatives involving a shift of location. Intuition on this point can be gained by comparing the Wilcoxon test statistic to the classical t statistic for testing equality of two population means,

$$t = (n_x n_y/n)^{1/2}\left[(\bar{Y} - \bar{X})/s\right] \tag{3}$$

where

$$s = (n - 2)^{-1/2}\left[\sum_{i=1}^{n_x}(X_i - \bar{X})^2 + \sum_{j=1}^{n_y}(Y_j - \bar{Y})^2\right]^{1/2} \tag{4}$$

The t statistic is appropriate for testing the null hypothesis that $E(X) = E(Y)$ when the underlying populations are normally distributed. Unfortunately, normality is a distinctly inappropriate distributional assumption for duration data. The Wilcoxon test may be interpreted as a distribution-free t test, obtained by replacing the observations

---

[9] Critical values are also tabulated in John V. Bradley (1968) for $n_x, n_y \leq 25$.

$\{X_1, \ldots, X_{n_x}, Y_1, \ldots, Y_{n_y}\}$ by their ranks $\{R_1, \ldots, R_n\}$, which yields

$$t^* = (n_x n_y/n)^{1/2}\left[\left(\overline{R}_y - \overline{R}_x\right)/s^*\right] \tag{5}$$

where $\overline{R}_x$ and $\overline{R}_y$ denote the mean ranks of the X and Y samples, and

$$s^* = (n-2)^{-1/2} \times \left[\sum_{i=1}^{n_x}\left(R_i - \overline{R}_x\right)^2 + \sum_{j=n_x+1}^{n}\left(R_j - \overline{R}_x\right)^2\right]^{1/2}. \tag{6}$$

Straightforward but tedious algebra reveals t^* to be a monotonic transformation of W.

Because the Wilcoxon test is exact, we are assured of correct test size, even in small samples. Surprisingly, the test also has good power against a variety of alternatives. The trade-off between the relaxation of distributional assumptions and the loss of power is extremely favorable: the Wilcoxon test is only slightly less powerful than the t test when the distributional assumption (normality) underlying the t test is true, and it may be much more powerful when the distributional assumption is false.[10]

Under the maintained assumption that the distributions of durations differ only by a shift in location [i.e., $G(k) = F(k + \Delta)$ for all k], we can also produce a confidence interval for the location shift, Δ. Consider the $n_x n_y$-element sequence of differences $\{D_{ij}\}$, $i = 1, \ldots, n_x$, $j = 1, \ldots, n_y$, where $D_{ij} = Y_j - X_i$, and order them so that $D_{(1)} < D_{(2)} < \cdots < D_{(n_x n_y)}$. For a given significance level α, let k_α be an integer defined from the confidence interval

$$P(k_\alpha \leq U \leq n_x n_y - k_\alpha) = 1 - \alpha \tag{7}$$

where

$$U = W - n_y(n_y + 1)/2 \tag{8}$$

is the Mann-Whitney U statistic, a monotonic transformation of W.[11] Then it can be shown (Bickel and Doksum, 1977) that

$$P(D_{(k_\alpha)}) \leq \Delta \leq D_{(n_x n_y - k_\alpha + 1)} = 1 - \alpha. \tag{9}$$

---

[10] See Peter J. Bickel and Kjell A. Doksum (1977) for a discussion of the comparative performance of the Wilcoxon and t tests.

[11] The finite-sample distribution of U is tabulated in Bickel and Doksum (1977).

Thus, a two-sided $(1 - \alpha)$-percent confidence interval for Δ is $(D_{(k_\alpha)}, D_{(n_x n_y - k_\alpha + 1)})$. Alternatively, the two $(1 - \alpha)$-percent one-sided confidence intervals are $(D_{(k_{2\alpha})}, \infty)$ and $(-\infty, D_{(n_x n_y - k_{2\alpha} + 1)})$.

3. Empirical Results

Before applying the Wilcoxon test, we first must verify two features of the data in order to ensure the validity of the testing procedure: first, the independence of duration observations and, second, the constancy of trend growth in the prewar and postwar periods. The independence assumption, which was required to obtain appropriate critical values for the Wilcoxon test, appears to be a good working assumption. The correlations between the lengths of successive expansions or between the lengths of successive contractions (over the entire sample) are insignificantly different from zero at even the 20-percent level.

The second pretest issue reflects the fact that business cycles are delineated on a non-trend-adjusted basis; thus, any differences in the trend growth of the economy in the prewar and postwar periods would affect duration comparisons. If the postwar economy had a higher average rate of growth than the prewar economy and each economy had identical trend-adjusted cyclical movements, the duration of postwar expansions would be longer and the duration of postwar contractions would be shorter than their prewar counterparts. However, as shown in Table 2.3, the mean growth rate of real output in the postwar period was little different than in the prewar period. (The prewar growth rates are calculated over several ranges that roughly correspond to our prewar duration samples, whose mnemonics are given in parentheses in Table 2.3).[12] Thus, any evidence for duration stabilization does not reflect changes in trend growth.

With these two issues settled, results from the Wilcoxon tests for expansions and contractions appear in Tables 2.4 and 2.5, respectively. For each pair of prewar and postwar samples, we report sample sizes, mean durations, the Wilcoxon statistic and its one-sided p value, and approximate 90-percent and 80-percent one-sided confidence intervals for the location shift.[13] For example, the top row of Table 2.4 compares the prewar expansion sample A1 (with 21 observations and a mean duration of 26.5 months) and the postwar expansion sample Z (with

---

[12] Note that we rely on the prewar measure of GNP only for average growth estimates, rather than using it for the more contentious assessment of properties of cyclical fluctuations.

[13] The obvious alternatives of longer postwar expansions and shorter postwar contractions make one-sided tests and confidence intervals appropriate.

TABLE 2.3
Mean Growth Rate of Real GNP

Sample	Mean ($\Delta \log Y_t$)
Postwar sample:	
1946–1989 (Z)	0.025
Prewar samples:	
1870–1938 (A1)	0.031
1886–1938 (A2)	0.027
1870–1929 (B1)	0.037
1886–1929 (B2)	0.034
1870–1914 (C1)	0.038
1886–1914 (C2)	0.033

Note: The real GNP sample from 1869 to 1929 comes from Romer (1989 pp. 22–3); the later data come from the national income and product accounts (NIPA).

nine observations and a mean duration of 49.9 months). For these two samples, the exact Wilcoxon p value under the null hypothesis of no change in distribution is less than 0.01, and the confidence-interval estimates suggest that we can be 90-percent certain that the postwar increase in mean expansion duration was at least 9 months. Results are shown for the other pairs of expansion samples in Table 2.4 and for contraction samples in Table 2.5. Almost without exception, the tests reject the null hypothesis of no stabilization in favor of longer postwar expansions or shorter postwar contractions. For contractions, rejection is always at the 1-percent level or better. For expansions, the evidence is slightly less overwhelming: 12 of 18 Wilcoxon p values for expansions are less than or equal to 0.02, but one sample rejects at only the 20-percent level, and two other samples reject at about the 10-percent level.

Even more persuasive evidence is provided by a test of the joint hypothesis of both longer expansions and shorter contractions. Given a postwar duration stabilization that results in either (or both) longer expansions and shorter contractions, expansion-to-contraction ratios will be larger in the postwar period. In light of the separate results for expansions and contractions, it is not surprising that the Wilcoxon statistics for their ratios, which test a joint stabilization hypothesis, are generally less than 0.001. We interpret these results as the most compelling evidence supporting overall postwar duration stabilization.

It is unusual in empirical macroeconomics to obtain such strong results, particularly with small samples. But what of the more important

TABLE 2.4
Wilcoxon Test for Expansions

Sample		Sample Size		Mean Duration		Wilcoxon Test		Confidence Interval	
x	y	n_x	n_y	$\bar{x}$	$\bar{y}$	W	$P_1(W)$	90-percent	80-percent
A1	Z	21	9	26.5	49.9	193.5	0.006	< -9	< -12
A2	Z	15	9	24.7	49.9	154.0	0.006	< -12	< -14
A3	Z	13	9	30.8	49.9	127.5	0.055	< -3	< -8
A1*	Z*	19	7	24.5	42.6	132.5	0.013	< -5	< -9
A2*	Z*	14	7	23.3	42.6	106.0	0.015	< -6	< -12
A3*	Z*	12	7	29.8	42.6	85.5	0.098	< 0	< -4
B1	Z	20	9	25.3	49.9	190.5	0.004	< -10	< -14
B2	Z	14	9	22.9	49.9	151.0	0.003	< -13	< -15
B3	Z	12	9	29.3	49.9	124.5	0.035	< -4	< -12
B1*	Z*	18	7	23.1	42.6	130.5	0.007	< -6	< -10
B2*	Z*	13	7	21.2	42.6	104.0	0.007	< -10	< -12
B3*	Z*	11	7	27.9	42.6	83.5	0.063	< -3	< -6
C1	Z	15	9	25.5	49.9	154.5	0.005	< -9	< -12
C2	Z	9	9	21.8	49.9	56.0	0.004	< -12	< -15
C3	Z	7	9	32.4	49.9	47.5	0.105	< 4	< -4
C1*	Z*	14	7	24.0	42.6	106.5	0.012	< -5	< -7
C2*	Z*	9	7	21.8	42.6	80.0	0.016	< -6	< -12
C3*	Z	7	7	32.4	42.6	45.5	0.191	< 6	< 0

Note: Samples are identified in Table 2.2. The mean durations and the Wilcoxon test statistic are given in months. $P_1(W)$ is a one-sided p value for the null hypothesis of no postwar duration stabilization.

question: are the postwar shifts significant from an *economic* perspective? Clearly, the answer is yes. Our results indicate that while less than 20 percent of the postwar period was spent in recession, more than 40 percent of the prewar period was spent in recession. Furthermore, the mean postwar expansion duration is *double* that of its prewar counterpart, while the mean postwar contraction duration is *half* that of its prewar counterpart.

The results are very different for whole cycles, whether measured from trough to trough or from peak to peak. Table 2.6 provides the statistics for cycles measured from peak to peak; similar results were obtained for trough-to-trough cycles. The p values of the Wilcoxon tests rarely indicate significant change in the postwar period; in fact, they are typically greater than 0.2. Thus, the data suggest an unchanged

TABLE 2.5
Wilcoxon Test for Contractions

| Sample | | Sample Size | | Mean Duration | | Wilcoxon Test | | Confidence Interval | |
x	y	n_x	n_y	$\bar{x}$	$\bar{y}$	W	$P_1(W)$	90-percent	80-percent
A1	Z	21	9	21.2	10.7	75.0	0.001	> 3	> 5
A2	Z	15	9	17.8	10.7	68.0	0.003	> 3	> 3
A3	Z	13	9	18.2	10.7	66.0	0.006	> 3	> 3
B1	Z	19	9	20.5	10.7	73.0	0.002	> 3	> 5
B2	Z	13	9	16.2	10.7	66.0	0.006	> 2	> 3
B3	Z	11	9	16.4	10.7	64.0	0.010	> 2	> 3
C1	Z	15	9	22.5	10.7	61.0	0.001	> 6	> 7
C2	Z	9	9	17.7	10.7	117.0	0.002	> 4	> 5
C3	Z	7	9	18.3	10.7	84.0	0.004	> 5	> 7

Note: Samples are identified in Table 2.2. The mean duration and the Wilcoxon test statistic are given in months. P_1W is a one-sided p value for the null hypothesis of no postwar duration stabilization.

distribution of whole-cycle durations but with a revised allocation of time so that postwar expansions are longer, and contractions shorter.

4. Summary

We have investigated the postwar-stabilization hypothesis from the perspective of *duration*, or frequency, as opposed to volatility, or amplitude. Our analysis made use of the qualitative information contained in the NBER's business-cycle chronology and was robust to criticisms of conventional measures of prewar aggregate data. Using a distribution-free statistical procedure, we found strong evidence of a postwar shift toward longer expansions and shorter contractions, which is consistent with a broad interpretation of the stabilization hypothesis. Moreover, we found no evidence for a postwar shift in the distribution of whole-cycle durations.

To the extent that postwar volatility was stabilized, one expects, ceteris paribus, concomitant duration stabilization due to the upward trend in aggregate economic activity. To see this, consider an extreme case: in an upwardly trending economy, as volatility approaches zero, expected expansion duration grows without bound, and expected con-

TABLE 2.6
Wilcoxon Test for Peak-to-Peak Cycles

Sample		Sample Size		Mean Duration		Wilcoxon Test		Confidence Interval	
x	y	n_x	n_y	$\bar{x}$	$\bar{y}$	W	$P_2(W)$	90-percent	80-percent
A1	Z	20	9	47.9	60.6	158.0	0.294	$(-24, 7)$	$(-19, 3)$
A2	Z	14	9	43.0	60.6	134.0	0.110	$(-34, 0)$	$(-26, -5)$
A3	Z	12	9	46.8	60.6	115.0	0.278	$(-33, 9)$	$(-26, 3)$
A1*	Z*	18	7	46.6	53.3	101.5	0.534	$(-18, 10)$	$(-15, 7)$
A2*	Z*	13	7	41.2	53.3	89.5	0.210	$(-32, 7)$	$(-17, 0)$
A3*	Z*	11	7	45.0	53.3	75.5	0.426	$(-28, 11)$	$(-17, 7)$
B1	Z	19	9	45.6	60.6	156.0	0.224	$(-28, 4)$	$(-20, 0)$
B2	Z	13	9	39.2	60.6	132.0	0.060	$(-38, 3)$	$(-32, -6)$
B3	Z	11	9	42.6	60.6	113.0	0.176	$(-38, 4)$	$(-30, -1)$
B1*	Z*	17	7	43.8	53.3	100.5	0.418	$(-22, 8)$	$(-15, 5)$
B2*	Z*	12	7	36.8	53.3	88.5	0.120	$(-33, 2)$	$(-28, -3)$
B3*	Z*	10	7	40.2	53.3	74.5	0.270	$(-32, 7)$	$(-27, 3)$
C1	Z	14	9	47.6	60.6	123.0	0.368	$(-24, 7)$	$(-19, 4)$
C2	Z	8	9	38.8	60.6	54.0	0.092	$(-39, 0)$	$(-32, -5)$
C3	Z	6	9	45.0	60.6	40.0	0.388	$(-38, 11)$	$(-26, 7)$
C1*	Z*	13	7	47.2	53.3	78.5	0.700	$(-18, 11)$	$(-14, 8)$
C2*	Z*	8	7	38.6	53.3	66.5	0.232	$(-34, 7)$	$(-18, 0)$
C3*	Z*	6	7	45.0	53.3	38.5	0.628	$(-19, 14)$	$(-17, 11)$

Note: Samples are identified in Table 2.2. The mean durations and the Wilcoxon test statistic are given in months. $P_2(W)$ is a one-sided p value for the null hypothesis of no postwar change in the duration distribution.

traction duration collapses to zero.[14] However, we believe that it is highly unlikely that all of the postwar duration stabilization is associated with volatility stabilization. To the extent that volatility actually was reduced, previous research has found that the reduction was small and hard to detect. The postwar shift toward duration stabilization, however, is large and difficult to deny. It is likely, therefore, that duration stabilization arose, at least in part, independently of volatility stabilization. Furthermore, some of the structural changes in the economy that have been cited as possible sources for volatility stabilization may actually impede duration stabilization. For example, it is fairly well

---

[14] However, it should be stressed that the link between volatility stabilization and duration stabilization may be affected by other changes in the nature of business cycles, notably in the asymmetry of the cycle.

established that the existence of a countercyclical entitlement program such as unemployment insurance *increases* individual unemployment durations by reducing the adverse effect of unemployment on personal income (e.g., Bruce D. Meyer, 1990). Such a program, although an "automatic stabilizer" in the sense of reducing the severity of contractions and the variability of fluctuations, may not generally shorten the durations of contractions or lead to duration stabilization.

References

Ayres, Leonard, *Turning Points in Business Cycles*, New York: Macmillan, 1939.

Baily, Martin Neal, "Stabilization Policy and Private Economic Behavior," *Brookings Papers on Economic Activity*, 1978, (1), 11–60.

Balke, Nathan S. and Gordon, Robert J., "The Estimation of Prewar Gross National Product: Methodology and New Evidence," *Journal of Political Economy*, February 1989, 97, 38–92.

Bickel, Peter J. and Doksum, Kjell A., *Mathematical Statistics*, San Francisco: Holden-Day, 1977.

Bradley, John V., *Distribution-Free Statistical Tests*, Englewood Cliffs, NJ: Prentice-Hall, 1968.

Burns, Arthur F., "Progress Toward Economic Stability," *American Economic Review*, March 1960, 50, 1–19.

—— and Mitchell, Wesley C., *Measuring Business Cycles*, New York: National Bureau of Economic Research, 1946.

Cloos, George W., (1963a) "How Good are the National Bureau's Reference Dates?" *Journal of Business*, January 1963, 36, 14–32.

—— (1963b) "More on Reference Dates and Leading Indicators," *Journal of Business*, July 1963, 36, 352–64.

De Long, J. Bradford and Summers, Lawrence H., "The Changing Cyclical Variability of Economic Activity in the United States," in Robert J. Gordon, ed., *The American Business Cycle: Continuity and Change*, Chicago: University of Chicago Press, 1986, pp. 679–719.

—— and Summers, Lawrence H., "How Does Macroeconomic Policy Affect Output?" *Brookings Papers on Economic Activity*, 1988, (2), 433–80.

Diebold, Francis X. and Rudebusch, Glenn D., "A Nonparametric Investigation of Duration Dependence in the American Business Cycle," *Journal of Political Economy*, June 1990, 98, 596–616.

——, —— and Tanizaki, Hisashi, "On the Comparative Size and Power Properties of the Fisher, Wilcoxon, and *t* Tests," unpublished manuscript, University of Pennsylvania, 1992.

Eckler, A. Ross, "A Measure of the Severity of Depressions, 1873–1932," *Review of Economics and Statistics*, May 1933, 15, 75–81.

Fels, Rendigs, *American Business Cycles, 1865–1897*, Chapel Hill: University of North Carolina Press, 1959.

Hamilton, James, "A New Approach to the Economic Analysis of Nonstationary Time Series and the Business Cycle," *Econometrica*, March 1989, 57, 357–84.

Kitchin, Joseph, "Cycles and Trends in Economic Factors," *Review of Economics and Statistics*, January 1923, 5, 10–16.

Lebergott, Stanley, "Discussion" [Diffusion and Timing of Business Cycle Turning Points], *Journal of Economic History*, June 1986, 46, 367–71.

Meyer, Bruce D., "Unemployment Insurance and Unemployment Spells," *Econometrica*, July 1990, 58, 757–82.

Moore, Geoffrey H., "Discussion," *Proceedings of the ASA, Business and Economic Statistics Section, 1961*, Washington, DC: American Statistical Association, 1961, pp. 34–7.

—— and Zarnowitz, Victor, "The Development and Role of the NBER's Business Cycle Chronologies," in Robert J. Gordon, ed., *The American Business Cycle: Continuity and Change*, Chicago: University of Chicago Press, 1986, pp. 735–79.

Persons, Warren M., *Forecasting Business Cycles*, New York: Wiley, 1931.

Romer, Christina D., (1986a) "Spurious Volatility in Historical Unemployment Data," *Journal of Political Economy*, February 1986, 94, 1–37.

—— (1986b) "Is the Stabilization of the Postwar Economy a Figment of the Data?" *American Economic Review*, June 1986, 76, 314–34.

—— (1986c) "New Estimates of Prewar Gross National Product and Unemployment," *Journal of Economic History*, June 1986, 46, 341–52.

——, "World War I and the Postwar Depression: A Reinterpretation Based on Alternative Estimates of GNP," *Journal of Monetary Economics*, July 1988, 22, 91–115.

——, "The Prewar Business Cycle Reconsidered: New Estimates of Gross National Product, 1869–1908," *Journal of Political Economy*, February 1989, 97, 1–37.

Shapiro, Matthew D., "The Stabilization of the U.S. Economy: Evidence from the Stock Market," *American Economic Review*, December 1988, 78, 1067–79.

Sheffrin, Steven M., "Have Economic Fluctuations Been Dampened? A Look at Evidence Outside the United States," *Journal of Monetary Economics*, January 1988, 21, 73–83.

Sichel, Daniel E., "Business Cycle Duration Dependence: A Parametric Approach," *Review of Economics and Statistics*, May 1991, 73, 254–60.

Stock, James H. and Watson, Mark W., "New Indexes of Coincident and Leading Economic Indicators," in O. Blanchard and S. Fischer, eds., *NBER Macroeconomics Annual, 1989*, Cambridge, MA: MIT Press, 1989, pp. 351–94.

Trueblood, Lorman C., "The Dating of Postwar Business Cycles," *Proceedings of The ASA, Business and Economic Statistics Section, 1961*, Washington, DC: American Statistical Association, 1961, pp. 16–26.

Weir, David R., "The Reliability of Historical Macroeconomic Data for Comparing Cyclical Stability," *Journal of Economic History*, June 1986, 46, 353–65.

Zarnowitz, Victor, (1963a) "On the Dating of Business Cycles," *Journal of Business*, April 1963, 36, 179–99.

—— (1963b) "Cloos on Reference Dates and Leading Indicators: A Comment," *Journal of Business*, October 1963, 36, 461–3.

——, "Business Cycles and Growth: Some Reflections and Measures," in W. J. Muckl and A. E. Ott, eds., *Wirtschaftstheorie und Wirtschaftspolitik: Gedenkenschrift fur Erich Preiser*, Passau: Passavia Universitatsverlag, 1981, pp. 475–508.

—— "Facts and Factors in the Recent Evolution of Business Cycles in the United States," National Bureau of Economic Research (Cambridge, MA) Working Paper No. 2865, 1989.

—— and Moore, Geoffrey H., "The Recession and Recovery of 1973–1976," *Explorations in Economic Research*, Fall 1977, 4, 471–577.

—— and ——, "The Timing and Severity of the 1980 Recession," in G. H. Moore, ed., *Business Cycles, Inflation and Forecasting*, Cambridge, MA: Ballinger, 1983, pp. 11–17.

3

Shorter Recessions and Longer Expansions

FRANCIS X. DIEBOLD AND GLENN D. RUDEBUSCH

HAVE THE PATTERNS of U.S. business cycles changed since World War II? And if so, have they changed in ways consistent with the hypothesis that postwar business cycles have been more stable than prewar cycles? These questions are difficult to answer, and different researchers have arrived at sharply divergent conclusions.

Earlier research, which failed to produce a consensus, focused almost exclusively on business-cycle *volatility*. Recent research, however, examines business cycles from the different (and complementary) perspective of duration, focusing in particular on the lengths of expansions, contractions, and whole cycles. The duration perspective—unlike its volatility counterpart—reveals striking changes in the nature of postwar business cycles.

The Stability Debate: Volatility Perspective

Steady growth in the 1960s produced a generally accepted view that the U.S. economy had become more stable in the period after World War II. This consensus was reinforced by formal studies that focused on business-cycle volatility and concluded that it had decreased in the postwar period.[1]

---

[1] The focus was typically on fluctuations in measures of aggregate economic activity, such as real GNP, industrial production, or the unemployment rate. The variability, or volatility, of such aggregates was defined as the variance of the detrended series—that is, the average squared deviation from trend. Two well-known and representative studies are Martin N. Baily, "Stabilization Policy and Private Economic Behavior," *Brookings Papers on Economic Activity* (1978:1), pp. 11–60; and J. Bradford Delong and Lawrence H. Summers, "The Changing Cyclical Variability of Economic Activity in the United States," in R. J. Gordon, ed., *The American Business Cycle: Continuity and Change* (University of Chicago Press for NBER, 1986). See also Robert J. Gordon, "Postwar Macroeconomics: The Evolution of Events and Ideas," in M. Feldstein, ed., *The American Economy in Transition* (University of Chicago Press for NBER, 1980).

But the consensus on postwar volatility stabilization has been seriously challenged by Christina D. Romer, in a provocative and stimulating series of papers.[2] Romer argues that the higher volatility displayed by prewar aggregates—whether real GNP, industrial production, or the unemployment rate—reflects differences in methods of prewar and postwar data construction, and that the difference between prewar and postwar volatility is greatly lessened if similar methods are employed for both periods. In Romer's interpretation, the apparent moderation of the business cycle is largely an artifact of inconsistent data.

Romer's contention has not gone undisputed. Various authors have constructed alternative versions of prewar aggregates and have reached traditional conclusions about volatility stabilization.[3] Still others have argued that Romer's reconstructed aggregates—like the original series —depend significantly on unverifiable assumptions and therefore are not unambiguously superior to the original series.[4]

Currently, then, the debate focusing on volatility stabilization is deadlocked. The lesson emerging from the literature is that, given the limited availability of prewar data, it is difficult to measure quantitative prewar U.S. economic aggregates, even annually. Moreover, because the size of fluctuations in these macroeconomic aggregates will be crucial for resolving the volatility debate, inadequate measures of prewar aggregates make any comparison of pre- and postwar volatility rather uncertain.

The Stability Debate: Duration Perspective

It is possible, however, to provide new evidence on the stability of the postwar economy by investigating a different aspect of stabilization and employing a different type of data.

The different aspect of stability concerns the relative *duration*, rather than the relative volatility, of pre- and postwar business cycles. In other

[2] See her papers, "Spurious Volatility in Historical Unemployment Data," *Journal of Political Economy* 94 (1986), pp. 1–37; "Is the Stabilization of the Postwar Economy a Figment of the Data?" *American Economic Review* 76 (1986), pp. 314–34; and "The Prewar Business Cycle Reconsidered: New Estimates of Gross National Product, 1869–1908," *Journal of Political Economy* 97 (1989), pp. 1–37.

[3] David R. Weir, for example, considers historical unemployment series in "The Reliability of Historical Macroeconomic Data for Comparing Cyclical Stability," *Journal of Economic History* 46 (1986), pp. 353–65, while Nathan S. Balke and Robert J. Gordon consider GNP in "The Estimation of Prewar Gross National Product: Methodology and New Evidence," *Journal of Political Economy* 97 (1989), pp. 38–92.

[4] See, for example, Stanley Lebergott's discussion of Romer's paper in *Journal of Economic History* 46 (1986), pp. 367–71.

words, the duration perspective considers explicitly the *lengths* of phases of the business cycle, whereas the volatility perspective focuses on amplitude.[5]

The different data are a chronology of business-cycle turning points. Compared to an aggregate measure of economic activity, a business-cycle chronology contains both less information, because the chronology is qualitative rather than quantitative, and more information, because the chronology can incorporate more sources of cyclical information. The former attribute is obvious: identification of turning points requires only a qualitative sense of the direction of general business activity. Thus, it is easier to determine, for example, that the second quarter of 1894 was a cyclical peak than it is to determine that real GNP rose *x* percent and fell *y* percent in the second and third quarters of that year.

At the same time, because only qualitative information is required, a business-cycle chronology can be constructed from a broader set of indicators of business activity than just the components of aggregate measures such as real GNP or industrial production. For example, the National Bureau of Economic Research (NBER) business-cycle chronology, which we use, incorporates a variety of sources of cyclical information, including the price movements of stocks and other assets as well as descriptive accounts of economic activity from historical business annals. Such sources have necessarily been ignored in the volatility stabilization debate, which has focused only on aggregate measures; thus, the NBER business-cycle chronology implicitly brings new information to the debate about the changing nature of business fluctuations.

Documenting Duration Stabilization

Duration stabilization is suggested by even a casual examination of the history of U.S. expansions and contractions, shown in Figure 3.1, in which recessions appear in black. The period before World War II

---

[5] This idea is developed more fully in "Have Postwar Economic Fluctuations Been Stabilized?" by Francis X. Diebold and Glenn D. Rudebusch, Economic Activity Working Paper 116, Board of Governors of the Federal Reserve System (1991). The present article is largely a nontechnical synopsis of that paper, which in turn builds upon our earlier work in "Scoring the Leading Indicators," *Journal of Business* 62 (1989), pp. 369–92, and "A Nonparametric Investigation of Duration Dependence in the American Business Cycle," *Journal of Political Economy* 98 (1990), pp. 596–616. See also our paper with Daniel E. Sichel, "Further Evidence on Business Cycle Duration Dependence," forthcoming in J. H. Stock and M. W. Watson, eds., *New Research on Business Cycles, Indicators and Forecasting* (University of Chicago Press for NBER, 1991).

1855 1865   1875 1885 1895 1905 1915 1925 1935 1945 1955 1965 1975 1985   1995

Note: Recessionary episodes are shaded.

Fig. 3.1. NBER business-cycle chronology, 1855–1991.

contains a great deal more black; however, formal statistical analysis
can assess the likelihood that the apparent postwar change in the
business cycle is *real* rather than merely good luck.

Statistical analyses of data on lengths of expansions and contractions
reveal that the apparent shifts in duration patterns following World
War II are real. Statistically speaking, we can reject the hypothesis of no
change in the behavior of expansion and contraction durations at the
0.1 percent level; that is, the probability that the rejection is incorrect is
no larger than one-tenth of 1 percent. Furthermore, the nature of
postwar change is clear: expansions have become longer, and contractions have become shorter.

It is unusual in empirical macroeconomics to obtain such high significance levels, particularly with such small samples as the number of
expansions or contractions since World War II. But what of the more
important question: are the postwar shifts significant from an economic,
as opposed to statistical, perspective? Clearly, the answer is yes, as can
be seen from three related perspectives.

First, consider average duration. The average duration of a prewar
expansion is about 25 months, whereas that for postwar expansions is
about 50 months; thus, the average duration of expansions has roughly
doubled. Conversely, the average duration of prewar contractions is
about 20 months, whereas that for postwar contractions is about 10

months; thus, the average duration of contractions has roughly been *halved*.

Second, consider the ratio of expansion duration relative to the duration of the preceding contraction. The prewar average of this ratio is 1.5, whereas the postwar average is a much larger 4.5.

Third, consider the amount of time spent in recession. More than 40 percent of the prewar period was spent in recession, compared to a much smaller 20 percent for the postwar period.

The striking changes in expansion and contraction duration patterns are readily seen by comparing the cumulative proportion of expansions and contractions lasting no longer than k months, for various values of k. We call the cumulative proportion $F(k)$ in the prewar period and $G(k)$ in the postwar period. Our interest centers on the overall shapes of $F(k)$ and $G(k)$ for expansions and contractions, and particularly on the relative speeds with which they rise from zero to 1. A fast rise corresponds to durations that are short on average, and conversely.

The pre- and postwar cumulative proportions $F(k)$ and $G(k)$ are graphed in Figures 3.2 (expansions) and 3.3 (contractions). The axes in each figure are scaled identically, so the two figures are comparable. Duration stabilization shows clearly in the rightward shift of the cumu-

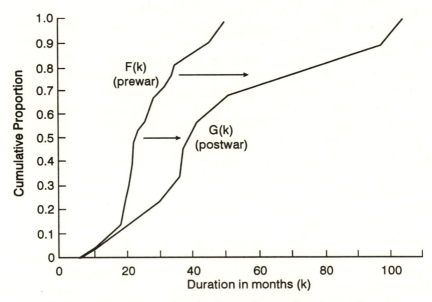

Fig. 3.2. Proportion of expansions lasting no longer than k months.

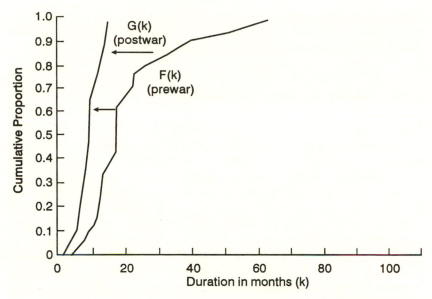

Fig. 3.3. Proportion of contractions lasting no longer than k months.

lative proportion for expansions, and by the leftward shift of the cumulative proportion for contractions. For example, Figure 3.2 shows that in the prewar period about 80 percent of expansions lasted less than 40 months, whereas in the postwar period only 50 percent lasted less than 40 months.

The behavior of whole-cycle duration patterns (whether measured peak-to-peak or trough-to-trough) is very different. Unlike the expansions and contractions of which they are composed, whole cycles show no evidence of postwar change. In fact, the hypothesis of no change cannot be rejected even at the 20 percent level. Thus, a reasonable distillation of the results is that the lengthening of postwar expansions and shortening of postwar contractions approximately cancel one another, leaving the patterns of whole-cycle durations unchanged. The time per business cycle has remained approximately constant, but *within* each cycle much more time is now spent in expansion.

All of the conclusions discussed here are robust to 1) changes in the ending date for the prewar sample (June 1938, August 1929, December 1914) to exclude the influence of the Great Depression or the interwar period in general; 2) exclusion of the pre-1885 turning-point dates in order to avoid potentially unreliable dates in the very early period; 3) exclusion of the 1887 and 1899 recessions, to account for the possibility that these were merely growth recessions; and 4) exclusion of wartime expansions (and whole cycles that include wartime expansions) to avoid the possibility of spuriously long observations.

Understanding Duration Stabilization

One obvious potential source of duration stabilization, ironically enough, is volatility stabilization! That is, to the extent that postwar volatility actually *was* stabilized, one expects, *ceteris paribus*, concomitant duration stabilization because of the upward trend in aggregate economic activity.[6] Therefore, potential sources of postwar volatility stabilization are also potential sources, at least in part, for postwar duration stabilization.[7] It is unlikely, however, that *all* of the postwar duration stabilization is associated with volatility stabilization. To the extent that volatility actually was stabilized, previous research has found that the reduction was small and hard to detect. The postwar shift toward duration stabilization, however, is large and difficult to deny. It is therefore likely that at least some of the duration stabilization arose independently of volatility stabilization.

The remaining potential factors underlying postwar duration stabilization can be broadly classified into three categories: 1) postwar changes in the nature of macroeconomic shocks; 2) postwar improvements in discretionary government policy; and 3) structural changes in the postwar economy. It is conceivable that these factors may have produced concomitant volatility and duration stabilization, or duration stabilization alone.

The first possibility—a direct change in the nature of postwar shocks—is certainly a logical possibility, but no evidence, either econometric or anecdotal, has been given as support. In particular, we know of no evidence indicating that macroeconomic shocks have changed in a way that led either to duration stabilization independent of volatility stabilization (a change in pattern but not size), or to concomitant duration and volatility stabilization (a change in size and perhaps pattern).

As for the second possibility, the start of the postwar period saw both a significant strengthening of the powers of monetary and fiscal policy and of the public commitment to use them to stabilize the economy. There is some evidence that this commitment alleviated fears of

---

[6] To see this, note that if the volatility of fluctuations around an upward trend is decreased, expansions are lengthened and contractions are shortened. In the limit, when volatility is zero, the economy is in permanent expansion, growing at the trend rate.

[7] Even the estimates least favorable to the volatility stabilization hypothesis—Romer's—indicate the possibility of some volatility stabilization in the postwar period.

macroeconomic catastrophes, by eliminating very long, deep recessions.[8] However, attempts to smooth the postwar period's moderate swings in business activity have been judged, even by those who normally might be somewhat sympathetic, as neutral at best, with successes offset by failures.[9] Overall, it would appear that if discretionary government policy in the postwar period produced duration stabilization, it did so independently of volatility stabilization. Such a scenario is not unreasonable, if policymakers perceived a link between the durations of expansions and contractions and welfare, perhaps along the lines discussed below, and took (successful) policy action accordingly.

The last set of factors—postwar structural changes in the economy—also includes likely sources of duration stabilization. Some of those changes have occurred independently of policy, such as the increased share of services (which have a very moderate cycle), increased availability of consumer credit (with a reduction in the number of liquidity-constrained households), and technical improvements leading to better inventory management. Others represent part of the postwar Keynesian institutional order, such as the introduction of "automatic stabilizers" (countercyclical entitlement programs, such as unemployment insurance, and an increasing marginal tax rate) and deposit insurance and regulation (which act indirectly through stabilization of the financial system).

Welfare Effects of Duration Stabilization

A natural question is whether duration stabilization improves welfare. A proper evaluation of this issue requires an economic model, and different models clearly produce different welfare rankings. Thus, an incontrovertible specification of the welfare gains and losses of duration stabilization will have to await a consensus theory.

From a Keynesian perspective, the lengthy periods of reduced output and low utilization of capital and labor inputs during recessions represent inefficient coordination failures; in particular, the additional unemployment and idleness incurred by workers during recessions is involuntary. The welfare cost of recessions in the Keynesian framework is

---

[8] See J. Bradford Delong and Lawrence H. Summers, "How Does Macroeconomic Policy Affect Output?" *Brookings Papers on Economic Activity* 2 (1988), pp. 433–80.

[9] See Robert J. Gordon, "Postwar Macroeconomics: The Evolution of Events and Ideas," in Martin Feldstein, ed., *The American Economy in Transition* (University of Chicago Press for NBER, 1980); Alan S. Blinder, *Economic Policy and the Great Stagflation* (New York: Academic Press, 1981); and Arthur M. Okun, "Postwar Macroeconomic Performance," in M. Feldstein, ed., *The American Economy in Transition*.

clearly evident in the shortfall of actual output from potential output. In this framework, the duration stabilization of the postwar period is welfare-improving.

In contrast, a different welfare assessment may be obtained from a neoclassical perspective. Models in the neoclassical tradition treat economic fluctuations as efficient outcomes of free-market competition; for example, the additional unemployment incurred during recessions represents a voluntary—and optimal—response by workers to changing opportunities. Thus, for neoclassical economists, duration stabilization need not be associated with increased welfare.

Recent work has tended to focus on equilibrium interpretations of economic fluctuations. However, an important subset of this work has stressed the existence of multiple equilibria: the economy may end up at a low level of output with higher unemployment or at a high level of output with lower unemployment. These outcomes are rankable in terms of welfare, suggesting that duration stabilization improves welfare because less time is spent in the low-output equilibrium.[10]

One condition associated with multiple equilibria is the presence of a complementarity or spillover between aggregate conditions and the actions or opportunities of individual agents.[11] A natural technological spillover occurs when the level of aggregate activity in one period affects firms' production functions in the next. For example, knowledge accumulated in one production period may affect subsequent production possibilities.[12] Furthermore, the accumulation of knowledge can be linked to the level of activity.[13] Indeed, a large literature suggests that the costs of idleness on human capital are substantial, because a crucial factor in accumulating human capital is the opportunity to maintain and update skills through employment. In contrast, unemployment results in an atrophy of skills, which reduces the effective supply of labor.[14] Thus, the shorter durations of postwar contractions may have curtailed the

---

[10] See, for example, Steven N. Durlauf, "Nonergodic Economic Growth," NBER Working Paper 3719 (1991).

[11] See, for example, Russell Cooper and Andrew John, "Coordinating Coordination Failures in Keynesian Models," *Quarterly Journal of Economics* 103 (1988), pp. 441–63.

[12] Paul Romer, for example, focuses on spillovers associated with human capital accumulation in "Increasing Returns and Long-Run Growth," *Journal of Political Economy* 94 (1986), pp. 1002–37.

[13] See Kenneth J. Arrow, "The Economic Implications of Learning by Doing," *Review of Economic Studies* 29 (1962), pp. 155–73.

[14] Extensive discussion of these effects can be found in Edward Phelps, *Inflation Policy and Unemployment Theory* (New York: Norton, 1972), and in Robert E. Hall, "The Phillips Curve and Macroeconomic Policy," *Carnegie-Rochester Conference Series on Economic Policy* 1 (1976), pp. 127–48.

loss of human capital and raised the level of production during subsequent expansions.

Conclusion

Investigating the stabilization hypothesis from the perspective of duration (or length), as opposed to volatility (or amplitude), has proved fruitful. There is strong evidence of a postwar shift toward longer expansions and shorter contractions, which is consistent with a broad interpretation of the stabilization hypothesis. Moreover, there is no evidence of a postwar shift in the distribution of whole-cycle durations, which suggests a reallocation of business-cycle time away from contraction and toward expansion.

Much less is known, however, about the sources and welfare effects of duration stabilization. Although it is easy to list potential sources of duration stabilization and potential welfare effects, deciding among them is difficult. Additional research along those lines will likely prove useful.

4

A Nonparametric Investigation of Duration Dependence in the American Business Cycle

FRANCIS X. DIEBOLD AND GLENN D. RUDEBUSCH*

1. Introduction

Several authors have recently modeled the business cycle as the out-come of a Markov process that switches between two discrete states, with one of the states representing expansions and the other represent-ing recessions. However, very different specifications have been adopted for the transition probability matrix governing the movement of the economy between these two states. For example, Neftci (1982) assumed that the transition probabilities were duration dependent; in particular, he assumed that the longer the economy remained in one state, the more likely it was to change to the other.[1] In contrast, Hamilton (1989) assumed that the state transition probabilities were duration indepen-dent so that, for example, after a long expansion (i.e., a long time in the expansion state), the economy was no more likely to switch to the recession state than after a short expansion.[2]

To resolve the question of the duration dependence of expansions and contractions, we investigate the nature of the probability process that generates their lengths. In addition, we consider the evidence for duration dependence in the lengths of whole cycles measured from peak to peak and from trough to trough. Whole-cycle duration dependence is obviously related to the question of half-cycle duration dependence, but it can also be interpreted in terms of a weak definition of stochastic periodicity, namely, that business cycle lengths tend to cluster around a

* We are grateful to two anonymous referees and an editor, as well as to seminar participants at Cornell, Montreal, Northwestern, Queen's, and Stanford, for constructive comments. Particular thanks go to Steve Durlauf, Eric Ghysels, Bob Hall, Nick Kiefer, Salih Neftci, Dave Runkle, Dan Sichel, Mark Watson, and David Wilcox. Diebold gratefully acknowledges financial support from the National Science Foundation and the University of Pennsylvania Research Foundation.

[1] This view has been expressed often in the popular press, e.g., with the suggestion that a very long expansion is unstable and is unusually likely to end.

[2] This is also the assumption of Diebold and Rudebusch (1989b).

certain duration. We argue that this notion of periodicity was implicit in an earlier literature on business cycles. For example, the classical "8-year" business cycle was distinguished as a cycle by its tendency to endure 8 years.

Of interest, of course, is the *significance* of the tendency of business fluctuations to maintain a fixed cyclical length. Early on, Irving Fisher (1925) argued that business cycles had no such tendency, but that instead they resembled "Monte Carlo cycles," the phantom cycles of luck perceived by gamblers at a casino. Similarly, to a casual observer of a repeated coin toss, runs of consecutive heads or tails may appear more likely to end as they grow longer, but the termination probability of a run actually remains constant. As Fisher would argue, one may tabulate the number of consecutive heads in repeated trials and find the average length of these runs, but there is no intrinsic clustering of run lengths, or periodicity, in the process. It is precisely this interpretation of weak business cycle periodicity that we shall test as our null hypothesis.

In Section 2, we explore more fully the notion of duration dependence in a macroeconomic context. In Section 3, we provide a weak definition of periodicity that will be useful in interpreting the duration dependence of whole cycles. Section 4 describes our empirical methodology, which employs nonparametric tests for duration dependence. These tests are based on the conformity of the lengths of half cycles and whole cycles to the exponential distribution, which corresponds to an absence of duration dependence. Empirical results are presented in Section 5, and Section 6 concludes with an interpretation in the light of recent developments in macroeconomics.

2. Macroeconomic Duration Dependence

A large statistical and econometric literature has addressed the interpretation of duration data.[3] A basic element of this analysis is the hazard function, denoted here as $\lambda(\tau)$, which is the conditional probability that a process will end after a duration of length τ, given that it has not terminated earlier. For example, microeconomic data indicate that lengths of employment for individuals exhibit a decreasing hazard function $(d\lambda(\tau)/d\tau < 0)$ or negative duration dependence; that is, the longer a job is held, the less likely it is to be lost. This section presents some aspects of duration analysis that are relevant for macroeconomics.

---

[3] This literature is well surveyed in Kiefer (1988).

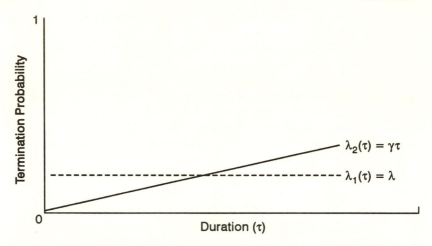

Fig. 4.1. Increasing and constant hazard functions.

Two examples of hazard functions are shown in figure 4.1. The constant hazard function, $\lambda_1(\tau) = \lambda$ (dashed line), reflects a termination probability with no duration dependence. The linearly increasing hazard function, $\lambda_2(\tau) = \gamma\tau$ (solid line), reflects a termination probability with positive duration dependence, so that termination probability increases with time. The question of the appropriate specification of a Markov model of the business cycle can be reduced to determining whether expansions and contractions are governed by a constant hazard, as assumed by Hamilton (1989), or by a nonconstant hazard such as $\lambda_2(\tau)$, as assumed by Neftci (1982).[4]

A given hazard function, $\lambda(\tau)$, provides a complete characterization of the unconditional density of durations, $f(\tau)$, since

$$f(\tau) = \lambda(\tau)\exp\left[-\int_0^\tau \lambda(u)\,du\right]. \tag{1}$$

Figure 4.2 displays the duration densities associated with the hazard functions given in figure 4.1. The constant hazard implies an exponen-

[4] As a related issue, Neftci (1984) investigates whether the hazard rates of expansions and contractions are the same, i.e., whether the state transition matrix and hence business cycles are symmetric. In contrast to his earlier work, Neftci performs the analysis under an assumption of time-invariant transition probabilities.

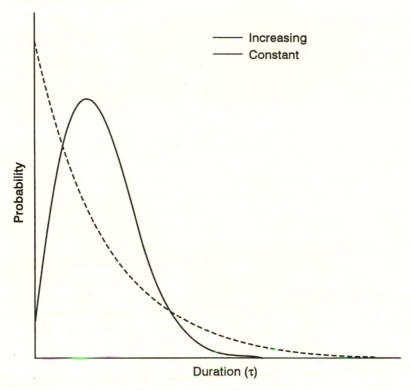

Fig. 4.2. Duration distributions associated with increasing and constant hazards.

tial density of durations (dashed line),[5]

$$f_1(\tau) = \lambda \exp(-\lambda\tau), \tau \geq 0. \tag{2}$$

Thus given a constant probability λ of termination, the density of durations is monotonically declining. Alternatively, the linearly upward-sloping hazard implies a particular nonexponential density of durations (solid line),

$$f_2(\tau) = \gamma\tau \exp\left(-\frac{\gamma}{2}\tau^2\right), \tau \geq 0. \tag{3}$$

This density is nonmonotonic and unimodal, and there is a clear concentration of probability mass around the modal value.

[5] In discrete time, the corresponding probability distribution is geometric, $f(\tau) = (1 - \lambda)^{\tau-1}\lambda$, $\tau = 1, 2, 3, \ldots$, which has the obvious coin toss interpretation of Fisher.

The specific distribution of durations corresponding to a nonconstant hazard will of course depend on that hazard's particular form. In general, however, the probability mass associated with a hazard displaying positive duration dependence is more concentrated around its mean than that associated with the exponential distribution of the same mean.[6] This is an implication of the turning point probability's rising with duration. Consider, for example, the increasing hazard, $\lambda_2(\tau) = \gamma\tau$, which implies a duration density with mean $E(\tau) = (\pi/2\gamma)^{1/2}$ and variance $\mathrm{var}(\tau) = (4 - \pi)/2\gamma$. Note that $d\lambda(\tau)/d\tau$ is positive and increasing in γ, while $\mathrm{var}(\tau)$ is decreasing in γ. That is, as the amount of positive duration dependence increases, the variance of the durations decreases. In addition, the exponential density with an identical mean has a larger variance since the exponential density with mean duration $(\pi/2\gamma)^{1/2}$ has variance $\pi/2\gamma$, which is of course greater than $(4 - \pi)/2\gamma$ for all positive γ.

To summarize, a constant hazard implies an exponential distribution of durations. Thus an exponential distribution of historical lengths of expansions and contractions is precisely the null hypothesis implicit in Fisher (1925) and Hamilton (1989), and it is the one that we shall test below. Furthermore, the positive duration dependence of an increasing hazard induces duration "clustering" around the mean duration, relative to the constant-hazard case. As we describe in the next section, for durations of whole cycles, this clustering has a natural interpretation.

3. Business Cycle Periodicity

In this section, whole-cycle positive duration dependence is related to a weak definition of periodicity, an interpretation that provides intuitive content to the former and empirical content to the latter. To both motivate and clarify our discussion, we shall elucidate several different forms of periodicity, including deterministic and stochastic and strong and weak.

---

[6]This general proposition can be proved, as suggested to us by Martin Wells, by noting the strict concavity of the log survivor function, $\log[1 - F(\tau)]$, when $\lambda(\tau)$ is strictly increasing. Marshall and Olkin (1979, p. 494) show that this concavity implies that the rth moments about the origin, μ_r, are concave in logs when normalized by r factorial ($r!$). In particular, $\log(\mu_1) > 1/2\log(\mu_0) + 1/2\log(\mu_2/2)$. After rearrangement, this implies that $\mathrm{var}(\tau)$ is less than $[E(\tau)]^2$, which is equal to the variance of the exponential distribution with mean $E(\tau)$.

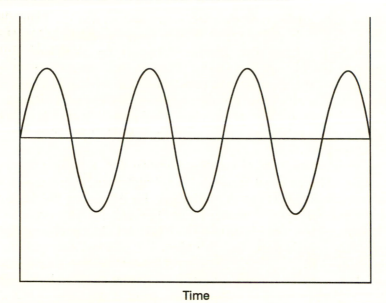

Time

Fig. 4.3. Deterministic strong periodicity.

We shall say that a variable X_t displays *deterministic strong periodicity* of period T if $X_{t+T} = X_t$, for all t.[7] This type of periodicity is found in many early macroeconomic models, such as the multiplier-accelerator and inventory systems of Samuelson (1939) and Metzler (1947). Samuelson's well-known analysis, for example, uses a multiplier-accelerator system to derive a deterministic second-order difference equation for aggregate output. Over a certain range of parameters, this equation produces stable deterministic cycles with a constant period of the type shown in figure 4.3.

A stochastic framework provides a more realistic basis for analysis of periodicity in economics. The definition of *stochastic strong periodicity* of period T is a straightforward generalization that replaces the equality of X_t and X_{t+T} with a high correlation between these values for all t. Such periodicity has a more precise frequency domain definition as a peak in the spectral density at the frequency corresponding to period T. Frisch (1933) demonstrated that a structural propagation mechanism can convert uncorrelated stochastic impulses into cyclical output with stochastic strong periodicity. This idea of a stochastic, periodic cycle

---

[7] This definition and the ones that follow abstract from considerations of growth; we also disregard trivial cases such as a constant $X_t = k$.

obtained from a perturbed macroeconomic system was the foundation for large-scale macroeconometric models (see, e.g., Klein 1983). However, there has been little empirical support for stochastic strong periodicity in economic fluctuations. Perhaps the most influential evidence against such periodicity is provided by the spectra of macroeconomic variables, which are typically monotonically declining from low to high frequencies (except at seasonal frequencies) with little power concentration at business cycle frequencies (e.g., Granger 1966; Sargent 1987, chap. 11).[8]

We shall attempt to assess the evidence for a weaker form of periodicity. The essential feature of a strongly periodic process is the close relationship between X_t and X_{t+T} for all t. For the irregular cycles of business activity, weaker forms of periodicity, which depend on periodic repetition for only certain t, are useful. For example, we define *deterministic peak-to-peak weak periodicity* (of period T) to exist for a series if for every t such that X_t is a peak in the series, X_{t+T} is also a peak.[9] This is shown in figure 4.4 with a series that has uniformly spaced cyclical peaks but is not periodic at every point in the cycle as in figure 4.3. In particular, note that this series does not exhibit deterministic *trough-to-trough* weak periodicity, which is exhibited when a trough at time t is always followed by a trough at time $t + T$.[10]

The concept of weak periodicity can be extended to a stochastic framework. A series displays *stochastic* peak-to-peak weak periodicity (of period T) if for every X_t that is a peak in the series, $X_{t+\tau}$ is also a peak, where τ is a random variable with mean T and variance

---

[8] This evidence should be interpreted with caution, however, given the small samples involved and the sensitivity of the results to various types of trend adjustment. Furthermore, spectral methods are intrinsically lienar and are not compatible with the Markov framework of Neftci (1982) and Hamilton (1989) (see also Neftci 1986; Diebold and Rudebusch 1989b).

[9] This definition can be formalized with a function, $TP(\cdot)$, that signals turning points. Specifically, if $Y_t = TP(X_t)$, then Y_t is a sequence that is always zero except at a peak in X_t, when $Y_t = 1$, and at a trough in X_t, when $Y_t = -1$. The series X_t displays deterministic peak-to-peak weak periodicity if, for each t such that $Y_t = 1$, $Y_{t+T} = 1$.

[10] Clearly, strong periodicity implies weak periodicity but not conversely; however, the two definitions of periodicity can be closely linked by a time deformation. Stock (1987) argues that macroeconomic variables appear to evolve on an economic time scale that may speed up or slow down relative to the observed calendar time scale. In such a setting, a cyclical process that is strongly periodic in economic time would be distorted by the nonlinear time deformation into a nonperiodic process in calendar time. However, if the speeding up and slowing down of economic time relative to calendar time averaged out over the cycle, the process would still display weak periodicity in the constancy of peak-to-peak or trough-to-trough durations. Indeed, fig. 4.4 is generated by applying precisely such a time deformation to fig. 4.3.

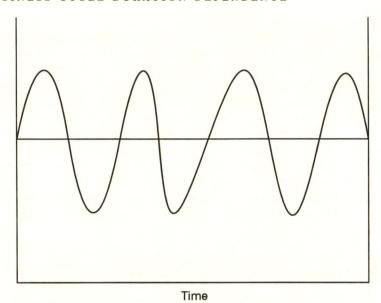

Fig. 4.4. Deterministic peak-to-peak weak periodicity.

σ^2.[11] Stochastic peak-to-peak weak periodicity implies that there is a tight distribution of observed peak-to-peak cycle durations (τ) around the mean period; that is, σ^2 is small. Deterministic peak-to-peak periodicity emerges, of course, when $\sigma^2 = 0$. More generally, however, a natural metric with which to evaluate the size of σ^2, and hence the extent of periodicity, is provided by the exponential distribution. Recall from the last section the close relationship between positive duration dependence and duration clustering relative to an exponential distribution. In particular, if the durations of cycles from peak to peak are clustered around a period of 4 years, then a 2-year-old cycle is less likely to end (i.e., more likely to survive 2 more years) and a 6-year-old cycle is more likely to end (i.e., less likely to survive even longer than 4 years) than a 4-year-old cycle. Thus, for periodic cycles, the probability of a peak is increasing with the length of the ongoing cycle. Nonperiodic cycles, on the other hand, have no particular interval after which they are more likely to end; their turning points are not positively related to the age of the cycle. In this sense, the exponential distribution provides a metric for the extent of periodicity; it allows one to ask whether the distribution of actual business cycle durations is more closely clustered than would be expected from a constant hazard probability model with the same mean duration.

---

[11] The stochastic form of weak trough-to-trough periodicity is similarly straightforward.

The stochastic weak form of periodicity, defined in terms of a cluster-ing tendency of intervals between turning points, has been used implic-itly in many previous discussions of business fluctuations. For example, Matthews (1959, p. 216), in a chapter on business cycle periodicity, implicitly adopts this definition when describing the path of British investment: "Apart from the minor wobbles in the curve around 1877 and 1902, the durations of the cycles measured from trough to trough are 6, 8, 10, 5 years; measured from peak to peak they are 9, 7, 10, 7 years. This is not precisely a seven to ten-year cycle, but it is as near to it as anyone could reasonably expect." The data he presents are sugges-tive of a clustering of cycle lengths, that is, weak periodicity.[12] We shall examine more rigorously the empirical distributions of durations of whole cycles and half cycles with procedures detailed in the next section.

4. Nonparametric Tests for Duration Dependence

We use nonparametric methods to directly test observed durations for conformity to the exponential distribution. Our analysis is intentionally nonparametric since we do not estimate and test a particular hazard model. The imposition of incorrect parametric forms can distort the available departures from the null hypothesis, and it is now well known that incorrect parameterizations of the hazard function can lead to severely misleading inferences (see, e.g., Heckman and Singer 1984).

A description of our testing methodology first requires discussion of the data. The lengths of expansions, contractions, and whole cycles are derived from business cycle turning dates since 1854, as designated by the National Bureau of Economic Research (NBER). These durations (in months) are given in table 4.1 and provide the raw data for our analysis.[13] By definition, a cycle is designated in the NBER methodology

---

[12] For other examples, see Adelman and Adelman (1959, p. 614) (who note approvingly the equivalence of peak-to-peak and trough-to-trough durations in the Klein-Goldberger model and in historical cycles), Zarnowitz (1985, pp. 525–26), and Britton (1986, p. 3). The last of these, which is devoted exclusively to an examination of business cycle periodicity, states that "this 'central tendency' [of cyclical durations]... is another way of describing the phenomenon with which the present study is concerned."

[13] In our samples that include postwar expansions, there is a right-censoring problem associated with the current expansion. We have assumed that this last duration is 80 months instead of its unknown, but longer, true length. This affects the durations of the last expansion, the last peak-to-peak cycle, and, with the additional assumption of a following 9-month contraction, the last trough-to-trough cycle. Since the current expan-sion is already quite long by historical standards, any additional length would shift the results slightly in the direction of no duration dependence. All our results are robust to varying the length of this final expansion over a wide range.

TABLE 4.1
NBER Business Cycle Reference Dates and Durations

Trough	Peak	Contractions	Expansions	Trough to Trough	Peak to Peak
December 1854	June 1857	NA	30	NA	NA
December 1858	October 1860	18	22	48	40
June 1861	April 1865	8	**46**	30	**54**
December 1867	June 1869	32	18	**78**	50
December 1870	October 1873	18	34	36	52
March 1879	March 1882	65	36	99	101
May 1885	March 1887	38	22	74	60
April 1888	July 1890	13	27	35	40
May 1891	January 1893	10	20	37	30
June 1894	December 1895	17	18	37	35
June 1897	June 1899	18	24	36	42
December 1900	September 1902	18	21	42	39
August 1904	May 1907	23	33	44	56
June 1908	January 1910	13	19	46	32
January 1912	January 1913	24	12	43	36
December 1914	August 1918	23	**44**	35	**67**
March 1919	January 1920	7	10	**51**	17
July 1921	May 1923	18	22	28	40
July 1924	October 1926	14	27	36	41
November 1927	August 1929	13	21	40	34
March 1933	May 1937	43	50	64	93
June 1938	February 1945	13	**80**	63	**93**
October 1945	November 1948	8	37	**88**	45
October 1949	July 1953	11	**45**	48	**56**
May 1954	August 1957	10	39	**55**	49
April 1958	April 1960	8	24	47	32
February 1961	December 1969	10	**106**	34	**116**
November 1970	November 1973	11	36	**117**	47
March 1975	January 1980	16	58	52	74
July 1980	July 1981	6	12	64	18
November 1982	?	16	80	28	96
?		NA	NA	89	NA

Note: The 80-month duration of the last expansion, the 96-month duration of the last peak-to-peak cycle, and the 89-month duration of the last trough-to-trough cycle are conservative estimates. They assume a peak in July 1989 and, for the last of these, a trough 9 months later. Wartime expansions and cycles containing wartime expansions are boldfaced.

only if it has achieved a certain maturity. Burns and Mitchell (1946, pp. 57–58) describe this criterion: "We do not recognize a rise and fall as a specific cycle unless its duration is at least fifteen months, whether measured from peak to peak or trough to trough. Fluctuations lasting less than two years are scrutinized with special care." Forty years later, Moore and Zarnowitz (1986), in a survey of the NBER methodology, reaffirm this maturity criterion. They indicate that full cycles of less than 1 year in duration and contractions of less than 6 months would be very unlikely to qualify for selection.

Previous examinations of macroeconomic duration dependence, including McCulloch (1975), Savin (1977), and de Leeuw (1987), also have recognized this maturity criterion. However, these earlier studies are limited in two major respects. First, previous analyses examine only the durations of expansions and contractions, but not whole cycles; thus the evidence provided is incomplete.[14] Second, the earlier work obtains evidence on duration dependence from the goodness of fit of estimated sample histograms to a null constant hazard distribution. The power of these tests has been questioned in small sample sizes (see Sichel 1989), and the results obtained with this method often depend on the arbitrary number of cells used in histogram construction (see the sensitivity analysis of Diebold and Rudebusch [1990]).

We shall apply nonparametric tests that have greater power and do not involve the arbitrary factors involved with histogram construction. Rather than grouping observations into histogram bins and thereby discarding information, these tests compare the observations with their ordered rank. The null hypothesis is

$$H_0: f(\tau) = \lambda \exp[-\lambda(\tau - t_0)], \ \tau \geq t_0, \lambda \text{ unknown}, t_0 \text{ unknown}. \quad (4)$$

That is, the duration random variable τ has an exponential probability density function, where λ has the earlier interpretation as the constant hazard and t_0 is the unknown minimum possible duration from the NBER maturity criterion, which will differ for expansions, contractions, and whole cycles. Shapiro and Wilk (1972) extended their well-known test for normality to provide a similar test for the exponential null H_0.

---

[14] Expansion and contraction durations individually could show no duration dependence but be negatively correlated during the cycle so as to induce duration dependence in whole cycles.

Renumber the durations in ascending order, so that $x_1 \leq x_2 \leq \cdots \leq x_N$; then

$$W = \frac{(\bar{x} - x_1)^2}{(N - 1)\hat{\sigma}^2},\tag{5}$$

where $\bar{x} = \sum_{i=1}^{N} x_i/N$ and $\hat{\sigma}^2 = \sum_{i=1}^{N}(x_i - \bar{x})^2/N$. The W statistic is a scaled ratio of the squared difference between the mean and shortest duration to the sample variance. The distribution of W is invariant to the true values of λ and t_0, and its exact finite-sample critical values have been tabulated by Shapiro and Wilk for N ranging from three to 100.

Also relevant to our investigation is a modified W statistic developed by Stephens (1978) for testing exponentially conditional on an assumed known minimum duration, $t_0 = \gamma$, so that the null hypothesis becomes

$$H_0': f(\tau) = \lambda \exp[-\lambda(\tau - \gamma)], \quad \tau \geq \gamma, \lambda \text{ unknown}, \gamma \text{ known.}\tag{6}$$

Define $A = \sum_{i=1}^{N}(x_i - \gamma)$ and $B = \sum_{i=1}^{N}(x_i - \gamma)^2$. Then the new statistic, denoted $W(t_0 = \gamma)$, is given by

$$W(t_0 = \gamma) = \frac{A^2}{N[(N + 1)B - A^2]}.\tag{7}$$

The statistic $W(t_0 = \gamma)$ has the same distribution for a sample of size N as the W statistic has for a sample of size $N + 1$, so the same table of finite-sample critical values can be used. Both of these statistics allow for the absence of short durations, but the W statistic incorporates a true but unknown t_0 value into the null hypothesis, while $W(t_0 = \gamma)$ *conditions* on an *assumed* t_0 value. The $W(t_0 = \gamma)$ test is useful given information about the NBER maturity criterion and the likely range of the minimum allowable duration t_0; furthermore, a sensitivity analysis that varies t_0 is readily performed.[15]

Finally, we examine another class of nonparametric tests for the exponential distribution. Consider first the null hypothesis H_0 and

---

[15] A clear trade-off emerges between W and $W(t_0 = \gamma)$. If the conditioning information employed in the latter is correct, it is expected to have higher power; if it is incorrect, nominal and empirical size will diverge. Since the validity of a chosen t_0 value cannot be ascertained exactly a priori in our application, the W and $W(t_0 = \gamma)$ tests are useful in conjunction.

define the normalized spacings between the ordered durations as

$$Y_i = (N - i + 1)(x_i - x_{i-1}), i = 2, \ldots, N. \tag{8}$$

A plot of Y_i versus i provides a mirror image of the plot of the hazard function; that is, increasing spacings imply a decreasing hazard function. Thus in a regression of normalized spacings on order, namely, $Y_i = \alpha + \beta i$, the exponential hypothesis implies that $\beta = 0$. Brain and Shapiro (1983) exploit this result to obtain a test statistic for exponentiality, denoted Z. Let $\tilde{i}$ and $\tilde{Y}_i$ denote the "de-meaned" variables $i - (N/2)$ and $Y_i - \bar{Y}$. Then

$$Z = \frac{\displaystyle\sum_{i=1}^{N-1} \tilde{i}\tilde{Y}_{i+1}}{\displaystyle\sum_{i=1}^{N-1} Y_{i+1}\left[\sum_{i=1}^{N-1} \tilde{i}^2/N(N-1)\right]^{1/2}}. \tag{9}$$

The distribution of the Z statistic is asymptotically $N(0,1)$, which it quickly approaches even in quite small samples. Furthermore, an assumed known minimum duration $t_0 = \gamma$ also can be conditioned on with the Z statistic to test null hypothesis H_0'. Simply consider γ as an additional observation and include as the first weighted spacing $Y_2 = N(x_1 - \gamma)$ in the calculations in equation (9) (running the iteration from one to N). The modified test statistic is denoted $Z(t_0 = \gamma)$. Brain and Shapiro also provide an alternative statistic, denoted Z^*, that is intended to be more sensitive to alternative duration distributions associated with nonlinear hazard functions.[16] The statistic Z^* is constructed from a linear regression *and* a quadratic regression of Y_i on order and has an asymptotic chi-squared distribution that appears, from the simulation study in Brain and Shapiro, to be appropriate even in small samples.

A number of Monte Carlo studies have examined the power of the W and Z tests against various alternatives, including the Weibull, chi-squared, half-normal, and lognormal distributions.[17] Overall, the W and Z tests appear to be comparable in their ability to detect departures from exponentially, with small comparative advantages for one or the other against specific alternative distributions. Both appear to have

---

[16] For example, with a hump-shaped hazard function, the slope of the fitted linear regression line, $Y_i = \alpha + \beta i$, may be close to zero. Thus the Z and $Z(t_0 = \gamma)$ statistics, which are based on this slope, may not be sensitive to such alternatives.

[17] Besides power studies in the papers cited above by Shapiro, Wilk, Brain, and Stephens, there are also relevant results in Samanta and Schwarz (1988).

excellent power in the range of small sample sizes relevant for our analysis.

5. Empirical Results

Besides performing the constant hazard tests on the full samples of expansions, contractions, and peak-to-peak and trough-to-trough cycles, we also examine a variety of subsamples. These include only pre- or post-World War II observations and may exclude wartime expansions and the whole cycles that contain them. The various duration samples investigated are listed in table 4.2 with their associated sample size,

TABLE 4.2
Business Cycle, Expansion, and Contraction Samples

Sample	Sample Size	Mean Duration	Standard Error
Expansions:			
E1. Entire sample	31	34.6	21.8
E2. Entire sample, excluding wars	26	28.9	15.3
E3. Post-WWII	9	48.6	28.9
E4. Post-WWII, excluding wars	7	40.9	22.3
E5. Pre-WWII	21	26.5	10.7
E6. Pre-WWII, excluding wars	19	24.5	9.2
Contractions:			
C1. Entire sample	30	18.1	12.5
C2. Post-WWII	9	10.7	3.4
C3. Pre-WWII	21	21.2	13.6
Peak to peak:			
PP1. Entire sample	30	52.8	24.9
PP2. Entire sample, excluding wars	25	47.9	22.0
PP3. Post-WWII	9	59.2	31.0
PP4. Post-WWII, excluding wars	7	51.6	26.0
PP5. Pre-WWII	20	47.9	20.3
PP6. Pre-WWII, excluding wars	18	46.6	20.9
Trough to trough:			
TT1. Entire sample	31	52.3	22.1
TT2. Entire sample, excluding wars	26	47.4	17.8
TT3. Post-WWII	9	59.0	27.5
TT4. Post-WWII, excluding wars	7	51.3	19.3
TT5. Pre-WWII	21	47.7	18.1
TT6. Pre-WWII, excluding wars	19	45.9	17.6

mean duration, and standard error.[18] The variation in the standard error, one measure of dispersion, anticipates some of our later statistical results, which will also account for sample size, mean duration, and minimum duration.

Our study of various subsamples is an attempt to control for possible heterogeneity across cycles. We are interested in duration dependence induced by economic behavior, and the chosen sample should reflect intrinsic macroeconomic forces rather than special factors. That is, the *systematic* mechanism of business cycles, which are properly considered a modern phenomenon of market economies, should be distinguished from *accidental* and episodic crises associated with wars, bad harvests, and foreign manipulation of oil prices.[19] Although one can always find circumstances specific to each cycle, to the extent that all business cycles are alike in their essentials, any intrinsic duration dependence should be evident. In the absence of any clear information on the size or direction of the bias associated with large, episodic exogenous shocks, we have some preference for complete samples.[20]

Probability values for the test statistics are given in tables 4.3 and 4.4. These *p*-values represent the likelihood of obtaining the value of the test statistic actually obtained under the null of no duration dependence.[21] Small *p*-values therefore indicate significant departures from exponentiality. We generally prefer the third column of each table, that is, the $W(t_0 = \gamma)$ and $Z(t_0 = \gamma)$ tests, which assume a minimum duration equal to the shortest observed duration (i.e., 17 months for cycles, 10 for expansions, and 6 for contractions). The first two columns in each table check the robustness of the results with smaller t_0 values, while the W, Z, and Z^* columns do not incorporate information regarding the likely range of t_0. We also generally prefer the W statistics over the Z statistics since their exact finite-sample critical values are available.

---

[18] It can be argued that the success of macroeconomics and macroeconomic policy has been the halving of the mean duration of contractions in the postwar period. This point is different from the one Baily (1978) made about diminished postwar amplitudes, which was disputed by Romer (1989) but reaffirmed by Balke and Gordon (1989).

[19] See Burns and Mitchell (1946, chap. 1). For an evaluation of the role that such shocks have played in directing the path of U.S. economic fluctuations, see Blanchard and Watson (1986).

[20] Large, exogenous shocks may bias the evidence for weak economic periodicity in either direction. For example, the coincidence of two oil price shocks in 1974 and 1979 or the existence of a quadrennial political business cycle may spuriously strengthen the evidence. (See Britton [1986, chap. 6] for a discussion.)

[21] The tests employed require that the observations are independent. In fact the correlations between successive durations in table 4.1 are quite low and are not statistically significant at even the 20 percent level.

TABLE 4.3
W and $W(t_0 = \gamma)$ Tests for Exponentiality (p-Values under the Null of No Duration Dependence)

	Statistic			
Sample	$W(t_0 = 8)$	$W(t_0 = 9)$	$W(t_0 = 10)$	W
Expansions:				
E1	.360	.533	.699	.573
E2	.113	.194	.410	.211
E3	.512	.573	.633	.420
E4	.524	.592	.660	.310
E5	< .01	.019	.044	.015
E6	< .01	.018	.043	< .01
	$W(t_0 = 4)$	$W(t_0 = 5)$	$W(t_0 = 6)$	W
Contractions:				
C1	.725	.990	.672	.810
C2	.044	.150	.580	.188
C3	.436	.548	.859	.904
	$W(t_0 = 13)$	$W(t_0 = 15)$	$W(t_0 = 17)$	W
Peak to peak:				
PP1	< .01	.016	.037	.017
PP2	.015	.039	.085	.042
PP3	.351	.467	.581	.250
PP4	.509	.625	.741	.317
PP5	.010	.028	.057	.021
PP6	.040	.079	.151	.073
	$W(t_0 = 13)$	$W(t_0 = 15)$	$W(t_0 = 17)$	W
Trough to trough:				
TT1	< .01	< .01	< .01	.698
TT2	< .01	< .01	< .01	.748
TT3	.136	.182	.280	.735
TT4	.086	.117	.162	.523
TT5	< .01	< .01	.010	.778
TT6	< .01	< .01	.026	.971

Note: These finite-sample p-values are obtained by linearly interpolating the tables in Shapiro and Wilk (1972). The samples are identified in Table 4.2.

TABLE 4.4
Z, Z^*, and $Z(t_0 = \gamma)$ Tests for Exponentiality (p-Values under the Null of No Duration Dependence)

Sample	Statistic				
	$Z(t_0 = 8)$	$Z(t_0 = 9)$	$Z(t_0 = 10)$	Z	Z^*
Expansions:					
E1	.383	.574	.818	.579	.077
E2	.165	.292	.491	.291	.028
E3	.705	.781	.862	.547	.320
E4	.701	.780	.866	.488	.382
E5	.021	.043	.090	.033	.008
E6	.022	.047	.099	.034	< .005
	$Z(t_0 = 4)$	$Z(t_0 = 5)$	$Z(t_0 = 6)$	Z	Z^*
Contractions:					
C1	.587	.952	.453	.662	.052
C2	.096	.252	.672	.268	.351
C3	.393	.633	.956	.974	.067
	$Z(t_0 = 13)$	$Z(t_0 = 15)$	$Z(t_0 = 17)$	Z	Z^*
Peak to peak:					
PP1	.011	.027	.067	.028	< .005
PP2	.018	.043	.103	.043	< .005
PP3	.535	.653	.792	.406	.357
PP4	.677	.814	.972	.487	.431
PP5	.018	.038	.080	.028	< .005
PP6	.045	.087	.169	.064	< .005
	$Z(t_0 = 13)$	$Z(t_0 = 15)$	$Z(t_0 = 17)$	Z	Z^*
Trough to trough:					
TT1	< .005	< .005	.009	.964	.633
TT2	< .005	< .005	.006	.960	.416
TT3	.294	.371	.467	.921	.502
TT4	.210	.269	.346	.713	.709
TT5	< .005	.008	.018	.943	.162
TT6	.006	.014	.031	.838	.050

Note: The p-values are obtained using the asymptotic distributions of the Z and $Z(t_0 = \gamma)$ statistics, which are $N(0,1)$, and of the Z^* statistic, which is χ^2 with two degrees of freedom. The samples are identified in table 4.2.

Consider first the W, Z, and Z^* tests that do not condition on a particular choice of t_0. When the expansion sample is taken as a whole, the case for positive duration dependence appears very slight.[22] Exclusion of wartime expansions leads to a reduced p-value, but we still fail to reject the null of no duration dependence at conventional significance levels. Significant duration dependence is indicated for prewar expansions, especially when wars are excluded, while postwar expansions show no evidence of duration dependence, regardless of whether wars are excluded. There is no evidence for duration dependence in any of the samples of contractions; however, in contrast to expansions, there is more evidence for duration dependence in the postwar period (though not significant at conventional levels) than in the prewar period.[23] It is interesting to note that, while there is generally little evidence of duration dependence in either expansions or contractions, there is significant duration dependence over the entire cycle, measured peak to peak.[24]

The Z test results are in solid agreement with those of the W test. The Z^* test results also accord quite closely, leading us to suspect that most departures from the constant-hazard null hypothesis are monotone.

We now report the results of the $W(t_0 = \gamma)$ and $Z(t_0 = \gamma)$ tests, which make use of conditioning information on t_0. An upper bound (and, in fact, a reasonable choice) for t_0 is the actual shortest observed duration. Thus our preferred t_0 value is 6 months for contractions and 10 months for expansions. For peak-to-peak cycles, the shortest duration is 17 months, which is about the sum of the shortest contraction and expansion lengths. For trough-to-trough cycles, the shortest duration is 28 months; however, with no evidence of a distinction

---

[22] The nature of the deviation from exponentiality, if any, can be inferred from the sign of the Z statistics, which were negative for all significant or near-significant departures from the null. The sign of the Z statistic is the same as the slope of the regression of the normalized spacings on the order, which is the inverse of the regression of the durations on the order. Thus negative Z statistics are associated with positive duration dependence.

[23] One interpretation of this result is that postwar countercyclical policy has been at least partially successful in terms of increasing duration dependence in contractions: i.e., contractions cluster around the smaller mean.

[24] As will be seen shortly, there is also strong evidence of duration dependence in trough-to-trough cycles, which the W, Z, and Z^* tests fail to detect. This is due to the minimum duration of 28 months for most of the trough-to-trough cycles, which are implicitly used by the W, Z, and Z^* tests as the minimum duration. The tests with lower, more reasonable, minimum durations do detect duration dependence in trough-to-trough cycles.

by the NBER in designating the two types of cycles,[25] we prefer a t_0 of 17 months for each type of complete cycle. This conditioning information has one important effect. The results for trough-to-trough cycles now closely match those obtained for peak-to-peak cycles and imply positive duration dependence in most samples.

The results from the $Z(t_0 = \gamma)$ test are very similar to those obtained with the $W(t_0 = \gamma)$ test. The differences between the first three columns of tables 4.3 and 4.4 are very slight. Notably, the $Z(t_0 = 17)$ column for whole cycles closely agrees with the $W(t_0 = 17)$ column.

We believe that our results, which for the most part suggest whole-cycle positive duration dependence and half-cycle duration independence, can be fruitfully reconciled. Whole-cycle duration dependence can take several different forms. Clearly, if both halves of the cycle exhibit duration dependence, so will the whole cycle. In addition, duration dependence of just expansions or of just contractions (with no duration dependence for the other half cycle) could generate cyclical duration dependence. Finally, if neither half cycle displays duration dependence but their lengths are negatively correlated, the whole cycle may display duration dependence. If duration dependence and weak periodicity were an important and intrinsic feature of the business cycle, one would expect that one of the forms would predominate over the sample. Our results on half-cycle duration dependence indicate that this is not the case; instead, the significant whole-cycle duration dependence appears to be a mixture of all these possibilities. The slightly significant prewar expansion duration dependence and the almost significant postwar contraction duration dependence coupled with a slight negative correlation between half-cycle durations drive the whole-cycle results.[26] This clearly qualifies our whole-cycle results since it admits the possibility that they are a spurious coincidence of several factors.

6. Conclusion

Our examination of the complete samples of expansions and contractions uncovered little evidence for duration dependence, which suggests that the maintained assumption of constant Markov transition probabilities in Hamilton (1989) is legitimate. In the postwar sample, our results indicate that this assumption appears to be particularly valid for expan-

---

[25] Recall the Burns and Mitchell statement of Sec. IV.

[26] Over the whole sample, the correlation between an expansion and the following contraction is $-.21$, and for a contraction with the following expansion it is $-.04$. Neither of these, however, is significant.

sions and perhaps less so for contractions, although the very small size of these samples may impair the power of the tests.

In contrast to our results for expansions and contractions, we have found some indication of duration dependence in whole cycles, although these results must be qualified by the uncertain and varying nature of the duration dependence. However, if durations of cycles are indeed more tightly clustered than those associated with an exponential distribution, then this appears to provide evidence against Fisher's hypothesis of a "Monte Carlo" business cycle. The positive cyclical duration dependence suggests weakly periodic behavior and hence a business cycle that cannot be completely characterized only by examination of *comovements* among macroeconomic aggregates (as in Lucas [1977]). Stochastic weak periodicity, as manifested by positive duration dependence, may be an important feature of American business fluctuations, in addition to the obvious multivariate interactions. Here, however, more research is required to assess the economic significance of any duration dependence rather than just its statistical significance.

By directly examining durations of NBER-designated expansions, contractions, and cycles, we beneficially avoided conditioning on a particular model. However, it will be of interest to ascertain the duration dependence properties of various theoretical macroeconomic models. Models of recent vintage, whether of the new-classical, new-Keynesian, or real business cycle variety, are simple Frischian impulse propagation mechanisms. The nature of the fluctuations implied by such models therefore depends, of course, on the propagation structure of the system and the nature of the impulses driving the system. It is a relatively straightforward exercise to explore the nature of duration dependence in the intertemporal equilibria implied by various economic models, given a filter for identifying turning points. There is, however, little agreement on the appropriate form of such a filter. The judgmental NBER filter, for example, does not have an exact, explicit representation.

Similarly, it will also be of interest to ascertain the duration dependence properties of various statistical models commonly used as reduced-form descriptions of business cycle dynamics. In particular, although we have used the nonlinear Markov switching model to motivate the issues treated in this paper, questions of duration dependence arise naturally in many other contexts as well. Given a definition of turning points, for example, one would like to inquire about the nature of duration dependence associated with various linear and nonlinear, stationary and nonstationary, dynamic statistical models. This is especially interesting in the light of the fact that there is little agreement regarding an appropriate statistical model, whether linear or nonlinear. For example, among linear models, consensus has not yet been reached on the existence and importance of shock persistence associated with unit roots; the relative importance of the permanent and transient components in gross national product has been the subject of considerable debate (see, e.g., Campbell and Mankiw 1987; Cochrane 1988; Diebold and Rudebusch 1989a). The notions of business cycle duration dependence introduced here may aid in discrimination among such competing models, via their introduction of a fresh metric for comparing economic models to data.

References

Adelman, Frank L., and Adelman, Irma. "The Dynamic Properties of the Klein-Goldberger Model." *Econometrica* 27 (October 1959): 596–625.

Baily, Martin N. "Stabilization Policy and Private Economic Behavior." *Brookings Papers Econ. Activity*, no. 1 (1978), pp. 11–50.

Balke, Nathan S., and Gordon, Robert J. "The Estimation of Prewar Gross National Product: Methodology and New Evidence." *J.P.E.* 97 (February 1989): 38–92.

Blanchard, Olivier J., and Watson, Mark W. "Are Business Cycles All Alike?" In *The American Business Cycle: Continuity and Change*, edited by Robert J. Gordon. Chicago: Univ. Chicago Press (for NBER), 1986.

Brain, Carlos W., and Shapiro, Samuel S. "A Regression Test for Exponentiality: Censored and Complete Samples." *Technometrics* 25 (February 1983): 69–76.

Britton, Andrew J. C. *The Trade Cycle in Britain, 1958–1982*. Cambridge: Cambridge Univ. Press, 1986.

Burns, Arthur F., and Mitchell, Wesley C. *Measuring Business Cycles*. New York: Columbia Univ. Press (for NBER), 1946.

Campbell, John Y., and Mankiw, N. Gregory. "Permanent and Transitory Components in Macroeconomic Fluctuations." *A.E.R. Papers and Proc.* 77 (May 1987): 111–17.

Cochrane, John H. "How Big Is the Random Walk in GNP?" *J.P.E.* 96 (October 1988): 893–920.

de Leeuw, Frank. "Do Expansions Have Memory?" Discussion Paper no. 16. Washington: U.S. Dept. Commerce, Bur. Econ. Analysis, 1987.

Diebold, Francis X., and Rudebusch, Glenn D. "Long Memory and Persistence in Aggregate Output." *J. Monetary Econ.* 24 (September 1989): 189–209. (a).

——, "Scoring the Leading Indicators." *J. Bus.* 62 (July 1989): 369–91. (b)

——, "Evaluation of Ex Ante Turning Point Forecasts from the Composite Leading Index." In *Leading Economic Indicators: New Approaches and Forecasting Records*, edited by K. Lahiri and G. H. Moore. Cambridge: Cambridge Univ. Press, 1990, in press.

Fisher, Irving. "Our Unstable Dollar and the So-Called Business Cycle." *J. American Statis. Assoc.* 20 (June 1925): 179–202.

Frisch, Ragnar. "Propagation Problems and Impulse Problems in Dynamic Economics." In *Economic Essays in Honour of Gustav Cassel*. London: Allen and Unwin, 1933.

Granger, Clive W. J. "The Typical Spectral Shape of an Economic Variable." *Econometrica* 34 (January 1966): 150–61.

Hamilton, James D. "A New Approach to the Economic Analysis of Nonstationary Time Series and the Business Cycle." *Econometrica* 57 (March 1989): 357–84.

Heckman, James J., and Singer, Burton. "A Method for Minimizing the Impact of Distributional Assumptions in Econometric Models for Duration Data." *Econometrica* 52 (March 1984): 271–320.

Kiefer, Nicholas M. "Economic Duration Data and Hazard Functions." *J. Econ. Literature* 26 (June 1988): 646–79.

Klein, Lawrence R. *Lectures in Econometrics*. Amsterdam: North-Holland, 1983.

Lucas, Robert E., Jr. "Understanding Business Cycles." In *Stabilization of the Domestic and International Economy*, edited by Karl Brunner and Allan H. Meltzer. Carnegie-Rochester Conference Series on Public Policy, vol. 5. Amsterdam: North-Holland, 1977.

McCulloch, J. Huston. "The Monte Carlo Cycle in Business Activity." *Econ. Inquiry* 13 (September 1975): 303–21.

Marshall, Albert W., and Olkin, Ingram. *Inequalities: Theory of Majorization and Its Applications*. New York: Academic Press, 1979.

Matthews, Robert C. O. *The Business Cycle*. Chicago: Univ. Chicago Press, 1959.

Metzler, Lloyd A. "Factors Governing the Length of Inventory Cycles." *Rev. Econ. Statis.* 29 (February 1947): 1–15.

Moore, Geoffrey H., and Zarnowitz, Victor. "The Development and Role of the National Bureau of Economic Research's Business Cycle Chronologies." In *The American Business Cycle: Continuity and Change*, edited by Robert J. Gordon. Chicago: Univ. Chicago Press (for NBER), 1986.

Neftci, Salih N. "Optimal Prediction of Cyclical Downturns." *J. Econ. Dynamics and Control* 4 (August 1982): 225–41.

——, "Are Economic Time Series Asymmetric over the Business Cycle?" *J.P.E.* 92 (April 1984): 307–28.

——, "Is There a Cyclical Time Unit?" *Carnegie-Rochester Conf. Ser. Public Policy* 24 (Spring 1986): 11–48.

Romer, Christina D. "The Prewar Business Cycle Reconsidered: New Estimates of Gross National Product, 1869–1908." *J.P.E.* 97 (February 1989): 1–37.

Samanta, M., and Schwarz, C. J. "The Shaprio-Wilk Test for Exponentiality Based on Censored Data." *J. American Statis. Assoc.* 83 (June 1988): 528–31.

Samuelson, Paul A. "Interactions between the Multiplier Analysis and the Principle of Acceleration." *Rev. Econ. Statis.* 21 (May 1939): 75–78.

Sargent, Thomas J. *Macroeconomic Theory*. 2d ed. Orlando, Fla.: Academic Press, 1987.

Savin, N. Eugene. "A Test of the Monte Carlo Hypothesis: Comment." *Econ. Inquiry* 15 (October 1977): 613–17.

Shapiro, Samuel S., and Wilk, M. B. "An Analysis of Variance Test for the Exponential Distribution (Complete Samples)." *Technometrics* 14 (May 1972): 355–70.

Sichel, Daniel. "Business Cycle Duration Dependence: A Parametric Approach." Economic Activity Working Paper no. 98. Washington: Board Governors, Fed. Reserve System, May 1989.

Stephens, M. A. "On the *W* Test for Exponentiality with Origin Known." *Technometrics* 20 (February 1978): 33–35.

Stock, James H. "Measuring Business Cycle Time." *J.P.E.* 95 (December 1987): 1240–61.

Zarnowitz, Victor. "Recent Work on Business Cycles in Historical Perspective: A Review of Theories and Evidence." *J. Econ. Literature* 23 (June 1985): 523–80.

5

Further Evidence on Business Cycle Duration Dependence

FRANCIS X. DIEBOLD, GLENN D. RUDEBUSCH,
AND DANIEL E. SICHEL*

DO BUSINESS CYCLES exhibit duration dependence? That is, are expansions, contractions, or whole cycles more likely or less likely to end as they grow older? In recent work (Diebold and Rudebusch 1990; Sichel 1991), we argued that understanding business-cycle duration dependence is important for understanding macroeconomic fluctuations, we provided a framework for answering the questions posed above, and we provided some preliminary answers. More generally, we argued that the duration perspective may furnish fresh insight on important and long-standing questions in macroeconomics, such as the existence and the extent of a postwar stabilization of business cycles (Diebold and Rudebusch 1992).

Our earlier findings on the attributes of U.S. business cycles from a duration perspective can be compactly summarized:

1a. Prewar expansions exhibit positive duration dependence.

1b. Postwar expansions exhibit no duration dependence.

2a. Prewar contractions exhibit no duration dependence.

2b. Postwar contractions exhibit positive duration dependence.

3a. Postwar expansions are longer than prewar expansions, regardless of any shift in duration dependence pattern.

* Discussions with Christian Gourieroux, Jim Hamilton, Bo Honore, Nick Kiefer, Peter Schotman, and James Stock were extremely valuable. Participants at the World Congress of the Econometric Society, the 1990 NBER Summer Institute, the 1991 NBER Conference on Common Elements of Growth and Fluctuations, and the 1991 NBER Conference on New Research on Business Cycles, Indicators, and Forecasting provided useful input, as did seminar participants at Yale, Columbia, Stockholm, Georgetown, Washington, Santa Barbara, Maryland, Virginia, Pittsburgh, Johns Hopkins, and Michigan State. Diebold thanks the National Science Foundation (grant SES 89-2715), the University of Pennsylvania Research Foundation (grant 3-71441), the Institute for Empirical Macroeconomics, and the Federal Reserve Bank of Philadelphia for financial support. Hisashi Tanizaki provided superlative research assistance.

3b. Postwar contractions are shorter than prewar contractions, regardless of any shift in duration dependence pattern.

In this paper, we extend our earlier work in two ways. First, we reassess and elaborate on our earlier findings for U.S. data. We use a parsimonious yet flexible exponential-quadratic hazard model, developed for this paper and potentially applicable in other contexts. This model provides a good compromise between nonparametric hazard estimation procedures, for which the available samples are too small, and commonly used parametric hazard estimation procedures, which may impose undesirable restrictions on admissible hazard shapes.

Second, we confront our earlier findings for prewar U.S. business-cycle duration dependence (points 1a and 2a) with prewar data for three additional countries. This is desirable because there have been only about thirty U.S. business cycles since 1854; therefore, only a limited number of duration observations are available. An obvious strategy for obtaining more information about business-cycle duration dependence is to expand the information set by using the NBER chronologies of business cycles in other countries.[1] Such chronologies are available for France, Germany, and Great Britain during the prewar period.

1. Methodology

The distribution function of a duration random variable, $F(\tau)$, gives the probability of failure at or before time τ. The survivor function, defined as

$$S(\tau) = 1 - F(\tau),$$

gives the probability of failure at or after time τ. The hazard function is then defined as

$$\lambda(\tau) = f(\tau)/S(\tau),$$

so that an integral of the hazard over a small integral Δ gives the probability of failure in Δ, conditional on failure not having occurred earlier. If the hazard function is increasing (decreasing) in an interval,

---

[1] Similarly, international data have been used in attempts to refine estimates of macroeconomic persistence (see, e.g., Campbell and Mankiw 1989; and Kormendi and Meguire 1990).

then it is said to exhibit positive (negative) duration dependence in that interval.

The obvious reference hazard, to which we shall compare our estimated hazards, is flat. That is,

$$\lambda(\tau) = \lambda, \quad \text{if } \tau > 0,$$

where λ is an unknown constant that will of course be different for expansions, contractions, and whole cycles. The associated duration density, $f(\tau)$, for the constant hazard is exponential.

Various hazard models that nest the constant hazard are in common use and could be used to study business-cycle dynamics. Consider, for example, the hazard[2]

$$\lambda(\tau) = \lambda\alpha\tau^{\alpha-1}, \quad \text{if } \tau > 0.$$

This hazard function nests the constant hazard (when $\alpha = 1$, $\lambda(\tau) = \lambda$). The associated duration density is Weibull; thus, the log likelihood (without censoring) is

$$\ln L(\alpha, \lambda; \tau_1, \ldots, \tau_T) = T \ln(\alpha\lambda) + (\alpha - 1) \sum_{t=1}^{T} \ln(\tau_t) = \lambda \sum_{t=1}^{T} (\tau_t)^\alpha,$$

on which estimation and inference may be based for a given sample of observed durations $\tau_1, \tau_2, \tau_3, \ldots, \tau_T$.

However, this hazard model, like other commonly used parameterizations, imposes strong restrictions on admissible hazard shapes. In particular, if $\alpha > 1$, the hazard is monotone increasing, and conversely for $\alpha < 1$. Nonmonotone hazard shapes (e.g., U or inverted U) are excluded. Although such restrictions may be natural in certain contexts, they appear unjustified in the business-cycle context.

Here we discuss a class of hazard models, developed for this paper but potentially more widely applicable, that we feel strikes a good balance between parsimony and flexibility of approximation, and on which we rely heavily in our subsequent empirical work. Consider the hazard

$$\lambda(\tau) = \exp(\beta_0 + \beta_1\tau + \beta_2\tau^2), \quad \text{if } \tau > 0.$$

This parsimonious hazard, which we call the exponential-quadratic hazard, is not necessarily monotone and is best viewed as a low-ordered

---

[2] For further details, see Sichel (1991).

series approximation to an arbitrary hazard.[3] In particular, the constant-hazard case of no duration dependence occurs for $\beta_1 = \beta_2 = 0$. Nonmonotone hazards occur when $\beta_1 \neq 0$, $\beta_2 \neq 0$, and sign (β_1) $\neq$ sign (β_2). The hazard is U shaped, for example, when $\beta_2 > 0$ and $\beta_1 < 0$ and inverted U shaped when $\beta_2 < 0$ and $\beta_1 > 0$.

The precise shape of the hazard is easily deduced. Immediately, $\lambda(0) = \exp(\beta_0)$, and rewriting the hazard as

$$\lambda(\tau) = \exp\left[\beta_2\left(\tau + \frac{\beta_1}{2\beta_2} \right)^2 - \frac{(\beta_1^2 - 4\beta_0\beta_2)}{4\beta_2} \right], \quad \beta_2 \neq 0,$$

makes obvious the fact that, when an interior maximum or minimum is achieved (i.e., when $\beta_1 \neq 0$, $\beta_2 \neq 0$, and sign $[\beta_1] \neq$ sign $[\beta_2]$), its location is at

$$\tau^* = -(\beta_1/2\beta_2),$$

with associated hazard value

$$\lambda(\tau^*) = \exp\left[-\frac{(\beta_1^2 - 4\beta_0\beta_2)}{4\beta_2} \right].$$

Before constructing the likelihood, we record a few familiar definitions that will be used repeatedly. First, by definition of the survivor function, we have

$$d \ln S(\tau)/d\tau = -f(\tau)/[1 - F(\tau)],$$

so that

$$\lambda(\tau) = -d \ln S(\tau)/d\tau.$$

We also define the integrated hazard as

$$\Lambda(\tau) = \int_0^\tau \lambda(x)\, dx,$$

which is related to the survivor function by

$$S(\tau) = \exp[-\Lambda(\tau)].$$

[3] Kiefer (1988) suggests that future research on hazard models of the form $\exp(\beta_0 + \beta_1\tau + \cdots + \beta_p\tau^p)$ would be useful. The exponential-quadratic hazard is, of course, a leading case of interest ($p = 2$). This hazard is also a special case of the Heckman-Walker (1990) hazard and is similar to the logistic-quadratic hazard of Nickell (1979).

It is interesting to note that, for a hazard $\lambda(\tau)$ to be proper, it cannot be negative on a set of positive measure (otherwise, the positivity of probabilities would be violated) and it must satisfy $\lim_{\tau \to \infty} \Lambda(\tau) = \infty$ (otherwise, the distribution function would not approach unity). Thus, certain parameterizations of the exponential-quadratic hazard do not, strictly speaking, qualify as proper hazard functions. This is of little consequence for the results presented below, however, in which the exponential-quadratic hazard is used only as a *local* approximation.[4]

Construction of the log likelihood allowing for right censoring (as, e.g., with the last postwar trough-to-trough duration) is straightforward. Let $\beta = (\beta_0, \beta_1, \beta_2)'$. Then

$$\ln L(\beta; \tau_1, \ldots, \tau_T) = \sum_{t=1}^{T} \{d_t \ln[f(\tau_t; \beta)] + (1 - d_t)\ln[1 - F(\tau_t; \beta)]\},$$

where d_t equals one if the tth duration is uncensored, and zero otherwise. The form of the log likelihood is a manifestation of the simple fact that the contribution of a noncensored observation to the log likelihood is the log density, while the contribution of a censored observation to the log likelihood is the log survivor. But

$$f(\tau_t; \beta) = \lambda(\tau_t; \beta)[1 - F(\tau_t; \beta)],$$

so

$$\ln L(\beta, \tau_1, \ldots, \tau_T) = \sum_{t=1}^{T} \{d_t \ln[\lambda(\tau_t; \beta)] + \ln[1 - F(\tau_t; \beta)]\}.$$

Moreover,

$$[1 - F(\tau_t; \beta)] = \exp\left[-\int_0^{\tau_t} \lambda(x; \beta)\, dx\right],$$

insertion of which in the log likelihood yields

$$\ln L(\beta; \tau_1, \ldots, \tau_T) = \sum_{t=1}^{T} \left\{d_t \ln[\lambda(\tau_t; \beta)] - \int_0^{\tau_t} \lambda(x; \beta)\, dx\right\}.$$

[4] Moreover, Heckman and Walker (1990) argue that, in certain contexts, it may be economically reasonable to place positive probability mass on durations of ∞.

Differentiating, we obtain the score

$$\partial \ln L / \partial \beta = \sum_{t=1}^{T} \left\{ [d_t / \lambda(\tau_t; \beta)][\partial \lambda(\tau_t; \beta) / \partial \beta] - \int_0^{\tau_t} \partial \lambda(x; \beta) / \partial \beta \, dx \right\}$$

and the Hessian

$$\partial^2 \ln L / \partial \beta \partial \beta' = \sum_{t=1}^{T} \left\{ [d_t / \lambda(\tau_t; \beta)][\partial^2 \lambda(\tau_t; \beta) / \partial \beta \partial \beta'] \right.$$

$$- [d_t / \lambda^2(\tau_t; \beta)][\partial \lambda(\tau_t; \beta) / \partial \beta][\partial \lambda(\tau_t; \beta) / \partial \beta']$$

$$\left. - \int_0^{\tau_1} \partial^2 \lambda(x; \beta) / \partial \beta \partial \beta' \, dx \right\}.$$

Thus, specialization to the exponential-quadratic case yields the log likelihood

$$\ln L(\beta; \tau_1, \ldots, \tau_T) = \sum_{t=1}^{T} \left[d_t (\beta_0 + \beta_1 \tau_t + \beta_2 \tau_t^2) \right.$$

$$\left. - \int_0^{\tau_t} \exp(\beta_0 + \beta_1 x + \beta_2 x^2) \, dx \right].$$

The derivatives of the exponential-quadratic hazard are

$$\partial \lambda(\tau_t; \beta) / \partial \beta = \begin{bmatrix} 1 \\ \tau_t \\ \tau_t^2 \end{bmatrix} \exp(\beta_0 + \beta_1 \tau_t + \beta_2 \tau_t^2)$$

and

$$\partial^2 \lambda(\tau_t; \beta) / \partial \beta \partial \beta' = \begin{bmatrix} 1 & \tau_t & \tau_t^2 \\ \tau_t & \tau_t^2 & \tau_t^3 \\ \tau_t^2 & \tau_t^3 & \tau_t^4 \end{bmatrix} \exp(\beta_0 + \beta_1 \tau_t + \beta_2 \tau_t^2).$$

Insertion of the exponential-quadratic hazard derivatives into the general score and Hessian expressions yields the exponential-quadratic score and hazard

$$\partial \ln L / \partial \beta = \sum_{t=1}^{T} \left\{ \left(d_t \begin{bmatrix} 1 \\ \tau_t \\ \tau_t^2 \end{bmatrix} \right) - \int_0^{\tau_t} \begin{bmatrix} 1 \\ x \\ x^2 \end{bmatrix} \exp(\beta_0 + \beta_1 x + \beta_2 x^2) \, dx \right\}$$

and

$$\partial^2 \ln L / \partial \beta \partial \beta' = - \sum_{t=1}^{T} \int_0^{\tau_t} \begin{bmatrix} 1 & x & x^2 \\ x & x^2 & x^3 \\ x^2 & x^3 & x^4 \end{bmatrix} \exp(\beta_0 + \beta_1 x + \beta_2 x^2) \, dx.$$

Although construction of the likelihood, score, and Hessian is straightforward, it is not clear that *maximization* of the likelihood will be numerically tractable, owing to the lack of a closed-form likelihood expression and the resulting necessity of numerically evaluating thousands of integrals en route to finding a likelihood maximum. It happens, however, that (1) the evaluation of the required integrals presents only a very modest computational burden, (2) the expressions derived earlier for the score and Hessian facilitate likelihood maximization, and (3) the likelihood is globally concave, which promotes speed and stability of numerical likelihood maximization and guarantees that any local maximum achieved is global.

First, consider the requisite integral evaluation. This is done in standard fashion by approximating the integrand by a step function with steps at each integer duration value and adding the areas in the resulting rectangles. Thus, for example, the integral

$$\int_0^{\tau_t} x \exp(\beta_0 + \beta_1 x + \beta_2 x^2) \, dx$$

is evaluated as

$$\sum_{j=1}^{\tau_t} \left[x_j \exp\left(\beta_0 + \beta_1 x_j + \beta_2 x_j^2 \right) + x_{j-1} \exp\left(\beta_0 + \beta_1 x_{j-1} + \beta_2 x_{j-1}^2 \right) \right]$$

$$\times (x_j - x_{j-1})/2,$$

where $x_j = j$.

Second, consider numerical likelihood maximization. Given our ability to compute the likelihood value for any parameter configuration β, we climb the likelihood via the Newton-Raphson algorithm,

$$\beta^{(i+1)} = \beta^{(i)} - [\partial^2 \ln L^{(i)}/\partial\beta\partial\beta']^{-1} \partial \ln L^{(i)}/\partial\beta.$$

Convergence is deemed to have occurred if the change in the log likelihood from one iteration to the next is less than 0.01 percent.

Finally, global concavity of the likelihood (i.e., $\partial^2\lambda(\tau; \beta)/\partial\beta\partial\beta' < 0$, for all β in R^3) is easily established. To prove global concavity, let H denote the Hessian of the exponential-quadratic model. We must show that $y'Hy \leq 0$, with equality, if and only if $y = 0$. Now,

$$y'Hy = - \sum_{t=1}^{T} \int_0^{\tau_t} y' \begin{bmatrix} 1 & x & x^2 \\ x & x^2 & x^3 \\ x^2 & x^3 & x^4 \end{bmatrix} y \exp(\beta_0 + \beta_1 x + \beta_2 x^2)\, dx$$

$$= - \sum_{t=1}^{T} \int_0^{\tau_t} \left[(a'y)^2 \exp(\beta_0 + \beta_1 x + \beta_2 x^2)\right] dx,$$

where $a = (1, x, x^2)' \gg 0$, and $y = (y_1, y_2, y_3)'$. Note that the integrand is nonnegative and zero if and only if $y = 0$. But the integral of a nonnegative function is nonnegative, as is the sum of such integrals. Thus, the entire expression is nonpositive and zero if and only if $y = 0$.

Finally, we note that we have obtained various generalizations and specializations of our results, which are not of particular interest in the present application but may be of interest in others. All are treated in the appendix. First, confidence intervals for the true but unknown hazard function may be computed. Second, models with covariates, Z, may be entertained, such as

$$\lambda(\tau, Z; \beta, \gamma) = \exp(\beta_0 + \beta_1\tau + \beta_2\tau^2 + Z\gamma).$$

Third, if it can be maintained that (locally) $\beta_2 < 0$, then the log likelihood can be written as a function of integrals of standard normal random variables, and numerical integration is not required.

2. Empirical Results

We take as given the NBER chronologies of business-cycle peaks and troughs for the prewar and postwar United States as well as for prewar France, Germany, and Great Britain, which are shown in tables 5.1 and 5.2.[5] The tables show durations of expansions, contractions, and whole

---

[5] These dates are taken from Moore and Zarnowitz (1986), which are the same as those in Burns and Mitchell (1946, 78–79), with minor revisions for some of the U.S. dates.

TABLE 5.1
Business Cycle Chronology and Durations: United States

Trough	Peak	Contractions	Expansions	Trough to Trough	Peak to Peak
			Prewar		
December 1854	June 1857	. . .	30	. . .	. . .
December 1858	October 1860	18	22	48	40
June 1861	April 1865	8	46	30	54
December 1867	June 1869	32	18	78	50
December 1870	October 1873	18	34	36	52
March 1879	March 1882	65	36	99	101
May 1885	March 1887	38	22	74	60
April 1888	July 1890	13	27	35	40
May 1891	January 1893	10	20	37	30
June 1894	December 1895	17	18	37	35
June 1897	June 1899	18	24	36	42
December 1900	September 1902	18	21	42	39
August 1904	May 1907	23	33	44	56
June 1908	January 1910	13	19	46	32
January 1912	January 1913	24	12	43	36
December 1914	August 1918	23	44	35	67
March 1919	January 1920	7	10	51	17
July 1921	May 1923	18	22	28	40
July 1924	October 1926	14	27	36	41
November 1927	August 1929	13	21	40	34
March 1933	May 1937	43	50	64	93
June 1938	. . .	13	. . .	63	. . .
			Postwar		
	February 1945	. . .	. . .	. . .	. . .
October 1945	November 1948	8	37	. . .	45
October 1949	July 1953	11	45	48	56
May 1954	August 1957	10	39	55	49
April 1958	April 1960	8	24	47	32
February 1961	December 1969	10	106	34	116
November 1970	November 1973	11	36	117	47
March 1975	January 1980	16	58	52	74
July 1980	July 1981	6	12	64	18
November 1982	?	16	90	28	106
?		. . .	. . .	98	. . .

TABLE 5.2
Prewar Business Cycle Chronologies and Durations: Germany, France,
and Great Britain

Trough	Peak	Contractions	Expansions	Trough to Trough	Peak to Peak
		France, 1865–1938			
December 1865	November 1867	...	23	...	...
October 1868	August 1870	11	22	34	33
February 1872	September 1873	18	19	40	37
August 1876	April 1878	35	20	54	55
September 1879	December 1881	17	27	37	44
August 1887	January 1891	68	41	95	109
January 1895	March 1900	48	62	89	110
September 1902	May 1903	30	8	92	38
October 1904	July 1907	17	33	25	50
February 1909	June 1913	19	52	52	71
August 1914	June 1918	14	46	66	60
April 1919	September 1920	10	17	56	27
July 1921	October 1924	10	39	27	49
June 1925	October 1926	8	16	47	24
June 1927	March 1930	8	33	24	41
July 1932	July 1933	28	12	61	40
April 1935	June 1937	21	26	33	47
August 1938	...	14	...	40	...
		Germany, 1879–1932			
February 1879	January 1882	...	35	...	...
August 1886	January 1890	55	41	90	96
February 1895	March 1900	61	61	102	122
March 1902	August 1903	24	17	85	41
February 1905	July 1907	18	29	35	47
December 1908	April 1913	17	52	46	69
August 1914	June 1918	16	46	68	62
June 1919	May 1922	12	35	58	47
November 1923	March 1925	18	16	53	34
March 1926	April 1929	12	37	28	49
August 1932	...	40	...	...	77

TABLE 5.2
(*Continued*)

Trough	Peak	Contractions	Expansions	Trough to Trough	Peak to Peak
		Great Britain, 1854–1938			
December 1854	September 1857	. . .	33	. . .	. . .
March 1858	September 1860	6	30	39	36
December 1862	March 1866	27	39	57	66
March 1868	September 1872	24	54	63	78
June 1879	December 1882	81	42	135	123
June 1886	September 1890	42	51	84	93
February 1895	June 1900	53	64	104	117
September 1901	June 1903	15	21	79	36
November 1904	June 1907	17	31	38	48
November 1908	December 1912	17	49	48	66
September 1914	October 1918	21	49	70	70
April 1919	March 1920	6	11	55	17
June 1921	November 1924	15	41	26	56
July 1926	March 1927	20	8	61	28
September 1928	July 1929	18	10	26	28
August 1932	September 1937	37	61	47	98
September 1938	. . .	12	. . .	73	. . .

cycles measured both peak to peak and trough to trough. The U.S. chronology in table 5.1 includes a ninety-month duration for the last expansion, a 106-month duration for the last peak-to-peak cycle, and a ninety-eight-month duration for the last trough-to-trough cycle. In the empirical work that follows, we treat them as right censored; that is, they are taken as lower bounds for the true durations, the values of which are as yet unknown.[6]

We are limited to prewar samples with the French, German, and British data because of the scarcity of true recessions, involving actual declines in output, in Europe during the 1950s and 1960s. After the devastation of Europe during World War II, there was a reconstruction of extraordinary pace; thus, it is often impossible to identify the classic business cycle in the early postwar period in the European countries. In the postwar period, growth cycles, which refer to periods of rising and falling activity relative to trend growth, have been identified for the European countries (see Moore and Zarnowitz 1986). However, the

---

[6] Thus, we assume that the great expansion of the 1980s ended no sooner than May 1990 and that the subsequent contraction ended no earlier than January 1991.

timing, and hence duration dependence, of these cycles is not comparable with the prewar business cycles.

Summary statistics, including the sample size, minimum observed duration, mean duration, and standard error, for each of the four samples from each country, are displayed in table 5.3. Also included in table 5.3 are summary statistics from pooled samples of all expansions,

TABLE 5.3
Business Cycle Summary Statistics

Sample	Sample Size (N)	Minimum Duration	Mean Duration	Standard Error
		Prewar		
France, 1865–1938:				
F1: Expansions	17	8	29.2	14.8
F2: Contractions	17	8	22.1	15.9
F3: Peak to peak	16	24	52.2	25.3
F4: Trough to trough	17	24	51.3	23.0
Germany, 1879–1932:				
G1: Expansions	10	16	36.9	14.2
G2: Contractions	10	12	27.3	18.1
G3: Peak to peak	10	34	64.4	27.5
G4: Trough to trough	9	28	62.8	25.5
Great Britain, 1854–1938:				
GB1: Expansions	16	8	37.1	17.8
GB2: Contractions	16	6	25.7	19.4
GB3: Peak to peak	15	17	64.0	32.9
GB4: Trough to trough	16	26	62.8	28.6
United States, 1854–1938:				
US1: Expansions	21	10	26.5	10.7
US2: Contractions	21	7	21.2	13.6
US3: Peak to peak	20	17	47.9	20.3
US4: Trough to trough	21	28	47.7	18.1
All countries:				
Expansions	64	8	31.5	14.8
Contractions	64	6	23.5	16.3
Peak to peak	61	17	55.7	26.7
Trough to trough	63	24	54.7	23.9
		Postwar		
United States, 1945–present:				
US1′: Expansions	9	12	49.9	29.0
US2′: Contractions	9	6	10.7	3.2
US3′: Peak to peak	9	18	60.6	28.2
US4′: Trough to trough	9	28	60.7	30.9

contractions, and whole cycles. We shall not conduct our empirical investigation, however, on pooled samples. Although it might be appealing to pool durations across countries to expand the sample, the conformity of business-cycle timing across countries suggests that the observations across countries are not independent.[7] Hence, simple pooling would be inappropriate. Estimation and testing procedures that control for the degree of interdependence are likely to be very complicated, particularly because so little is known about the transmission of business cycles from one country to another.

There is one area, however, in which we *do* pool information from the four countries, namely, in the specification of a lower bound on admissible durations. This lower-bound criterion, which is denoted t_0, is necessary because, *by definition*, the NBER does not recognize an expansion or a contraction unless it has achieved a certain maturity. The exact required maturity is not spelled out by the NBER, but, in describing the guidelines enforced since Burns and Mitchell (1946), Moore and Zarnowitz (1986) indicate that full cycles of less than one year in duration and contractions of less than six months in duration would be very unlikely to qualify for selection.[8] Because this is a criterion of the NBER definition of business cycles, the choice of t_0 should be, not country specific, but uniform across countries. In particular, we set t_0 for expansions, contractions, or whole cycles equal to one less than the minimum duration actually observed in any of the four countries. We also require t_0 to be identical for peak-to-peak and trough-to-trough cycles, given evidence that the NBER makes no distinction between these two types of whole cycles (see Diebold and Rudebusch 1990). Operationally, the minimum duration criterion is incorporated into estimation of the hazard functions by subtracting t_0 from each of the observed durations before implementing the methodology described in section 1.

Let us first consider the United States, for which we can contrast the prewar and postwar experiences. We start with prewar half-cycle hazards, estimates of which are graphed in figure 5.1. Each graph in this figure—and those in all subsequent figures—consists of three superimposed estimated hazards: the exponential constant ($\exp[\beta_0]$), exponential linear ($\exp[\beta_0 + \beta_1\tau]$), and exponential quadratic ($\exp[\beta_0 + \beta_1\tau + \beta_2\tau^2]$). These may be viewed as progressively more flexible approximations to the true hazard and are useful, in particular, for visually gauging the conformity of business-cycle durations to the constant-

[7] For qualitative descriptions of the conformity of international business cycles, see Moore and Zarnowitz (1986) and Morgenstern (1959).

[8] Note that Geoffrey Moore and Victor Zarnowitz are two of the eight members of the NBER Business Cycle Dating Committee.

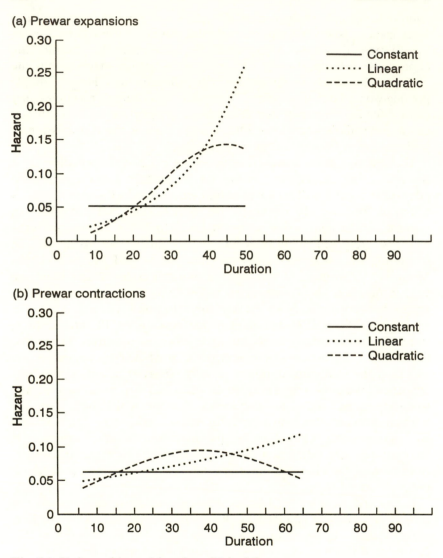

Fig. 5.1. Estimated hazard functions, United States.

hazard model. The numerical values underlying the figures are given in tables 5.4–5.6, along with maximum-likelihood estimates of the underlying hazard function parameters. In keeping with our interpretation of the exponential hazard as a local approximation, the ranges of the tables and graphed hazard functions have been chosen to reflect observed historical maximum durations.

TABLE 5.4
Estimated Exponential-Constant Hazard Functions

Sample	β_0	$\exp(\beta_0)$	Sample	β_0	$\exp(\beta_0)$
	Prewar Expansions			*Prewar Trough to Trough*	
F1	− 3.099	.045	F4	− 3.564	.028
G1	− 3.398	.033	G4	− 3.875	.021
GB1	− 3.405	.033	GB4	− 3.846	.021
US1	− 2.969	.051	US4	− 3.457	.032
	Prewar Contractions			*Postwar*	
F2	− 2.840	.058	US1′	− 3.871	.021
G2	− 3.105	.045	US2′	− 1.735	.177
GB2	− 3.030	.048	US3′	− 3.910	.020
US2	− 2.787	.062	US4′	− 3.904	.020
	Prewar Peak to Peak				
F3	− 3.589	.028			
G3	− 3.850	.021			
GB3	− 3.871	.021			
US3	− 3.464	.031			

Note: For sample descriptions, see table 5.3.

Prewar U.S. expansions display strong evidence of duration dependence. The estimated exponential-linear expansion hazard rises sharply, from .03 to .25 after fifty months. The estimated exponential-quadratic expansion hazard rises more sharply at first, but subsequently less sharply, reaching .15 after fifty months. The *p*-values in table 5.7 indicate that we can soundly reject the constant-hazard null; the *p*-value for the null that $\beta_1 = 0$ in the exponential-linear model (p_1), for example, is .001.[9] The evidence against the linear-quadratic model, however, is less strong; the *p*-value for the null hypothesis that $\beta_2 = 0$ in the exponential-quadratic model (p_2) is .18.

Conversely, prewar U.S. contractions do not show strong evidence of duration dependence. The estimated exponential-linear expansion hazard rises only slowly, from .06 to .12 after seventy months. The estimated exponential-quadratic contraction hazard is inverted-U

---

[9] We report asymptotic *p*-values associated with the Wald statistics in the exponential-linear and exponential-quadratic models. The *p*-values give the probability of obtaining a sample test statistic at least as large in absolute value as the one actually obtained, under the null of no duration dependence. Small *p*-values therefore indicate significant departures from the null. p_1 is the *p*-value for the null hypothesis that $\beta_1 = 0$ in the exponential-linear model. p_2 is the *p*-value for the null hypothesis that $\beta_2 = 0$ in the exponential-quadratic model.

TABLE 5.5
Estimated Exponential-Linear Hazard Functions

Sample	β_0	β_1	12	18	24	36	48	72	96
			Duration in Months						
			Prewar Expansions						
F1	−3.76	.035	.028	.034	.042	.065	.099	.231	...
G1	−4.93	.065	.010	.015	.022	.047	.102	.481	...
GB1	−4.66	.050	.012	.016	.022	.041	.074	...	...
US1	−3.91	.060	.027	.039	.055	.113	.231	...	...
			Prewar Contractions						
F2	−2.95	.007	.055	.057	.060	.065	.070	.083	...
G2	−3.48	.019	.035	.039	.044	.055	.069	.108	...
GB2	−3.14	.005	.045	.047	.048	.051	.055	.062	.071
US2	−2.99	.014	.055	.060	.065	.077	.091	.127	...
			Prewar Peak to Peak						
F3	−4.06	.015	...	.018	.019	.023	.028	.040	.058
G3	−4.61	.020	...	.010	.012	.015	.019	.030	.048
GB3	−4.59	.018	...	.011	.012	.014	.018	.027	.041
US3	−4.05	.022	...	.018	.021	.027	.035	.060	.101
			Prewar Trough to Trough						
F4	−4.27	.024	...	.015	.017	.023	.030	.053	.093
G4	−5.35	.038	...	.005	.006	.010	.016	.040	.100
GB4	−4.55	.018	...	.011	.012	.015	.019	.029	.046
US4	−4.17	.028	...	.016	.019	.027	.037	.073	.142
			Postwar						
US1′	−4.20	.010	.016	.017	.018	.020	.022	.028	.035
US2′	−2.65	.195	.278	.897	...	...	...	...	...
US3′	−4.20	.008	...	.015	.016	.018	.019	.024	.029
US4′	−4.36	.013	...	.013	.014	.017	.019	.027	.036

Note: For sample descriptions, see table 5.3

shaped, achieving a maximum of .09 after thirty-six months, but dropping back to .03 after seventy-two months. The *p*-values indicate that the constant-hazard null is hard to reject; p_1 is .17, and p_2 is .20.

The postwar U.S. results provide striking contrast. Postwar U.S. expansions display no duration dependence, while postwar U.S. contractions display strong positive duration dependence. In short, postwar duration dependence patterns, cataloged in figure 5.2 and tables 5.4–5.6, are precisely *opposite* those of the prewar period!

TABLE 5.6
Estimated Exponential-Quadratic Hazard Functions

Sample	β_0	β_1	β_2	\multicolumn{7}{c}{Duration in Months}
				12	18	24	36	48	72	96
\multicolumn{11}{c}{*Prewar Expansions*}
F1	−3.80	.039	−.0001	.027	.034	.043	.066	.099	.207	...
G1	−5.13	.083	−.0003	.009	.014	.022	.050	.103	.340	...
GB1	−3.74	−.041	.0016	.020	.018	.019	.027	.063	...	...
US1	−4.44	.132	−.0017	.022	.041	.067	.124	.139	...	...
\multicolumn{11}{c}{*Prewar Contractions*}
F2	−2.98	.011	−.0001	.055	.058	.061	.066	.070	.074	...
G2	−3.24	−.014	.0006	.037	.036	.038	.047	.070	.270	...
GB2	−3.14	.006	−.0001	.045	.047	.048	.051	.055	.062	.070
US2	−3.28	.056	−.0009	.053	.067	.080	.093	.085	.033	...
\multicolumn{11}{c}{*Prewar Peak to Peak*}
F3	−4.54	.050	−.0004	...	.012	.016	.025	.035	.051	.047
G3	−5.16	.052	−.0003	...	.006	.008	.014	.022	.039	.048
GB3	−4.17	−.008	.0002	...	.015	.015	.015	.016	.022	.040
US3	−4.73	.075	−.0007	...	.010	.015	.030	.049	.069	.045
\multicolumn{11}{c}{*Prewar Trough to Trough*}
F4	−4.29	.026	.0000	...	.014	.017	.023	.030	.053	.089
G4	−5.06	.021	.0002	...	.007	.008	.010	.015	.037	.114
GB4	−5.14	.049	−.0003	...	.006	.009	.014	.021	.038	.050
US4	−5.10	.101	−.0010	...	.007	.013	.031	.055	.077	.034
\multicolumn{11}{c}{*Postwar*}
US1'	−4.32	.018	−.0001	.015	.016	.018	.021	.024	.029	.032
US2'	−2.72	.235	−.0034	.287	...	...	...	...	...	...
US3'	−4.17	.006	.0000	...	.016	.016	.018	.019	.023	.029
US4'	−4.76	.040	−.0003	...	.009	.012	.017	.023	.032	.033

Note: For sample descriptions, see table 5.3

The estimated exponential-linear and exponential-quadratic hazard functions for postwar U.S. expansions are hardly distinguishable from each other or from the estimated exponential-constant hazard, rising from .02 to only .03 after ninety-six months. Moreover, the *p*-values indicate that the data conform closely to the exponential-constant model ($p_1 = .23$, $p_2 = .43$). Conversely, the estimated hazards for postwar U.S. contractions rise extremely sharply. The estimated exponential-linear and exponential-quadratic hazards cannot be distinguished

TABLE 5.7
p-Values for Null Hypotheses That Hazard Parameters Equal Zero

Sample	p_1	p_2	Sample	p_1	p_2
Prewar Expansions			*Prewar Trough to Trough*		
F1	.017	.472	F4	.015	.480
G1	.002	.425	G4	.004	.375
GB1	.002	.055	GB4	.010	.161
US1	.001	.181	US4	.002	.049
Prewar Contractions			*Postwar*		
F2	.330	.468	US1'	.223	.433
G2	.169	.319	US2'	.027	.460
GB2	.328	.496	US3'	.264	.484
US2	.172	.201	US4'	.149	.295
Prewar Peak to Peak					
F3	.048	.176			
G3	.037	.245			
GB3	.024	.203			
US3	.011	.090			

Note: We report asymptotic p-values associated with the Wald statistics in the exponential-linear and exponential-quadratic models. p_1 is the p-value for the null hypothesis that $\beta_1 = 0$ in the exponential-linear model. p_2 is the p-value for the null hypothesis that $\beta_2 = 0$ in the exponential-quadratic model. For sample descriptions, see table 5.3.

from each other but are readily distinguished from the constant hazard, rising from .07 to .29 in just twelve months. The deviation from constant-hazard behavior is highly statistically significant, with $p_1 = .03$.

It is important to note that the differences between prewar and postwar expansion and contraction hazards are not limited to average *slopes*, although, as we have stressed, the slope changes are large and important. In particular, differences between the overall level of prewar and postwar expansion and contraction hazards exist—expansion hazards are higher in the prewar period, whereas contraction hazards are higher in the postwar period. These insights from the conditional perspective of hazard analysis—also noted in Sichel (1991)—lead to a deeper understanding of the unconditional distributional shifts documented in Diebold and Rudebusch (1992).[10]

[10] Using exact finite-sample procedures, Diebold and Rudebusch (1992) also document the high statistical significance of the prewar-postwar change in business-cycle dynamics and establish the robustness of that conclusion to issues of prewar data quality, the definition of *prewar*, and allowance for heterogeneity.

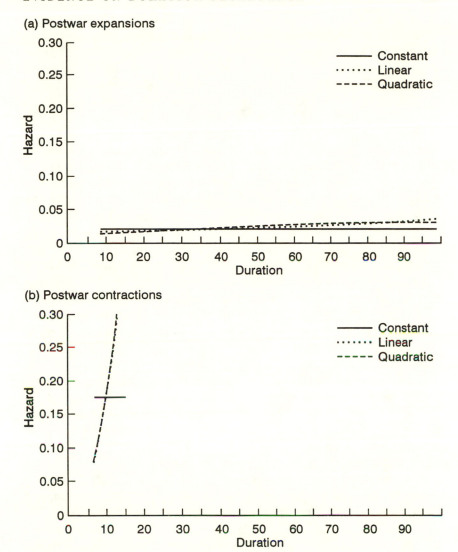

Fig. 5.2. Estimated hazard functions, United States.

Evidence of duration dependence in U.S. whole cycles, whether measured peak to peak or trough to trough, is also present in the prewar data. Moreover, the *p*-values indicate significance of the quadratic hazard term in the U.S. case. Finding duration dependence in prewar whole cycles is not surprising, in light of our finding of duration dependence in prewar expansions.[11] It is rather surprising, however, not to find significant duration dependence in postwar whole cycles, in light of our finding of significant duration dependence in postwar contractions. This may be due to low power, related to the fact that postwar whole-cycle behavior is dominated by expansion behavior (more than 80 percent of the postwar period was spent in the expansion state, as opposed to approximately 50 percent of the prewar period).

Now let us consider the evidence for France, Germany, and Great Britain. The estimated international exponential-constant, exponential-linear, and exponential-quadratic prewar hazard functions, shown in figures 5.3–5.5 and tables 5.4–5.6, indicate striking cross-country conformity in prewar business-cycle duration dependence patterns. All expansion hazards show strong positive duration dependence. The estimated hazard for German expansions, for example, rises from near zero after twelve months to .34 after seventy-two months. France and Great Britain also show substantial slope in their expansion hazard functions. Like that of the U.S. hazard, the departures of the French, German, and British hazards from constancy are highly significant, the respective values of p_1 being .02, .00, and .00. Also like the U.S. hazard, the quadratic term does not play a very important role, the respective values of p_2 being .47, .43, and .06.

For contractions, the U.S. prewar findings are again mimicked in France, Germany, and Britain: no evidence of duration dependence is found. All estimated contraction hazards are nearly constant, and the deviations from constancy are never significant. In contrast to the estimated expansion hazards, which start near zero and grow relatively quickly (and at increasing rates), the estimated contraction hazards start near .05 and grow less quickly (and at decreasing rates).

Evidence for duration dependence in prewar whole cycles, which is strong in the U.S. samples, is also strong in the French, German, and British samples. For both peak-to-peak and trough-to-trough samples, all values of p_1 are less than .05. As in the United States, it would appear that the significant international prewar whole-cycle duration dependence is a manifestation of the significant half-cycle (expansion) duration dependence.

---

[11] In fact, as pointed out by Mudambi and Taylor (1991), whole cycles may be expected to show duration dependence even in the absence of half-cycle duration dependence because the distribution of the time to *second* failure is not exponential when the distribution of the time to first failure is. (Moreover, the failure probabilities are of course different in expansions and contractions.)

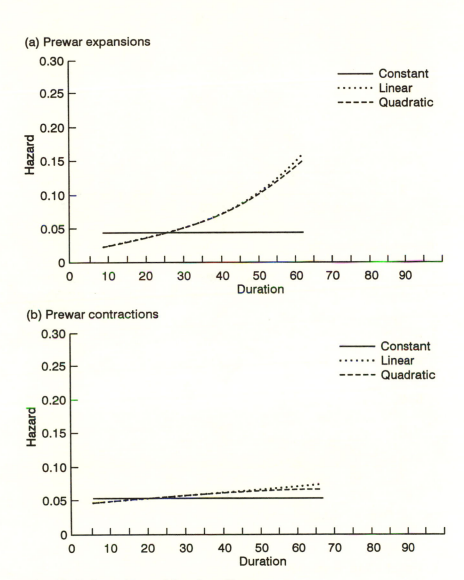

Fig. 5.3. Estimated hazard functions, France.

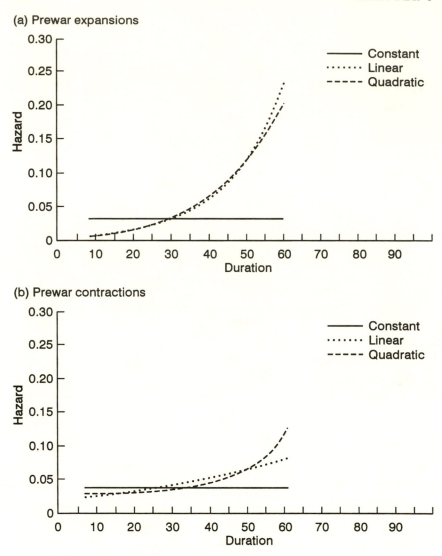

Fig. 5.4. Estimated hazard functions, Germany.

3. Concluding Remarks

We began this paper by asking whether expansions, contractions, or whole cycles are more likely or less likely to end as they grow older, a question whose answer is of importance both methodologically and substantively. Methodologically, for example, the answer has implica-

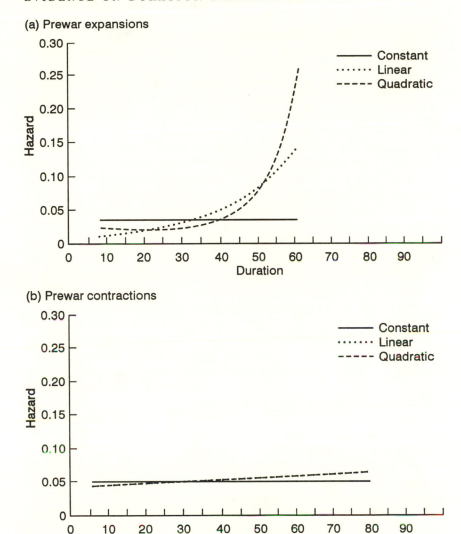

Fig. 5.5. Estimated hazard functions, Great Britain.

tions for the proper specification of empirical macroeconomic models, such as the Markov-switching models proposed recently by Hamilton (1989). Substantively, for example, the answer has implications for turning-point prediction and business-cycle dating, as pointed out by Diebold and Rudebusch (1989, 1991).

Here we have investigated the patterns of duration dependence in U.S. prewar and postwar business cycles using a parsimonious yet flexible hazard model, deepening our understanding of the nature of postwar stabilization documented in Diebold and Rudebusch (1992). We presented evidence of a postwar shift in U.S. business-cycle duration dependence patterns: postwar expansion hazards display less duration dependence and are lower on average, while postwar contraction hazards display more duration dependence and are higher on average.

Moreover, we compared our prewar U.S. results with those obtained using prewar data from France, Germany, and Great Britain. We found that, for prewar expansions, all four countries exhibit evidence of positive duration dependence. For prewar contractions, none of the countries do. The results paint a similar prewar picture for each country; statistically significant and economically important positive duration dependence is consistently associated with expansions and never associated with contractions. The similarities in the prewar pattern of duration dependence across countries suggest conformity across countries in the characteristics of business cycles.

The empirical results in this paper and in our earlier papers pose substantial challenges for the construction of macroeconomic models; we hope that our measurement stimulates fresh theory. Obvious questions abound: What types of economic propagation mechanisms induce duration dependence in aggregate output, and what types do not? What are the theoretical hazard functions associated with the equilibria of various business-cycle models, and how do they compare with those estimated from real data? What types of models are capable of generating equilibria with differing expansion and contraction hazard functions, and how do they relate to existing linear and nonlinear models? How can we explain and model secular variation in the degree of duration dependence in expansions and contractions? Some recent work has begun to address various of these questions (e.g., Murphy, Shleifer, and Vishny 1989 develop a model in which cyclical duration is influenced by the stock of durables), but much remains to be done.

Appendix: Specialization and Generalization of the Exponential-Quadratic Hazard Model

Confidence Intervals

Confidence intervals for the true but unknown hazard may be obtained in straightforward fashion. Taylor series expansion of $\lambda(\tau_t, \hat{\beta})$ around $\lambda(\tau_t, \beta)$ yields

$$\lambda\left(\tau_t; \hat{\beta}\right) \approx \lambda(\tau_t; \beta) + \partial\lambda(\tau_t; \beta)/\partial\beta'\left(\hat{\beta} - \beta\right),$$

where $\hat{\beta}$ denotes the maximum likelihood estimate of β. Mean squared error is therefore approximated by

$$E\left[\lambda(\tau_t; \hat{\beta}) - \lambda(\tau_t; \beta)\right]^2$$

$$\approx \partial\lambda(\tau_t; \beta)/\partial\beta' E\left[(\hat{\beta} - \beta)(\hat{\beta} - \beta)'\right]\partial\lambda(\tau_t; \beta)/\partial\beta.$$

By asymptotic unbiasedness of the maximum likelihood estimate, $E[(\hat{\beta} - \beta)(\hat{\beta} - \beta)']$ is asymptotically just $\text{cov}(\hat{\beta})$, which we estimate in standard fashion as $-(\partial^2 \ln L/\partial\beta\partial\beta')^{-1}$ evaluated at $\beta = \hat{\beta}$. Thus, as $T \to \infty$,

$$E\left[\lambda(\tau_t; \hat{\beta}) - \lambda(\tau_t; \beta)\right]^2 \to \text{var}\left[\lambda(\tau_t; \hat{\beta})\right].$$

For the exponential-quadratic hazard, recall that the first derivate of the hazard is

$$\partial\lambda(\tau_t; \beta)/\partial\beta = \begin{bmatrix} 1 \\ \tau_t \\ \tau_t^2 \end{bmatrix} \exp(\beta_0 + \beta_1\tau_t + \beta_2\tau_t^2)$$

and that the Hessian is

$$\partial^2 \ln L/\partial\beta\partial\beta' = -\sum_{t=1}^{T} \int_0^{\tau_1} \begin{bmatrix} 1 & x & x^2 \\ x & x^2 & x^3 \\ x^2 & x^3 & x^4 \end{bmatrix} \exp(\beta_0 + \beta_1 x + \beta_2 x^2)\, dx,$$

thus producing the asymptotic variance of the estimated hazard

$$\text{var}\left[\lambda(\tau_t; \hat{\beta})\right]$$

$$\approx \exp\left[2(\beta_0 + \beta_1\tau_t + \beta_2\tau_t^2)\right]\left[1, \tau_t, \tau_t^2\right]$$

$$\times \left\{\sum_{t=1}^{T} \int_0^{\tau_t} \begin{bmatrix} 1 & x & x^2 \\ x & x^2 & x^3 \\ x^2 & x^3 & x^4 \end{bmatrix} \exp(\beta_0 + \beta_1 x + \beta_2 x^2)\, dx\right\}^{-1} \begin{bmatrix} 1 \\ \tau_t \\ \tau_t^2 \end{bmatrix}.$$

The Likelihood Function for the Model with Negative Quadratic Coefficient

The log likelihood in hazard form is

$$\ln L(\beta; \tau_1, \ldots, \tau_T) = \sum_{t=1}^{T} [d_t \ln \lambda(\tau_t) - \Lambda(\tau_t)],$$

which in the exponential-quadratic hazard case is

$$\ln L(\beta; \tau_1, \ldots, \tau_T) = \sum_{t=1}^{T} \left[d_t(\beta_0 + \beta_1 \tau_t + \beta_2 \tau_t^2) \right.$$

$$\left. - \int_0^{\tau_t} \exp(\beta_0 + \beta_1 x + \beta_2 x^2)\, dx \right], \quad (A1)$$

evaluation of which requires evaluation of the integrated hazard. The integration must be done numerically. Under the assumption that $\beta_2 < 0$, however, the integration may be greatly simplified because, as we shall show, the likelihood may be rewritten in terms of the standard normal cumulative density function (c.d.f.). The standard normal c.d.f. has been extensively tabulated and is available, for example, as a primitive function in many FORTRANs. We proceed by noting that

$$\Lambda(\tau_t) = \int_0^{\tau_t} \exp(\beta_0 + \beta_1 x + \beta_2 x^2)\, dx$$

$$= \int_0^{\tau_t} \exp\left\{ \beta_2 [x + \beta_1/(2\beta_2)]^2 - \beta_1^2/(4\beta_2) + \beta_0 \right\} dx$$

$$= \exp\left[\beta_0 - \beta_1^2/(4\beta_2) \right]$$

$$\times \int_0^{\tau_t} \exp\left[(-1/\{2[-1/(2\beta_2)]\})[x + \beta_1/(2\beta_2)]^2 \right] dx$$

$$= \exp\left[\beta_0 - \beta_1^2/(4\beta_2) \right] (2\pi)^{1/2} [-1/(2\beta_2)]^{1/2}$$

$$\times \int_0^{\tau_t} (2\pi)^{-1/2} [-1/(2\beta_2)]^{-1/2}$$

$$\times \exp\left[(-1/\{2[-1/(2\beta_2)]\})[x + \beta_1/(2\beta_2)]^2 \right] dx, \quad (A2)$$

which contains an integral of a normal density function with mean $-\beta_1/(2\beta_2)$ and variance $-1/(2\beta_2)$. (Recall our assumption that $\beta_2 < 0$, which is needed to ensure positivity of the variance.)

The integral may be rewritten as the difference of two integrals with left integration limit $-\infty$; that is,

$$\int_0^{T_t} (2\pi)^{-1/2} [-1/(2\beta_2)]^{-1/2}$$

$$\times \exp\left[(-1/\{2[-1/(2\beta_2)]\})[x + \beta_1/(2\beta_2)]^2 \right] dx$$

$$= \int_{-\infty}^{T_t} (2\pi)^{-1/2} [-1/(2\beta_2)]^{-1/2}$$

$$\times \exp\left[(-1/\{2[-1/(2\beta_2)]\})[x + \beta_1/(2\beta_2)]^2 \right] dx$$

$$- \int_{-\infty}^{0} (2\pi)^{-1/2} [-1/(2\beta)]^{-1/2}$$

$$\times \exp\left[(-1/\{2[-1/(2\beta_2)]\})[x + \beta_1/(2\beta_2)]^2 \right] dx.$$

By standardizing appropriately, we can rewrite the difference of integrals as

$$[-1/(2\beta_2)]^{-1/2} \Phi\left\{ [x + \beta_1/(2\beta_2)]/[-1/(2\beta_2)]^{1/2} \right\}$$

$$- [-1/(2\beta_2)]^{-1/2} \Phi\left\{ [\beta_1/(2\beta_2)]/[-1/(2\beta_2)]^{-1/2} \right\}$$

$$= [-1/(2\beta_2)]^{-1/2} \Phi\left\{ [x + \beta_1/(2\beta_2)]/[-1/(2\beta_2)]^{1/2} \right\}$$

$$- [-1/(2\beta_2)]^{-1/2} \Phi\left\{ [-\beta_1/(-2\beta_2)]^{-1/2} \right\}. \qquad \text{(A3)}$$

where

$$\Phi(x) = \int_{-\infty}^{x} (2\pi)^{-1/2} \exp(-y^2/2)\, dx$$

denotes the standard normal c.d.f. Insertion of (A3) into (A2) yields

$$\Lambda(\tau_t) = \exp\left[\beta_0 - \beta_1^2/(4\beta_2) \right] (2\pi)^{1/2}$$

$$\times \left(\Phi\left\{ [x + \beta_1/(2\beta_2)]/[-1/(2\beta_2)]^{1/2} \right\} \right.$$

$$\left. - \Phi\left\{ [-\beta_1/(-2\beta_2)]^{1/2} \right\} \right),$$

which, when evaluated for $t = 1, 2, \ldots, T$ and inserted into (A1), yields the log likelihood function.

The Likelihood Function for the Model with Covariates

Consider the introduction of a vector of covariates into the hazard function; that is, consider

$$\lambda(Z_{\tau_t + s_t}, \tau_t; \beta),$$

where $s_t = \sum_{j=1}^{t-1} \tau_j$. Note that the total period used for estimation is $\sum_{t=1}^{T} \tau_t$. The log likelihood is

$$\ln L(\beta; \tau_1, \ldots, \tau_T)$$

$$= \sum_{t=1}^{T} \left\{ d_t \ln[\lambda(Z_{\tau_t + s_t}, \tau_t; \beta)] - \int_0^{\tau_t} \lambda(Z_{x + s_t}, x; \beta) \, dx \right\}.$$

The score is

$$\partial \ln L / \partial \beta = \sum_{t=1}^{T} \left\{ [d_t / \lambda(Z_{\tau_t + s_t}, \tau_t; \beta)] [\partial \lambda(Z_{\tau_t + s_t}, \tau_t; \beta) / \partial \beta] \right.$$

$$\left. - \int_0^{\tau_t} \partial \lambda(Z_{t + s_t}, x; \beta) / \partial \beta \, dx \right\},$$

and the Hessian is

$$\partial^2 \ln L / \partial \beta \partial \beta' = \sum_{t=1}^{T} \left\{ [d_t / \lambda(Z_{\tau_t + s_t}, \tau_t; \beta)] [\partial^2 \lambda(Z_{\tau_t + s_t}, \tau_t; \beta) / \partial \beta \partial \beta'] \right.$$

$$- [d_t / \lambda^2(Z_{\tau_t + s_{tt}}, \tau_t; \beta)] [\partial \lambda(Z_{\tau_t + s_t}, \tau_t; \beta) / \partial \beta']$$

$$\left. - \int_0^{\tau_t} \partial^2 \lambda(Z_{x + s_t}, x; \beta) / \partial \beta \partial \beta' \, dx \right\}.$$

In the exponential-quadratic case, we have

$$\lambda(Z_{\tau_t + s_t}, \tau_t; \beta) = \exp\left(\beta_0 + \beta_1 \tau_t + \beta_2 \tau_t^2 + Z_{\tau_t + s_t} \gamma \right),$$

where both $Z_{\tau_t + s_t}$ and γ are vectors, so that the score and Hessian are

$\partial \ln L / \partial \beta$

$$= \sum_{t=1}^{T} \left\{ \left(d_t \begin{bmatrix} 1 \\ \tau_t \\ \tau_t^2 \\ Z_{\tau_t + s_t} \end{bmatrix} \right) \right.$$

$$\left. - \int_0^{\tau_t} \begin{bmatrix} 1 \\ x \\ x^2 \\ Z_{x+s_t} \end{bmatrix} \exp\left(\beta_0 + \beta_1 x + \beta_2 x^2 + Z_{x+s_t} \gamma \right) dx \right\}$$

and

$$\partial^2 \ln L / \partial\beta\partial\beta' = - \sum_{t=1}^{T} \int_0^{\tau_t} \begin{bmatrix} 1 \\ x \\ x^2 \\ Z_{x+s_t} \end{bmatrix} \left(1, x, x^2, Z_{x+s_t} \right)$$

$$\times \exp\left(\beta_0 + \beta_1 x + \beta_2 x^2 + Z_{x+s_t} \gamma \right) dx.$$

Each integration may be evaluated numerically as discussed in the text. Thus, for example,

$$\int_0^{\tau_t} Z_{x+s_t} \exp\left(\beta_0 + \beta_1 x + \beta_2 x^2 + Z_{x+s_t} \gamma \right) dx$$

is evaluated as

$$\sum_{j=1}^{\tau_t} \left[Z_{x_j + s_t} \exp\left(\beta_0 + \beta_1 x + \beta_2 x_j^2 + Z_{x_j + s_t} \gamma \right) \right.$$

$$\left. + Z_{s_{j-1} + s_t} \exp\left(\beta_0 + \beta_1 x_{j-1} + \beta_2 x_{j-1}^2 + Z_{x_{j-1} + s_t} \gamma \right) \right] (x_j + x_{j-1})/2,$$

where $x_j = j$.

References

Burns, A. F., and W. C. Mitchell. 1946. *Measuring business cycles*. New York: NBER.

Campbell, J. Y., and N. G. Mankiw. 1989. International evidence on the persistence of macroeconomic fluctuations. *Journal of Monetary Economics* 23:319–33.

Diebold, F. X., and G. D. Rudebusch. 1989. Scoring the leading indicators. *Journal of Business* 62:369–92.

——. 1990. A nonparametric investigation of duration dependence in the American business cycle. *Journal of Political Economy* 98:596–616.

——. 1991. Ex ante forecasting with the leading indicators. In *Leading economic indicators: New approaches and forecasting records*, ed. K. Lahiri and G. H. Moore. Cambridge: Cambridge University Press.

——. 1992. Have postwar economic fluctuations been stabilized? *American Economic Review* 82:993–1005.

Hamilton, J. H. 1989. A new approach to the analysis of nonstationary time series and the business cycle. *Econometrica* 57:357–84.

Heckman, J. J., and J. R. Walker. 1990. The relationship between wages and income and the timing and spacing of births: Evidence from Swedish longitudinal data. *Econometrica* 58:1411–42.

Kiefer, N. M. 1988. Economic duration data and hazard functions. *Journal of Economic Literature* 26:646–79.

Kormendi, R. C., and P. G. Meguire. 1990. A multicountry characterization of the nonstationarity of aggregate output. *Journal of Money, Credit and Banking* 22:77–93.

Moore, G. H., and V. Zarnowitz. 1986. The development and role of the National Bureau of Economic Research's business cycle chronologies. In *The American business cycles*, ed. R. J. Gordon, Chicago: University of Chicago Press.

Morgenstern, O. 1959. *International financial transactions and business cycles*. New York: NBER.

Mudambi, R., and L. W. Taylor. 1991. A nonparametric investigation of duration dependence in the American business cycle: A note. *Journal of Political Economy* 99:654–56.

Murphy, K. M., A. Shleifer, and R. W. Vishny. 1989. Building blocks of market-clearing business cycle models [with discussion]. *NBER Macroeconomics Annual*, 247–86.

Nickell, S. 1979. Estimating the probability of leaving unemployment, *Econometrica* 47:1249–66.

Sichel, D. E. 1991. Business cycle duration dependence: A parametric approach. *Review of Economics and Statistics* 71:254–60.

6

Measuring Business Cycles: A Modern Perspective

FRANCIS X. DIEBOLD AND GLENN D. RUDEBUSCH*

1. Introduction

It is desirable to know the facts before attempting to explain them; hence, the attractiveness of organizing business-cycle regularities within a model-free framework. During the first half of this century, much research was devoted to obtaining just such an empirical characterization of the business cycle. The most prominent example of this work was Burns and Mitchell (1946), whose summary empirical definition was:

> Business cycles are a type of fluctuation found in the aggregate economic activity of nations that organize their work mainly in business enterprises: a cycle consists of expansions occurring at about the same time in many economic activities, followed by similarly general recessions, contractions, and revivals which merge into the expansion phase of the next cycle. (p. 3)

Burns and Mitchell's definition of business cycles has two key features. The first is the comovement among individual economic variables. Indeed, the comovement among series, taking into account possible leads and lags in timing, was the centerpiece of Burns and Mitchell's methodology. In their analysis, Burns and Mitchell considered the historical concordance of hundreds of series, including those measuring commodity output, income, prices, interest rates, banking transactions, and transportation services. They used the clusters of turning points in these individual series to determine the monthly dates of the turning

* This paper benefited from participants' comments at the NBER Economic Fluctuations Meeting on Developments in Business-Cycle Research, as well as a number of other meetings and seminars. We thank the referees for their constructive comments, and we also thank Alan Auerbach, Michael Boldin, Antúlio Bomfim, Russell Cooper, Steve Durlauf, René Garcia, Jim Hamilton, Danny Quah, Neil Shephard, and Mark Watson. The hospitality of the University of Chicago, where parts of this work were completed, is gratefully acknowledged. We are also grateful to José Lopez and Marcelle Chauvet, who provided assistance with many of the computations. We thank the National Science Foundation, the Sloan Foundation, and the University of Pennsylvania Research Foundation for support.

points in the overall business cycle.[1] Similarly, the early emphasis on the consistent pattern of comovement among various variables over the business cycle led directly to the creation of *composite* leading, coincident, and lagging indexes (e.g., Shishkin, 1961).

The second prominent element of Burns and Mitchell's definition of business cycles is their division of business cycles into separate phases or regimes. Their analysis, as was typical at the time, treats expansions separately from contractions. For example, certain series are classified as leading or lagging indicators of the cycle, depending on the general state of business conditions.

Both of the features highlighted by Burns and Mitchell as key attributes of business cycles were less emphasized in postwar business-cycle models—particularly in empirical models where the focus was on the time-series properties of the cycle. Most subsequent econometric work on business cycles followed Tinbergen (1939) in using the linear difference equation as the instrument of analysis. This empirical work has generally focused on the time-series properties of just one or a few macroeconomic aggregates, ignoring the pervasive comovement stressed by Burns and Mitchell. Likewise, the linear structure imposed eliminated consideration of any nonlinearity of business cycles that would require separate analyses of expansions and contractions.

Recently, however, empirical research has revived consideration of each of the attributes highlighted by Burns and Mitchell. Notably, Stock and Watson (1989, 1991, 1993) have used a dynamic factor model to capture comovement by obtaining a single common factor from a set of many macroeconomic series, and Hamilton (1989) has estimated a nonlinear model for real GNP with discrete regime switching between periods of expansion and contraction.

This paper is part survey, part interpretation, and part new contribution. We describe the dynamic-factor and regime-switching models in some detail in sections 2 and 3, and we sketch their links to recent developments in macroeconomics in section 4. The modern dynamic-factor and regime-switching literatures, however, have generally considered the comovement and regime-switching aspects of the business cycle in isolation of each other. We view that as unfortunate, as scholars of the cycle have simultaneously used both ideas for many decades. Thus, in section 5, we attempt an empirical synthesis in a comprehensive framework that incorporates *both* factor structure and regime switching. We conclude in section 6.

---

[1] See Diebold and Rudebusch (1992) for further discussion of the role of comovement in determining business-cycle turning points.

2. Comovement: Factor Structure

In a famous essay, Lucas (1976) drew attention to a key business-cycle fact: outputs of broadly-defined sectors move together. Lucas' view is part of a long tradition that has stressed the coordination of activity among various economic actors and the resulting comovement in sectoral outputs.

Analysis of comovement in dynamic settings typically makes use of two nonparametric tools, the autocorrelation function and the spectral density function. In the time domain, one examines multivariate dynamics via the autocorrelation function, which gives the correlations of each variable with its own past and with the past of all other variables in the system. Such analyses are now done routinely, as in Backus and Kehoe (1992), who characterize the dynamics of output, consumption, investment, government purchases, net exports, money, and prices across ten countries and a hundred years.

Alternatively, one examines dynamics in the frequency domain via the spectral density function, the Fourier transform of the autocovariance function, which presents the same dynamic information but in a complementary fashion. The spectral density matrix decomposes variation and covariation among variables by frequency, permitting one to concentrate on the dynamics of interest (business-cycle dynamics, for example, correspond to periods of roughly 2–8 years). Transformations of both the real and imaginary parts of the spectral density matrix have immediate interpretation in business-cycle analysis; the *coherence* between any two economic time series effectively charts the strength of their correlation by frequency, while the *phase* charts lead/lag relationships by frequency. A good example of business-cycle analysis in the frequency domain is Sargent (1987), who examines the spectral density matrix of seven U.S. data series: real GNP, the unemployment rate, the interest rate, the change in real money stock, inflation, productivity, and real wages.[2]

Of course, one can analyze business-cycle data parametrically as well, by approximating the dynamic relationships with a particular statistical model. In this regard, the vector autoregression, introduced by Sims (1980), is ubiquitous. The moving-average representation (that is, the impulse-response function) of a vector autoregression of a set of macroeconomic variables provides a readily interpretable characteriza-

---

[2] In the frequency domain, Sargent (1987, p. 282) offers the following update of Burns and Mitchell's definition: "...the business cycle is the phenomenon of a number of important economic aggregates (such as GNP, unemployment, and layoffs) being characterized by high pairwise coherences at the low business cycle frequencies."

tion of dynamics, by charting the response of each variable to shocks to itself and the other variables.

Unfortunately, a vector-autoregressive study that attempts to capture the pervasive comovement among hundreds of series emphasized by Burns and Mitchell requires more degrees of freedom than are available in macroeconomic samples. Recent work provides crucial dimensionality reduction, however, because the dynamic comovements among large sets of macroeconomic variables are often well-described by a particular configuration of the vector autoregression associated with *index structure*, or *factor structure*.

Factor models have a long history of use in cross-sectional settings, and their generalization to dynamic environments is due to Sargent and Sims (1977), Geweke (1977) and Watson and Engle (1983). Important recent contributions include Stock and Watson (1989, 1991, 1993) and Quah and Sargent (1993), among others. The idea is simply that the comovement of contemporaneous economic variables may be due to the fact that they are driven in part by common shocks. In a one-factor model, for example, the behavior of the set of N variables is qualitatively similar to the behavior of just *one* variable, the common factor. This allows parsimonious modeling while nevertheless maintaining fidelity to the notion of pervasive macroeconomic comovement.[3]

Let us focus on the dynamic factor model of Stock and Watson (1991), which was developed as a modern statistical framework for computing a composite index of coincident indicators. In their one-factor model, movements in the N macroeconomic variables of interest, x_t, are determined by changes in the one-dimensional unobserved common factor, f_t, and by the N-dimensional idiosyncratic component, u_t:

$$
\begin{array}{ccccccc}
x_t & = & \beta & + & \lambda & f_t & + & u_t \\
N \times 1 & & N \times 1 & & N \times 1 & 1 \times 1 & & N \times 1
\end{array}
$$

$$
\begin{array}{ccc}
D(L) & u_t & = & \epsilon_t \\
N \times N & N \times 1 & & N \times 1
\end{array}
$$

$$
\begin{array}{ccc}
\phi(L) & (f_t - \delta) & = & \eta_t. \\
1 \times 1 & 1 \times 1 & & 1 \times 1
\end{array}
$$

All idiosyncratic stochastic dynamics are driven by ϵ_t, while all common stochastic dynamics, which are embodied in the common factor, are

---

[3] It is interesting to note that parallel structures may exist in many financial markets, which makes sense to the extent that asset prices accurately reflect fundamentals, which themselves have factor structure. See Singleton (1980), Bollerslev, Engle and Woolridge (1988), and Diebold and Nerlove (1989), among others, for examples of factor structure in both the conditional means and conditional variances of various asset returns.

driven by η_t. Identification may be achieved in many ways. Stock and Watson, for example, impose (1) orthogonality at all leads and lags of $\{u_{1t}, \ldots, u_{Nt}, f_t\}$ (which is achieved by making $D(L)$ diagonal and $\{\epsilon_{1t}, \ldots, \epsilon_{Nt}, \eta_t\}$ orthogonal at all leads and lags), and (2) $\text{var}(\eta_t) = 1$.

3. Nonlinearity: Regime Switching

Underlying much of the traditional business-cycle literature is the notion that a good statistical characterization of business-cycle dynamics may require some notion of regime switching between "good" and "bad" states.[4] Models incorporating regime switching have a long tradition in dynamic econometrics.[5] One recent time-series model squarely in line with the regime-switching tradition is the "threshold" model (e.g., Tong, 1983; Potter, 1995). In a threshold model, the regime switches according to the observable past history of the system.

Although threshold models are of interest, models with *latent* states as opposed to observed states may be more appropriate for business-cycle modeling. Hamilton (1989, 1990, 1994) develops such models. In Hamilton's regime-switching setup, time-series dynamics are governed by a finite-dimensional parameter vector that switches (potentially each period) depending upon which of two unobservable states is realized, with state transitions governed by a first-order Markov process.

To make matters concrete, let's take a simple example. Let $\{s_t\}_{t=1}^T$ be the (latent) sample path of two-state first-order Markov process, taking values 0 or 1, with transition probability matrix given by[6]

$$M = \begin{bmatrix} p_{00} & 1 - p_{00} \\ 1 - p_{11} & p_{11} \end{bmatrix}.$$

---

[4] Again, parallel structures may exist in financial markets. Regime switching has been found, for example, in the conditional mean dynamics of interest rates (Hamilton, 1988; Cecchetti, and Lam and Mark, 1990) and exchange rates (Engel and Hamilton, 1990), and in the conditional variance dynamics of stock returns (Hamilton and Susmel, 1994).

[5] Key early contributions include the early work of Quandt (1958) and Goldfeld and Quandt (1973).

[6] The ij^{th} element of M gives the probability of moving from state i (at time $t - 1$) to state j (at time t). Note that there are only two free parameters, the "staying probabilities" p_{00} and p_{11}.

Let $\{y_t\}_{t=1}^T$ be the sample path of an observed time series that depends on $\{s_t\}_{t=1}^T$ such that the density of y_t conditional upon s_t is

$$f(y_t \mid s_t; \theta) = \frac{1}{\sqrt{2\pi}\,\sigma} \exp\left[\frac{-(y_t - \mu_{s_t})^2}{2\sigma^2}\right].$$

Thus, y_t is Gaussian white noise with a potentially switching mean. The two means around which y_t moves are of particular interest and may, for example, correspond to episodes of differing growth rates ("expansions" and "contractions").

The central idea of regime switching is simply that expansions and contractions may be usefully treated as different probabilistic objects. This idea has been an essential part of the Burns-Mitchell-NBER tradition of business-cycle analysis and is also manifest in the great interest in the popular press, for example, in identifying and predicting turning points in economic activity. Yet it is only within a regime-switching framework that the concept of a turning point has intrinsic meaning. Recent contributions that have emphasized the use of probabilistic models in the construction and evaluation of turning-point forecasts and chronologies include Neftci (1984) and Diebold and Rudebusch (1989).

Various seemingly disparate contributions may be readily interpreted within the context of the basic switching model. One example is Neftci's (1984) well-known analysis of business-cycle asymmetry, which amounts to asking whether the transition probability matrix is symmetric. Another example is Potter's (1995) and Sichel's (1994) evidence for the existence of a "recovery" regime of very fast growth at the beginning of expansions, which corresponds to a "third state" in business-cycle dynamics.

Yet another class of examples concerns recent analyses of business-cycle duration dependence, which amount to asking whether the transition probabilities vary with length-to-date of the current regime. Diebold and Rudebusch (1990), Diebold, Rudebusch, and Sichel (1993), and Filardo (1994) have found positive duration dependence in postwar U.S. contractions; that is, the longer a contraction persists, the more likely it is to end soon. Similar results have been obtained by Durland and McCurdy (1994) using the technology of semi-Markov processes. Other forms of time-variation in business-cycle transition probabilities may be important as well. Ghysels (1993, 1994), in particular, argues that business-cycle transition probabilities vary seasonally and provides formal methods for analyzing such variation.[7]

---

[7] See also De Toldi, Gourieroux, and Monfort (1992).

The business-cycle duration dependence literature highlights the fact that economic considerations may suggest the potential desirability of allowing the transition probabilities to vary through time. The duration dependence literature focuses on trend and seasonal variation in transition probabilities, but in certain contexts it may be desirable to allow for more general time-variation, as in Diebold, Lee, and Weinbach (1994) and Filardo (1994), who let the transition probabilities evolve as logistic functions of exogenous variables, z_t:

$$M_t = \begin{bmatrix} \dfrac{\exp(z_t' \beta_0)}{1 + \exp(z_t' \beta_0)} & 1 - \dfrac{\exp(z_t' \beta_0)}{1 + \exp(z_t' \beta_0)} \\ 1 - \dfrac{\exp(z_t' \beta_1)}{1 + \exp(z_t' \beta_1)} & \dfrac{\exp(z_t' \beta_1)}{1 + \exp(z_t' \beta_1)} \end{bmatrix}.$$

4. Factor Structure and Regime Switching: Links to Macroeconomic Theory

In this section, as further motivation, we describe some of the links between macroeconomic theory and factor structure and regime switching. We use convex equilibrium business-cycle models to motivate the appearance of factor structure and non-convex models with multiple equilibria to motivate regime switching; however, we hasten to add that these pairings are by no means exclusive. Moreover, of course, our ultimate interest lies in models that simultaneously display factor structure and regime-switching behavior, which as the following discussion suggests, might occur in a variety of ways.

A. Macroeconomic Theory and Factor Structure

The econometric tradition of comovement through factor structure is consistent with a variety of modern dynamic macroeconomic models. Here we highlight just one—a linear-quadratic equilibrium model—in order to motivate the appearance of factor structure. We follow the basic setup of Hansen and Sargent (1993), which although arguably rigid in some respects, has two very convenient properties. First, the discounted dynamic programming problem associated with the model may be solved easily and *exactly*. Second, the equilibria of such models are *precisely* linear (that is, precisely a vector autoregression), thereby bringing theory into close contact with econometrics.

Preferences are quadratic and are defined over consumption of services, s_t, and work effort, l_t, with preference shocks, b_t, determining a stochastic bliss point. There are four linear constraints on the utility maximization. The first represents the linear technology: a weighted average of the output of consumption goods, c_t, intermediate goods, g_t, and investment goods, i_t, equals a linear combination of lagged capital stock, k_{t-1}, and work effort, plus the technology shock, d_t. The second is the law of motion for the capital stock: Capital accumulates through additional net investment. The third is the law of motion for "household capital," h_t, which is driven by consumption expenditures. The last specifies that current consumption services depend on both lagged household capital and current consumption.

Formally, the planning problem associated with this model is

$$\max -\frac{1}{2} E \sum_{t=0}^{\infty} \beta^t \left[(s_t - b_t) + l_t^2 \right]$$

subject to the four constraints[8]

$$\alpha_1 c_t + \alpha_2 g_t + \alpha_3 i_t = \alpha_4 k_{t-1} + \alpha_5 l_t + d_t$$

$$k_t = \beta_1 k_{t-1} + \beta_2 i_t$$

$$h_t = \gamma_1 h_{t-1} + \gamma_2 c_t$$

$$s_t = \delta_1 h_{t-1} + \delta_2 c_t.$$

The exogenous uncertainty (e_{t+1}) in the model evolves according to

$$e_{t+1} = \rho_1 e_t + w_{t+1},$$

where w_{t+1} is zero-mean white noise. The preference and technology shocks (b_t and d_t) are linear transformations of the e_t,

$$b_t = U_b e_t$$

$$d_t = U_d e_t.$$

Importantly for our purposes, note that this framework can potentially describe the determination of a large set of series. All variables (except l_t) can be considered as vectors of different goods or services with the parameters interpreted as conformable matrices.

---

[8] Consumption appears in both of the last two equations in order to capture both its durable and nondurable aspects.

The equilibrium of this economy is a *linear* stochastic process and can be presented by a vector autoregression constrained by cross-equation restrictions, with state-space form

$$\alpha_{t+1} = A\alpha_t + Cw_{t+1}$$

$$o_t = G\alpha_t,$$

where the state vector α_t contains h_t, k_t, and e_t. o_t can contain any variable that can be expressed as a linear function of the state variables. Note that this vector autoregression will be singular so long as the number of shocks is less than the number of variables in the system. Fewer shocks than observables is the rule in economic models. The standard setups have just a few preference and technology shocks driving a comparatively large number of decision variables, thereby building in singularity. In fact, in the leading case of a single technology shock and no preference shocks, one shock is responsible for all variation in the choice variables, resulting in an equilibrium that maps into a special (singular) case of the one-factor model discussed earlier. In that special case, there are no idiosyncratic shocks (or equivalently, they have zero variance).

To reconcile the singular equilibrium from the model economy with the clearly non-singular nature of the data, measurement error is often introduced.[9] The state-space representation becomes

$$\alpha_{t+1} = A\alpha_t + Cw_{t+1}$$

$$o_t = G\alpha_t + v_t,$$

where v_t is a martingale-difference sequence. In single-shock linear-quadratic models with measurement error, the equilibria are precisely of the single-factor form, with nondegenerate idiosyncratic effects.

Feeling constrained by linear technology and quadratic preferences, many authors have recently focused on models that are *not* linear-quadratic.[10] The formulation is basically the same as in the linear-quadratic case, but the mechanics are more complicated. The discounted dynamic programming problem associated with the recursive competitive equilibrium can only be solved *approximately*; however, the decision rules are nevertheless well-approximated linearly near the steady state. Under regularity conditions, the equilibrium is a Markov process in the state variables, and if that Markov process converges to

---

[9] See Sargent (1989) and Hansen and Sargent (1993), among others.

[10] See, for example, Kydland and Prescott (1982), Hansen (1985), Cooley and Hansen (1989), and Cooley (1995).

an invariant distribution, then a vector-autoregressive representation exists. Again, the vector autoregression is only an approximation to the generally *nonlinear* decision rules, and its computation can be tedious. However, the availability of a factor structure for modelling this approximation remains.

B. Macroeconomic Theory and Regime Switching

Regime-switching behavior is also consistent with a variety of macroeconomic models. Here we focus on models with coordination failures, which produce multiple equilibria. In what follows, we shall provide a brief overview of this theoretical literature and its relation to the regime-switching model.

Much has been made of the role of spillovers and strategic complementarities in macroeconomics (Cooper and John, 1988). "Spillover" simply refers to a situation in which others' strategies affect one's own *payoff*. "Strategic complementarity" refers to a situation in which others' strategies affect one's own *optimal strategy*. Spillovers and strategic complementarities arise, for example, in models of optimal search (e.g., Diamond, 1982), where thick-market externalities ensure that the likelihood of successful search depends on the intensity of search undertaken by others, which in turn affects one's own optimal search intensity. In short, search is more desirable when other agents are also searching, because it is likely to be more productive.

Spillovers and strategic complementarities may have important macroeconomic effects. For example, the appearance of aggregate increasing returns to scale (e.g., Hall, 1991) may simply be an artifact of the positive externalities associated with high output levels in the presence of spillovers and strategic complementarities rather than true increasing returns in firms' technologies. Indeed, Caballero and Lyons (1992) find little evidence of increasing returns at the individual level, yet substantial evidence at the aggregate level, suggesting the importance of spillovers and strategic complementarities.

Spillovers and strategic complementarities can produce multiple equilibria, the dynamics of which may be well-approximated by statistical models involving regime switching.[11] In fact, Cooper and John (1988) stress the existence of multiple equilibria, with no coordination mechanism, as a common theme in a variety of seemingly unrelated models displaying spillovers and strategic complementarities. Moreover, the

---

[11] Durlauf (1991) and Cooper and Durlauf (1993) provide insightful discussion of this point.

equilibria are frequently Pareto-rankable. Situations arise, for example, in which an economy is in a low-output equilibrium such that all agents would be better off at higher output levels, but there is no coordination device to facilitate the change.[12]

Recent work has provided some mechanisms for endogenizing switches between equilibria. One approach involves variations on Keynesian "animal spirits," or self-fulfilling waves of optimism and pessimism, as formalized by Azariadis (1981) and Cass and Shell (1983). Notably, Diamond and Fudenberg (1989) demonstrate in a search framework the existence of rational-expectations sunspot equilibria in which agents' beliefs about cycles are self-fulfilling. Howit and McAfee (1992) obtain results even more in line with our thesis in a model in which waves of optimism and pessimism evolve according to a Markov process. The statistical properties of equilibria from their model are well-characterized by a Markov regime-switching process.[13]

Finally, Cooper (1994) proposes a history-dependent selection criterion in an economy with multiple Nash equilibria corresponding to different levels of productivity. The Cooper criterion reflects the idea that history may create a focal point: a person's recent experience is likely to influence her expectations of others' future strategic behavior, resulting in a slow evolution of conjectures about others' actions. Cooper's analysis highlights the importance of learning to respond optimally to the strategic actions of others. The Cooper criterion leads to persistence in the equilibrium selected, with switching occurring as a consequence of large shocks, phenomena which again may be well-characterized by statistical models involving regime switching.

Other history-dependent theoretical models have been proposed by Startz (1994) and Acemoglu and Scott (1993). These include the same "learning-by-doing" dynamic externality that drives the "new growth theory" models. Again, shocks cause endogenous switching between high-growth and low-growth states.

5. Synthesis: Regime Switching in a Dynamic Factor Model

We have argued that both comovement through factor structure and nonlinearity through regime switching are important elements to be considered in an analysis of business cycles. It is unfortunate, therefore,

---

[12] In many respects, such equilibria are reminiscent of the traditional Keynesian regimes of "full employment" and "underemployment" discussed, for example, in DeLong and Summers (1988).

[13] Related approaches have been proposed by Durlauf (1995) and Evans and Honkapohja (1993), among others.

that the two have recently been considered largely in isolation from each other. In what follows, we sketch a framework for the analysis of business-cycle data that incorporates both factor structure and regime switching in a natural way. This framework, although not formally used before, may be a good approximation to the one implicitly adopted by many scholars of the cycle.

A. A Prototypical Model

Consider a dynamic factor model in which the factor switches regimes. First consider a switching model for the factor f_t; we work with a slightly richer model than before, allowing for p^{th}-order autoregressive dynamics. Again let $\{s_t\}_{t=1}^T$ be the sample path of a latent Markov process, taking on values 0 and 1, let $\{f_t\}_{t=1}^T$ be the sample path of the factor (which depends on $\{s_t\}_{t=1}^T$), and collect the relevant history of the factor and state in the vector $h_t = (s_{t-1}, \ldots, s_{t-p}, f_{t-1}, \ldots, f_{t-p})'$. The probabilistic dependence of f_t on h_t is summarized by the conditional density,

$$P(f_t \mid h_t; \theta) = \frac{1}{\sqrt{2\pi}\,\sigma} \exp \frac{-\left[(f_t - \mu_{s_t}) - \sum_{i=1}^{p} \phi_i(f_{t-i} - \mu_{s_{t-i}})\right]^2}{2\sigma^2}.$$

The latent factor, then, follows a pth-order Gaussian autoregression with potentially changing mean. The two means around which the factor moves are of particular interest; call them μ_0 (slow growth) and μ_1 (fast growth).

We then assemble the rest of the model around the regime-switching factor. We write

$$\underset{N \times 1}{\Delta x_t} = \underset{N \times 1}{\beta} + \underset{N \times 1}{\lambda} \underset{1 \times 1}{f_t} + \underset{N \times 1}{u_t}$$

$$\underset{N \times N}{D(L)} \underset{N \times 1}{u_t} = \underset{N \times 1}{\epsilon_t}$$

as earlier. In Frischian terms, the model as written has a regime-switching "impulse" with a stable "propagation mechanism." Many variations on the theme of this basic setup are of course possible.

B. A Look at the Data

Let us first describe the data. We examine quarterly economic indicators, 1952.I–1993.I, as described in detail in table 6.1. The data include three composite indexes of coincident indicators, corresponding to three alternative methodologies: Commerce Department, modified Commerce Department, and Stock-Watson. The component indicators underlying the Commerce Department and modified Commerce Department indexes are identical (personal income less transfer payments, index of industrial production, manufacturing and trade sales, and employees on non-agricultural payrolls); only their processing differs slightly (see Green and Beckman, 1992). The Stock-Watson index introduces a change in the list of underlying indicators (employees on nonagricultural payrolls is replaced by hours of employees on nonagricultural payrolls) and processes the underlying component indicators differently than either the Commerce Department or modified Commerce Department indexes. We obtained qualitatively similar results from all of the indexes; thus, we shall focus here on the Commerce Department's modified Composite Coincident Index. Henceforth, we shall refer to it simply as "the Composite Coincident Index."

We graph the log of the Composite Coincident Index in figure 6.1. It tracks the business cycle well, with obvious and pronounced drops corresponding to the NBER-designated recessions of 1958, 1960, 1970, 1974, 1980, 1982 and 1990. We similarly graph the logs of the four components of the Composite Coincident Index in figure 6.2.[14] Their behavior closely follows that of the Composite Coincident Index; in particular, there seems to be commonality among switch times.

We shall not provide maximum-likelihood estimates (or any other estimates) of a fully specified dynamic-factor model with regime-switching factor. To do so would be premature at this point. Instead, we shall sift the data in two simple exercises to provide suggestive evidence as to whether the data accord with our basic thesis.

First, we work directly with the Composite Coincident Index, which is essentially an estimate of the common factor underlying aggregate economic activity.[15] We ask whether its dynamics are well approximated by a Markov-switching model. We fit a switching model to one hundred

---

[14] Each of the four component indicators is graphed on a different scale to enable their presentation in one graph. For this reason, no scale appears on the vertical axis of the graph.

[15] Stock and Watson motivate and derive their index in precisely this way. The Commerce indexes are attempts at the same methodology, albeit less formally.

TABLE 6.1
Data Description

Composite Indexes of Coincident Indicators, Alternative Methodologies

CCI: Composite Index of Four Coincident Indicators, Commerce Department Methodology, 1982 = 100

CCIM: Experimental Composite Index of Four Coincident Indicators, Modified Commerce Department Methodology, 1982 = 100

CCISW: Experimental Composite Index of Four Coincident Indicators, Stock-Watson Methodology, August 1982 = 100

Components of the Composite Index of Four Coincident Indicators Commerce Department Methodology (CCI) and Modified Commerce Department Methodology (CCIM)

PILTP: Personal Income Less Transfer Payments, Seasonally Adjusted at an Annual Rate, Trillions of 1987 Dollars

MIP: Index of Industrial Production, Seasonally Adjusted, 1987 = 100

MTS: Manufacturing and Trade Sales, Seasonally Adjusted at an Annual Rate, Millions of 1982 Dollars

ENAP: Employees on Non-Agricultural Payrolls, Seasonally Adjusted at an Annual Rate, Millions of People

Components of the Composite Index of Four Coincident Indicators Stock-Watson Methodology (CCISW)

Same as CCI, except Employees on Nonagricultural Payrolls (ENAP) is replaced by:

HENAP: Hours of Employees on Nonagricultural Payrolls, Seasonally Adjusted at an Annual Rate, Billions of Hours

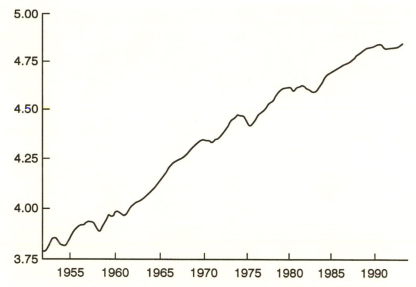

Fig. 6.1. Log of composite coincident index.

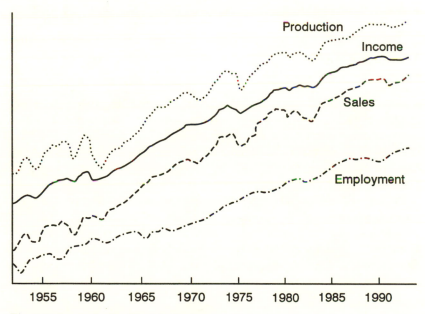

Fig. 6.2. Logs of coincident indicators.

TABLE 6.2
Estimated AR(1) Markov-Switching Models

	START	CCIM	PILTP	ENAP	IP	MTS
μ_0	−0.50	−0.91	−0.75	−0.54	−4.12	−2.26
		(0.17)	(0.45)	(0.13)	(0.70)	(0.96)
μ_1	0.50	0.97	0.88	0.61	1.16	1.01
		(0.11)	(0.15)	(0.09)	(0.29)	(0.27)
ϕ_1	0.40	0.66	0.35	0.97	0.52	0.38
		(0.10)	(0.10)	(0.08)	(0.09)	(0.11)
σ^2	0.80	0.31	0.48	0.10	2.04	2.13
		(0.04)	(0.08)	(0.01)	(0.24)	(0.38)
p_{00}	0.75	0.70	0.68	0.63	0.57	0.45
		(0.10)	(0.16)	(0.11)	(0.15)	(0.28)
p_{11}	0.90	0.92	0.96	0.95	0.96	0.95
		(0.02)	(0.03)	(0.02)	(0.02)	(0.04)

Notes: The column labeled "START" contains the startup values used for itera-
tions. The other column labels denote the variable (defined in table 1) to which the
Markov-switching model is fitted. Asymptotic standard errors appear in parentheses.
The sample period is 1952.I–1993.I.

times the change in the natural logarithm of the Composite Coincident
Index, with one autoregressive lag and a potentially switching mean.

The results appear in the second column of table 6.2.[16] Several points
are worth mentioning. First, the state-0 mean is significantly negative,
and the state-1 mean is significantly positive, and the magnitudes of the
estimates are in reasonable accord with our priors. Second, the within-
state dynamics display substantial persistence. Third, the estimates of
p_{00} and p_{11} accord with the well-known fact that expansion durations
are longer than contraction durations on average. Fourth, the smoothed
(that is, conditional upon all observations in the sample) probabilities
that the Composite Coincident Index was in state 0 (graphed in figure
6.3) are in striking accord with the professional consensus as to the
history of U.S. business cycles.[17]

In our second exercise, we fit switching models to the individual
indicators underlying the Composite Coincident Index and examine the
switch times for commonality. In a similar fashion to our analysis of the
Composite Coincident Index, we fit models to one hundred times the
change in the natural logarithm of each of the underlying coincident
indicators, with one autoregressive lag and potentially switching means.

[16] We give the startup values for iteration in the first column of table 6.2.
[17] They follow the NBER chronology closely, for example.

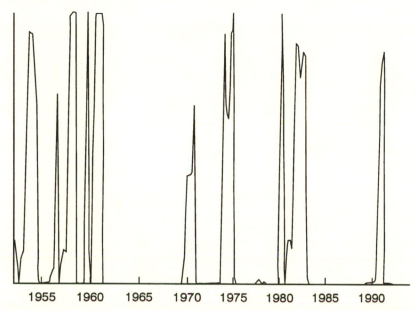

Fig. 6.3. Smoothed probability of being in state 0 composite coincident index.

The results appear in columns three through six of table 6.2.[18] The component-by-component results are qualitatively similar to those for the Composite Coincident Index, as would be expected in the presence of a regime-switching common factor. Further evidence in support of factor structure emerges in figure 6.4, in which we graph the time series of smoothed state-0 probabilities for each of the four component coincident indicators. There is commonality in switch times, which is indicative of factor structure. Note, however, that the ability of the individual component indicators to track the business cycle (as captured in the smoothed state-0 probabilities for each of the component indicators) is inferior to that of the Composite Coincident Index. This is consistent with the switching-factor argument. Individual series are swamped by measurement error and hence provide only very noisy information on the state of the business cycle, but moving to a multivariate framework enables more precise tracking of the cycle.

---

[18] Again, we use the startup values shown in the first column of table 6.2.

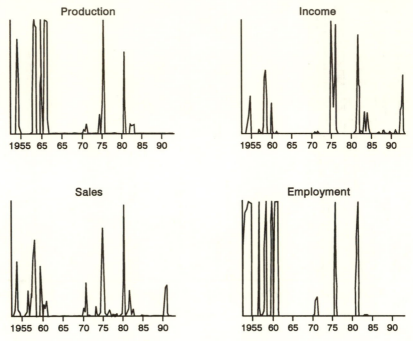

Fig. 6.4. Smoothed probability of being in state 0 coincident indicators.

C. Assessing Statistical Significance

Thus far, our empirical work has proceeded under the *assumption* of regime switching. It is also of obvious interest to test for regime switching—that is, to *test* the null hypothesis of one state against the alternative of two. The vast majority of the dozens of papers fitting Markov switching models make no attempt to test that key hypothesis.[19] This is because the econometrics are nonstandard. Boldin (1990), Hansen (1992, 1996a, 1996b) and Garcia (1992) point out that the transition probabilities that govern the Markov switching are not identified under the one-state null, and moreover, that the score with respect to the mean parameter of interest is identically zero if the probability of staying in state 1 is either 0 or 1. In either event, the information matrix is singular.

Hansen proposes a bounds test that is valid in spite of these difficulties, but its computational difficulty has limited its applicability. A closely related approach, suggested by Garcia, is operational, however.

---

[19] See Hamilton's (1994) survey, and the many papers cited there.

The key is to treat the transition probabilities as nuisance parameters (ruling out from the start the problematic boundary values 0 and 1) and to exploit another of Hansen's (1992) results, namely that the likelihood ratio test statistic for the null hypothesis of one state is the supremum over all admissible values of the nuisance parameters (the transition probabilities).

Let $\theta = (\mu_0, \mu_1, \phi_1, \ldots, \phi_p, \sigma^2)'$ be the set of all model parameters other than p_{00} and p_{11}. We write the log likelihood as a function of three parameters (one vector parameter, and two scalar parameters),

$$\ln L(\theta, p_{00}, p_{11}) = \ln P(y_1, \ldots, y_T; \theta, p_{00}, p_{11}).$$

If we let a "hat" denote a maximum-likelihood estimator, then the maximized value of the log likelihood is $\ln L(\hat{\theta}, \hat{p}_{00}, \hat{p}_{11})$. Now consider maximizing the likelihood under the constraint (corresponding to the null hypothesis of one state) that $\mu_0 = \mu_1$. In that case, p_{00} and p_{11} are unidentified, so the maximized value of the log likelihood function is the same for any values of p_{00} and p_{11}. Therefore, we simply write $\ln L(\theta^*)$, where θ^* is the constrained maximum-likelihood estimator of θ. Assembling all of this, we write the likelihood-ratio statistic for the null hypothesis of one state as

$$LR = 2\left[\ln L\left(\hat{\theta}, \hat{p}_{00}, \hat{p}_{11}\right) - \ln L(\theta^*)\right].$$

Now consider a different constrained likelihood maximization problem, in which we maximize the likelihood for arbitrary fixed values of p_{00} and p_{11}. We denote the constrained maximum-likelihood estimator by $\hat{\theta}(p_{00}, p_{11})$; the resulting maximized value of the constrained log likelihood is $\ln L(\hat{\theta}(p_{00}, p_{11}), p_{00}, p_{11})$. Now form the likelihood-ratio statistic that compares the restrictions associated with $\hat{\theta}(p_{00}, p_{11})$ to those associated with θ^*, namely

$$LR(p_{00}, p_{11}) = 2\left[\ln L\left(\hat{\theta}(p_{00}, p_{11}), p_{00}, p_{11}\right) - \ln L(\theta^*)\right].$$

Garcia (1992), building on Hansen (1996a), establishes that

$$LR = \sup_{p_{00}, p_{11}} LR(p_{00}, p_{11}),$$

where p_{00} and p_{11} are restricted to the interior of the unit interval. This makes clear the intimate connection of this testing problem to Andrews' (1993) test of structural change with breakpoint identified from the

TABLE 6.3
Likelihood-Ratio Statistics for the Null Hypothesis of No Regime Switching

	CCIM	PILTP	ENAP	IP	MTS
AR(1)	43.4[a]	52.0[a]	52.8[a]	32.9[a]	17.1[a]
AR(2)	50.6[a]	51.5[a]	62.9[a]	32.0[a]	18.7[a]
AR(3)	49.9[a]	36.2[a]	65.9[a]	33.9[a]	18.2[a]
AR(4)	60.2[a]	39.8[a]	73.5[a]	33.7[a]	27.3[a]

Note: We report the likelihood-ratio statistics for the null hypothesis of a one-state model against the alternative of a two-state model.
[a] Significant at the 1% level using the Garcia (1992) critical values.

data, and not surprisingly, the limiting distribution of *LR* is of precisely the same form.[20]

Table 6.3 reports *LR* statistics calculated for the Composite index as well as its components. For the AR(1) case, which is the one relevant to the estimation results presented earlier, the asymptotic distribution of *LR* has been characterized and tabulated by Garcia (1992) and shown to be accurate in samples of our size.[21] Using the Garcia critical values, it is clear that the null hypothesis of no switching is overwhelmingly rejected for the CCI and each of its components.

A battery of diagnostic tests revealed that the AR(1) specification is typically quite good, although for some series (particularly manufacturing and trade sales) there is evidence that inclusion of a few more lags may improve the approximation. This raises the question of whether the AR(1) model is inducing serial correlation in the error, which is spuriously being picked up by the regime-switching dynamics. Thus, as a robustness check, we also present LR statistics for higher orders of autoregressive approximation in table 6.3. As in the AR(1) case, the asymptotic null distribution of LR depends on nuisance parameters (the autoregressive coefficients), but also as before, the dependence appears to be minor. Garcia, for example, calculates the 1% critical value for a particular AR(4) to be 11.60, which is little different than the AR(1) critical values. Each of our test statistics in table 6.3 is so much larger than the range of available critical values that even though they may not be strictly applicable, a strong rejection of the null hypothesis of one

---

[20] The results of Giné and Zinn (1990) and Stinchcombe and White (1993), used by Diebold and Chen (1996) to argue the validity of the bootstrap in Andrews' (1993) case, are relevant here as well.

[21] The null distribution depends, even asymptotically, on the (unknown) true value of the autoregressive parameter. Fortunately, however, the dependence is slight; for example, Garcia's 1% critical values only vary from 11.54 to 11.95 over an autoregressive parameter range of −0.5 to 0.8.

state appears unavoidable for the Composite Coincident Index as well as for all of its components.

6. Concluding Remarks and Directions for Future Research

We have argued that a model with factor structure and regime switching is a useful modern distillation of a long tradition in the analysis of business-cycle data. We proposed one stylized version of such a model, and we suggested its compatibility with macroeconomic data and macroeconomic theory.

Let us summarize our stance on the importance of the two attributes of the business cycle on which we have focused. It appears to us that comovement among business-cycle indicators is undeniable. This comovement could perhaps be captured by a VAR representation, if very long time series were available. The factor structure that we have advocated goes further, in that it implies *restrictions* on the VAR representation, restrictions that *could* be at odds with the data. Although more research is needed on that issue, the factor model is nothing more than a simple and parsimonious way of empirically implementing the common idea of fewer sources of uncertainty than variables.

The alleged nonlinearity of the business cycle is open to more dispute. The linear model has two key virtues: (1) it works very well much of the time, in economics as in all the sciences, in spite of the fact that there is no compelling a priori reason why it should, and (2) there is only *one* linear model, in contrast to the many varieties of nonlinearity. Why worry, then, about nonlinearity in general, and regime switching in particular?

First, a long tradition in macroeconomics, culminating with the earlier-discussed theories of strategic complementarities and spillovers in imperfectly competitive environments, thick-market externalities in search, self-fulfilling prophesies, and so on, makes predictions that seem to accord with the regime-switching idea.

Second, regime-switching models seem to provide a good fit to aggregate output data. Our rejections of the no-switching null hypothesis, in particular, appear very strong.

Third, the cost of ignoring regime switching, if in fact it occurs, may be large. Business people, for example, want to have the best assessments of current and likely future economic activity, and they are particularly concerned with turning points. Even tiny forecast improvements that may arise from recognizing regime switching may lead to large differences in profits. Similarly, for policy makers, if regime switching corresponds to movements between Pareto-rankable equilibria, there are important policy implications.[22]

Fourth, macroeconomists, more generally, are interested in a host of issues impinged upon by the existence or non-existence of regime switching. Optimal decision rules for consumption and investment (including inventory investment), for example, may switch with regime, as may agents' ability to borrow.

There are many directions for future research. The obvious extension is computation of full system estimates for the full dynamic-factor/Markov-switching model, which is straightforward conceptually but has been computationally infeasible thus far. Two avenues appear promising. One approach employs a multimove Gibbs sampler, in conjunction with a partially non-Gaussian state-space representation and a simulated EM algorithm, as developed recently by Shephard (1994) and de Jong and Shephard (1995). A similar approach from a Bayesian perspective is proposed in Kim (1994b).

A second approach involves using Kim's (1994a) filtering algorithm for a general class of models in state-space form, of which ours is a special case. The Kim algorithm maximizes an approximation to the likelihood rather than the exact likelihood, but the algorithm is fast and the approximation appears accurate. Presently, Chauvet (1995) is using the Kim algorithm to estimate the model and extract estimates of the factor (the "coincident index"), using both quarterly and monthly data and a variety of detrending procedures.

References

Acemoglu, Daron, and Andrew Scott, "A Theory of Economic Fluctuations: Increasing Returns and Temporal Agglomeration," Discussion Paper 163, Centre for Economic Performance, London School of Economics (1993).

Andrews, Donald W. K., "Tests for Parameter Instability and Structural Change with Unknown Change Point," *Econometrica* 61 (July 1993), 821–856.

Azariadis, Costas, "Self-Fulfilling Prophecies," *Journal of Economic Theory* 25 (Dec. 1981), 380–396.

Backus, David K., and Patrick J. Kehoe, "International Evidence on the Historical Properties of Business Cycles," *American Economic Review* 82 (Sept. 1992), 864–888.

Becketti, Sean, and John Haltiwanger, "Limited Countercyclical Policies: An Exploratory Study," *Journal of Public Economics* 34 (Dec. 1987), 311–328.

---

[22] Moreover, countercyclical policy may *itself* introduce nonlinearities if it is applied only in extreme situations. See Zarnowitz and Moore (1982) and Becketti and Haltiwanger (1987).

Boldin, Michael D., *Business Cycles and Stock Market Volatility: Theory and Evidence of Animal Spirits*, Ph.D. Dissertation, Department of Economics, University of Pennsylvania (1990).

Bollerslev, Tim, Robert F. Engle, and Jeffrey M. Wooldridge, "A Capital Asset Pricing Model with Time Varying Covariances," *Journal of Political Economy* 96 (Feb. 1988), 116–131.

Burns, Arthur F., and Wesley C. Mitchell, *Measuring Business Cycles* (New York: National Bureau of Economic Research, 1946).

Caballero, Ricardo J., and Richard K. Lyons, "External Effects in U.S. Procyclical Productivity," *Journal of Monetary Economics* 30 (Apr. 1992), 209–225.

Cass, David, and Karl Shell, "Do Sunspots Matter?" *Journal of Political Economy* 91 (Apr. 1983), 193–227.

Cecchetti, Stephen G., Pok-sang Lam, and Nelson C. Mark, "Mean Reversion in Equilibrium Asset Prices," *American Economic Review* 80 (June 1990), 398–418.

Chauvet, Marcelle, "An Econometric Characterization of Business Cycle Dynamics with Factor Structure and Regime Switching," Ph.D. Dissertation in progress, University of Pennsylvania (1995).

Cooley, Thomas F. (ed.), *Frontiers of Business Cycle Research* (Princeton: Princeton University Press, 1995).

Cooley, Thomas F., and Gary D. Hansen, "The Inflation Tax in a Real Business Cycle Model," *American Economic Review* 79 (Sept. 1989), 733–748.

Cooper, Russell, "Equilibrium Selection in Imperfectly Competitive Economies with Multiple Equilibria," *Economic Journal* 104 (Sept. 1994), 1106–1122.

Cooper, Russell, and Andrew John, "Coordinating Coordination Failures in Keynesian Models," *Quarterly Journal of Economics* 103 (Aug. 1988), 441–463.

Cooper, Suzanne J., and Steven N. Durlauf, "Multiple Regimes in U.S. Output Fluctuations," manuscript, Kennedy School of Government, Harvard University, and Department of Economics, University of Wisconsin (1993).

De Jong, P., and Neil Shephard, "The Simulation Smoother for Time Series Models," *Biometrika* 82 (1995), 339–350.

DeLong, J. Bradford, and Lawrence H. Summers, "How Does Macroeconomic Policy Affect Output?," *Brookings Papers on Economic Activity* (1988: 2), 433–480.

De Toldi, M., Christian Gourieroux, and Alain Monfort, "On Seasonal Effects in Duration Models," Working Paper No. 9216, INSEE, Paris (1992).

Diamond, Peter A., "Aggregate Demand Management in Search Equilibrium," *Journal of Political Economy* 90 (1982), 881–894.

Diamond, Peter A., and Drew Fudenberg, "Rational Expectations Business Cycles in Search Equilibrium," *Journal of Political Economy* 97 (June 1989), 606–619.

Diebold, Francis X., and Celia Chen, "Testing Structural Stability with Endogenous Break Point: A Size Comparison of Analytic and Bootstrap Procedures," *Journal of Econometrics* (1996), forthcoming.

Diebold, Francis X., Joon-Haeng Lee, and Gretchen C. Weinbach, "Regime Switching with Time-Varying Transition Probabilities," in C. Hargreaves (ed.), *Nonstationary Time-Series Analysis and Cointegration (Advanced Texts in*

Econometrics, C. W. J. Granger and G. Mizon (series eds.) (Oxford: Oxford University Press, 1994), 283–302.

Diebold, Francis X., and Marc Nerlove, "The Dynamics of Exchange Rate Volatility: A Multivariate Latent-Factor ARCH Model," *Journal of Applied Econometrics* 4 (Jan.–Mar. 1989), 1–22.

Diebold, Francis X., and Glenn D. Rudebusch, "Scoring the Leading Indicators," *Journal of Business* 64 (July 1989), 369–391.

——, "A Nonparametric Investigation of Duration Dependence in the American Business Cycle," *Journal of Political Economy* 98 (June 1990), 596–616.

——, "Have Postwar Economic Fluctuations Been Stabilized?," *American Economic Review* 82 (Sept. 1992), 993–1005.

Diebold, Francis X., Glenn D. Rudebusch, and Daniel E. Sichel, "Further Evidence on Business Cycle Duration Dependence," in J. H. Stock and M. W. Watson (eds.), *Business Cycles, Indicators and Forecasting* (Chicago: University of Chicago Press for NBER, 1993), 255–284.

Durland, J. Michael, and Thomas H. McCurdy, "Duration-Dependent Transitions in a Markov Model of U.S. GNP Growth," *Journal of Business and Economic Statistics* 12 (July 1994), 279–288.

Durlauf, Steven N., "Multiple Equilibria and Persistence in Aggregate Fluctuations," *American Economic Review* 81 (May 1991), 70–74.

——, "An Incomplete Markets Theory of Business Cycle Fluctuations," manuscript, Department of Economics, University of Wisconsin (1995).

Engel, Charles, and James D. Hamilton, "Long Swings in the Dollar: Are They in the Data and Do Markets Know It?," *American Economic Review* 80 (Sept. 1990), 689–713.

Evans, George W., and Seppo Honkapohja, "Increasing Social Returns, Learning and Bifurcation Phenomena," in A. Kirman and M. Salmon (eds.), *Learning and Rationality in Economics* (Oxford: Basil Blackwell, 1994).

Filardo, Andrew J., "Business-Cycle Phases and Their Transitional Dynamics," *Journal of Business and Economic Statistics* 12 (July 1994), 299–308.

Garcia, René, "Asymptotic Null Distribution of the Likelihood Ratio Test in Markov Switching Models," manuscript, Department of Economics, University of Montreal (1992).

Giné, Evarist, and Joel Zinn, "Bootstrapping General Empirical Measures," *Annals of Probability* 18 (1990), 851–869.

Geweke, John, "The Dynamic Factor Analysis of Economic Time-Series Models," in D. J. Aigner and A. S. Goldberger (eds.), *Latent Variables in Socioeconomic Models* (Amsterdam: North-Holland, 1977), 365–383.

Ghysels, Eric, "A Time-Series Model with Periodic Stochastic Regime Switching," Discussion Paper No. 84, Institute for Empirical Macroeconomics (1993).

——, "On the Periodic Structure of the Business Cycle," *Journal of Business and Economic Statistics* 12 (July 1994), 289–298.

Goldfeld, Stephen M., and Richard E. Quandt, "A Markov Model for Switching Regressions," *Journal of Econometrics* 1 (Mar. 1973), 3–15.

Green, George R., and Barry A. Beckman, "The Composite Index of Coincident Indicators and Alternative Coincident Indexes," *Survey of Current Business* 72 (June 1992), 42–45.

Hall, Robert E., *Booms and Recessions in a Noisy Economy* (New Haven, CT: Yale University Press, 1991).

Hamilton, James D., "Rational-Expectations Econometric Analysis of Changes in Regime: An Investigation of the Term Structure of Interest Rates," *Journal of Economic Dynamics and Control* 12 (June/Sept. 1988), 385–423.

——, "A New Approach to the Economic Analysis of Nonstationary Time Series and the Business Cycle," *Econometrica* 57 (Mar. 1989), 357–384.

——, "Analysis of Time Series Subject to Changes in Regime," *Journal of Econometrics* 45 (July/Aug. 1990), 39–70.

——, "State-Space Models," in R. F. Engle and D. McFadden (eds.), *Handbook of Econometrics*, Volume 4 (Amsterdam: Elsevier Science B. V., 1994).

Hamilton, James D., and R. Susmel, "Autoregressive Conditional Heteroskedasticity and Changes in Regime," *Journal of Econometrics* 64 (Sept.–Oct. 1994), 307–333.

Hansen, Bruce E., "The Likelihood Ratio Test Under Non-Standard Conditions: Testing the Markov Trend Model of GNP," *Journal of Applied Econometrics* 7 (1992), S62–S82.

——, "Inference When a Nuisance Parameter Is Not Identified Under the Null Hypothesis," *Econometrica* (1996a), forthcoming.

——, "Erratum: The Likelihood Ratio Test Under Non-Standard Conditions: Testing the Markov Trend Model of GNP," *Journal of Applied Econometrics* (1996b), forthcoming.

Hansen, Gary D., "Indivisible Labor and the Business Cycle," *Journal of Monetary Economics* 16 (Nov. 1985), 309–327.

Hansen, Lars P., and Thomas J. Sargent, *Recursive Linear Models of Dynamic Economies* (Princeton: Princeton University Press, forthcoming).

Howit, Peter, and Preston McAfee, "Animal Spirits," *American Economic Review* 82 (June 1992), 493–507.

Kim, Chan-Jin, "Dynamic Linear Models with Markov Switching," *Journal of Econometrics* 60 (Jan.–Feb. 1994a), 1–22.

——, "Bayes Inference via Gibbs Sampling of Dynamic Linear Models with Markov Switching," Department of Economics, Korea University and York University (1994b).

Kydland, Finn E., and Edward C. Prescott, "Time to Build and Aggregate Fluctuations," *Econometrica* 50 (Nov. 1982), 1345–1370.

Lucas, Robert E., "Understanding Business Cycles," in K. Brunner and A. Meltzer (eds.), *Stabilization of the Domestic and International Economy, Carnegie-Rochester Series on Public Policy* 5 (Amsterdam: North-Holland, 1976), 7–29.

Neftci, Salih N., "Are Economic Time Series Asymmetric Over the Business Cycle?," *Journal of Political Economy* 92 (Apr. 1984), 307–328.

Potter, Simon M., "A Nonlinear Approach to U.S. GNP," *Journal of Applied Econometrics* 10 (Apr./June 1995), 109–125.

Quah, Danny, and Thomas J. Sargent, "A Dynamic Index Model for Large Cross Sections," in J. H. Stock and M. W. Watson (eds.), *Business Cycles, Indicators and Forecasting* (Chicago: University of Chicago Press for NBER, 1993), 285–310.

Quandt, Richard E., "The Estimation of Parameters of Linear Regression System Obeying Two Separate Regimes," *Journal of the American Statistical Association* 55 (1958), 873–880.

Sargent, Thomas J., *Macroeconomic Theory*, 2nd edition (Boston: Academic Press, 1987).

——, "Two Models of Measurements and the Investment Accelerator," *Journal of Political Economy* 97 (Apr. 1989), 251–287.

Sargent, Thomas J., and Christopher Sims, "Business Cycle Modeling without Pretending to Have Too Much a priori Theory," in C. Sims (ed.), *New Methods of Business Cycle Research* (Minneapolis: Federal Reserve Bank of Minneapolis, 1977).

Shephard, Neil, "Partial Non-Gaussian State Space," *Biometrika* 81 (Mar. 1994), 115–131.

Shishkin, Julius, *Signals of Recession and Recovery*, NBER Occasional Paper No. 77 (New York: NBER, 1961).

Sichel, Daniel E., "Inventories and the Three Phases of the Business Cycle," *Journal of Business and Economic Statistics* 12 (July 1994), 269–277.

Sims, Christopher A., "Macroeconomics and Reality," *Econometrica* 48 (1980), 1–48.

Singleton, Kenneth J., "A Latent Time-Series Model of the Cyclical Behavior of Interest Rates," *International Economic Review* 21 (Oct. 1980), 559–575.

Startz, Richard, "Growth States and Sectoral Shocks," manuscript, Department of Economics, University of Washington (1994).

Stinchcombe, Maxwell B., and Halbert White, "Consistent Specification Testing with Unidentified Nuisance Parameters Using Duality and Banach Space Limit Theory," Discussion Paper 93-14, Department of Economics, University of California, San Diego (1993).

Stock, James H., and Mark W. Watson, "New Indexes of Coincident and Leading Economic Indicators," in O. Blanchard and S. Fischer (eds.), *NBER Macroeconomics Annual* (Cambridge, MA: MIT Press, 1989), 351–394.

——, "A Probability Model of the Coincident Economic Indicators," in K. Lahiri and G. H. Moore (eds.), *Leading Economic Indicators: New Approaches and Forecasting Records* (Cambridge: Cambridge University Press, 1991), 63–89.

——, "A Procedure for Predicting Recessions with Leading Indicators: Econometric Issues and Recent Experience," in J. H. Stock and M. W. Watson (eds.), *Business Cycles, Indicators and Forecasting* (Chicago: University of Chicago Press for NBER, 1993), 255–284.

Tinbergen, Jan, *Statistical Testing of Business Cycle Theories, Volume II: Business Cycles in the United States of America, 1919–1932* (Geneva: League of Nations, 1939).

Tong, Howell, *Threshold Models in Non-linear Time-Series Analysis* (New York: Springer-Verlag, 1983).

Watson, Mark W., and Robert F. Engle, "Alternative Algorithm for the Estimation of Dynamic Factor, Mimic and Varying Coefficient Models," *Journal of Econometrics* 15 (Dec. 1983), 385–400.

Zarnowitz, Victor, and Geoffrey H. Moore, "Sequential Signals of Recession and Recovery," *Journal of Business* 55 (Jan. 1982), 57–85.

7

Regime Switching with Time-Varying Transition Probabilities

FRANCIS X. DIEBOLD, JOON-HAENG LEE,
AND GRETCHEN C. WEINBACH*

1. Introduction

Models incorporating nonlinearities associated with regime switching have a long tradition in empirical macroeconomics and dynamic econometrics.[1] Key methodological contributions include the early work of Quandt (1958) and Goldfeld and Quandt (1973) and the more recent work of Hamilton (1990). Recent substantive applications include Hamilton (1988) (interest rates), Hamilton (1989) (aggregate output), Cecchetti, Lam and Mark (1990) and Abel (1992) (stock returns), and Engel and Hamilton (1990) (exchange rates), among many others.

Our attention here focuses on Hamilton's Markov switching model, which has become very popular. In Hamilton's model, time-series dynamics are governed by a finite-dimensional parameter vector, which switches (potentially each period) depending upon which of two states is realised, with state transitions governed by a first-order Markov process with constant transition probabilities.

Although the popularity of Hamilton's model is well deserved, it nevertheless incorporates a potentially severely binding constraint, the constancy of state transition probabilities. Economic considerations suggest the desirability of allowing the transition probabilities to vary. As an example, consider the process of exchange rate revaluation. It is plausible that the likelihood of exchange rate revaluation increases under progressively more severe over- or undervaluation on the basis of economic fundamentals, and certainly, one would not want to exclude that possibility from the outset.

* Financial support from the U.K. Economic and Social Research Council under grant R000233447 is gratefully acknowledged by both authors. We are indebted to Neil Ericsson for helpful comments.

[1] For a survey of the nonlinear tradition in empirical macroeconomics, with particular attention paid to regime switching, see Diebold and Rudebusch (1993).

We therefore propose in this paper a class of Markov switching models in which the transition probabilities are endogenous.[2] We discuss the model in Section 2, develop an EM algorithm for parameter estimation in Section 3, and illustrate the methodology with a simulation example in Section 4. We conclude with a discussion of directions for future research in Section 5.

2. The Model

Let $\{s_t\}_{t=1}^{T}$ be the sample path of a first-order, two-state Markov process with transition probability matrix illustrated in Figure 7.1. As is apparent in the figure, the two transition probabilities are time-varying, evolving as logistic functions of $x'_{t-1}\beta_i$, $i = 0, 1$, where the $(k \times 1)$ conditioning vector x_{t-1} contains economic variables that affect the state transition probabilities. It will be convenient to stack the two sets of parameters governing the transition probabilities into a $(2k \times 1)$ vector, $\beta = (\beta_0', \beta_1')'$.

It is obvious, but worth noting, that when the last $(k - 1)$ terms of the $(1 \times k)$ transition probability parameter vectors, β_0 and β_1, are set to zero, the transition probability functions are time-invariant so that p_t^{00}

$$
\begin{array}{c}
\text{Time } t \\
\begin{array}{cc}
\text{State 0} & \text{State 1}
\end{array} \\
\text{Time } t-1 \quad
\begin{array}{c}
\text{State 0} \\[2em]
\\
\text{State 1}
\end{array}
\left[
\begin{array}{c:c}
p_t^{00} & p_t^{01} = (1 - p_t^{00}) \\
P(s_t = 0 \mid s_{t-1} = 0, x_{t-1}; \beta_0) & P(s_t = 1 \mid s_{t-1} = 0, x_{t-1}; \beta_0) \\
\dfrac{\exp(x'_{t-1}\beta_0)}{1 + \exp(x'_{t-1}\beta_0)} & 1 - \dfrac{\exp(x'_{t-1}\beta_0)}{1 + \exp(x'_{t-1}\beta_0)} \\
\hdashline
p_t^{10} = (1 - p_t^{11}) & p_t^{11} \\
P(s_t = 0 \mid s_{t-1} = 1, x_{t-1}; \beta_1) & P(s_t = 1 \mid s_{t-1} = 1, x_{t-1}; \beta_1) \\
1 - \dfrac{\exp(x'_{t-1}\beta_1)}{1 + \exp(x'_{t-1}\beta_1)} & \dfrac{\exp(x'_{t-1}\beta_1)}{1 + \exp(x'_{t-1}\beta_1)}
\end{array}
\right]
\end{array}
$$

Note: $x_{t-1} = (1, x_{1,t-1}, \ldots, x_{(k-1),t-1})'$ and $\beta_i = (\beta_{i0}, \beta_{i1}, \ldots, \beta_{i(k-1)})'$, $i = 0, 1$.

Fig. 7.1. Transition Probability Matrix

[2] The first work in this area is Lee (1991), from which this paper draws. Related subsequent literature includes Fillardo (1991), who considers Markov-switching business-cycle models with transition probabilities that change with movements in an index of leading indicators, as well as Ghysels (1992) and De Toldi, Gourieroux and Monfort (1992), who consider duration models with hazard rates that vary across seasons.

and p_t^{11} are simply constants; our model collapses to that of Hamilton (1990).

Let $\{y_t\}_{t=1}^T$ be the sample path of a time series that depends on $\{s_t\}_{t=1}^T$ as follows:

$$(y_t \mid s_t = i; \; \alpha_i) \overset{iid}{\sim} N(\mu_i, \sigma_i^2), \tag{1}$$

where $\alpha_i = (\mu_i, \sigma_i^2)'$, $i = 0, 1$.[3] Thus, the density of y_t conditional upon s_t is:

$$f(y_t \mid s_t = i; \; \alpha_i) = \frac{1}{\sqrt{2\pi}\,\sigma_i} \exp\left(\frac{-(y_t - \mu_i)^2}{2\sigma_i^2}\right), \tag{2}$$

$i = 0, 1$. It will be convenient to stack the two sets of parameters governing the densities into a (4×1) vector, $\alpha = (\alpha_0', \alpha_1')'$.

As we shall see, a quantity of particular interest in the likelihood function is $P(s_1)$, which denotes $P(S_1 = s_1)$. Regarding x_t, there are two cases to consider, stationary and nonstationary. In the stationary case,

$$P(s_1) = P(s_1 \mid \underline{x}_T; \theta) = P(s_1; \beta).$$

That is, $P(s_1)$ is simply the long-run probability of $S_1 = s_1$, which in turn is determined by β. In the nonstationary case, the long-run probability does not exist, and so $P(S_1 = s_1)$ must be treated as an additional parameter to be estimated. It turns out, as we show subsequently, that $P(S_1 = 1)$ is all that is needed to construct the first likelihood term. We shall call this quantity 'ρ' in both the stationary and nonstationary cases, remembering that in the stationary case ρ is *not* an additional parameter to be estimated, but rather is determined by β, while the nonstationary case ρ *is* an additional parameter to be estimated.[4] In certain situations, computation of ρ in the stationary case may be done via simulation; see Diebold and Schuermann (1992).

---

[3] Generalisations to allow for more than two states and/or intra-state dynamics are straightforward but tedious, so we shall not consider them here.

[4] Alternatively, if prior information is available, ρ may be set accordingly. The issues are analogous to those that arise with initialisation of the Kalman filter in the nonstationary case.

Let $\theta = (\alpha', \beta', \rho)'$ be the $(2k + 5 \times 1)$ vector of all model parameters. The complete-data likelihood is then[5]

$$f(\underline{y}_T, \underline{s}_T \mid \underline{x}_T; \theta)$$

$$= f(y_1, s_1 \mid \underline{x}_T; \theta) \prod_{t=2}^{T} f(y_t, s_t \mid \underline{y}_{t-1}, \underline{s}_{t-1}, \underline{x}_T; \theta)$$

$$= f(y_1 \mid s_1, \underline{x}_T; \theta) P(s_1) \prod_{t=2}^{T} f(y_t \mid s_t, \underline{y}_{t-1}, \underline{s}_{t-1}, \underline{x}_T; \theta)$$

$$\times P(s_t \mid \underline{y}_{t-1}, \underline{s}_{t-1}, \underline{x}_t; \theta)$$

$$= f(y_1 \mid s_1; \alpha) P(s_1) \prod_{t=2}^{T} f(y_t \mid s_t; \alpha) P(s_t \mid s_{t-1}, x_{t-1}; \beta),$$

here f denotes any density and underlining denotes past history of the variable from $t = 1$ to the variable subscript.

It will prove convenient to write the complete-data likelihood in terms of indicator functions,

$$f(\underline{y}_T, \underline{s}_T \mid \underline{x}_T; \theta) = [\mathrm{I}(s_1 = 1) f(y_1 \mid s_1 = 1; \alpha_1) \rho$$

$$+ \mathrm{I}(s_1 = 0) f(y_1 \mid s_1 = 0; \alpha_0)(1 - \rho)]$$

$$\times \prod_{t=2}^{T} \{ \mathrm{I}(s_t = 1, s_{t-1} = 1) f(y_t \mid s_t = 1; \alpha_1) p_t^{11}$$

$$+ \mathrm{I}(s_t = 0, s_{t-1} = 1) f(y_t \mid s_t = 0; \alpha_0)(1 - p_t^{11})$$

$$+ \mathrm{I}(s_t = 1, s_{t-1} = 0) f(y_t \mid s_t = 1; \alpha_1)(1 - p_t^{00})$$

$$+ \mathrm{I}(s_t = 0, s_{t-1} = 0) f(y_t \mid s_t = 0; \alpha_0) p_t^{00} \}.$$

Conversion to log form yields

$$\log f(\underline{y}_T, \underline{s}_T \mid \underline{x}_T; \theta)$$

$$= \mathrm{I}(s_1 = 1)[\log f(y_1 \mid s_1 = 1; \alpha_1) + \log \rho]$$

$$+ \mathrm{I}(s_1 = 0)[\log f(y_1 \mid s_1 = 0; \alpha_0) + \log(1 - \rho)]$$

$$+ \sum_{t=2}^{T} \{ \mathrm{I}(s_t = 1) \log f(y_t \mid s_t = 1; \alpha_1)$$

---

[5]'Complete-data' refers to the (hypothetical) assumption that both $\{y_t\}$ and $\{s_t\}$ are observed.

$$+ \mathrm{I}(s_t = 0)\log f(y_t \mid s_t = 0; \alpha_0)$$

$$+ \mathrm{I}(s_t = 1, s_{t-1} = 1)\log(p_t^{11})$$

$$+ \mathrm{I}(s_t = 0, s_{t-1} = 1)\log(1 - p_t^{11})$$

$$+ \mathrm{I}(s_t = 1, s_{t-1} = 0)\log(1 - p_t^{00})$$

$$+ \mathrm{I}(s_t = 0, s_{t-1} = 0)\log(p_t^{00})\}.$$

The complete-data log likelihood cannot be constructed in practice, because the complete data are not observed. Conceptually, the fact that the states are unobserved is inconsequential, because the incomplete-data log likelihood may be obtained by summing over all possible state sequences,

$$\log f(\underline{y}_T \mid \underline{x}_T; \theta) = \log\left(\sum_{s_1=0}^{1} \sum_{s_2=0}^{1} \cdots \sum_{s_T=0}^{1} f(\underline{y}_T, \underline{s}_T \mid \underline{x}_T; \theta) \right),$$

and then maximised with respect to θ. In practice, however, construction and numerical maximisation of the incomplete-data log likelihood in this way is computationally intractable, as $\{s_t\}_{t=1}^{T}$ may be realised in 2^T ways. Therefore, following Hamilton's (1990) suggestion for the case of constant transition probabilities, we propose an EM algorithm for maximisation of the incomplete-data likelihood.

3. Model Estimation: The EM Algorithm

The EM algorithm is a stable and robust procedure for maximising the incomplete-data log likelihood via iterative maximisation of the expected complete-data log likelihood, conditional upon the observable data.[6] The procedure, shown schematically in Figure 7.2, amounts to the following.[7]

---

[6] Insightful discussions of the EM algorithm may be found in Dempster, Laird and Rubin (1977), Watson and Engle (1983), and Ruud (1991).

[7] Parameter superscripts count iterations.

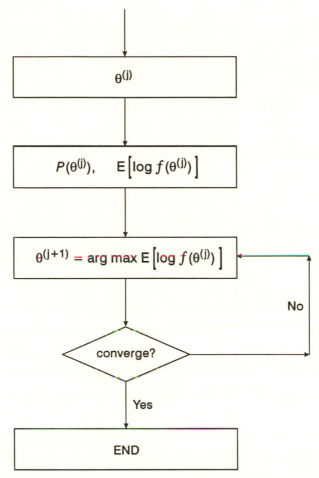

Fig. 7.2. The EM algorithm (notation discussed in the text).

(1) Pick $\theta^{(0)}$,
(2) Get:

$$P\left(s_t = 1 \mid \underline{y}_T, \underline{x}_T; \theta^{(0)}\right) \quad \forall t,$$

$$P\left(s_t = 0 \mid \underline{y}_T, \underline{x}_T; \theta^{(0)}\right) \quad \forall t,$$

$$P\left(s_t = 1, s_{t-1} = 1 \mid \underline{y}_T, \underline{x}_T; \theta^{(0)}\right) \quad \forall t,$$

$$P\left(s_t = 0, s_{t-1} = 1 \mid \underline{y}_T, \underline{x}_T; \theta^{(0)}\right) \quad \forall t,$$

$$P\left(s_t = 1, s_{t-1} = 0 \mid \underline{y}_T, \underline{x}_T; \theta^{(0)}\right) \quad \forall t,$$

$$P\left(s_t = 0, s_{t-1} = 0 \mid \underline{y}_T, \underline{x}_T; \theta^{(0)}\right) \quad \forall t;$$

construct $E \log f(\underline{y}_T, \underline{s}_T \mid \underline{x}_T; \theta^{(0)})$ by replacing I's with P's.

(3) Set $\theta^{(1)} = \arg\max_{\theta} E[\log f(\underline{y}_T, \underline{s}_T \mid \underline{x}_T; \theta^{(0)})]$.

(4) Iterate to convergence.

Step (1) simply assigns an initial guess to the parameter vector, $\theta^{(0)}$, in order to start the EM algorithm. Step (2) is the 'E' (expectation) part of the algorithm, which produces smoothed state probabilities conditional upon $\theta^{(0)}$, while step (3) is the 'M' (maximisation) part, which produces an updated parameter estimate, $\theta^{(1)}$, conditional upon the smoothed state probabilities obtained in step (2). The convergence criterion adopted in (4) may be based upon various standard criteria, such as the change in the log likelihood from one iteration to the next, the value of the gradient vector, or $\|\theta^{(j)} - \theta^{(j-1)}\|$, for various norms $\|\bullet\|$.

3.1. The Expectation Step

We wish to take expectations of the complete-data log likelihood, conditional upon the observed data. As in Hamilton (1990), this amounts to substitution of smoothed state probabilities (to be derived below) for indicator functions in the complete-data log likelihood,

$$
\begin{aligned}
& E\left[\log f\left(\underline{y}_T, \underline{s}_T \mid \underline{x}_T; \theta^{(j-1)}\right)\right] \\
&= \rho^{(j-1)}\left[\log f(y_1 \mid s_1 = 1; \alpha_1^{(j-1)}) + \log \rho^{(j-1)}\right] \\
&\quad + (1 - \rho^{(j-1)})\left[\log f(y_1 \mid s_1 = 0; \alpha_0^{(j-1)}) + \log(1 - \rho^{(j-1)})\right] \\
&\quad + \sum_{t=2}^{T} \left\{ P\left(s_t = 1 \mid \underline{y}_T, \underline{x}_T; \theta^{(j-1)}\right) \log f(y_t \mid s_t = 1; \alpha_1^{(j-1)}) \right. \\
&\quad + P\left(s_t = 0 \mid \underline{y}_T, \underline{x}_T; \theta^{(j-1)}\right) \log f(y_t \mid s_t = 0; \theta_0^{(j-1)}) \\
&\quad + P\left(s_t = 1, s_{t-1} = 1 \mid \underline{y}_T, \underline{x}_T; \theta^{(j-1)}\right) \log(p_t^{11}) \\
&\quad + P\left(s_t = 0, s_{t-1} = 1 \mid \underline{y}_T, \underline{x}_T; \theta^{(j-1)}\right) \log(1 - p_t^{11}) \\
&\quad + P\left(s_t = 1, s_{t-1} = 0 \mid \underline{y}_T, \underline{x}_T; \theta^{(j-1)}\right) \log(1 - p_t^{00}) \\
&\quad \left. + P\left(s_t = 0, s_{t-1} = 0 \mid \underline{y}_T, \underline{x}_T; \theta^{(j-1)}\right) \log(p_t^{00}) \right\},
\end{aligned}
\tag{3}
$$

where the smoothed state probabilities are obtained from the optimal nonlinear smoother, conditional upon the current 'best guess' of θ, $\theta^{(j-1)}$.

Given $\theta^{(j-1)}$, $\underline{y}_T$, and $\underline{x}_T$, the algorithm for calculating the smoothed state probabilities for iteration j is as follows:

1. Calculate the sequence of conditional densities of y_t given by (2.2) (a $(T \times 2)$ matrix), and transition probabilities given by Figure 7.1 (a $(T - 1 \times 4)$ matrix).

2. Calculate filtered joint state probabilities (a $(T - 1 \times 4)$ matrix) by iterating on steps 2a–2d below for $t = 2, \ldots, T$:

2a. Calculate the joint conditional distribution of (y_t, s_t, s_{t-1}) given $\underline{y}_{t-1}$ and $\underline{x}_{t-1}$ (four numbers): For $t = 2$, the joint conditional distribution is given by

$$f(y_2, s_2, s_1 \mid y_1, x_1; \theta^{(j-1)})$$

$$= f(y_2 \mid s_2; \alpha^{(j-1)})P(s_2 \mid s_1, x_1; \beta^{(j-1)})P(s_1).$$

For subsequent time t, the joint conditional distribution is

$$f\left(y_t, s_t, s_{t-1} \mid \underline{y}_{t-1}, \underline{x}_{t-1}; \theta^{(j-1)}\right)$$

$$= \sum_{s_{t-2}=0}^{1} f(y_t \mid s_t; \alpha^{(j-1)})P(s_t \mid s_{t-1}, x_{t-1}; \beta^{(j-1)})$$

$$\times P\left(s_{t-1}, s_{t-2} \mid \underline{y}_{t-1}, \underline{x}_{t-1}; \theta^{(j-1)}\right)$$

where the conditional density $f(y_t \mid s_t; \alpha^{(j-1)})$ and transition probabilities $P(s_t \mid s_{t-1}, x_{t-1}; \beta^{(j-1)})$ are given by step 1, and $P(s_{t-1}, s_{t-2} \mid \underline{y}_{t-1}, \underline{x}_{t-1}; \theta^{(j-1)})$ is the filtered probability resulting from execution of step 2 for the previous t value.

2b. Calculate the conditional likelihood of y_t (one number):

$$f\left(y_t \mid \underline{y}_{t-1}, \underline{x}_{t-1}; \theta^{(j-1)}\right)$$

$$= \sum_{s_t=0}^{1} \sum_{s_{t-1}=0}^{1} f\left(y_t, s_t, s_{t-1} \mid \underline{y}_{t-1}, \underline{x}_{t-1}; \theta^{(j-1)}\right).$$

2c. Calculate the time-t filtered state probabilities (four numbers):

$$P\left(s_t, s_{t-1} \mid \underline{y}_t, \underline{x}_t; \theta^{(j-1)}\right) = \frac{f\left(y_t, s_t, s_{t-1} \mid \underline{y}_t, \underline{x}_t; \theta^{(j-1)}\right)}{f\left(y_t \mid \underline{y}_t, \underline{x}_t; \theta^{(j-1)}\right)},$$

where the numerator is the joint conditional distributional of (y_t, s_t, s_{t-1}) from step 2a and the denominator is the conditional likelihood of y_t from step 2b above.

2d. These four filtered probabilities are used as input for step 2a to calculate the filtered probabilities for the next time period, and steps 2a–2d are repeated $(T-2)$ times.

3. Calculate the smoothed joint state probabilities as follows (a $(T-1 \times 6)$ matrix):

3a. For $t = 2$ and a given valuation of (s_t, s_{t-1}), sequentially calculate the joint probability of $(s_\tau, s_{\tau-1}, s_t, s_{t-1})$ given $\underline{y}_\tau$ and $\underline{x}_\tau$, for $\tau = t + 2, t + 3, \ldots, T.$[8]

$$P\left(s_\tau, s_{\tau-1}, s_t, s_{t-1} \mid \underline{y}_\tau, \underline{x}_\tau; \theta^{(j-1)}\right)$$

$$= \frac{\sum_{s_{\tau-2}=0}^{1} f(y_\tau \mid s_\tau; \alpha^{(j-1)}) P(s_\tau \mid s_{\tau-1}, x_{\tau-1}; \beta^{(j-1)}) \times P\left(s_{\tau-1}, s_{\tau-2}, s_t, s_{t-1} \mid \underline{y}_{\tau-1}, \underline{x}_{\tau-1}; \theta^{(j-1)}\right)}{f\left(y_\tau \mid \underline{y}_{\tau-1}, \underline{x}_{\tau-1}; \theta^{(j-1)}\right)}$$

where the first two terms in the numerator are given by step 1, the third by the previous step 3a computation, and the denominator by step 2b. When $\tau = t + 2$, the third term in the numerator is initialised with the following expression:

$$P\left(s_{t+1}, s_t, s_{t-1} \mid \underline{y}_{t+1}, \underline{x}_{t+1}; \theta^{(j-1)}\right)$$

$$= \frac{f(y_{t+1} \mid s_{t+1}; \alpha^{(j-1)}) P(s_{t+1} \mid s_t, x_t; \beta^{(j-1)}) \times P\left(s_t s_{t-1} \mid \underline{y}_t, \underline{x}_t; \theta^{(j-1)}\right)}{f\left(y_{t+1} \mid \underline{y}_t, \underline{x}_t; \theta^{(j-1)}\right)}.$$

For each τ value we produce a (4×1) vector of probabilities corresponding to the four possible valuations of $(s_\tau, s_{\tau-1})$. Thus, upon reaching $\tau = T$, we have computed and saved a $(T-3) \times 4$ matrix, the last row of which is used in step 3b below.

---

[8] There are of course four possible (s_t, s_{t-1}) sequences: $(0, 0)$, $(0, 1)$, $(1, 0)$ and $(1, 1)$.

3b. Upon reaching $\tau = T$, the smoothed joint state probability for time t and the chosen valuation of (s_t, s_{t-1}) is calculated as

$$P\left(s_t, s_{t-1} \mid \underline{y}_T, \underline{x}_T; \theta^{(j-1)}\right)$$

$$= \sum_{s_T=0}^{1} \sum_{s_{T-1}=0}^{1} P\left(s_T, s_{T-1}, s_t, s_{t-1} \mid \underline{y}_T, \underline{x}_T; \theta^{(j-1)}\right).$$

3c. Steps 3a and 3b are repeated for all possible time t valuations (s_t, s_{t-1}), until a smoothed probability has been calculated for each of the four possible valuations. At this point we have a (1×4) vector of smoothed joint state probabilities for (s_t, s_{t-1}).

3d. Steps 3a–3c are repeated for $t = 3, 4, \ldots, T$, yielding a total of $(T - 1 \times 4)$ smoothed joint state probabilities.

4. Smoothed marginal state probabilities are found by summing over the smoothed joint state probabilities. For example,

$$P\left(s_t = 1 \mid \underline{y}_T, \underline{x}_T; \theta^{(j-1)}\right) = P\left(s_t = 1, s_{t-1} = 1 \mid \underline{y}_T, \underline{x}_T; \theta^{(j-1)}\right)$$

$$+ P\left(s_t = 1, s_{t-1} = 0 \mid \underline{y}_T, \underline{x}_T; \theta^{(j-1)}\right).$$

These $(T - 1 \times 6)$ smoothed state probabilities are used as input for the maximisation step, which we now describe.

3.2. The Maximisation Step

Given the smoothed state probabilities, the expected complete-data log likelihood, given by (3), is maximised directly with respect to the model parameters. The resulting $2k + 5$ first-order conditions are linear both in ρ and the conditional density parameter vector α, and nonlinear in the transition probability parameter vector β. Moreover, these two sets of parameters appear in distinctly different terms in the likelihood function. Due to this separability, five of the first-order conditions are linear in the parameters:

$$\sum_{t=1}^{T} P\left(s_t = i \mid \underline{y}_T, \underline{x}_T; \theta^{(j-1)}\right)\left(y_t - \mu_i^{(j)}\right) = 0$$

$$\sum_{t=1}^{T} P\left(s_t = i \mid \underline{y}_T, \underline{x}_T; \theta^{(j-1)}\right)\left(\frac{(y_t - \mu_i^{(j)})^2}{(\sigma_i^2)^{(j)}} - 1\right) = 0$$

$$P\left(s_1 = 1 \mid \underline{y}_T, \underline{x}_T; \theta^{(j-1)}\right)\left(\frac{1}{\rho}\right) - 1 = 0,$$

and yield immediate closed-form expressions for the maximum likelihood estimators.

$$\mu_i^{(j)} = \frac{\sum_{t=1}^{T} y_t P\left(s_t = i \mid \underline{y}_T, \underline{x}_T; \theta^{(j-1)}\right)}{\sum_{t=1}^{T} P\left(s_t = i \mid \underline{y}_T, \underline{x}_T; \theta^{(j-1)}\right)}$$

$$(\sigma_i^2)^{(j)} = \frac{\sum_{t=1}^{T} (y_t - \mu_i^{(j)})^2 P\left(s_t = i \mid \underline{y}_T, \underline{x}_T; \theta^{(j-1)}\right)}{\sum_{t=1}^{T} P\left(s_t = i \mid \underline{y}_T, \underline{x}_T; \theta^{(j-1)}\right)}$$

$$\rho^{(j)} = P\left(s_1 = 1 \mid \underline{y}_T, \underline{x}_T; \theta^{(j-1)}\right),$$

$i = 0, 1.$

However, given our use of logit transition probability functions, the remaining $2k$ first-order conditions are *nonlinear* in β, and are given by[9]

$$\sum_{t=2}^{T} x_{t-1} \left\{ P\left(s_t = 0, s_{t-1} = 0 \mid \underline{y}_T, \underline{x}_T; \theta^{(j-1)}\right) \right.$$

$$\left. -p_t^{00} P\left(s_{t-1} = 0 \mid \underline{y}_T, \underline{x}_T; \theta^{(j-1)}\right) \right\} = 0$$

$$\sum_{t=2}^{T} x_{t-1} \left\{ P\left(s_t = 1, s_{t-1} = 1 \mid \underline{y}_T, \underline{x}_T; \theta^{(j-1)}\right) \right.$$

$$\left. -p_t^{11} P\left(s_{t-1} = 1 \mid \underline{y}_T, \underline{x}_T; \theta^{(j-1)}\right) \right\} = 0.$$

Closed-form solutions are found by linearly approximating p_t^{00} and p_t^{11} using a first-order Taylor series expansion around $\beta_0^{(j-1)}$ and $\beta_1^{(j-1)}$,

---

[9] A variety of alternative functional forms, in addition to the logit, are examined in Lee (1991).

respectively. These linear approximations are given by

$$p_t^{00}(\beta_0^{(j-1)}) \approx p_t^{00}(\beta_0^{(j-1)}) + \left.\frac{\partial p_t^{00}(\beta_0)}{\partial \beta_0}\right|_{\beta_0 = \beta_0^{(j-1)}} (\beta_0 - \beta_0^{(j-1)})$$

$$p_t^{11}(\beta_1^{(j-1)}) \approx p_t^{11}(\beta_1^{(j-1)}) + \left.\frac{\partial p_t^{11}(\beta_1)}{\partial \beta_1}\right|_{\beta_1 = \beta_1^{(j-1)}} (\beta_1 - \beta_1^{(j-1)}).$$

For simplicity, we adopt the following notation:

$$p_{it}^{00}(\beta_0^{(j-1)}) = \left.\frac{\partial p_t^{00}(\beta_0)}{\partial \beta_{i0}}\right|_{\beta_0 = \beta_0^{(j-1)}}, \ i = 0, \dots, k-1$$

$$p_{it}^{11}(\beta_1^{(j-1)}) = \left.\frac{\partial p_t^{11}(\beta_1)}{\partial \beta_{i1}}\right|_{\beta_1 = \beta_1^{(j-1)}}, \ i = 0, \dots, k-1,$$

so that the vectors of partials are $(1 \times k)$ row vectors given by

$$\left.\frac{\partial p_t^{00}(\beta_0)}{\partial \beta_0}\right|_{\beta_0 = \beta_0^{(j-1)}} = \left[p_{0t}^{00}(\beta_0^{(j-1)}), p_{1t}^{00}(\beta_0^{(j-1)}), \dots, p_{(k-1)t}^{00}(\beta_0^{(j-1)}) \right]$$

$$\left.\frac{\partial p_t^{11}(\beta_1)}{\partial \beta_1}\right|_{\beta_1 = \beta_1^{(j-1)}} = \left[p_{0t}^{11}(\beta_1^{(j-1)}), p_{1t}^{11}(\beta_1^{(j-1)}), \dots, p_{(k-1)t}^{11}(\beta_1^{(j-1)}) \right],$$

and the individual partials are given by

$$p_{it}^{00}(\beta_0^{(j-1)}) = x_{i,t-1}\left[p_t^{00}(\beta_0^{(j-1)}) - p_t^{00}(\beta_0^{(j-1)})^2 \right], \ i = , \dots, k-1$$

$$p_{it}^{11}(\beta_1^{(j-1)}) = x_{i,t-1}\left[p_t^{11}(\beta_1^{(j-1)}) - p_t^{11}(\beta_1^{(j-1)})^2 \right], \ i = 0, \dots, k-1,$$

where $x_{i,t-1}$ is the ith element of x_{t-1}.

Substituting these linear approximations for the transition probabilities into the $2k$ nonlinear first-order conditions results in $2k$ *linear* first-order conditions given by

$$
\sum_{t=2}^{T} x_{t-1} \left\{ P\left(s_t = 0, s_{t-1} = 0 \mid \underline{y}_T, \underline{x}_T; \theta^{(j-1)}\right) \right.
$$

$$
- P\left(s_{t-1} = 0 \mid \underline{y}_T, \underline{x}_T; \theta^{(j-1)}\right)
$$

$$
\left. \times \left[p_t^{00}(\beta_0^{(j-1)}) + \frac{\partial p_t^{00}(\beta_0)}{\partial \beta_0} (\beta_0 - \beta_0^{(j-1)}) \right] \right\} = 0
$$

$$
\sum_{t=2}^{T} x_{t-1} \left\{ P\left(s_t = 1, s_{t-1} = 1 \mid \underline{y}_T, \underline{x}_T; \theta^{(j-1)}\right) \right.
$$

$$
- P\left(s_{t-1} = 1 \mid \underline{y}_T, \underline{x}_T; \theta^{(j-1)}\right)
$$

$$
\left. \times \left[p_t^{11}(\beta_1^{(j-1)}) + \frac{\partial p_t^{11}(\beta_1)}{\partial \beta_1} (\beta_1 - \beta_1^{(j-1)}) \right] \right\} = 0,
$$

where all derivatives are understood to be evaluated at $\beta_0^{(j-1)}$ or $\beta_1^{(j-1)}$, as relevant. Solving these, we obtain a closed-form solution for $\beta_0^{(j)}$,

$$
\beta_0^{(j)} = \left(\sum_{t=2}^{T} x_{t-1} P\left(s_{t-1} = 0 \mid \underline{y}_T, \underline{x}_T; \theta^{(j-1)}\right) \frac{\partial p_t^{00}(\beta_0)}{\partial \beta_0} \right)^{-1}
$$

$$
\times \left(\sum_{t=2}^{T} x_{t-1} \left\{
\begin{array}{l}
P\left(s_t = 0, s_{t-1} = 0 \mid \underline{y}_T, \underline{x}_T; \theta^{(j-1)}\right) \\
\quad - P\left(s_{t-1} = 0 \mid \underline{y}_T, \underline{x}_T; \theta^{(j-1)}\right) \\
\quad \times \left[p_t^{00}(\beta_0^{(j-1)}) - \frac{\partial p_t^{00}(\beta_0)}{\partial \beta_0} \beta_0^{(j-1)} \right]
\end{array}
\right\} \right).
$$

Similarly the closed-form solution for $\beta_1^{(j)}$ is

$$
\beta_1^{(j)} = \left(\sum_{t=2}^{T} x_{t-1} P\left(s_{t-1} = 1 \mid \underline{y}_T, \underline{x}_T; \theta^{(j-1)}\right) \frac{\partial p_t^{11}(\beta_1)}{\partial \beta_1} \right)^{-1}
$$

$$
\times \left(\sum_{t=2}^{T} x_{t-1} \left\{
\begin{array}{l}
P\left(s_t = 1, s_{t-1} = 1 \mid \underline{y}_T, \underline{x}_T; \theta^{(j-1)}\right) \\
\quad - P\left(s_{t-1} = 1 \mid \underline{y}_T, \underline{x}_T; \theta^{(j-1)}\right) \\
\quad \times \left[p_t^{11}(\beta_1^{(j-1)}) - \frac{\partial p_t^{11}(\beta_1)}{\partial \beta_1} \beta_1^{(j-1)} \right]
\end{array}
\right\} \right).
$$

The cases of $k = 2$ and $k = 3$ are of particular interest in applied work. For this reason, we catalog explicit expressions for $\beta_0^{(j)}$ and $\beta_1^{(j)}$ in those cases in the appendix.

4. Simulation Results

In order to demonstrate the methodology, we present the results of a simulation exercise. Sample size is 100. We set $k = 2$ so that the time-varying transition probabilities are driven by one x series. The transition probability parameters, α, are chosen and the x series constructed so that the (true) probabilities of staying in state, p_t^{00} and p_t^{11}, each alternate between 0.40 and 0.90 over successive sets of twenty sample observations, beginning with $p_t^{00} = 0.40$ and $p_t^{11} = 0.90$. The chosen parameter values are shown in Table 7.1, the simulated y and s sequences are shown in Figure 7.3, the x sequence is shown in Figure 7.4, and the resultant probabilities of staying in state are shown in Figure 7.7 (labeled 'actual').

Parameter estimation using the EM algorithm begins at the true parameter values. Convergence of the EM algorithm is checked as follows. Upon the calculation of each new parameter vector, say the jth, a comparison is make with the previous vector, the $(j - 1)^{\text{st}}$. If the

TABLE 7.1
Estimation Results

Parameter	θ_0	$\hat{\theta}$	$\hat{\theta}_H$
μ_0	-1.00	-1.62	-0.38
σ_0^2	4.00	2.83	3.73
μ_1	1.00	1.27	2.25
σ_1^2	4.00	2.97	2.24
β_{00}	0.79	-1.53	1.72
β_{01}	-2.00	-2.89	NA
β_{10}	1.00	0.94	0.49
β_{11}	2.00	2.07	NA
ρ	1.00	0.97	0.29
MSE		0.13	0.27
Iterations		462	208
lnL		-238.17	-247.53

Notes: θ_0 is the true parameter vector; $\hat{\theta}$ is the estimated parameter vector, and $\hat{\theta}_H$ is the estimated parameter vector for the Hamilton model, obtained by constraining β_{01} and β_{11} to be zero.

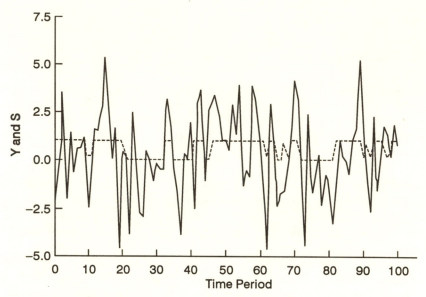

Fig. 7.3. Y and S sequences.

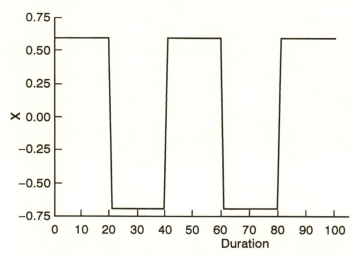

Fig. 7.4. X sequence.

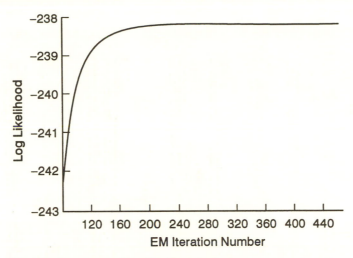

Fig. 7.5. Sequence of log-likelihood values.

absolute value of the maximal difference in like elements of $\theta^{(j)}$ and $\theta^{(j-1)}$ is less than $10e^{-8}$, iteration is terminated. Convergence was obtained in 462 iterations, and the location of the likelihood maximum obtained was robust to a variety of alternative start up parameters. As shown in Figure 7.5, the EM algorithm gets close to the likelihood maximum very quickly, but then takes more iterations to reach convergence.[10]

The resultant maximum likelihood parameter estimates are given in Table 7.1, labelled $\hat{\theta}$. Given the small sample size, the likelihood maximum is fairly close to the true parameter vector, the main exception being the estimate of β_{00}, which diverges from the true value by a rather large amount.

In Figure 7.6 we graph the time series of true states and smoothed state probabilities produced by the EM algorithm. The smoothed state probabilities, which are the EM algorithm's best guess at the state each period based on our time-varying transition probability model (Figure 7.6(a)), track the true states quite well. The mean-squared state extraction error using our model is 0.13.[11]

Next, we use the EM algorithm to fit a Hamilton model, which does not allow for time-varying transition probabilities, to the same dataset. The Hamilton model parameter estimates are given in Table 7.1,

---

[10] This behaviour is noted frequently in the literature.

[11] The mean squared state extraction error using the *true* parameter values, which may be viewed as a lower bound, is 0.11.

(a) Time-varying probabilities, MSE = 0.13

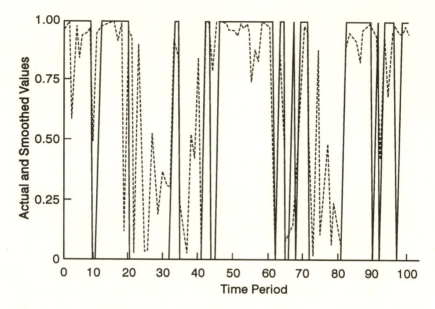

(b) Constant probabilities, MSE = 0.27

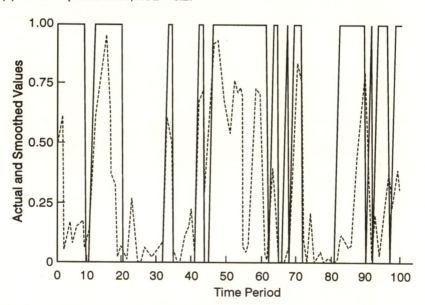

Fig. 7.6. Actual and smoothed state sequences.

labelled $\hat{\theta}_H$. The likelihood ratio test statistic clearly rejects the null of constant transition probabilities. The time series of true states and smoothed state probabilities that result from the fitted Hamilton model appear in Figure 7.6(b). The mean-squared state extraction error is 0.27, more than twice as large as that resulting from our time-varying transition probability model.

The fitted values of the transition probabilities for our model and the Hamilton model appear in Figures 7.7(a) and (b), along with the true probabilities. Our estimates do a reasonable job of tracking the time-varying probabilities, whereas, needless to say, the Hamilton estimates do not. As intuition suggests, the Hamilton estimates lie between the actual 'high' and 'low' values. Their restriction to constancy is responsible for the higher mean-squared state extraction error associated with the Hamilton model.

5. Concluding Remarks

This paper has been largely methodological, and numerous additional methodological issues are currently under investigation, including formal asymptotic distribution theory, elimination of the linear approximation employed in solving the first-order conditions, model specification tests, and analytic determination of ergodic probabilities. We shall not dwell on those issues here; instead, we shall briefly discuss two potentially fruitful areas of application.

The first concerns exchange rate dynamics. Engel and Hamilton (1990) have suggested that exchange rates may follow a switching process. We agree. But certainly, it is highly restrictive to require constancy of the transition probabilities. Rather, they should be allowed to vary with fundamentals, such as relative money supplies, relative real outputs, interest rate differentials, and so forth. Moreover, Mark (1992) produces useful indexes of fundamentals, which may be exploited to maintain parsimony. We shall provide a detailed report on this approach in a future paper.

The second concerns aggregate output dynamics. Diebold, Rudebusch and Sichel (1993) have found strong duration dependence in postwar U.S. contractions. That is, the longer a contraction persists, the more likely it is to end. That suggests allowing the transition probabilities in a Markov switching model of aggregate output dynamics to depend on length-to-date of the current regime, which can readily be achieved by expanding the state space of the process.[12]

---

[12] We thank Atsushi Kajii and Jim Hamilton for pointing this out.

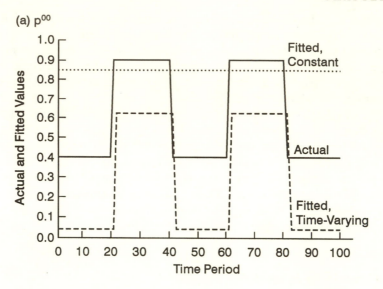

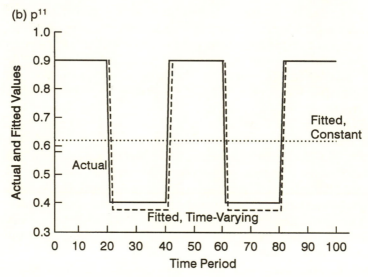

Fig. 7.7. Actual and fitted values.

Appendix

The general form of the maximum expected complete-data likelihood estimators for the $2k$ transition probability function parameters, $\beta_0^{(j)}$ and $\beta_1^{(j)}$, is given in Section 3.2. Here we include the explicit expressions for the cases of $k = 2$ and $k = 3$, which are of particular interest in applied work. Due to space limitations, it is understood that in the expressions that follow all smoothed probabilities are conditional on y_T and $\underline{x}_T$ given $\theta^{(j-1)}$, and that transition probabilities p_t^{00}, p_t^{11} and their derivatives are evaluated at $\beta_0^{(j-1)}$ and $\beta_1^{(j-1)}$, respectively.

$$\underline{k = 2}$$

$$\beta_0^{(j)} = \begin{pmatrix} \beta_{00}^{(j)} \\ \beta_{01}^{(j)} \end{pmatrix}$$

$$= \begin{pmatrix} \sum_{t=2}^T x_{0,t-1} P(s_{t-1} = 0) p_{0t}^{00} & \sum_{t=2}^T x_{0,t-1} P(s_{t-1} = 0) p_{1t}^{00} \\ \sum_{t=2}^T x_{1,t-1} P(s_{t-1} = 0) p_{0t}^{00} & \sum_{t=2}^T x_{1,t-1} P(s_{t-1} = 0) p_{1t}^{00} \end{pmatrix}^{-1}$$

$$\times \begin{pmatrix} \sum_{t=2}^T x_{0,t-1} \left\{ P(s_t = 0, s_{t-1} = 0) - P(s_{t-1} = 0) \left[p_t^{00} - \dfrac{\partial p_t^{00}}{\partial \beta_0} \beta_0^{(j-1)} \right] \right\} \\ \sum_{t=2}^T x_{1,t-1} \left\{ P(s_t = 0, s_{t-1} = 0) - P(s_{t-1} = 0) \left[p_t^{00} - \dfrac{\partial p_t^{00}}{\partial \beta_0} \beta_0^{(j-1)} \right] \right\} \end{pmatrix}$$

$$\beta_1^{(j)} = \begin{pmatrix} \beta_{10}^{(j)} \\ \beta_{11}^{(j)} \end{pmatrix}$$

$$= \begin{pmatrix} \sum_{t=2}^T x_{0,t-1} P(s_{t-1} = 1) p_{0t}^{11} & \sum_{t=2}^T x_{0,t-1} P(s_{t-1} = 1) p_{1t}^{11} \\ \sum_{t=2}^T x_{1,t-1} P(s_{t-1} = 1) p_{0t}^{11} & \sum_{t=2}^T x_{1,t-1} P(s_{t-1} = 1) p_{1t}^{11} \end{pmatrix}^{-1}$$

$$\times \begin{pmatrix} \sum_{t=2}^T x_{0,t-1} \left\{ P(s_t = 1, s_{t-1} = 1) - P(s_{t-1} = 1) \left[p_t^{11} - \dfrac{\partial p_t^{11}}{\partial \beta_1} \beta_1^{(j-1)} \right] \right\} \\ \sum_{t=2}^T x_{1,t-1} \left\{ P(s_t = 1, s_{t-1} = 1) - P(s_{t-1} = 1) \left[p_t^{11} - \dfrac{\partial p_t^{11}}{\partial \beta_1} \beta_1^{(j-1)} \right] \right\} \end{pmatrix}$$

$$\underline{k = 3}$$

$$\beta_0^{(j)} = \begin{pmatrix} \beta_{00}^{(j)} \\ \beta_{01}^{(j)} \\ \beta_{02}^{(j)} \end{pmatrix}$$

$$= \begin{pmatrix} \sum_{t=2}^T x_{0,t-1} P(s_{t-1} = 0) p_{0t}^{00} & \sum_{t=2}^T x_{0,t-1} P(s_{t-1} = 0) p_{1t}^{00} \\ \sum_{t=2}^T x_{1,t-1} P(s_{t-1} = 0) p_{0t}^{00} & \sum_{t=2}^T x_{1,t-1} P(s_{t-1} = 0) p_{1t}^{00} \\ \sum_{t=2}^T x_{2,t-1} P(s_{t-1} = 0) p_{0t}^{00} & \sum_{t=2}^T x_{2,t-1} P(s_{t-1} = 0) p_{1t}^{00} \end{pmatrix}$$

$$\left.\begin{array}{c}\Sigma_{t=2}^{T}x_{0,t-1}P(s_{t-1}=0)p_{2t}^{00}\\ \Sigma_{t=2}^{T}x_{1,t-1}P(s_{t-1}=0)p_{2t}^{00}\\ \Sigma_{t=2}^{T}x_{2,t-1}P(s_{t-1}=0)p_{2t}^{00}\end{array}\right)^{-1}$$

$$\times \left(\begin{array}{c}\Sigma_{t=2}^{T}x_{0,t-1}\left\{P(s_t=0,s_{t-1}=0)-P(s_{t-1}=0)\left[p_t^{00}-\dfrac{\partial p_t^{00}}{\partial \beta_0}\beta_0^{(j-1)}\right]\right\}\\[2ex] \Sigma_{t=2}^{T}x_{1,t-1}\left\{P(s_t=0,s_{t-1}=0)-P(s_{t-1}=0)\left[p_t^{00}-\dfrac{\partial p_t^{00}}{\partial \beta_0}\beta_0^{(j-1)}\right]\right\}\\[2ex] \Sigma_{t=2}^{T}x_{2,t-1}\left\{P(s_t=0,s_{t-1}=0)-P(s_{t-1}=0)\left[p_t^{00}-\dfrac{\partial p_t^{00}}{\partial \beta_0}\beta_0^{(j-1)}\right]\right\}\end{array}\right)$$

$$\beta_1^{(j)}=\left(\begin{array}{c}\beta_{10}^{(j)}\\ \beta_{11}^{(j)}\\ \beta_{12}^{(j)}\end{array}\right)$$

$$=\left(\begin{array}{cc}\Sigma_{t=2}^{T}x_{0,t-1}P(s_{t-1}=1)p_{0t}^{00} & \Sigma_{t=2}^{T}x_{0,t-1}P(s_{t-1}=1)p_{1t}^{00}\\ \Sigma_{t=2}^{T}x_{1,t-1}P(s_{t-1}=1)p_{0t}^{00} & \Sigma_{t=2}^{T}x_{1,t-1}P(s_{t-1}=1)p_{1t}^{00}\\ \Sigma_{t=2}^{T}x_{2,t-1}P(s_{t-1}=1)p_{0t}^{00} & \Sigma_{t=2}^{T}x_{2,t-1}P(s_{t-1}=1)p_{1t}^{00}\end{array}\right.$$

$$\left.\begin{array}{c}\Sigma_{t=2}^{T}x_{0,t-1}P(s_{t-1}=1)p_{2t}^{00}\\ \Sigma_{t=2}^{T}x_{1,t-1}P(s_{t-1}=1)p_{2t}^{00}\\ \Sigma_{t=2}^{T}x_{2,t-1}P(s_{t-1}=1)p_{2t}^{00}\end{array}\right)^{-1}$$

$$\times \left(\begin{array}{c}\Sigma_{t=2}^{T}x_{0,t-1}\left\{P(s_t=1,s_{t-1}=1)-P(s_{t-1}=1)\left[p_t^{11}-\dfrac{\partial p_t^{11}}{\partial \beta_1}\beta_1^{(j-1)}\right]\right\}\\[2ex] \Sigma_{t=2}^{T}x_{1,t-1}\left\{P(s_t=1,s_{t-1}=1)-P(s_{t-1}=1)\left[p_t^{11}-\dfrac{\partial p_t^{11}}{\partial \beta_1}\beta_1^{(j-1)}\right]\right\}\\[2ex] \Sigma_{t=2}^{T}x_{2,t-1}\left\{P(s_t=1,s_{t-1}=1)-P(s_{t-1}=1)\left[p_t^{11}-\dfrac{\partial p_t^{11}}{\partial \beta_1}\beta_1^{(j-1)}\right]\right\}\end{array}\right)$$

References

Cecchetti, S. G., P. Lam and N. C. Mark (1990), "Mean Reversion in Equilibrium Asset Prices," *American Economic Review*, 80, 3, pp. 398–418.

Dempster, A. P., N. M. Laird and D. B. Rubin (1977), "Maximum Likelihood from Incomplete Data via the EM Algorithm," *Journal of the Royal Statistical Society*, 39, pp. 1–38.

De Toldi, M., C. Gourieroux and A. Monfort (1992), "On Seasonal Effects in Duration Models," Working Paper #9216, INSEE, Paris.

Diebold, F. X. and G. D. Rudebusch (1993), "Measuring Business Cycles: A Modern Perspective," Manuscript, Dept. of Economics, University of Pennsylvania.

Diebold, F. X., G. D. Rudebusch and D. Sichel (1993), "Further Evidence on Business Cycle Duration Dependence," in J. H. Stock and M. W. Watson (eds.), *New Research on Business Cycles, Indicators and Forecasting*, University of Chicago Press for NBER, Chicago, pp. 255–84.

Diebold, F. X. and T. Schuermann (1992), "Exact Maximum Likelihood Estimation of ARCH Models," Manuscript, Dept. of Economics, University of Pennsylvania.

Engel, C. and J. D. Hamilton (1990), "Long Swings in the Dollar: Are They in the Data and do Markets Know it?," *American Economic Review*, 80, 4, pp. 689–713.

Fillardo, A. J. (1991), "Business Cycle Phases and Their Transitions," Manuscript, Dept. of Economics, University of Chicago.

Ghysels, E. (1992), "A Time Series Models of Growth Cycles and Seasonals with Stochastic Regime Switches," Manuscript, CRDE, Dept. of Economics, University of Montreal.

Goldfeld, S. M. and R. E. Quandt (1973), "A Markov Model for Switching Regressions," *Journal of Econometrics*, 1, pp. 3–16.

Hamilton, J. D. (1988), "Rational-Expectations Econometric Analysis of Changes in Regime: An Investigation of the Term Structure of Interest Rates," *Journal of Economic Dynamics and Control*, 12, pp. 385–423.

—— (1989), "A New Approach to the Economic Analysis of Nonstationary Time Series and the Business Cycle," *Econometrica*, 57, pp. 357–84.

—— (1990), "Analysis of Time Series Subject to Changes in Regime," *Journal of Econometrics*, 45, pp. 39–70.

Lee, J.-H. (1991), "Nonstationary Markov Switching Models of Exchange Rates: The Pound-Dollar Exchange Rate," PhD Dissertation, University of Pennsylvania.

Mark, N. C. (1992), "Exchange Rates and Fundamentals: Evidence on Long-Horizon Predictability and Overshooting," Manuscript, Dept. of Economics, Ohio State University.

Quandt, R. E. (1958), "The Estimation of Parameters of Linear Regression System Obeying Two Separate Reigmes," *Journal of the American Statistical Association*, 55, pp. 873–80.

Ruud, P. A. (1991), "Extension of Estimation Methods Using the EM Algorithm," *Journal of Econometrics*, 49, pp. 305–41.

Watson, M. W. and R. F. Engle (1983), "Alternative Algorithms for the Estimation of Dynamic Factor, Mimic and Varying Coefficient Models," *Journal of Econometrics*, 15, pp. 385–400.

Part III

BUSINESS CYCLE DYNAMICS

The chapters in this section use linear time-series methods to model business cycles. They are also all largely examinations of the persistence of economic shocks. Chapters 8, 9, and 10 summarize and contribute to the debate about the choice between models of the economy that assume a fixed trend rate of growth and models with no such fixed trend. The popular Dickey–Fuller test is found to be of limited value in distinguishing between these models using postwar data, although longer samples are more informative. Chapters 11, 12, and 13 introduce a fractionally integrated model that nests the fixed and variable trend specifications as special cases. Again, however, in the postwar period, insufficient information appears to be available to pin down definitively the long-run dynamic of the economy.

8

Trends and Random Walks in Macroeconomic Time Series: A Reexamination

GLENN D. RUDEBUSCH*

1. Introduction

One of the most influential papers in macroeconomics during the last decade, in terms of its effect on research agendas and methodology, was "Trends and Random Walks in Macroeconomic Time Series" by Charles Nelson and Charles Plosser (1982). Nelson and Plosser were unable to reject the hypothesis of a single unit root in the autoregressive representations of a wide variety of macroeconomic time series, including employment, GNP, prices, interest rates, and stock prices. Following Nelson and Plosser's lead, macroeconomics has often been preoccupied, for better or worse, by unit roots.

The ramifications of unit roots have been widely felt. For example, application of unit root tests resulted in reevaluations of the permanent income hypothesis of consumption (e.g., Mankiw and Shapiro 1985, Deaton 1987, and Diebold and Rudebusch 1991), the sustainability of government deficits (e.g., Hamilton and Flavin 1986), and the efficiency of stock markets and foreign exchange markets (e.g., Poterba and Summers 1987 and Meese and Singleton 1982). In addition, the general inability to reject a unit root was considered by many to be proof of the *existence* of a permanent component whose fluctuations are not eventually eliminated through reversion to trend. This naturally spurred attempts to determine the importance of that permanent component. Thus, Nelson and Plosser's work can be seen as a precursor to research on the closely related questions of the persistence of macroeconomic shocks (e.g., Campbell and Mankiw 1987, Cochrane 1988, and Diebold and Rudebusch 1989 in univariate contexts, and Shapiro and Watson

* David Wilcox, Danny Quah, Doug Steigerwald, Gene Savin, Spencer Krane, Steve Durlauf, Frank Diebold, and two anonymous referees provided helpful comments. Michelle Phillips and Roberto Sella provided research assistance.

1988 and Blanchard and Quah 1989 in multivariate ones) and the decomposition of macroeconomic dynamics into trend and cycle (e.g., Harvey 1985).

Nelson and Plosser's results have also influenced the direction of business cycle theorizing. Under the condition that monetary shocks have only temporary real effects, Nelson and Plosser asserted that their evidence of a permanent component in real output suggested that the source of business fluctuations is nonmonetary. This argument was one factor in the early popularity of real business cycle models (e.g., King and Plosser 1984).[1]

Finally, Nelson and Plosser's work helped to stimulate a general interest in econometrics about issues related to stationarity. The associated research led to several advances that have been widely applied, notably cointegration (e.g., Engle and Granger 1987) and new tests for unit roots (e.g., Phillips 1987).

In light of the influence of Nelson and Plosser (1982), this paper reexamines the data set used in their analysis to delineate the evidence regarding the existence and economic significance of a unit root. To examine existence, I estimate a difference-stationary (DS) null model and a trend-stationary (TS) alternative model for each variable and use resampling techniques to obtain the distributions of unit root test statistics under each model. The distributions obtained from the estimated DS models provide the appropriate small-sample size of the tests, while the distributions from the estimated TS models provide, for specific and plausible alternatives, the power of the tests, that is, their ability to reject a false null. By simulating specific DS and TS models estimated from the data, this study uses the most relevant models, initial conditions, sample sizes, and error distributions available for calculation of size and power.

However, an examination merely of test power is not enough. Although unit root tests may have low power against particular TS alternatives, that inadequacy does not necessarily compromise Nelson and Plosser's results. As Nelson and Plosser (1982, p. 152) note, no unit root test "can have power against a TS alternative with an [autoregressive] root arbitrarily close to unity. However, if we are observing stationary deviations from linear trends in these series, then the tendency to return to the trend line must be so weak as to avoid detection even in samples as long as sixty years to over a century." Thus, Nelson and Plosser argue that the evidence they provide against the DS models is so weak that plausible alternative TS models most likely exhibit

---

[1] Recently, others have noted that substantial persistence in output is compatible with a wide range of theoretical models, including monetary ones (e.g., West 1988).

persistence properties that are similar to those of the DS models over economically relevant horizons. I examine the persistence properties of the estimated TS and DS models at a variety of horizons in order to assess the validity of this argument.

Section 2 describes the two unit root tests that I will employ and introduces a measure of persistence. The simulation technique used to obtain the small-sample distributions of the test statistics is outlined in Section 3. Section 4 contains empirical results from the Nelson and Plosser data set; for each series, I compare likelihoods of the estimated DS and TS models and contrast their persistence properties. Section 5 examines the consequences of small-sample bias in the estimates of the parameters of the TS models; examination of median-unbiased TS models qualifies some of the earlier results, notably for the nominal series. Section 6 offers some concluding comments and discusses the relationship of my results to recent related work.

2. The Permanent Component: Existence and Importance

Consider the k-th order autoregressive representation ($AR(k)$),

$$x_t = \mu + \gamma t + \sum_{i=1}^{k} \rho_i x_{t-i} + \varepsilon_t, \tag{1}$$

where ε_t is a white noise innovation (and $k \geq 1$). There are two special cases of interest: (1) the *trend-stationary* (TS) model, where stationarity is assumed around a linear deterministic trend, so the roots of the lag operator polynomial $\rho(L) = 1 - \rho_1 L - \cdots - \rho_k L^k$ lie outside the unit circle, which implies that the sum of the autoregressive coefficients is less than one ($\sum_{i=1}^{k} \rho_i < 1$); and (2) the *difference-stationary* (DS) model, where $\gamma = 0$ and $\rho(L)$ contains one (positive, real) unit root, which implies $\sum_{i=1}^{k} \rho_i = 1$.[2] Note that equation (1) can be rearranged as[3]

$$x_t = \mu + \gamma t + \left(\sum_{i=1}^{k} \rho_i \right) x_{t-1} + \sum_{i=1}^{k-1} \left(- \sum_{j=i+1}^{k} \rho_j \right) \Delta x_{t-i} + \varepsilon_t. \tag{2}$$

---

[2] More precisely, these models are integrated of orders zero and one, respectively.

[3] If $k = 1$, summations over $i = 1, \ldots, k - 1$ are ignored; the DS model is simply a random walk with drift.

Thus, the DS model has the $AR(k - 1)$ representation in first differences,

$$\Delta x_t = \mu + \sum_{i=1}^{k-1} \phi_i \Delta x_{t-i} + \varepsilon_t, \qquad (3)$$

where $\phi_i \equiv -\sum_{j=i+1}^{k} \rho_j$.

A test to distinguish the TS model from the DS model, assuming the order k is known, is easily constructed.[4] Estimate equation (2), the "augmented Dickey-Fuller" regression, as

$$x_t = \hat{\mu} + \hat{\gamma} t + \hat{\delta} x_{t-1} + \sum_{i=1}^{k-1} \hat{\phi}_i \Delta x_{t-i} + \hat{\varepsilon}_t, \qquad (4)$$

and the test unit root (or DS model) null hypothesis, H_0: $\delta = 1$.[5] A natural test statistic for this hypothesis is the t-test, defined as $\hat{\tau} \equiv (\hat{\delta} - 1)/SE(\hat{\delta})$, where $SE(\hat{\delta})$ is the standard error of the estimated coefficient. However, Dickey (1976) and Fuller (1976) show that this statistic does not have the usual Student-t distribution but has a distribution that is skewed toward negative values. For $k = 1$, Dickey and Fuller report critical values for this test at conventional significance levels for a variety of sample sizes. For the case of k greater than one, Dickey and Fuller show that $\hat{\tau}$ will have an *asymptotic* distribution that is the same as when $k = 1$; thus, their reported asymptotic critical values for $\hat{\tau}$ with $k = 1$ can be applied in the case of arbitrary k.

In addition to the augmented Dickey-Fuller $\hat{\tau}$ test for stationarity, which was employed by Nelson and Plosser (1982), I also consider a second, more recent, test of stationarity that has been developed by Phillips (1987) and Phillips and Perron (1988). To test for a unit root in the $AR(k)$ process (1),[6] they estimate the first-order regression,

$$x_t = \tilde{\mu} + \tilde{\gamma} t + \tilde{\delta} x_{t-1} + \tilde{\eta}_t, \qquad (5)$$

---

[4] Like Nelson and Plosser (1982), I only consider unit root tests that allow for a trend under the alternative. Such tests appear to be appropriate for most macroeconomic time series (note the time trend coefficients in the estimated TS models below); furthermore, West (1987) has shown that the tests without a trend have no power asymptotically against a trend alternative.

[5] The analysis below was also conducted with the Dickey-Fuller normalized bias and likelihood ratio tests, and qualitatively similar results were obtained.

[6] Following Nelson and Plosser, I limit consideration in this paper to pure autoregressive models. Both the augmented Dickey-Fuller test (as noted by Said and Dickey 1984) and the Phillips test can be applied to more general mixed ARMA processes. I consider the issue of model specification in more detail below.

but modify—in a nonparametric way—the t-statistic $\tilde{\tau} \equiv (\tilde{\delta} - 1)/SE(\tilde{\delta})$ for likely serial correlation in residuals $\tilde{\eta}_t$. The Phillips test statistic (for sample size T) takes the form[7]

$$\tilde{Z} \equiv \tilde{\tau}(s_\eta/s_q) - \left(s_q^2 - s_\eta^2\right)T^3\left[4s_q(3D_{XX})^{1/2}\right]^{-1},$$

where D_{XX} is the determinant of the regressor cross-product matrix from (5) and

$$s_\eta^2 \equiv T^{-1} \sum_{t=1}^{T} \tilde{\eta}_t^2,$$

$$s_q^2 \equiv s_\eta^2 + 2T^{-1} \sum_{j=1}^{q} [1 - j/(1 + q)] \sum_{t=j+1}^{T} \tilde{\eta}_t \tilde{\eta}_{t-j},$$

where q is a parameter that determines the number of autocorrelations used in the estimate of s_q^2. Under the unit root null that $\delta = 1$, the Phillips t-test, $\tilde{Z}$, converges in the limit to the distribution of $\hat{\tau}$; thus, the asymptotic critical values tabulated in Dickey and Fuller are also appropriate for $\tilde{Z}$.

It should be emphasized that in the general case of the k-th order autoregression in equation (1), only asymptotic critical values are available for either the augmented Dickey-Fuller or the Phillips unit root test. In finite samples, the distributions of $\hat{\tau}$ and $\tilde{Z}$ under the null will depend on the sample size, the parameter values, and the distribution of the disturbances (see Evans and Savin 1984 and Schmidt 1990). The empirical section below reports critical values for $\hat{\tau}$ and $\tilde{Z}$ that account for these factors in the Nelson and Plosser data samples. In addition, in these same samples, I examine the power of the tests to reject the unit root null for plausible TS alternatives.

While $\hat{\tau}$ and $\tilde{Z}$ are able to test for the existence of a unit root, and hence test the DS model restrictions, these statistics will, of course, have low power against TS alternatives with an autoregressive root very close to unity. However, here, the assertion of Nelson and Plosser that was quoted in the introduction about the *economic importance* of trend reversion comes to the fore; the near-unit root in the TS model that makes it difficult to reject the unit root null may also imply that trend reversion in the TS model occurs only with a very long lag. Thus, it is necessary to supplement the unit root tests with a measure of the

[7] More precisely, this is the form that I use; see Schwert (1989) for a discussion of various estimators of s_η^2 and s_q^2.

persistence of shocks. A unit root simply implies a nonzero permanent response of the time series to an innovation, while an examination of the amount of trend reversion at various horizons allows one to distinguish the DS model from the TS model in terms of economic significance.

The measure of persistence that I use is the size (at a given horizon) of the impulse response of the time series to a unit innovation.[8] Consider the moving-average representation of the first difference of the (TS or DS) time series x_t,

$$\Delta x_t = k + A(L)\varepsilon_t = k + (1 + a_1 L + a_2 L^2 + \cdots)\varepsilon_t, \qquad (6)$$

where k is some constant. The measure of interest is the sum of the coefficients of the lag operator $A(L)$. A unit shock in period t affects the *change* in x at time $t + h$ by a_h and affects the *level* of x at time $t + h$ by $c_h \equiv 1 + a_1 + \cdots + a_h$. For various horizons, the cumulative response c_h answers the question of interest: "How does a shock today affect x in the short, medium, and long run?" For example, with annual data, c_{10} measures the impact of a shock today on the level of x ten years hence. In the limit, the effect of a unit shock today on the level of x infinitely far in the future is c_∞. For any TS series, $c_\infty = 0$, because the effect of any shock is transitory as reversion to the deterministic trend eventually dominates. For a DS series, $c_\infty \neq 0$; that is, each shock has a permanent component. At shorter horizons, the dynamic responses of particular TS and DS representations may be quite similar or quite different, and below, I shall investigate these responses for TS and DS models that are estimated from a common data sample.

3. Monte Carlo Methodology

My methodology is distinguished by careful construction of a sampling experiment that closely mimics the actual unit root inference problem for a typical macroeconomic time series. For each of the 14 macroeconomic variables used by Nelson and Plosser (1982), I formulate DS and TS data-generating processes with parameters and innovations that are obtained from regressions estimated from the data.[9] Doing so allows me to ascertain the DS model and TS model small-sample distributions of $\hat{\tau}$ and $\tilde{Z}$ for the Nelson and Plosser data samples and to describe the

---

[8] This measure is described in further detail in Diebold and Rudebusch (1989) and Diebold and Nerlove (1990).

[9] Section 5 will examine the implications of the small-sample bias in the coefficients of these estimated autoregressive models.

exact amount of support from the data for these models. In addition, and as importantly, I am able to clearly delineate the persistence properties, and thus the economic characteristics, of the relevant DS and TS models. In this section, I will illustrate the procedures using Nelson and Plosser's sample of real GNP.

The first step is to estimate both a TS and a DS model from the sample of the log of U.S. real GNP (Y_t), which consists of 62 annual observations (1909 through 1970). This requires specifying k, the order of the model, and I follow the choice of Nelson and Plosser (1982).[10] For real GNP, Nelson and Plosser set $k = 2$; thus, I estimate the TS model with a linear deterministic trend and second-order dependence for GNP as:

TS Model, $(k = 2)$

$$Y_t = .819 + .0056t + 1.24Y_{t-1} - .419Y_{t-2} + \hat{u}_t, \hat{\sigma}_u = .0583. \quad (7)$$
$$(.270) \ (.0019) \quad (.121) \quad\quad (.121)$$

The first two years of the sample are used up by initial conditions; the standard errors of the coefficients appear in parentheses. Estimating the DS model for this sample yields:

DS Model,

$$\Delta Y_t = .019 + .341\Delta Y_{t-1} + \hat{v}_t, \hat{\sigma}_v = .0618. \quad\quad\quad (8)$$
$$(.009) \ (.124)$$

As noted above, the DS model imposes two restrictions: (1) that the time trend coefficient is zero and (2) that the sum of the autoregressive coefficients is one (i.e., the unit root hypothesis).

Both models appear to fit the data quite well; the standard deviations of the fitted residuals, $\hat{u}_t$ and $\hat{v}_t$, are very close, and plots of the residuals are basically indistinguishable and suggest no obvious outliers. In addition, Q-statistics computed from the fitted residuals are similar at a variety of lags and provide little evidence against the null of no serial correlation. However, the two models have very different implications about the dynamics of GNP. I transform the estimated DS and TS models into moving average form (6) and calculate the cumulative impulse responses (c_h) for each model at a variety of horizons. These

---

[10] Nelson and Plosser implicitly specify k by selecting the number of Dickey-Fuller regression augmentation lags (which equals $k - 1$). Their selection is based on examination of the sample autocorrelation and partial autocorrelation functions; as noted below, uncertainty about the true value of k would only add to the uncertainty involved in the unit root inference.

TABLE 8.1
Cumulative Impulse Response of Real GNP

	Horizon (years)						
	1	*2*	*3*	*4*	*5*	*10*	*15*
DS Model	1.34	1.46	1.50	1.51	1.52	1.52	1.52
	(.12)	(.21)	(.25)	(.27)	(.28)	(.29)	(.29)
TS Model	1.24	1.12	.87	.61	.39	.00	.00
	(.12)	(.20)	(.24)	(.26)	(.27)	(.13)	(.01)

responses are shown in Table 8.1, with standard errors for the responses in parentheses.[11]

The impulse response of the DS model implies not only shock persistence but shock magnification, because an innovation is not reversed but eventually changes the level of real GNP by more than one and a half times the size of the innovation ($c_{10} = 1.52$). In contrast, the TS model exhibits fairly rapid reversion to trend, with the effect of a shock essentially completely disappearing after ten years ($c_{10} = 0$). The cumulative impulse responses for the two models, each estimated from a common data sample, are clearly very different in both economic and statistical terms.

Ideally, the unit root tests could distinguish between these two models. For this sample of real GNP, Nelson and Plosser (1982) report a $\hat{\tau}$ test statistic equal to -2.99, which is insignificant at even the 10 percent level, according to the asymptotic critical value of -3.12 given in Fuller (1976); thus, the data offer no evidence to reject the DS model. Nelson and Plosser (p. 160) go even further and argue that this result would be consistent with a TS model "only if the fluctuations around a deterministic trend are so highly autocorrelated as to be indistinguishable from nonstationary series themselves in realizations as long as one hundred years." Clearly, this statement would seem to rule out the TS model estimated for real GNP above in light of that model's rapid trend reversion displayed in Table 8.1.

I will, in effect, reexamine Nelson and Plosser's evidence and their assertion. By repeatedly simulating models (7) and (8), I calculate distributions of the unit root test statistics, under the DS model and under the TS model, that are precisely tailored to Nelson and Plosser's GNP data sample. For example, from the estimated DS model, I

---

[11] The standard errors are calculated as follows. Let the cumulative impulse response at horizon h be given by $c_h = F(\rho_1, \ldots, \rho_k)$, and let f denote the vector of partials of F with respect to the parameters. Then, the standard error equals $\sqrt{f'\Sigma f}$, where Σ is the estimated variance-covariance matrix of the autoregressive parameters.

generate 10,000 data sets. Each data set includes the historical levels of the log of GNP in 1909 and 1910 as initial conditions and evolves according to the estimated equation in (8) with disturbances obtained by random draws (with replacement) from the set of fitted residuals $\{\hat{v}_1, \ldots, \hat{v}_{60}\}$.[12] For each data set, $\hat{\tau}$ is computed, and the resulting 10,000 realizations of this statistic provide the appropriate DS model distribution. Similarly, using the parameters from the estimated TS model (7), I generate 10,000 data sets using disturbances obtained by random draws from $\{\hat{u}_1, \ldots, \hat{u}_{60}\}$. The resulting 10,000 realizations of $\hat{\tau}$ provide the sampling distribution of the augmented Dickey-Fuller statistic from a plausible TS model. Of interest for examining the existence of a unit root in this sample of real GNP are the probabilities of obtaining a value of $\hat{\tau}$ as extreme as -2.99 from these TS model and DS model test statistic distributions. The next section provides these probabilities and similar ones for the Phillips $\hat{Z}$ test. Application of this same methodology also provides DS and TS model probabilities for all of the other macroeconomic time series examined by Nelson and Plosser.

4. Empirical Evidence for the DS and TS Models

This section implements the resampling procedure described above for each of the fourteen data samples considered in Nelson and Plosser (1982).[13] The first step is to estimate TS and DS models, of form (1) and (3) respectively, for each series. The TS model estimates are shown in Table 8.2, with the real GNP estimates described above repeated in the first row. For each series, the selection of k, the number of autoregressive lags used in the TS model, follows the choice of Nelson and Plosser. Note that for all but one of the estimated models the sum of the autoregressive parameters is close to, but less than, unity. The exception

---

[12] I also obtained virtually identical results below from simulations using normal errors (with the variance of the residuals) instead of the actual redrawn (bootstrapped) residuals. Both simulation procedures, of course, assume that the disturbances are identically and independently distributed (iid). This last assumption was also maintained in Nelson and Plosser's application of the Dickey-Fuller test, and they selected k for each series to obtain iid residuals. Formal tests, such as the Ljung-Box Q-statistic and the Breusch-Pagan heteroskedasticity test generally support this assumption for each of the time series.

[13] The fourteen series are real GNP (sample size, $T = 62$), nominal GNP (62), real per capita GNP (62), industrial production (111), employment (81), unemployment rate (81), GNP deflator (82), consumer prices (111), nominal wages (71), real wages (71), money stock (82), velocity (102), bond yield (71), and an index of common stock prices (100). The series, which are annual and in logs (except for the bond yield), are described further in Nelson and Plosser (1982).

TABLE 8.2
Estimated Coefficients of TS Models[a]

Series	Const.	t	Y_{t-1}	y_{t-2}	y_{t-3}	y_{t-4}	Standard Error
Real GNP	.819	.0056	1.24	−.419			.0583
	(.270)	(.0019)	(.121)	(.121)			
Nominal GNP	1.06	.0056	1.39	−.489			.0871
	(.448)	(.0024)	(.117)	(.117)			
Real GNP, p.c.	1.28	.0035	1.23	−.410			.0590
	(.419)	(.0012)	(.122)	(.121)			
Industrial	.103	.0067	.931	−.134	.084	−.091	.0973
Prod.[b]	(.024)	(.0027)	(.099)	(.136)	(.136)	(.135)	
Employment	1.42	.0021	1.27	−.479	.072		.0353
	(.529)	(.0008)	(.117)	(.180)	(.116)		
Unemployment	.514	−.0005	1.09	−.585	.445	−.243	.4068
	(.183)	(.0021)	(.107)	(.148)	(.146)	(.105)	
GNP Deflator	.260	.0021	1.37	−.454			.0460
	(.102)	(.0008)	(.102)	(.101)			
Consumer	.090	.0006	1.66	−.953	.358	−.091	.0419
Prices	(.051)	(.0002)	(.094)	(.182)	(.180)	(.092)	
Wages	.566	.0038	1.45	−.604	.068		.0599
	(.246)	(.0017)	(.126)	(.208)	(.126)		
Real Wages	.488	.0035	1.08	−.252			.0346
	(.157)	(.0011)	(.118)	(.116)			
Money Stock	.133	.0049	1.58	−.663			.0468
	(.038)	(.0016)	(.086)	(.086)			
Velocity	.052	−.0003	.941				.0671
	(.052)	(.0018)	(.035)				
Bond Yield	−.187	.0032	1.13	.204	−.305		.2836
	(.197)	(.0018)	(.127)	(.189)	(.139)		
Stock Prices	.096	.0032	1.20	−.425	.134		.1543
	(.056)	(.0013)	(.104)	(.157)	(.105)		

[a] These models are estimated on the level of the series. All data, except bond yields, are in log form. Standard errors are given in parentheses.

[b] The coefficients on the fifth and sixth lags of the TS model for industrial production are −.175 and .222, respectively, with standard errors equal to .135 and .097.

is the model of the bond yield, where $\sum_{i=1}^{k} \rho_i > 1$, so the estimated TS model is not stationary; thus, I shall not include this series in the simulation below.

The DS models for the fourteen variables, estimated in first differences, are shown in Table 8.3. As was the case for real GNP, the standard errors of the TS and DS models for each of the series are very close in size.

TABLE 8.3
Estimated Coefficients of DS Models[a]

Series	Const.	Δy_{t-1}	Δy_{t-2}	Δy_{t-3}	Δy_{t-4}	Standard Error
Real GNP	.019	.341				.0618
	(.009)	(.124)				
Nominal GNP	.031	.439				.0897
	(.013)	(.118)				
Real GNP, p.c.	.011	.332				.0627
	(.008)	(.124)				
Industrial Prod.[b]	.069	.006	−.126	−.030	−.116	.0997
	(.014)	(.096)	(.096)	(.096)	(.095)	
Employment	.012	.375	−.171			.0365
	(.005)	(.113)	(.113)			
Unemployment	−.014	.217	−.352	.122		.4357
	(.050)	(.108)	(.102)	(.106)		
GNP Deflator	.012	.434				.0475
	(.006)	(.102)				
Consumer Prices	.005	.708	−.291	.078		.0432
	(.004)	(.094)	(.113)	(.093)		
Wages	.025	.533	−.150			.0614
	(.009)	(.123)	(.123)			
Real Wages	.014	.191				.0366
	(.005)	(.120)				
Money Stock	.022	.622				.0490
	(.008)	(.089)				
Velocity	−.012					.0684
	(.007)					
Bond Yield	.040	.178	.369			.2862
	(.036)	(.126)	(.130)			
Stock Prices	.027	.266	−.187			.1574
	(.016)	(.102)	(.102)			

[a] These models are estimated on the first difference of the series. All data, except bond yields, are in log form. Standard errors are given in parentheses.

[b] The coefficient on the fifth lag of the DS model for industrial production is −.286 with standard error equal to .096.

Table 8.4 provides cumulative impulse responses for the estimated TS and DS models shown in Tables 8.2 and 8.3, as well as, in the final column, the standard error (conditional on each model) for the 10-year response. The rapid divergence between the DS and TS model responses that was evident for real GNP is typical of the other series as well. There are some exceptions: after 30 years, the TS model for consumer prices displays substantial persistence, while the DS model

TABLE 8.4
Cumulative Impulse Responses of Estimated TS and DS Models[a]

Series	Model	Horizon (years)								$se(c_{10})$
		1	2	3	4	5	10	15	30	
Real GNP	DS	1.34	1.46	1.50	1.51	1.52	1.52	1.52	1.52	.29
	TS	1.24	1.12	.87	.61	.39	.00	.00	.00	.13
Nominal GNP	DS	1.44	1.63	1.72	1.75	1.77	1.78	1.78	1.78	.37
	TS	1.39	1.44	1.33	1.14	.93	.24	.04	.00	.35
Real GNP, p.c.	DS	1.33	1.44	1.48	1.49	1.50	1.50	1.50	1.50	.28
	TS	1.23	1.10	.85	.60	.38	.00	.00	.00	.12
Industrial Prod.	DS	1.01	.88	.85	.75	.75	.79	.79	.79	.06
	TS	.93	.73	.64	.49	.17	.22	.07	.01	.14
Employment	DS	1.38	1.35	1.27	1.25	1.25	1.26	1.26	1.26	.21
	TS	1.27	1.13	.90	.70	.53	.14	.04	.00	.20
Unemployment	DS	1.22	.91	.89	1.02	1.02	.98	.99	.99	.18
	TS	1.09	.60	.47	.40	.16	−.07	.00	.00	.08
GNP Deflator	DS	1.43	1.62	1.70	1.74	1.76	1.77	1.77	1.77	.32
	TS	1.37	1.42	1.33	1.17	1.00	.38	.13	.01	.31
Consumer	DS	1.71	1.92	1.94	1.95	1.96	1.98	1.98	1.98	.38
Prices	TS	1.66	1.80	1.77	1.72	1.67	1.28	.96	.41	.35
Wages	DS	1.53	1.67	1.66	1.63	1.62	1.62	1.62	1.62	.33
	TS	1.45	1.50	1.37	1.17	.98	.34	.12	.00	.36
Real Wages	DS	1.19	1.23	1.23	1.24	1.24	1.24	1.24	1.24	.18
	TS	1.08	.91	.72	.54	.41	.09	.02	.00	.12
Money Stock	DS	1.62	2.01	2.25	2.40	2.49	2.63	2.64	2.65	.59
	TS	1.58	1.83	1.85	1.71	1.47	.23	−.13	.01	.45
Velocity	DS	1.00	1.00	1.00	1.00	1.00	1.00	1.00	1.00	.00
	TS	.94	.89	.83	.78	.74	.54	.40	.16	.21
Stock Prices	DS	1.27	1.15	1.07	1.07	1.09	1.09	1.09	1.09	.15
	TS	1.20	1.02	.84	.74	.67	.38	.21	.04	.22

[a] The standard error of the estimated cumulative impulse response at a horizon of 10 years is given in the last column as $se(c_{10})$.

for industrial production displays some shock dampening. Overall, however, the estimated TS and DS models provide very different descriptions of the dynamics of each of the series, with the TS models rapidly reverting to trend after a unit innovation and the DS models exhibiting shock magnification.

Before considering the ability of the unit root tests to discriminate between the TS and DS models, I first examine the tests under the DS model in order to indicate how appropriate the widely used asymptotic Dickey-Fuller critical values are for statistical inference in the Nelson and Plosser data set. For a given critical value (of nominal size, say, 5 percent) the proportion of rejections among the 10,000 simulated DS model data sets, given the truth of the null in the data generation process, is the empirical size of a test. This empirical size may differ from nominal size because it accounts for several factors: (1) the finite size of the sample, (2) the estimated values of the parameters, and (3) the estimated error distribution. Using the asymptotic critical values reported in Dickey and Fuller, Table 8.5 provides, for each series, the actual percentage of rejections of the unit root null out of the 10,000 DS model replications. Critical values at the 1 percent and 5 percent level are used for both the $\hat{\tau}$ and $\tilde{Z}$ tests. Below these empirical sizes, Table 8.5 also provides the actual 1 percent and 5 percent cutoff values. The $\hat{\tau}$ test exhibits an empirical size that is very close to its nominal size for all variables and at both significance levels; at the nominal 5 percent level, for example, empirical size ranges from 4.29 to 6.51 percent. In contrast, the Phillips $\tilde{Z}$ test appears to be mis-sized in these small samples; at the nominal 5 percent level, the empirical size of $\tilde{Z}$ ranges from 0.58 to 27.62 percent.[14] Thus, Table 8.5 indicates that for classical hypothesis tests of the unit root null hypothesis in the Nelson and Plosser samples, the asymptotic critical values appear to be appropriate approximations for the $\hat{\tau}$ test but not for the $\tilde{Z}$ test.[15]

Of more interest, however, than just the appropriateness of the asymptotic critical values is the actual likelihood of obtaining the sample values of the test statistics, denoted $\hat{\tau}_s$ and $\tilde{Z}_s$, from their estimated DS model and TS model small-sample distributions. For real GNP, Figure 8.1 displays the estimated DS model density function for $\hat{\tau}$, denoted $f_{DS}(\hat{\tau})$, and the estimated TS model density function for $\hat{\tau}$, denoted $f_{TS}(\hat{\tau})$; these are empirical densities formed from the realizations of the test statistic in the 10,000 samples from each model. The sample value of the augmented Dickey-Fuller t-test for real GNP, which is equal to -2.99, is shown as a vertical dotted line. There are two areas in Figure 8.1 of special interest. The hatched area under $f_{DS}(\hat{\tau})$ and to the left of $\hat{\tau}_s$ represents the probability of obtaining a value of the t-test equal to or smaller than -2.99, conditional on the DS model. This probability, which equals 0.150 for real GNP, is denoted as

$$\text{DS } p\text{-value} \equiv \text{prob } (\hat{\tau} \leq \hat{\tau}_s \mid \text{DS model}).$$

---

[14] This is consistent with the results of Schwert (1989) that suggest the Phillips test is incorrectly sized in samples of ARIMA (0, 1, 1) processes. In the Phillips test, I set q equal to 6; however, the results were qualitatively identical with q equal to 10.

[15] It should be stressed that the $\hat{\tau}$ test, unlike the Phillips test, incorporates the order of the data-generating process, which is assumed to be known. If the incorrect order were used, it is likely that the divergence between the empirical and nominal size would be greater.

TABLE 8.5
Empirical Size of Unit Root Tests[a]

Series (k)	$\hat{\tau}$		$\tilde{Z}$	
	1%	*5%*	*1%*	*5%*
Real GNP (2)	1.66	6.40	.24	1.17
	−4.13	−3.53	−3.49	−2.93
Nominal GNP (2)	1.72	6.38	.43	1.19
	−4.23	−3.52	−3.54	−2.82
Real GNP, p.c. (2)	1.56	6.26	.22	1.25
	−4.12	−3.51	−3.50	−2.95
Industrial Prod. (6)	1.41	5.42	8.01	27.62
	−4.08	−3.45	−4.67	−4.12
Employment (3)	1.02	4.88	.11	.84
	−3.97	−3.40	−3.37	−2.97
Unemployment (4)	1.55	6.08	2.74	10.30
	−4.12	−3.50	−4.29	−3.73
GNP Deflator (2)	1.25	5.12	.50	1.50
	−4.05	−3.42	−3.58	−2.93
Consumer Prices (4)	1.46	5.93	.86	3.60
	−4.10	−3.47	−3.87	−3.27
Wages (3)	1.35	5.40	.11	.80
	−4.10	−3.45	−3.33	−2.85
Real Wages (2)	.99	4.29	.08	.58
	−3.96	−3.34	−3.30	−2.82
Money Stock (2)	1.78	6.51	.21	.87
	−4.14	−3.55	−3.38	−2.82
Velocity (1)	1.27	5.49	1.39	6.47
	−4.06	−3.45	−4.07	−3.51
Stock Prices (3)	1.14	5.02	.61	3.83
	−3.99	−3.42	−3.80	−3.32

[a]The upper number in each cell is the percentage of rejections using the asymptotic Dickey-Fuller critical values, namely, −3.96 at the 1% level and −3.41 at the 5% level. The actual cutoff value for the 1% or the 5% fractile is given as the lower number. The number of augmentation lags in the Dickey-Fuller test equals $k - 1$, while q equals 6 in each Phillips test.

This p-value is the marginal significance level for rejection of the DS model null hypothesis; that is, in a classical hypothesis testing framework, given the sample test statistic $\hat{\tau}_s$, we could not reject the DS model at anything less than the 15 percent level. This is consistent with the inability of Nelson and Plosser to reject the DS model.

The other area of interest is the shaded region under $f_{TS}(\hat{\tau})$ and to the right of $\hat{\tau}_s$, which represents the probability of obtaining a value of

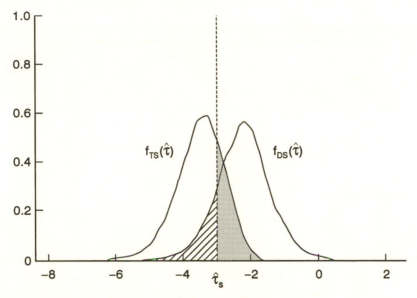

Fig. 8.1. Empirical densities of $\hat{\tau}$ from DS and TS models of real GNP.

the t-test equal to or greater than -2.99, conditional on the TS model. This probability is denoted

$$\text{TS } p\text{-value} \equiv \text{prob } (\hat{\tau} \geq \hat{\tau}_s \mid \text{TS model}).$$

For real GNP, the TS p-value is 0.216; in other words, it is quite possible that a sample statistic as large as -2.99 could have been generated from the estimated TS model.[16] In short, at conventional significance levels, there is very little evidence against either the DS model or the TS model for real GNP. The evidence in Nelson and Plosser (1982) on the DS model probabilities thus provides only one side of the story for inference regarding the unit root hypothesis. The other side is that the TS model is at least as consistent with the sample test statistic.

The other variables provide similar results. For each series, the estimated densities, f_{DS} and f_{TS}, have a substantial region of overlap, and the sample value, $\hat{\tau}_s$, falls into the range of this overlap. The overlap is obvious in Table 8.6, which gives $\hat{\tau}_s$ for each series with its associated DS p-value and TS p-value. Among all of the variables, there is only

[16] An equivalent statement of this result is that the $\hat{\tau}$ test of the DS null at the 15 percent significance level has a power against the TS alternative of only 78.4 percent.

TABLE 8.6
Sample $\hat{\tau}$ Test Statistics and Probabilities[a]

Series	$\hat{\tau}_s$	DS p-Value	TS p-Value
Real GNP	-2.99	.150	.216
Nominal GNP	-2.32	.429	.148
Real GNP, p.c.	-3.05	.137	.223
Industrial Prod.	-2.53	.301	.177
Employment	-2.66	.229	.196
Unemployment	-3.55	.045	.268
GNP Deflator	-2.52	.280	.228
Consumer Prices	-1.97	.613	.128
Wages	-2.24	.425	.165
Real Wages	-3.05	.094	.403
Money Stock	-3.08	.134	.261
Velocity	-1.66	.761	.075
Stock Prices	-2.12	.522	.104

[a] The sample augmented Dickey-Fuller test statistic, $\hat{\tau}_s$, is given with its
p-values from the TS and DS models. For each series, k equals the value given
in Table 8.5.

one model that can be rejected at the 5 percent level: the DS model for
the unemployment rate.

Table 8.7 provides, for each series, the sample Phillips test statistics,
$\tilde{Z}_s$, along with their p-values conditional on the DS or TS models. The
qualitative results are similar to those from the augmented Dickey-Fuller
test: there is a substantial region of overlap between the estimated DS
model and TS model densities of $\tilde{Z}$, and the sample test statistic falls
into this region of overlap. Only 2 of the 26 estimated models have
p-values less than 5 percent, namely, the TS models for velocity and
stock prices.

The conclusion to be drawn from Tables 8.6 and 8.7 is that there is
very little evidence to support the rejection of the DS model or the TS
model in *any* of the Nelson and Plosser time series. Given these data
and test statistics, little can be said about the choice between the DS
and TS models. The proper conclusion from application of the unit root
$\hat{\tau}$ test to these samples is that we cannot answer the question of the
existence of a unit root.

5. Correction of Bias in TS Model Estimates

There is one qualification to the preceding analysis that must be
considered. For each series, the specific alternative examined is the TS
model estimated from the available data sample with OLS. Is this model

TABLE 8.7

Sample $\tilde{Z}$ Test Statistics and Probabilities[a]

Series	$\tilde{Z}_s$	DS p-Value	TS p-Value
Real GNP	−2.25	.307	.131
Nominal GNP	−1.77	.592	.095
Real GNP, p.c.	−2.34	.255	.161
Industrial Prod.	−3.31	.321	.201
Employment	−2.39	.271	.156
Unemployment	−3.08	.198	.235
GNP Deflator	−2.34	.234	.263
Consumer Prices	−1.45	.814	.117
Wages	−2.05	.427	.212
Real Wages	−2.65	.094	.383
Money Stock	−2.33	.193	.341
Velocity	−1.47	.864	.047
Stock Prices	−1.96	.665	.044

[a] The sample Phillips test statistic, $\tilde{Z}_t$, is given with its p-values from the TS and DS models. For each series, q equals six.

the *most* plausible alternative? Perhaps not. Although the OLS estimates of the coefficients of the TS model are consistent and asymptotically normal, they are biased in small samples because of the presence of lagged dependent variables.[17] An arguably more plausible TS alternative would correct the coefficient estimates for this bias, and this section constructs and analyzes such an alternative.[18]

The small-sample bias of the OLS estimates of autoregressive model coefficients is most easily documented for an AR(1) process. The middle column of Table 8.8 provides the median value of the OLS estimate $\hat{\rho}_1$, based on repeated samples from the first-order process $y_t = \mu + \gamma t + \rho_1 y_{t-1} + \varepsilon_t$, for a variety of values of ρ_1 (with $\mu = \gamma = 0$). This estimate is downwardly biased over a wide range of ρ_1, with the deviation of the median estimate from the true value being particularly pronounced for values of ρ_1 that are just less than one.[19] The third

[17] This bias is most severe in the presence of a unit root, the so-called "Dickey-Fuller bias," but it is present for all autoregressions. For further discussion of this bias, see Evans and Savin (1984) and Stine and Shaman (1989).

[18] The coefficient estimates of the DS model, which is an autoregressive model in differences, are biased as well. However, because the roots of the DS model are distant from the unit circle, the biases in the DS model coefficients were small and inconsequential for the analysis.

[19] The distribution of $\hat{\rho}_1$ is negatively skewed, so the median is a better measure of central tendency than the mean: I use the term "bias" in this paper to denote the deviation of the *median* from the true value.

TABLE 8.8
Small-Sample Bias of OLS Estimate of AR(1) Model[a]

ρ_1	median $(\hat{\rho}_1)$	prob $(\hat{\rho}_1 \geq \rho_1)$
0.70	0.676	0.333
0.72	0.695	0.325
0.74	0.715	0.315
0.76	0.735	0.306
0.78	0.754	0.296
0.80	0.773	0.286
0.82	0.792	0.273
0.84	0.810	0.257
0.86	0.829	0.240
0.88	0.847	0.221
0.90	0.864	0.194
0.92	0.880	0.158
0.94	0.893	0.117
0.96	0.902	0.066
0.98	0.906	0.022
1.00	0.910	0.005
1.02	0.991	0.088

[a] Column 2 provides the median OLS estimate of ρ_1 in the regression $y_t = \hat{\mu} + \hat{\gamma} t + \hat{\rho}_1 y_{t-1} + \varepsilon_1$, while column 3 gives the proportion of estimates that are greater than or equal to ρ_1. These are based on 10,000 samples of size 100 generated from $y_t = \rho_1 y_{t-1} + \varepsilon_t$ with normal disturbances and $\sigma_\varepsilon = 0.1$ and an initial condition of zero.

column of Table 8.8 gives the probability of obtaining an OLS estimate equal to or greater than ρ_1; these probabilities also indicate that a given estimate is more likely to be below rather than above the true value of the autoregressive parameter.

Based on Table 8.8, it is likely that the methodology of Sections 4 and 5 would employ a TS model (when $k = 1$) that incorporated an estimate of ρ_1 that is lower than the true value of ρ_1. A more plausible TS model of the data-generating process would correct for this downward small-sample bias.[20] I define the "median-unbiased" TS model as the

[20] Several bias corrections have been proposed for the OLS estimates of the autoregressive model. For example, Orcutt and Winokur (1969) and Rudebusch (1993) recommend mean-unbiased estimators, and Andrews (1990), independently of the present paper, proposes a median-unbiased one. The simulation strategy pursued below can approximate these estimators to any desired degree of accuracy. One advantage to median-unbiased estimates of the parameters is that they imply a median-unbiased estimate of the cumulative impulse response (which is a nonlinear function of the parameters). This property does not hold for mean-unbiased estimates.

one that, across repeated simulations, has a median OLS estimate of each parameter that is equivalent to the actual sample estimate of that parameter. Formally, let the vector of median-unbiased TS model coefficients be denoted as $\Phi_{MUE} = (\mu, \gamma, \rho_1, \ldots, \rho_k)$; across repeated samples, the median OLS estimates of these coefficients is median $(\hat{\Phi}_{MUE})$. Let $\hat{\Phi}_s$ be the vector of OLS parameters estimated from the data sample under consideration (which formed the parameters of the TS data-generating processes in Table 8.2). The vector Φ_{MUE} is defined by the equality of median $(\hat{\Phi}_{MUE})$ and $\hat{\Phi}_s$; that is, the median-unbiased model has median OLS parameter estimates equal to the sample estimates.

For multi-parameter models, finding Φ_{MUE} is complicated by the covariance among estimated parameters. This problem can be solved by repeated simulations of a baseline model where each baseline model coefficient is changed by a fraction of the difference between the resulting median estimate of that coefficient and the actual sample value. Convergence occurs when all of the median estimates match the sample ones. Table 8.9 presents the coefficients of these median-unbiased TS models for each of the series.[21]

What are the consequences of using the median-unbiased TS model coefficients for inference about unit roots? Examination of the AR(1) case in Table 8.8 is instructive; the median-unbiased estimate of ρ_1 will be closer to one than the OLS estimate (assuming $\rho_1 < 1$). Thus, the median-unbiased model will exhibit a greater persistence of shocks than the uncorrected model;[22] thus, in economic terms, the median-unbiased model will behave more like the DS model. On the other hand, the median-unbiased TS model will be even harder to distinguish from the DS model using unit root tests; that is, the power of the unit root tests will even be lower against the median-unbiased alternative.

These two results—higher persistence and lower power—usually generalize to the higher-order median-unbiased models as well. The cumulative impulse response of the median-unbiased model is shown in Table 8.10 for each series. The responses of these models display greater persistence for each series than the responses of the uncor-

---

[21] To be precise, when 1000 samples are generated from the models in Table 8.9 (of size equal to the sample data size of the series given in footnote 14) the difference between the median OLS estimate for each coefficient and the sample OLS estimate (given in Table 8.2) is less than .001 (except for the time coefficient when it was less than .0001). The disturbances for the simulations are generated from a normal distribution with standard error equal to the OLS estimate of the regression standard error (given for each series in Table 8.2). Letting this standard error be a free parameter along with the other coefficients led to qualitatively identical results.

[22] For an $AR(1)$, $c_n = \rho_1^n$, so the cumulative impulse response is higher at all horizons.

TABLE 8.9
Median-Unbiased TS Model Coefficients[a]

Series	Const.	t	y_{t-1}	y_{t-2}	y_{t-3}	y_{t-4}
Real GNP	.507	.0035	1.296	−.398		
Nominal GNP	.657	.0031	1.449	−.503		
Real GNP, p.c.	.882	.0023	1.276	−.394		
Industrial Prod.[b]	.094	.0033	.976	−.127	.072	−.080
Employment	1.043	.0015	1.323	−.508	.085	
Unemployment	.402	−.0002	1.130	−.592	.456	−.221
GNP Deflator	.110	.0008	1.421	−.453		
Consumer Prices	.039	.0004	1.688	−.984	.360	−.079
Wages	.186	.0011	1.538	−.672	.108	
Real Wages	.292	.0020	1.144	−.231		
Money Stock	.096	.0032	1.616	−.669		
Velocity	−.025	.0003	.995			
Stock Prices	.029	.0010	1.269	−.446	.161	

[a] When simulated 1000 times, these models have median OLS parameter estimates equal to those of the corresponding TS models in Table 8.2.
[b] The coefficients on the fifth and sixth lags are −.184 and .262, respectively.

TABLE 8.10
Cumulative Impulse Responses of Median-Unbiased TS Models

Series	Horizon (years)							
	1	2	3	4	5	10	15	30
Real GNP	1.30	1.28	1.15	.98	.81	.28	.09	.00
Nominal GNP	1.45	1.60	1.59	1.49	1.37	.75	.38	.05
Real GNP, p.c.	1.28	1.24	1.07	.89	.71	.19	.05	.00
Industrial Prod.	.98	.83	.75	.62	.31	.42	.24	.12
Employment	1.32	1.24	1.06	.88	.73	.30	.13	.01
Unemployment	1.13	.69	.56	.52	.32	−.02	−.01	.00
GNP Deflator	1.42	1.57	1.58	1.54	1.47	1.10	.81	.32
Consumer Prices	1.69	1.87	1.85	1.81	1.78	1.54	1.31	.82
Wages	1.54	1.69	1.68	1.61	1.53	1.18	.92	.43
Real Wages	1.14	1.08	.97	.86	.76	.41	.22	.03
Money Stock	1.62	1.94	2.06	2.03	1.90	.86	.20	−.02
Velocity	1.00	.99	.99	.98	.98	.95	.93	.86
Stock Prices	1.27	1.16	1.07	1.04	1.04	.95	.86	.65

rected OLS TS models shown in Table 8.4. For example, the median-unbiased TS model of real GNP has a cumulative impulse response at a horizon of ten years (c_{10}) of .28 as compared to the zero response for the uncorrected model. However, for about half of the series, the median-unbiased TS alternative still has much less persistence than the DS model. In particular, for the real series (real GNP, real GNP per capita, industrial production, employment, unemployment, and real wages), reversion to trend is fairly rapid (c_{10} is well below 0.5). The median-unbiased TS models for the remaining nominal series show considerably more persistence; indeed, for velocity and stock prices, the median-unbiased TS model is virtually indistinguishable from the DS model.

Finally, from repeated simulations of the median-unbiased TS models, Table 8.11 provides the p-values of the sample values of the unit root test statistics.[23] For each series, the p-values of $\hat{\tau}_s$ and $\tilde{Z}_s$ are quite large and provide no evidence against the TS alternative. For each nominal series, the lack of evidence is not surprising because the median-unbiased alternative is so similar in economic terms to the DS model. However, for the real series, Table 8.11 reinforces the conclusion of Section 4 that there are plausible TS alternatives that are different from DS models in economic terms but which cannot be identified by unit root tests.

6. Conclusion

Until about a decade ago, economists were in broad agreement that macroeconomic variables were trend stationary; as a prominent example, the business cycle fluctuations of real output were treated as stationary deviations from a steadily growing trend. This general agreement was shattered by Nelson and Plosser (1982), and a new consensus was formed that macroeconomic variables were best modeled as difference stationary. The evidence above indicates that, at least for *real* macroeconomic variables, this new consensus has no firmer statistical foundation than the one it replaced. The Nelson and Plosser sample of data does not support the proposition that unit roots are a pervasive

---

[23] The simulation methodology was the same as described in Sections 3 and 4, with initial conditions equal to the first k observations for each series. However, the disturbances were drawn from normal distributions instead of bootstrapping, but as noted in footnote 12, this change should have negligible effect.

TABLE 8.11
Probabilities of Sample Test Statistics from Median-Unbiased TS Models

Series	p-Value ($\hat{\tau}_s$)	p-Value ($\bar{\bar{Z}}_s$)
Real GNP	.587	.458
Nominal GNP	.300	.223
Real GNP, p.c.	.504	.409
Industrial Prod.	.547	.623
Employment	.227	.159
Unemployment	.505	.441
GNP Deflator	.704	.807
Consumer Prices	.397	.358
Wages	.457	.500
Real Wages	.692	.607
Money Stock	.536	.588
Velocity	.394	.310
Stock Prices	.468	.347

element in real macroeconomic time series.[24] The unit root tests employed by Nelson and Plosser display low power, not against TS alternatives with a "root arbitrarily close to unity," but against plausible TS models estimated from the data. Furthermore, if the alternative TS model is true, the DS model does not provide a good approximation for even medium-term dynamic responses. For each nominal time series, the evidence is more ambiguous because the most plausible alternative TS model displays substantial persistence; however, in light of the impulse response of this TS model, an appropriate confidence interval around an estimate of medium-term persistence is much larger than the one suggested by conditioning on the DS model alone.[25]

The above analysis can be fruitfully contrasted with two other recent papers in this area. My results were obtained even though I limited the class of models under consideration to $AR(k)$ processes with specific and known k. Variation in the order of the model will likely lead to variation in the relative probabilities of the DS and TS models; thus, uncertainty about the underlying model would only add to the uncertainty about unit roots. This conjecture is supported by Christiano and Eichenbaum (1990) who examine a variety of ARMA representations for postwar U.S. real GNP. They argue that imposing the TS constraint

[24] Further evidence on this issue for real GNP (where the Nelson and Plosser data are of dubious origin) is given in Rudebusch (1993) using a sample of postwar quarterly data.
[25] This suggests the importance of measuring the confidence intervals for estimates of persistence without conditioning on the TS or DS model. Diebold and Rudebusch (1989b) provide a first step in this direction using a model of fractional integration.

that $c_\infty = 0$ leads to only small differences in likelihood and that errors in specifying the order of the model can greatly affect these differences and hence affect the inference about unit roots.[26]

DeJong, Nankervis, Savin, and Whiteman (1989) provide a complementary investigation of the power of unit root tests against a comprehensive array of first-order autoregressive alternatives (at the nominal 5 percent significance level). Their conclusion also stresses the difficulty of detecting a TS process. My analysis differs from their work in that it focuses on specific, but arguably the most relevant, higher-order null and alternative models and provides an assessment of power at the most relevant significance level (the empirical marginal significance level of the DS model). More importantly, however, my analysis goes beyond a study of power and contrasts the persistence properties of the relevant TS and DS models.

In sum, the evidence in this paper and in other recent work suggests that a new consensus should be formed that stresses the difficulty of knowing anything about the existence of unit roots in macroeconomic time series. This recommends careful scrutiny of all macroeconometric results for possible sensitivity to the modeling of the trend component. An example of this sensitivity is given by Shapiro and Watson (1988), who provide two sets of estimates of their model under deterministic and stochastic detrending that have very different implications about the source of macroeconomic fluctuations.

References

Andrews, D., "Exact Unbiased Estimation of First Order Autoregressive/Unit Root Models," manuscript, Yale University, 1990.

Blanchard, O., "What Is Left of the Multiplier Accelerator?" *American Economic Review, Papers and Proceedings* 71 (1981), 150–154.

—— and D. Quah, "The Dynamic Effects of Aggregate Demand and Supply Disturbances," *American Economic Review* 79 (1989), 655–673.

Campbell, J. Y. and N. G. Mankiw, "Are Output Fluctuations Transitory?" *Quarterly Journal of Economics* 102 (1987), 857–880.

Christiano, L. J. and M. Eichenbaum, "Unit Roots in Real GNP: Do We Know, and Do We Care?" in A. H. Meltzer, ed., *Unit Roots, Investment Measures, and Other Essays*, Carnegie-Rochester Conference Series on Public Policy 32 (1990), 7–62.

---

[26] However, the analysis of Christiano and Eichenbaum (1990) is subject to the criticism of Section 5 because their estimated TS models do not take into account the small-sample estimation bias.

Cochrane, J. H., "How Big Is the Random Walk in GNP?" *Journal of Political Economy* 96 (1988), 893–920.

Deaton, A., "Life Cycle Models of Consumption: Is the Evidence Consistent with the Theory?" in T. F. Bewley, ed., *Advances in Econometrics, Fifth World Congress*, Vol. 2 (Cambridge: Cambridge University Press, 1987).

DeJong, D. N., J. C. Nankervis, N. E. Savin, and C. H. Whiteman, "Integration Versus Trend Stationarity in Macroeconomic Time Series," Working Paper No. 89-31, Department of Economics, University of Iowa, 1989.

Diebold, F. X. and M. Nerlove, "Unit Roots in Economic Time Series: A Selective Survey," in T. B. Fomby and G. F. Rhodes, eds., *Advances in Econometrics: Co-Integration, Spurious Regressions, and Unit Roots* (Greenwich, Conn.: JAI Press, 1990).

——— and G. D. Rudebusch, "Long Memory and Persistence in Aggregate Output," *Journal of Monetary Economics* 24 (1989), 189–209.

——— and ———, "Is Consumption Too Smooth? Long Memory and the Deaton Paradox," *Review of Economics and Statistics* 73 (1991), 1–9.

Dickey, D. A., "Estimation and Hypothesis Testing in Nonstationary Time Series," Ph.D. Dissertation, Iowa State University, 1976.

——— and W. F. Fuller, "Likelihood Ratio Statistics for Autoregressive Time Series with a Unit Root," *Econometrica* 49 (1981), 1057–1072.

Engle, R. F. and C. W. J. Granger, "Co-Integration and Error Correction: Representation, Estimation, and Testing," *Econometrica* 55 (1987), 251–276.

Evans, G. B. A. and N. E. Savin, "Testing for Unit Roots II," *Econometrica* 52 (1984), 1241–1270.

Fuller, W. A., *Introduction to Statistical Time Series* (New York: Wiley, 1976).

Hamilton, J. D. and M. A. Flavin, "On the Limitations of Government Borrowing: A Framework for Empirical Testing," *American Economic Review* 76 (1986), 808–819.

Harvey, A. C., "Trends and Cycles in Macroeconomic Time Series," *Journal of Business and Economic Statistics* 3 (1985), 216–227.

King, R. G. nd C. I. Plosser, "Money, Credit, and Prices in a Real Business Cycle," *American Economic Review* 74 (1984), 363–380.

Kydland, F. and E. C. Prescott, "A Competitive Theory of Fluctuations and the Feasibility and Desirability of Stabilization Policy," in S. Fischer, ed., *Rational Expectations and Economic Policy* (Chicago: University of Chicago, 1980), 169–189.

Mankiw, N. G. and M. D. Shapiro, "Trends, Random Walks, and Tests of the Permanent Income Hypothesis," *Journal of Monetary Economics* 16 (1985), 165–174.

Meese, R. A. and K. J. Singleton, "On Unit Roots and the Empirical Modeling of Exchange Rates," *Journal of Finance* 37 (1982), 1029–1035.

Nelson, C. R. and C. I. Plosser, "Trends and Random Walks in Macroeconomic Time Series: Some Evidence and Implications," *Journal of Monetary Economics* 10 (1982), 139–162.

Orcutt, G. H. and H. S. Winokur, "First Order Autoregression: Inference, Estimation, and Prediction," *Econometrica* 37 (1969), 1–14.

Phillips, P. C. B., "Time Series Regression With a Unit Root," *Econometrica* 55 (1987), 277–301.

―― and P. Perron, "Testing for a Unit Root in Time Series Regression," *Biometrika* 75 (1988), 335–346.

Poterba, J. and L. Summers, "The Persistence of Volatility and Stock Market Fluctuations," *American Economic Review* 76 (1987), 1142–1151.

Rudebusch, G. D., "The Uncertain Unit Root in Real GNP," *American Economic Review* (forthcoming 1993).

Said, S. E. and D. A. Dickey, "Testing for Unit Roots in Autoregressive-Moving Average Models of Unknown Order," *Biometrika* 71 (1984), 599–607.

Schwert, G. W., "Tests for Unit Roots: A Monte Carlo Investigation," *Journal of Business and Economic Statistics* 7 (1989), 147–159.

Schmidt, P., "Dickey-Fuller Tests with Drift," in T. B. Fomby and G. F. Rhodes, eds., *Advances in Econometrics: Co-Integration, Spurious Regressions, and Unit Roots* (Greenwich: JAI Press, 1990).

Shapiro, M. and M. Watson, "Sources of Business Cycle Fluctuations," *NBER Macroeconomics Annual* 3 (1988), 111–156.

Stine, R. A. and P. Shaman, "A Fixed Point Characterization for Bias of Autoregressive Estimators," *Annals of Statistics* 17 (1989), 1275–1284.

Stock, J. H. and M. W. Watson, "Interpreting the Evidence on Money-Income Causality," *Journal of Econometrics* 40 (1989), 161–181.

West, K., "A Note on the Power of Least Squares Tests for a Unit Root," *Economics Letters* 24 (1987), 249–252.

――, "On the Interpretation of Near Random-Walk Behavior in GNP," *American Economic Review* 78 (1988), 202–209.

9

The Uncertain Unit Root in Real GNP

GLENN D. RUDEBUSCH*

THE IMPULSE and propagation mechanisms of business cycles have long been debated; however, until recently, economists were in fairly broad agreement that business fluctuations could be studied separately from the secular growth of the economy. This separation was justified because, to a first approximation, the factors underlying trend growth were assumed to be stable at business-cycle frequencies. Indeed, the common practice of macroeconomists of all theoretical persuasions was to model movements in real GNP as stationary fluctuations around a linear deterministic trend (e.g., Finn Kydland and Edward C. Prescott, 1980; Olivier J. Blanchard, 1981). Such a trend-stationary (TS) model of real GNP was the canonical empirical representation of aggregate output until the early 1980's.

In contrast to previous work, much of the research of the last ten years has assumed a unit root in the autoregressive representation of real GNP, which is inconsistent with a TS model of output. A model with a unit root, commonly termed a "difference-stationary" (DS) model, implies that any stochastic shock to output contains an element that represents a permanent shift in the level of the series. If real GNP is best represented by a DS model, the traditional separation between business cycles and trend growth is incorrect. In the usual empirical versions of the DS model estimated for real GNP, output behaves more like a random walk than like transitory deviations from a steadily growing trend (e.g., John Y. Campbell and N. Gregory Mankiw, 1987; Peter K. Clark, 1987). The long-run trend of these DS representations is not fixed, as in a TS model, but stochastic; indeed, in the typical DS model, almost all fluctuations in output represent permanent shifts in trend rather than transitory movements in cycle. From another perspective, the essential difference between the two models can be found in the persistence of their dynamic responses to random shocks. In the DS

* I thank two anonymous referees for comments as well as Bill Bell, Frank Diebold, Steve Durlauf, Spence Krane, Doug Steigerwald, and David Wilcox. Michelle Phillips and Roberto Sella provided research assistance.

model of output, the effect of a shock persists forever because the disturbance changes the trend component and thus affects the level of output in all future periods. In contrast, the impact of a shock in the TS model is transitory and is eliminated quite quickly as output reverts to its steady trend.

The widespread acceptance of a DS model for aggregate output was based on evidence that the hypothesis of a unit root in real GNP could not be rejected.[1] Although this evidence was extremely robust across various data samples and unit-root testing procedures (see, e.g., Charles R. Nelson and Charles I. Plosser, 1982; René M. Stulz and Walter Wasserfallen, 1985; James H. Stock and Mark W. Watson, 1986; Pierre Perron and Peter C. B. Phillips, 1987; Perron, 1988; George W. Evans, 1989), the distinct contrast between traditional TS models of output and recent DS models led many researchers to challenge the unit-root tests. In particular, some questioned the power of these tests, that is, their ability to reject the unit-root null hypothesis when it is indeed false.[2] However, the indictment of low power against unit-root tests has not been a decisive criticism. The fact that unit-root tests may have low power against certain TS alternatives does not *necessarily* compromise the results from those tests. It would not be at all surprising if unit-root tests had little power against TS alternatives that mimicked a DS model and reverted to trend extremely slowly; all statistical tests have low power against alternatives that are "local" to the null. The failure to reject near-unit-root TS alternatives is of little economic importance, however, because these alternatives are indistinguishable in economic terms from the DS null over the time horizons of practical macroeconomic interest (say, shorter than 10 years). Critics of unit-root tests must instead make the stronger claim that unit-root tests have low power against plausible TS alternatives that display substantially different macroeconomic behavior than a plausible DS null model. Simple power studies are not well suited to answering this question.

This note addresses the argument that unit-root tests have low power only against local alternatives. The goal is to select the most plausible DS and TS representations for output, determine whether these representations have different short-run persistence properties, and then examine whether unit-root tests can distinguish between these models.

---

[1] This acceptance was not generally shared by government and business economists. For example, the official series on potential output, which is used in policy and budget deliberations, has remained a smooth nonstochastic trend.

[2] Among many others, Bennett T. McCallum (1986), Francis X. Diebold and Rudebusch (1991), and David N. DeJong et al. (1992) have warned of the low power of unit-root tests. Other challenges have been made by DeJong and Whiteman (1991) from a Bayesian perspective and by Perron (1989) in a framework with structural breaks.

In the next section, I examine the ordinary least-squares (OLS) estimates of a TS model and a DS model for the postwar sample of real GNP. These models are plausible representations of the data generating process and yet imply very different economic dynamics at the horizons of economic relevance. In Section 2, I examine simulated data from these models and show that a unit-root test cannot distinguish between these particular TS and DS representations. Thus, the unit-root test has low power against a plausible TS model that is *not* local in economic terms to a plausible DS model. Section 3 extends the basic argument to account for small-sample bias in the estimated model coefficients.

1. DS and TS Models of Real GNP

Two obvious candidates for plausible TS and DS representations of the data generating process for real GNP are simply the OLS estimates of these models from the available data sample. The data consist of quarterly observations on U.S. postwar log real GNP per capita (denoted Y_t) from 1948:3 to 1988:4. Assuming second-order dependence,[3] the sample OLS estimate of the TS model of aggregate output with a linear deterministic trend is

$$Y_t = -0.321 + 0.00030t + 1.335Y_{t-1} \tag{1}$$
$$(0.109) \quad (0.00010) \quad (0.073)$$

$$-0.401Y_{t-2} + u_t \qquad \hat{\sigma}_u = 0.01013$$
$$(0.073)$$

(standard errors of the coefficients appear in parentheses).[4] I will refer to this specific model estimate for the sample as the TS_{OLS} model.

Under the assumption of a unit root, the DS model for this data sample is estimated in first differences as

$$\Delta Y_t = 0.003 + 0.369\Delta Y_{t-1} + \hat{v}_t \qquad \hat{\sigma}_t = 0.01035 \tag{2}$$
$$(0.001) \quad (0.074)$$

This particular sample DS model will be denoted as the DS_{OLS} model.

---

[3] The analysis was repeated assuming that the order of the model was four, six, and eight. Similar persistence and power results were obtained.
[4] The last two quarters of 1948 were used as fixed initial conditions.

The estimated models (1) and (2) both appear to fit real GNP per capita fairly well; the standard deviations of their residuals are quite close, and plots of the residuals suggest no obvious outliers. In addition, Q statistics computed from the fitted residuals provide little evidence against the null hypothesis of no serial correlation at a variety of lags.

However, the estimated TS_{OLS} and DS_{OLS} models have very different implications for the persistence of the dynamic response of output to a random disturbance. To measure this persistence, consider the moving-average representation for the first difference of output implied by a TS or DS model:

$$\Delta Y_t = k + \varepsilon_t + a_1 \varepsilon_{t-1} + a_2 \varepsilon_{t-2} + \cdots \qquad (3)$$

where k is some constant and ε_t is the innovation of the model. In this form, the sum of the a_i's measures the model response to a unit innovation.[5] A unit shock in period t affects ΔY_{t+h} by a_h and affects Y_{t+h} by $c_h \equiv 1 + a_1 + \cdots + a_h$. Thus, for various horizons, the cumulative response c_h answers the question: how does a shock today affect the level of real output in the short, medium, and long run? With quarterly data, for example, c_{20} measures the impact of a shock today on Y_t five years hence.

In the limit, the effect of a unit shock today on the level of output infinitely far in the future is given by c_∞. For any TS series, $c_\infty = 0$, because the effect of any shock is eliminated as reversion to the deterministic trend eventually dominates. For a DS series, $c_\infty \neq 0$; that is, each shock has some permanent effect. However, the impulse response of real output at an infinite horizon is of no practical economic significance; indeed, horizons of less than 10 years are usually of greatest interest. At these short horizons, the dynamic responses of TS and DS models may be quite similar or quite different depending on the values taken by the parameters of the models. Thus, the presence of a unit root determines whether c_∞ is positive or zero, but it does not determine all of the model properties of economic interest. It is in this sense that, as noted in the introduction, focusing solely on the existence of unit roots and on the power of unit-root tests against arbitrary TS alternatives is insufficient. What is of economic relevance is the ability of unit-root tests to recognize when data have been generated from TS models that differ substantially from the DS model at short horizons (i.e., the ability to identify economically nonlocal alternatives). Conse-

---

[5] This measure of persistence is described further in Campbell and Mankiw (1987) and Diebold and Rudebusch (1989).

TABLE 9.1
Cumulative Impulse Responses of OLS Models

Model	Horizon (quarters)								
	1	*2*	*4*	*8*	*12*	*16*	*20*	*30*	*40*
DS_{OLS}	1.37	1.51	1.57	1.59	1.59	1.59	1.59	1.59	1.59
	(0.07)	(0.13)	(0.17)	(0.19)	(0.19)	(0.19)	(0.19)	(0.19)	(0.19)
TS_{OLS}	1.33	1.38	1.19	0.73	0.43	0.25	0.15	0.04	0.01
	(0.07)	(0.13)	(0.18)	(0.23)	(0.23)	(0.20)	(0.15)	(0.07)	(0.02)

Note: Standard errors are given in parentheses.

quently, a comparison of the persistence properties of the estimated TS_{OLS} and DS_{OLS} models at relevant horizons is required.

The estimated model responses are shown in Table 9.1, with standard errors in parentheses.[6] The impulse response of the DS_{OLS} model implies not only shock persistence but shock magnification. The effect of an innovation is not reversed through time, and it eventually increases the level of real GNP by more than one and a half times the size of the innovation ($c_{20} = 1.59$). In contrast, the TS model exhibits fairly rapid reversion to trend, with 85 percent of a shock dissipated after five years ($c_{20} = 0.15$). Thus, the cumulative impulse responses of these two models, each estimated from the same data sample, imply very different economic dynamics at cyclical frequencies. Because the TS_{OLS} and DS_{OLS} models of aggregate output have such different persistence properties, it would be useful to have a test capable of distinguishing between them. The next section explores the ability of one commonly used unit-root test to accomplish this task.

2. Application of a Unit-Root Test

The augmented Dickey-Fuller unit-root test (David A. Dickey and Wayne F. Fuller, 1981) is often used to try to distinguish a TS model

---

[6] These standard errors are calculated as follows. Let the cumulative impulse response at horizon h be given by $c_h = F(\rho_1, \ldots, \rho_k)$, and let $\mathbf{f}$ denote the vector of partials of F with respect to the parameters; then, the standard error equals $\sqrt{\mathbf{f}'\Sigma\mathbf{f}}$, where Σ is the estimated variance-covariance matrix of the autoregressive parameters. The standard errors account for parameter uncertainty but not for unit-root uncertainty.

from a DS model.[7] For the second-order models under consideration, the augmented Dickey-Fuller regression takes the following form:

$$Y_t = \hat{\mu} + \hat{\gamma}t + \hat{\delta}Y_{t-1} + \hat{\phi}_1\Delta Y_{t-1} + \hat{\varepsilon}_t. \tag{4}$$

Under the unit-root (or DS model) null hypothesis, $\delta = 1$; thus, the Dickey-Fuller test statistic is simply the t test, $\hat{\tau} \equiv (\hat{\delta} - 1)/\mathrm{SE}(\hat{\delta})$, where $\mathrm{SE}(\hat{\delta})$ is the standard error of the estimated coefficient.

For the postwar real GNP data under consideration, the sample value of the Dickey-Fuller test, which is denoted as $\hat{\tau}_{\mathrm{samp}}$, is equal to -2.98. However, this statistic does not have the usual Student-t distribution, but is skewed toward negative values. At the 10-percent significance level, Dickey and Fuller (1981) calculate the appropriate asymptotic critical value to be -3.12. Thus, the evidence from this sample, in accordance with the findings of previous researchers, suggests that the DS model for real GNP cannot be rejected at even the 10-percent level.

However, the critical values provided by Dickey and Fuller (1981) for their augmented test are only valid asymptotically. In finite samples, the distribution of $\hat{\tau}$ will usually depend on the sample size and nuisance-parameter values (see, e.g., Gene Evans and Savin, 1984). These factors can be taken into account by examining simulated data from the $\mathrm{DS}_{\mathrm{OLS}}$ model and calculating the exact probability of obtaining the sample value of the test statistic from this particular null model. This ensures correct size for the test. More importantly, however, by simulating the $\mathrm{TS}_{\mathrm{OLS}}$ model, the exact probability of obtaining $\hat{\tau}_{\mathrm{samp}}$ from this particular alternative model can also be obtained. This allows correct assessment of test power against what is arguably one of the most interesting alternatives.

The test-statistic probability distributions conditional on the OLS models are exhibited in Figure 9.1. The distribution of $\hat{\tau}$ conditional on the $\mathrm{DS}_{\mathrm{OLS}}$ model is denoted $f_{\mathrm{DS}}(\hat{\tau})$, while the distribution of $\hat{\tau}$ conditional on the $\mathrm{TS}_{\mathrm{OLS}}$ model is denoted $f_{\mathrm{TS}}(\hat{\tau})$. Each distribution is formed from 10,000 realizations of the test statistic calculated from 10,000 simulated data samples generated from the particular model.[8]

---

[7] Similar results to those below were also obtained with the Dickey-Fuller normalized-bias and likelihood-ratio tests, as well as with the generalized Phillips test (Phillips and Perron, 1988).

[8] The samples are generated with normal independently and identically distributed errors with sample size and initial conditions that matched those in equations (1) and (2).

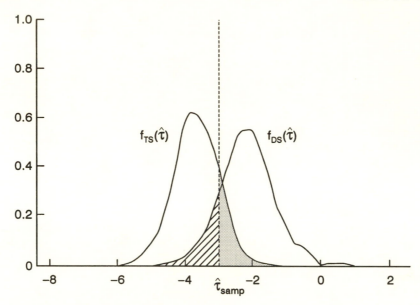

Fig. 9.1. Empirical densities of $\hat{\tau}$ from DS_{OLS} and TS_{OLS} models.

The actual sample value of the test statistic ($\hat{\tau}_{samp} = -2.98$) is shown as a vertical dotted line.

There are two areas in Figure 9.1 of special interest. The hatched area under $f_{DS}(\hat{\tau})$ and to the left of $\hat{\tau}_{samp}$ represents the probability of obtaining a value of the t test equal to or smaller than -2.98, conditional on the DS model of equation (2). This p value, is denoted as

$$DS_{OLS} \ p \text{ value} \equiv \text{prob}(\hat{\tau} \leq \hat{\tau}_{samp} \mid DS_{OLS} \text{ model})$$

and represents the marginal significance level for rejection of the null hypothesis for the DS_{OLS} model. This probability equals 0.15; that is, given the sample test statistic, one could not reject the DS model at anything less than the 15-percent level in a classical hypothesis test. This is consistent with the usual inability to reject the DS model for real GNP at conventional significance levels.

The other area of interest is the shaded region under $f_{TS}(\hat{\tau})$ and to the right of $\hat{\tau}_{samp}$. This area represents the probability of obtaining a value of the t test equal to or greater than -2.98, conditional on the TS model of equation (1). This probability is denoted as

$$TS_{OLS} \ p \text{ value} \equiv \text{prob}(\hat{\tau} \geq \hat{\tau}_{samp} \mid TS_{OLS} \text{ model}).$$

For real GNP, the TS_{OLS} p value is 0.22, so one would not be able to reject the estimated TS_{OLS} model at even the 20-percent significance level.[9]

In short, the sample statistic for the augmented Dickey-Fuller test does not provide strong evidence against either the estimated DS_{OLS} model or the TS_{OLS} model for real GNP. Earlier papers that are unable to reject a unit root in output provide only one side of the relevant evidence for inference regarding the DS model. The other side, namely, the inability to reject a plausible TS model that exhibits transitory cyclical dynamics of a traditional nature, is at least as convincing.

3. Unbiased DS and TS Models

At first glance, the DS_{OLS} and TS_{OLS} models might appear to be the most plausible candidates for DS and TS representations of the data generating process of real GNP. However, although the OLS estimates of these autoregressive models are consistent and asymptotically normal, they are biased in small samples because the presence of lagged dependent variables violates the assumption of nonstochastic regressors in the classical linear regression model. This bias is easy to illustrate for the OLS estimate of the autoregressive parameter of an AR(1) process,

$$x_t = \mu + \gamma t + \rho_1 x_{t-1} + \varepsilon_t. \tag{5}$$

Based on 10,000 samples of size 160 generated from equation (5), Table 9.2 provides the mean value of the OLS estimate, $\hat{\rho}_1$, as well as the proportion of estimates that are less than the true value of ρ_1.[10] For example, if the true ρ_1 is equal to 0.95, the mean OLS estimate is 0.90, and 89 percent of the estimates are less than 0.95. The size of the autoregressive parameter bias that pushes the average OLS estimate below its true value varies with the value of the true parameter, but it is most severe for near-unit-root models (i.e., those with ρ close to 1.0).

A significant bias in the OLS sample estimates is potentially a serious shortcoming of the simulation methodology pursued in the previous two sections. In particular, the estimation bias implies that the sample OLS models used above probably understate the actual amount of persistence in real output. Suppose, for example, that an AR(1) TS representation like equation (5) was fit to real output, and the resulting OLS

---

[9] An equivalent statement of this result is that the $\hat{\tau}$ test at the 15-percent significance level has power against the TS_{OLS} alternative of only 78 percent.

[10] Table 9.2 is generated with $\mu = \gamma = x_0 = 0$ and disturbances drawn from a standard normal distribution.

TABLE 9.2
Properties of the OLS Estimate of an AR(1) Model

Statistic	ρ_1						
	0.40	0.60	0.80	0.85	0.90	0.95	1.00
$E(\hat{\rho}_1)$	0.38	0.57	0.76	0.81	0.86	0.90	0.94
prob($\hat{\rho}_1 < \rho_1$)	0.61	0.65	0.72	0.76	0.81	0.89	0.99

Note: Each column is based on 10,000 samples (each with 160 observations) drawn from an AR(1) with an autoregressive coefficient equal to ρ_1.

sample estimate $\hat{\rho}_1$ was equal to 0.90; consequently, the associated estimate of the 10-period cumulative impulse response, $\hat{c}_{10}$, would be 0.34. Assuming that the OLS estimate was equal to its mean, $E(\hat{\rho}_1)$, then the true parameter would be 0.95, and the actual value of c_{10} would be 0.60. Thus, in this case, the OLS sample estimate, on average, understates the amount of persistence.

Arguably, more plausible candidates than the TS_{OLS} and DS_{OLS} models for the data-generating process would correct the parameters for small-sample bias.[11] First-order approximate bias corrections can be calculated for both the TS and DS models quite easily. The bias of the DS_{OLS} model, which is an AR(1) model with an unknown drift parameter, is treated in F. H. C. Marriott and J. A. Pope (1954). They show that, ignoring second-order terms, the expected value of the OLS estimate $\hat{\rho}_1$ is given by

$$E(\hat{\rho}_1) = \rho_1 - (1 + 3\rho_1)/T \tag{6}$$

where T is the sample size. Substituting the sample OLS estimate for its expected value provides a bias-corrected estimator

$$\tilde{\rho}_1 = (T\hat{\rho}_1 + 1)/(T - 3). \tag{7}$$

Note that, to a first-order approximation, this estimator is unbiased:[12]

$$E(\tilde{\rho}_1) = \rho_1.$$

---

[11] In this paper, I consider approximate mean-unbiased estimators of the TS and DS models. In Rudebusch (1992), I examine median-unbiased estimators obtained through repeated simulations, a procedure which would lead to qualitatively similar results if applied to the data set in this paper.

[12] Of course, reduced bias does not necessarily ensure that $\tilde{\rho}_1$ is a better estimator. However, Guy H. Orcutt and Herbert S. Winokur (1969) explore the properties of this estimator through simulations and find that it often has a smaller mean squared error than the OLS estimator. Theoretical results on this issue are provided in Hong-Ching Zhang (1989).

Applying (7) to the DS_{OLS} model for postwar real GNP given in (2), where $\hat{\rho}_1 = 0.369$, I calculate the autoregressive coefficient of the bias-corrected DS model (denoted as the DS_{BC} model) to be $\tilde{\rho}_1 = 0.383$.

Similarly, for the TS_{OLS} model, which is an AR(2) with linear trend, the (first-order) bias in the estimated parameters can be determined using the results in Robert A. Stine and Paul Shaman (1989). Correcting for bias gives a TS_{BC} model with autoregressive coefficients:

$$\tilde{\rho}_1 = (T\hat{\rho}_1 + 2 + 2\tilde{\rho}_2)/(T - 1) \tag{8}$$

for the one-period lag, and

$$\tilde{\rho}_2 = (T\hat{\rho}_2 + 3)/(T - 5) \tag{9}$$

for the two-period lag. For postwar real GNP, the TS_{BC} model has autoregressive coefficients $\tilde{\rho}_1 = 1.351$ and $\tilde{\rho}_2 = -0.395$.

The bias-corrected DS_{BC} and TS_{BC} models both display somewhat greater persistence than the DS_{OLS} and TS_{OLS} models. The bias correction embodied in the DS_{BC} model is in the same direction and of the same magnitude as the one suggested by Table 9.2. In particular, because the root of the associated lag-operator polynomial is so far from the unit circle, the bias of the DS_{OLS} model is quite modest.[13] For the second-order TS_{OLS} and TS_{BC} models, a useful metric with which to judge their closeness to a nonstationary model is simply the sum of the autoregressive coefficients (see, e.g., Phillips, 1991). The sum of the OLS estimates $\hat{\rho}_1$ and $\hat{\rho}_2$ equals 0.933, while the sum of the bias-corrected coefficients $\tilde{\rho}_1$ and $\tilde{\rho}_2$ equals 0.955—a clear, though somewhat small, shift toward nonstationarity.[14]

More specifically, the implications of the bias correction for judging the persistence of real GNP are given in Table 9.3, which contrasts the impulse responses of the DS_{BC} and TS_{BC} models. The impulse response of the DS_{BC} model implies a shock persistence that is virtually indistinguishable from that of the DS_{OLS} model, which is not surprising given the trivial size of the coefficient bias. Moreover, the TS_{BC} model

[13] The bias in the DS_{OLS} model is even smaller than the one in Table 9.2 because a linear trend is not estimated. With a linear trend, as in Table 9.2, the bias is given by $E(\hat{\rho}_1) - \rho_1 = -(2 + 4\rho_1)/T$.

[14] The bias correction in the AR(2) TS model may appear to be surprisingly small in light of the large biases shown for the AR(1) model in Table 9.2. However, as noted by Stine and Shaman (1989), the results for the AR(1) model do not generalize to higher-order models. Indeed, there are cases in which the bias (to a first-order approximation) moves the roots of the lag-operator polynomial *closer* to the unit circle.

TABLE 9.3

Cumulative Impulse Responses of Bias-Corrected Models

Model	Horizon (quarters)								
	1	*2*	*4*	*8*	*12*	*16*	*20*	*30*	*40*
DS_{BC}	1.38	1.53	1.61	1.62	1.62	1.62	1.62	1.62	1.62
TS_{BC}	1.35	1.43	1.32	0.97	0.70	0.51	0.37	0.16	0.07

exhibits reversion to trend only slightly less rapid than that of the TS_{OLS} model. For the TS_{BC} model, almost two-thirds of a shock is dissipated after five years ($c_{20} = 0.37$). Most importantly, it remains true that the DS_{BC} and TS_{BC} candidates for plausible representations of aggregate output have quite different implications about dynamic responses over fairly short horizons.

As a final step, one can ask whether the augmented Dickey-Fuller test can distinguish between these two models. Based on 10,000 samples generated from the DS_{BC} model,[15] I obtain the probability of the sample test statistic as

$$DS_{BC} \ p \ \text{value} \equiv \text{prob}\big(\hat{\tau} \leq \hat{\tau}_{\text{samp}} \mid DS_{BC} \ \text{model}\big) = 0.15.$$

In contrast, the probability of the test statistic under the bias-corrected alternative model is

$$TS_{BC} \ p \ \text{value} \equiv \text{prob}\big(\hat{\tau} \geq \hat{\tau}_{\text{samp}} \mid TS_{BC} \ \text{model}\big) = 0.24.$$

These probabilities provide further confirmation of the inability of unit-root tests to identify plausible TS alternative models for real output that display low persistence. In sum, the biases present in the OLS estimates are not substantial enough to change the conclusions from Sections 1 and 2.

4. Conclusion

Based on the usual unit-root tests, little can be said about the relative likelihood of the specific DS and TS models of real GNP given above. In particular, plausible TS alternatives that fit the data cannot be detected because of low test power. The appropriate conclusion from unit-root tests on this data sample is that the existence of a unit root is uncertain.

---

[15] The OLS estimates of the trend and intercept are used in generating data.

Furthermore, the unit-root tests employed display low power against plausible TS models that display quite different economic behavior than a plausible DS null model. If the TS models described above correctly portray the persistence of real GNP, then the DS model does not provide a good approximation of the dynamic response of output at even short-run cyclical horizons of, say, five years.

In light of the impulse responses of the TS models, the *appropriate* confidence intervals for estimates of short-term or medium-term persistence are much larger than ones given conditional on the existence of a unit root. This suggests the importance of measuring the confidence intervals for estimates of persistence without conditioning on the TS or DS model. In Diebold and Rudebusch (1989), approximate estimates of such intervals are obtained by using a model of fractional integration that nests the TS and DS models. Stock (1991) also provides a step in this direction by obtaining confidence intervals for the largest autoregressive root.

In sum, the evidence in this paper and in other recent work, notably Lawrence J. Christiano and Martin Eichenbaum (1990), suggests that a new consensus should be formed that stresses the uncertainty about the existence of a unit root in real output and the uncertainty about the amount of persistence of macroeconomic shocks.

References

Blanchard, Olivier J., "What is Left of the Multiplier Accelerator?" *American Economic Review*, May 1981 (*Papers and Proceedings*), 71, 150–4.

Campbell, John Y. and Mankiw, N. Gregory, "Are Output Fluctuations Transitory?" *Quarterly Journal of Economics*, November 1987, 102, 857–80.

Christiano, Lawrence J. and Eichenbaum, Martin, "Unit Roots in Real GNP: Do We Know, and Do We Care?" *Carnegie-Rochester Conference Series on Public Policy*, Spring 1990, 32, 7–62.

Clark, Peter K., "The Cyclical Component of U.S. Economic Activity," *Quarterly Journal of Economics*, November 1987, 102, 797–814.

DeJong, David N., Nankervis, John C., Savin, N. E. and Whiteman, Charles H., "Integration versus Trend Stationarity in Time Series," *Econometrica*, March 1992, 60, 423–33.

—— and Whiteman, Charles H., "Reconsidering 'Trends and Random Walks in Macroeconomic Time Series'," *Journal of Monetary Economics*, October 1991, 28, 221–54.

Dickey, David A. and Fuller, Wayne F., "Likelihood Ratio Statistics for Autoregressive Time Series with a Unit Root," *Econometrica*, July 1981, 49, 1057–72.

Diebold, Francis X. and Rudebusch, Glenn D., "Long Memory and Persistence in Aggregate Output," *Journal of Monetary Economics*, September 1989, 24, 189–209.

—— and ——, "On the Power of Dickey-Fuller Tests Against Fractional Alternatives," *Economics Letters*, 1991, 35 (2), 155–60.

Evans, Gene and Savin, N. E., "Testing for Unit Roots II," *Econometrica* September 1984, 52, 1241–70.

Evans, George W., "Output and Unemployment Dynamics in the United States: 1950–1985," *Journal of Applied Econometrics*, July–September 1989, 4, 213–37.

Kydland, Finn and Prescott, Edward C., "A Competitive Theory of Fluctuations and the Feasibility and Desirability of Stabilization Policy," in Stanley Fischer, ed., *Rational Expectations and Economic Policy*, Chicago: University of Chicago Press, 1980, pp. 169–89.

Marriott, F. H. C. and Pope, J. A., "Bias in the Estimation of Autocorrelations," *Biometrika*, December 1954, 41, 393–403.

McCallum, Bennett T., "On 'Real' and 'Sticky-Price' Theories of the Business Cycle," *Journal of Money, Credit, and Banking*, November 1986, 18, 397–414.

Nelson, Charles R. and Plosser, Charles I., "Trends and Random Walks in Macroeconomic Time Series: Some Evidence and Implications," *Journal of Monetary Economics*, September 1982, 10, 139–62.

Orcutt, Guy H. and Winokur, Herbert S., "First Order Autoregression: Inference, Estimation, and Prediction," *Econometrica*, January 1969, 37, 1–14.

Perron, Pierre, "Trends and Random Walks in Macroeconomic Time Series: Further Evidence from a New Approach," *Journal of Economic Dynamics and Control*, June/September 1988, 12, 297–332.

——, "The Great Crash, the Oil Price Shock, and the Unit Root Hypothesis," *Econometrica*, November 1989, 57, 1361–1402.

—— and Phillips, Peter C. B., "Does GNP Have a Unit Root? A Re-evaluation," *Economics Letters*, 1987, 23 (2), 139–45.

Phillips, Peter C. B., "Bayesian Routes and Unit Roots: De Rebus Prioribus Semper Est Disputandum," *Journal of Applied Econometrics*, October–December 1991, 6, 435–73.

—— and Perron, Pierre, "Testing for a Unit Root in Time Series Regression," *Biometrika*, 1988, 75 (2), 335–46.

Rudebusch, Glenn D., "Trends and Random Walks in Macroeconomic Time Series: A Re-examination," *International Economic Review*, August 1992, 33, 661–80.

Stine, Robert A. and Shaman, Paul, "A Fixed Point Characterization for Bias of Autoregressive Estimators," *Annals of Statistics*, 1989, 17 (3), 1275–84.

Stock, James H., "Confidence Intervals for the Largest Autoregressive Root in U.S. Macroeconomic Time Series," *Journal of Monetary Economics*, November 1991, 28, 435–59.

—— and Watson, Mark W., "Does GNP Have a Unit Root?" *Economics Letters*, 1986, 22 (2), 147–51.

Stulz, René M. and Wasserfallen, Walter, "Macroeconomic Time-Series, Business Cycles, and Macroeconomic Policies," *Carnegie-Rochester Conference Series on Public Policy*, Spring 1985, 22, 9–54.

Zhang, Hong-Ching, "Reduction of the Asymptotic Bias of Estimators of Parameters in the Autoregressive and Linear Trend Models," Ph.D. dissertation, Department of Statistics, University of Pennsylvania, 1989.

10

The Uncertain Unit Root in Real GNP: Comment

FRANCIS X. DIEBOLD AND ABDELHAK S. SENHADJI*

FIFTEEN YEARS after the seminal work of Charles R. Nelson and Charles I. Plosser (1982), the question of deterministic vs. stochastic trend in U.S. GNP (and other key aggregates) remains open. The surrounding controversy certainly is not due to lack of professional interest—the literature on the question is huge. Instead, the low power of tests of stochastic trend (or "difference stationarity" in the parlance of John H. Cochrane [1988]) against nearby deterministic-trend ("trend-stationary") alternatives, together with the fact that such nearby alternatives are the relevant ones, explains the lack of consensus.

In an important paper, Glenn D. Rudebusch (1993) contributes to the "we don't know" literature initiated by Lawrence J. Christiano and Martin Eichenbaum (1990) by arguing that unit-root tests applied to U.S. quarterly real GNP per capita lack power even against *distant* alternatives. First, Rudebusch shows that the best-fitting trend-stationary and difference-stationary models imply very different medium- and long-run dynamics. Then he shows with an innovative procedure that, regardless of which of the two models obtains, the exact finite-sample distributions of the Dickey-Fuller test statistics are very similar. Thus, Rudebusch concludes that unit-root tests are unlikely to be capable of discriminating between deterministic and stochastic trends.

The distinction between trend stationarity and difference stationarity is not critical in some contexts. Often, for example, one wants a broad gauge of the persistence in aggregate output dynamics, in which case one may be better informed by an interval estimate of the dominant root in an autoregressive approximation. Hence the importance of James H. Stock's (1991) clever procedure for computing such intervals. But the distinction between trend stationarity and difference stationarity is potentially important in other contexts, such as economic forecast-

*For constructive and insightful comments, we thank Craig Hakkio, Andy Postlewaite, Glenn Rudebusch, Chuck Whiteman, and two referees, as well as numerous seminar participants, but all errors remain ours alone. We gratefully acknowledge support from the National Science Foundation, the Sloan Foundation, and the University of Pennsylvania Research Foundation.

ing, because the trend- and difference-stationary models may imply very different dynamics and hence different point forecasts, as argued by Stock and Mark W. Watson (1988) and John Y. Campbell and Pierre Perron (1991).

Motivated by the potential importance of unit roots for the forecasting of aggregate output, as well as other considerations that we discuss later, we extend Rudebusch's (1993) analysis to several long spans of annual U.S. real GNP data, and we examine the robustness of all results to variations in the sample period and the particular GNP measure employed. As we shall show, the outcome is both surprising and robust.

1. Construction of Annual U.S. Real GNP Series, 1869–1993

Three annual "raw" data series underlie the annual series used in this paper. We create the first two, which are real GNP series, by splicing the 1869–1929 real GNP series of Nathan S. Balke and Robert J. Gordon (1989) or Christina D. Romer (1989) to the 1929–1993 real GNP series reported in table 1.10 of the National Income and Product Accounts of the United States, measured in billions of 1987 dollars. The two historical real GNP series are measured in billions of 1982 dollars, which we convert to 1987 dollars by multiplying by 1.166, which is the ratio of the 1987 dollar value to the 1982 dollar value in the overlap year 1929, at which time the Balke-Gordon and Romer series are in precise agreement.

The third series is total population residing in the United States (in thousands of people), as reported by the Bureau of the Census. For 1869–1970, we take the data from table A-7 of *Historical Statistics of the United States*. For 1971–1993, we take the data from the Census Bureau's *Current Population Reports*, Series P-25.

From these underlying series we create and use the following:

GNP-BG ("GNP, Balke-Gordon").—Gross national product, pre-1929 values from Balke-Gordon;

GNP-R ("GNP, Romer").—Gross national product, pre-1929 values from Romer;

GNP-BGPC ("GNP, Balke-Gordon, per capita").—Gross national product per capita, pre-1929 values from Balke-Gordon;

GNP-RPC ("GNP, Romer, per capita").—Gross national product per capita, pre-1929 values from Romer.

The post-1929 values of GNP-BG and GNP-R are identical, as are the post-1929 values of GNP-BGPC and GNP-RPC. Pre-1929, the series differ because of the differing assumptions underlying their construction.

As a guide to subsequent specification, we first estimate an extensive battery of conventional Dickey-Fuller regressions,

$$y_t = \hat{\mu} + \hat{\gamma}t + \hat{\delta}y_{t-1} + \sum_{j=1}^{k-1} \hat{\phi}_j \Delta y_{t-j} + \hat{\varepsilon}_t$$

for each of the four real GNP variables discussed above and for $k = 1$ through $k = 6$.[1] A unit root corresponds to $\delta = 1$, and the Dickey-Fuller statistic is $\hat{\tau} = (\hat{\delta} - 1)/\text{SE}(\hat{\delta})$, where $\text{SE}(\hat{\delta})$ is the standard error of the estimated coefficient, $\hat{\delta}$. The common sample period for all variables and for all values of k is 1875–1993. The selected lag order in the Dickey-Fuller regression for all four variables is $k = 2$, regardless of whether we used the Schwarz criterion, the Akaike criterion, or conventional hypothesis-testing procedures to determine k. More precisely, all diagnostics indicate that $k = 1$ is grossly inadequate and that $k > 2$ is unnecessary and therefore wasteful of degrees of freedom. Thus, in terms of a "reasonable range" in which to vary k, we focus throughout the paper on $k = 2$ through $k = 4$, and our attention centers on $k = 2$.

2. Evidence from Rudebusch's Exact Finite-Sample Procedure

We use Rudebusch's (1993) procedure throughout. In Table 10.1 we display the full-sample estimates of the selected trend-stationary and difference-stationary models for each of the four GNP series. For each series, the two models fit equally well, but they imply very different dynamics. This can be seen by comparing the forecasts shown in Figure 10.1, in which we show GNP per capita using Romer's (1989) pre-1929 values (GNP-RPC) for 1869–1933, followed by the forecasts from the best-fitting trend- and difference-stationary models for 1934–1993, made in 1933. The years 1932 and 1933 were years of severe recession, so the forecasts are made from a position well below trend. The forecasts from

---

[1] We gave particular care to the determination of k, the augmentation lag order, because it is well known that the results of unit-root analyses may vary with k. A number of authors have recently addressed this important problem, exploring the properties of various lag-order selection criteria. For example, Alastair Hall (1994) establishes conditions under which the Dickey-Fuller test statistic converges to the Dickey-Fuller distribution when data-based procedures are used to select k, and he verifies that the conditions are satisfied by the popular Schwarz information criterion. Serena Ng and Perron (1995), however, argue that t and F tests on the augmentation lag coefficients in the Dickey-Fuller regression are preferable, because they lead to less size distortion and comparable power.

TABLE 10.1
Estimated Best-Fitting Trend- and Difference-Stationary Models

Data Series	Regressor					
	c	t	$y(-1)$	$y(-2)$	$\Delta y(-1)$	SER
Trend-Stationary (Dependent Variable y)						
GNP-R	0.88	0.58	1.33	−0.51	—	0.043
	(0.18)	(0.12)	(0.08)	(0.08)		
GNP-RPC	−1.07	0.31	1.33	−0.51	—	0.043
	(0.24)	(0.07)	(0.08)	(0.08)		
					—	0.050
GNP-BG	0.90	0.59	1.21	−0.39		
	(0.20)	(0.14)	(0.09)	(0.09)		
GNP-BGPC	−1.14	0.33	1.20	−0.39	—	0.051
	(0.27)	(0.08)	(0.09)	(0.09)		
Difference-Stationary (Dependent Variable Δy)						
					0.43	0.046
ΔGNP-R	0.02	—	—	—	(0.08)	
	(0.01)					
ΔGNP-RPC	0.01	—	—	—	0.42	0.046
	(0.004)				(0.08)	
ΔGNP-BG	0.02	—	—	—	0.30	0.054
	(0.01)				(0.09)	
ΔGNP-BGPC	0.01	—	—	—	0.30	0.054
	(0.01)				(0.09)	

Notes: The regressor c is a constant term, t is a linear trend, and y is the log of Romer's (1989) gross national product (GNP-R), the log of Romer's gross national product per capita (CNP-RPC), the log of Balke and Gordon's (1989) gross national product (GNP-BG), or the log of Balke and Gordon's gross national product per capita (GNP-BGPC). All samples are annual, 1875–1993. Standard errors appear in parentheses. For the trend-stationary models, the trend coefficients and their standard errors have been multiplied by 100. The last column reports the standard error of the regression (SER).

the trend-stationary model revert to trend quickly, in sharp contrast to those from the difference-stationary model, which remain permanently lower.

For each series, we compute the exact finite-sample distribution of $\hat{\tau}$ under the best-fitting difference-stationary model and the best-fitting trend-stationary model, and then we check where the value of $\hat{\tau}$ actually obtained (call it $\hat{\tau}_{\text{sample}}$) lies relative to those distributions. The p values $\Pr[\hat{\tau} \le \hat{\tau}_{\text{sample}} \mid f_{\text{DS}}(\hat{\tau})]$ and $\Pr[\hat{\tau} \le \hat{\tau}_{\text{sample}} \mid f_{\text{TS}}(\hat{\tau})]$, where $f_{\text{DS}}(\hat{\tau})$ is the distribution of $\hat{\tau}$ under the difference-stationary model and $f_{\text{TS}}(\hat{\tau})$ is the distribution of $\hat{\tau}$ under the trend-stationary model, summarize the relevant information. In Table 10.2 we show the p values for $k = 2$

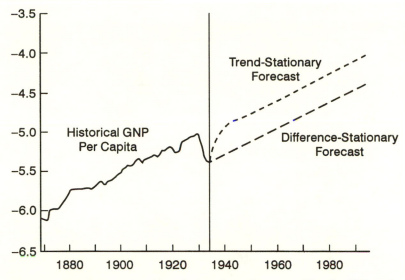

Fig. 10.1. GNP per capita, historical and two forecasts. We plot U.S. real GNP per capita, together with the optimal 1934–1993 forecasts (made in 1933) from the best-fitting trend-stationary model (short-dashed line) and from the best-fitting difference-stationary model (long-dashed line). Pre-1929 GNP data are from Romer (1989).

through $k = 4$. The results provide overwhelming support for the trend-stationary model. For each value of k and each aggregate output measure, the p value associated with $\hat{\tau}$ under the difference-stationary model is very small, while the p value associated with $\hat{\tau}$ under the trend-stationary model is large. In the leading case of $k = 2$, to which all diagnostics point, the p value under the difference-stationary model is consistently less than 0.01, while that under the trend-stationary model is consistently greater than 0.62. To illustrate the starkness of the results, we graph in Figure 10.2 the exact distributions of $\hat{\tau}$ for the best-fitting difference-stationary and trend-stationary models for GNP-RPC with $k = 2$. It is visually obvious that $\hat{\tau}_{sample}$ is tremendously unlikely relative to $f_{DS}(\hat{\tau})$ but very likely with respect to $f_{TS}(\hat{\tau})$.

We check the robustness of our results by varying the starting and ending dates over a wide range. We find no qualitative change in any result. In Figure 10.3, for example, we show the exact finite-sample p values of $\hat{\tau}$ under the best-fitting difference-stationary model for GNP-RPC, computed using the Rudebusch procedure over samples ranging from t_1 through t_T, with $t_1 = 1875, \ldots, 1895$ and $t_T = 1973, \ldots, 1993$. The p value always lies below 0.05 and typically falls well below 0.01.

TABLE 10.2
Exact p Values of the Dickey-Fuller Statistic

	p Value		
Data Series	$k = 2$	$k = 3$	$k = 4$
GNP-R			
$\Pr[\hat{\tau} \leq \hat{\tau}_{\text{sample}} \mid f_{\text{TS}}(\hat{\tau})]$	0.625	0.690	0.592
$\Pr[\hat{\tau} \leq \hat{\tau}_{\text{sample}} \mid f_{\text{DS}}(\hat{\tau})]$	0.001	0.005	0.012
GNP-RPC			
$\Pr[\hat{\tau} \leq \hat{\tau}_{\text{sample}} \mid f_{\text{TS}}(\hat{\tau})]$	0.668	0.673	0.695
$\Pr[\hat{\tau} \leq \hat{\tau}_{\text{sample}} \mid f_{\text{DS}}(\hat{\tau})]$	0.001	0.007	0.017
GNP-BG			
$\Pr[\hat{\tau} \leq \hat{\tau}_{\text{sample}} \mid f_{\text{TS}}(\hat{\tau})]$	0.651	0.616	0.657
$\Pr[\hat{\tau} \leq \hat{\tau}_{\text{sample}} \mid f_{\text{DS}}(\hat{\tau})]$	0.005	0.002	0.020
GNP-BGPC			
$\Pr[\hat{\tau} \leq \hat{\tau}_{\text{sample}} \mid f_{\text{TS}}(\hat{\tau})]$	0.692	0.656	0.711
$\Pr[\hat{\tau} \leq \hat{\tau}_{\text{sample}} \mid f_{\text{DS}}(\hat{\tau})]$	0.006	0.003	0.021

Notes: The Dickey-Fuller statistic is represented by $\hat{\tau}$; $f_{\text{TS}}(\hat{\tau})$ is the empirical distribution of $\hat{\tau}$ conditional on the trend-stationary model, $f_{\text{DS}}(\hat{\tau})$ is the empirical distribution of $\hat{\tau}$ conditional on the difference-stationary model, k is the augmentation lag order in the Dickey-Fuller regression, and $\Pr[\hat{\tau} \leq \hat{\tau}_{\text{sample}} \mid f_{\text{TS}}(\hat{\tau})]$ and $\Pr[\hat{\tau} \leq \hat{\tau}_{\text{sample}} \mid f_{\text{DS}}(\hat{\tau})]$ are the probabilities of obtaining $\hat{\tau} \leq \hat{\tau}_{\text{sample}}$ under the trend-stationary and the difference-stationary models. The variables are the log of Romer's (1989) gross national product (GNP-R), the log of Romer's gross national product per capita (GNP-RPC), the log of Balke and Gordon's (1989) gross national product (GNP-BG), or the log of Balke and Gordon's gross national product per capita (GNP-BGPC). All samples are annual, 1875–1993.

It is of particular interest to examine carefully the robustness to starting date, because the quality of the data deteriorates as one moves backward in time. Thus, in Figure 10.4 we show the exact finite-sample p values of $\hat{\tau}$ under the best-fitting difference-stationary model for each of the four aggregate output measures, computed using the Rudebusch procedure over samples ranging from t_1 through 1993, with $t_1 = 1875, \ldots, 1945$. Again, the p values are typically very small.

Finally, we wish to reconcile our results with those of Nelson and Plosser (1982). In Figure 10.5, we show U.S. real GNP per capita using GNP-RPC, together with a fitted linear trend. Nelson and Plosser use only the shaded subsample, 1909–1970. Two issues are relevant. First, the Nelson-Plosser sample is obviously much shorter than ours, and on that ground alone Nelson and Plosser had less power to detect deviations from difference stationarity. Second, Figure 10.5 makes clear that

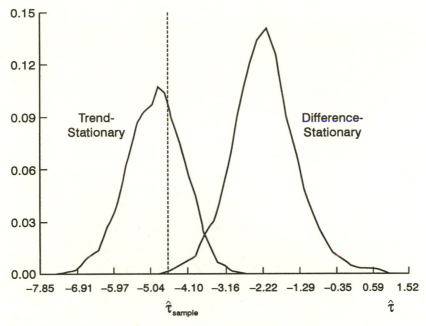

Fig. 10.2. Exact distributions of the Dickey-Fuller statistic. We show exact finite-sample distributions of the Dickey-Fuller statistic under the best-fitting trend-stationary and difference-stationary models for U.S. real GNP per capita. The sample period is 1875–1993. Pre-1929 GNP data are from Romer (1989). The value of the Dickey-Fuller statistic actually obtained is $\hat{\tau}_{\text{sample}}$.

the only prolonged, persistent deviation of output from trend is the Great Depression and the ensuing World War II, which sit squarely in the center of the Nelson-Plosser sample. If we restrict our analysis to the Nelson-Plosser years, we obtain $\hat{\tau} = -3.26$, and we would not reject the difference-stationary model at conventional levels. If we trim 15 years from each end of the Nelson-Plosser sample, using only 1924–1955, we obtain $\hat{\tau} = -2.71$, corresponding to even less evidence against the difference-stationary model. Conversely, as we expand the sample to include years both earlier and later than those used by Nelson and Plosser, the evidence against difference-stationarity grows quickly, because the earlier and later years are highly informative about the question of interest, as output clings tightly to trend. By the time we use the full sample, 1875–1993, we obtain $\hat{\tau} = -4.57$, and we reject difference-stationarity at any reasonable level.

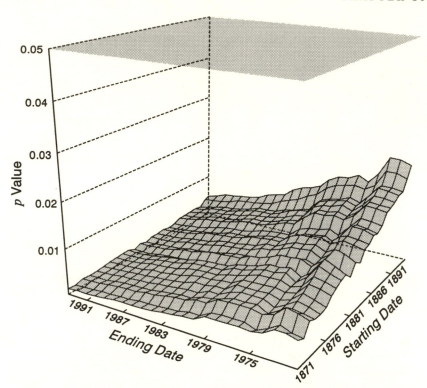

Fig. 10.3. Exact p values of the Dickey-Fuller statistic. We show exact finite-sample p values of the Dickey-Fuller statistic under the best-fitting difference-stationary model for U.S. real GNP per capita. Samples range from t_1 through t_N, with $t_1 = 1875, \ldots, 1895$ and $t_r = 1973, \ldots, 1993$. Pre-1929 GNP data are from Romer (1989). For visual reference, we also show the plane corresponding to $p = 0.05$.

3. Concluding Remarks

There is no doubt that unit-root tests do suffer from low power in many situations of interest. Rudebusch's (1993) analysis of postwar U.S. quarterly GNP illustrates that point starkly. We have shown, however, that Rudebusch's procedure produces evidence that distinctly favors trend-stationarity using long spans of annual data. Moreover, allowing for breaking trend in the spirit of Perron (1989) would only strengthen our results. Thus, the U.S. aggregate output data are not as uninformative as many believe. Interestingly, the same conclusion has been reached by very different methods in the Bayesian literature (e.g., David

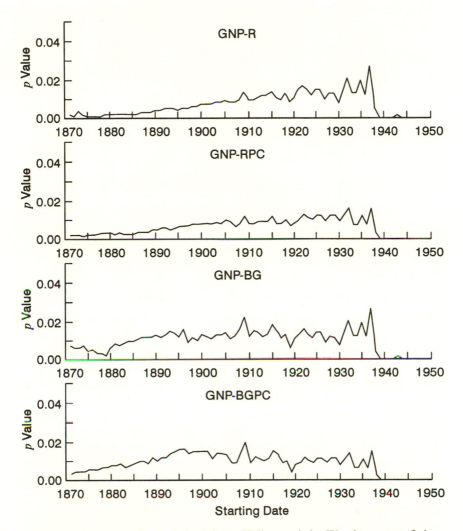

Fig. 10.4. Exact p values of the Dickey-Fuller statistic. We show exact finite-sample p values of the Dickey-Fuller statistic under the best-fitting difference-stationary model for the log of Romer's (1989) gross national product (GNP-R), the log of Romer's gross national product per capita (GNP-RPC), the log of Balke and Gordon's (1989) gross national product (GNP-BG), and the log of Balke and Gordon's gross national product per capita (GNP-BGPC). Samples range from t_1 through 1993, with $t_1 = 1875, \ldots, 1945$. To facilitate comparisons, each subplot is scaled to have a height of 0.05.

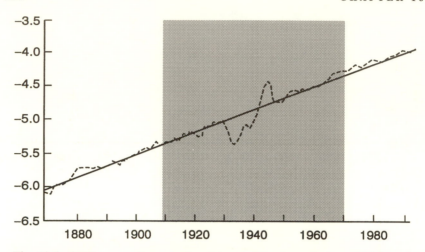

Fig. 10.5. GNP per capita, actual and trend. We show the log of U.S. real GNP per capita, together with a fitted linear trend. The Nelson and Plosser (1982) subsample, 1909–1970, is shaded. Pre-1929 GNP data are from Romer (1989).

N. DeJong and Charles H. Whiteman, 1991) and in out-of-sample forecasting competitions (e.g., John Geweke and Richard A. Meese, 1984; DeJong and Whiteman, 1994).

We have already stressed the importance of our results for forecasting aggregate output. They are also important for macroeconometric modeling more generally. For example, recent important work by Graham Elliott (1995) points to the nonrobustness of cointegration methods to deviations of variables from difference-stationarity. More precisely, Elliott shows that even very small deviations from difference-stationarity can invalidate the inferential procedures associated with conventional cointegration analyses. Our results suggest that U.S. aggregate output is not likely to be difference-stationary: the dominant autoregressive root is likely close to, but less than, unity. This points to the desirability of additional work on inference in macroeconometric models with dynamics that are long-memory but mean-reverting, as in Diebold and Rudebusch (1989), or short-memory with roots local to unity, as in Elliott et al. (1992).

Finally, let us summarize our contribution as we see it. We do not take issue with Rudebusch; we in fact study very different aggregate output series, and certainly we are not the first to notice that the use of longer GNP samples may produce sharper unit-root inference (see, e.g., Stock and Watson, 1986). Rather, we are skeptical of blanket generalizations of the Christiano-Eichenbaum-Rudebusch results, prevalent in the recent oral tradition. We have argued that, even for the famously recalcitrant aggregate output series, unit-root tests over long spans can be informative, and they may be important for point forecasting, among other things. Our results make clear that uncritical repetition of the "we don't know, and we don't care" mantra is just as scientifically irresponsible as blind adoption of the view that "all macroeconomic series are difference-stationary," or the view that "all macroeconomic series are trend-stationary." There is simply no substitute for serious, case-by-case, analysis.

References

Balke, Nathan S. and Gordon, Robert J. "The Estimation of Prewar Gross National Product: Methodology and New Evidence." *Journal of Political Economy*, February 1989, 97(1), pp. 38–92.

Bureau of the Census, U.S. Department of Commerce. *Historical statistics of the United States*. Washington, DC: U.S. Government Printing Office, various years.

——, *Current population reports*, Series P-25. Washington, DC: U.S. Government Printing Office, various years.

Campbell, John Y. and Perron, Pierre. "Pitfalls and Opportunities: What Macroeconomists Should Know About Unit Roots," in Olivier Blanchard and Stanley Fischer, eds., *NBER macroeconomics annual, 1991*. Cambridge, MA: MIT Press, 1991, pp. 141–201.

Christiano, Lawrence J. and Eichenbaum, Martin. "Unit Roots in Real GNP: Do We Know and Do We Care?" *Carnegie-Rochester Conference Series on Public Policy*, Spring 1990, 32, pp. 7–61.

Cochrane, John H. "How Big Is the Random Walk in GNP?" *Journal of Political Economy*, October 1988, 96(5), pp. 893–920.

DeJong, David N. and Whiteman, Charles H. "The Case for Trend-Stationarity Is Stronger Than We Thought." *Journal of Applied Econometrics*, October–December 1991, 6(4), pp. 413–421.

——, "The Forecasting Attributes of Trend- and Difference-Stationary Representations for Macroeconomic Time Series." *Journal of Forecasting*, April 1994, 13, pp. 279–97.

Diebold, Francis X. and Rudebusch, Glenn D. "Long Memory and Persistence in Aggregate Output." *Journal of Monetary Economics*, September 1989, 24(2), pp. 189–209.

Elliott, Graham. "On the Robustness of Cointegration Methods When the Regressors Almost Have Unit Roots." Unpublished manuscript, Department of Economics, University of California, San Diego, 1995.

Elliott, Graham; Rothenberg, Thomas J. and Stock, James H. "Efficient Tests for an Autoregressive Unit Root." National Bureau of Economic Research (Cambridge, MA) Technical Working Paper No. 130, 1992.

Geweke, John and Meese, Richard A. "A Comparison of Autoregressive Univariate Forecasting Procedures for Macroeconomic Time Series." *Journal of Business and Economic Statistics*, July 1984, 2(3), pp. 191–200.

Hall, Alastair. "Testing for a Unit Root in Time Series with Pretest Data-Based Model Selection." *Journal of Business and Economic Statistics*, October 1994, 12(4), pp. 461–70.

National income and product accounts of the United States. Washington, DC: U.S. Department of Commerce, various years.

Nelson, Charles R. and Plosser, Charles I. "Trends and Random Walks in Macroeconomic Time Series: Some Evidence and Implications." *Journal of Monetary Economics*, September 1982, 10(2), pp. 139–62.

Ng, Serena and Perron, Pierre. "Unit Root Tests in ARMA Models with Data-Dependent Methods for the Selection of the Truncation Lag." *Journal of the American Statistical Association*, March 1995, 90(429), pp. 268–81.

Perron, Pierre. "The Great Crash, the Oil Price Shock, and the Unit Root Hypothesis." *Econometrica*, November 1989, 57(6), pp. 1361–1401.

Romer, Christina D. "The Prewar Business Cycle Reconsidered: New Estimates of Gross National Product, 1869–1908." *Journal of Political Economy*, February 1989, 97(1), pp. 1–37.

Rudebusch, Glenn D. "The Uncertain Unit Root in Real GNP." *American Economic Review*, March 1993, 83(1), pp. 264–72.

Stock, James H. "Confidence Intervals for the Largest Autoregressive Root in U.S. Macroeconomic Time Series." *Journal of Monetary Economics*, December 1991, 28(3), pp. 435–59.

Stock, James H. and Watson, Mark W. "Does GNP Have a Unit Root?" *Economics Letters*, March 1986, 22, pp. 147–51.

——, "Variable Trends in Economic Time Series." *Journal of Economic Perspectives*, Summer 1988, 2(3), pp. 147–74.

11

Long Memory and Persistence in Aggregate Output

FRANCIS X. DIEBOLD AND GLENN D. RUDEBUSCH*

1. Introduction

In the last five years, the permanent nature of macroeconomic fluctuations has become the subject of intense debate. Starting with Nelson and Plosser (1982), some have taken issue with the traditional view that macroeconomic time series are well described as transitory deviations from a deterministic trend. Instead, it has been suggested that aggregate output contains a substantial permanent component; that is, a given movement in aggregate output will persist and will not necessarily be reversed in the future through reversion to trend. Campbell and Mankiw (1987a), for instance, fit autoregressive integrated moving-average (ARIMA) models to post-war real gross national product (GNP) and conclude that a 1 percent innovation to current GNP should change long-run forecasts of GNP by *more* than 1 percent.

We contribute to this debate by examining the low-frequency components in real output movements in greater detail than has been done previously. The results have implications for the nature and existence of business cycles, the persistence of macroeconomic shocks, and the specification of statistical models of economic fluctuations. We explore an approximation to the Wold representation that is more general than, and includes as special cases, the ARIMA and unobserved-components (UC) representations that have been used by others. We use long-memory, fractionally integrated representations that allow for increased flexibility in modeling low-frequency dynamics. The results provide a unification of existing disparate persistence estimates as well as, given the wide confidence intervals obtained, a cautionary note against focus-

* We thank the editors and an anonymous referee for constructive comments, as well as John Campbell, Rob Engle, Jim Hamilton, Lars Hansen, Salih Neftci, Tom Sargent, Fallaw Sowell, Jim Stock, Mark Watson, and seminar participants at Chicago, Virginia, Penn, Berkeley, Montreal, Cornell, and the NBER Summer Institute. Paula Decubellis provided persistently good research assistance.

ing on any point estimate of the permanent component on the basis of a limited span of macroeconomic data.

In the next section, we discuss the importance of understanding the nature of persistence in aggregate output and describe our measure of persistence. In section 3, the fractionally integrated ARIMA model is introduced and economic motivation is provided. Section 4 describes the estimation procedure employed. Empirical results are contained in section 5, and section 6 concludes.

2. Measuring the Permanent Component

A measurement of the permanent component in aggregate output is crucial to both the theory and practice of macroeconomics. The presence of a large permanent component would imply that a substantial portion of a given macroeconomic shock to the economy would persist through time. This conflicts with traditional formulations of both Keynesian and Classical macroeconomic theories, where output fluctuations, from a variety of causes, are temporary deviations from a slowly growing natural or equilibrium level of output. A large permanent component implies instead that almost al fluctuations in output represent permanent movements. Such fluctuations require description within an intrinsically stochastic economic theory, since deterministic models cannot be regarded as even approximately true when reversion to deterministic equilibrium paths is absent.[1] In addition, all of the standard econometric tasks—estimation, hypothesis testing, prediction, and control—are sensitive to the presence of a permanent component.

For policymakers, the implications of macroeconomic persistence are just as unsettling. Strong persistence would call into question, at a fundamental level, the appropriateness of countercyclical policy. If the cyclical component is insignificant in aggregate output and there is no steady trend to which to return the economy, attempts at countercyclical policy are at best misguided. In addition, when each movement in output is largely permanent, the costs and benefits of policy actions are far different than when movements are transitory; the price of higher or lower output over the whole future path of the economy must be weighed in the policy calculus.

Much of the empirical literature relevant to the persistence debate examines the *existence* of a permanent component, which provides, as

---

[1] Much recent work on stochastic growth models, such as King, Plosser, and Rebello (1988), is at least partially motivated by this fact.

we shall discuss below, a first step to the more interesting question of the *importance* of the permanent component. The existence of a permanent component is commonly examined by testing for unit roots in autoregressive lag-operator polynomials. If a unit root is found in an ARMA representation, then, as shown by Beveridge and Nelson (1981), the series may be decomposed into the sum of a random-walk component and a stationary component. The permanence of the random-walk movements implies a permanent component in the original series.

To formalize matters, consider the ARMA model

$$\Phi(L)Y_t = \Theta(L)\varepsilon_t, \qquad \varepsilon_t \sim (0, \sigma_\varepsilon^2), \tag{1}$$

where $\Phi(L) = 1 - \phi_1 L - \cdots - \phi_p L^p$, $\Theta(L) = 1 - \theta_1 L - \cdots - \theta_q L^q$, all roots of $\Phi(L)$ are on or outside the unit circle, and all roots of $\Theta(L)$ are outside the unit circle. If $\Phi(L)$ has a unit root, it is assumed to be positive and real, in which case we can difference the series and write $\Phi(L) = (1 - L)\Phi'(L)$, where $\Phi'(L)$ is of order $p - 1$; thus, the process is ARIMA($p - 1, 1, q$).

The Dickey–Fuller tests [e.g., Fuller (1976)] and generalizations by Phillips (1987) and others have been widely applied in economics to test the unit-root hypothesis. Most such studies conclude that real output and many other economic time series are well described by low-order ARMA processes with a single unit root.[2] Broad surveys such as Nelson and Plosser (1982) and Schwert (1987), which make use of a variety of unit-root tests on scores of economic variables, find pervasive and robust evidence of unit roots. In addition, the growing literature documenting cointegration in various economic relationships implicitly extends the above list, because cointegrated variables have unit roots in their univariate representations. In this paper, we provide qualification to the wide-ranging evidence on the existence of unit roots, and more crucially their importance, by considering more general models that allow for rich low-frequency dynamics and include unit roots as a special case.

While the presence of a unit root in real output provides evidence for the existence of persistence, the more relevant question for macroeconomic analysis involves quantifying the extent of that persistence. We are more interested in the size or importance of the response of output to a unit innovation than in the mere existence of some nonzero response. One measure of persistence, used by Watson (1986), Campbell and Mankiw (1987a,b), and others, is the cumulative impulse-

---

[2] See, for example, Stock and Watson (1986), Perron and Phillips (1987), and Campbell and Deaton (1987).

response function, i.e., the sum of the coefficients of the moving-average lag-operator polynomial of the first-differenced series. Specifically, consider

$$\Delta Y_t = A(L)\varepsilon_t = (1 + a_1 L + a_2 L^2 + \cdots)\varepsilon_t. \tag{2}$$

The impact of a unit shock in period t on the *growth rate* of Y at time $t + k$ is a_k, while the impact on the level of Y at time $t + k$ is $c_k \equiv 1 + a_1 + \cdots + a_k$. In the limit, we obtain c_∞, which is the effect of a unit shock today on the level of Y infinitely far in the future. For any stationary or trend-stationary series, $c_\infty = 0$, because the effect of any shock is transitory as reversion to mean or trend eventually dominates. For a random walk, $c_\infty = 1$; that is, the effect of any shock is exactly permanent. In general, unit roots lead to a nonzero long-run response; however, the particular value of c_∞ depends on the specific parameterization of the process.

Any reasonable persistence measure must be related to the form of the Wold-representation lag-operator polynomial $A(L)$, which completely characterizes the mapping from inputs $\{\varepsilon_t\}$ to outputs $\{Y_t\}$. This is true of all persistence measures that have appeared in the literature, including the height of the spectral density of ΔY at frequency zero, the proportion of variation in ΔY due to movements in the underlying random-walk component, or the limiting value of Cochrane's (1988) variance ratio.[3] In this paper, we part with the tradition of using the infinite cumulative response, c_∞, to measure persistence and instead examine the *entire* sequence of cumulative impulse responses, $C = \{1, c_1, c_2, c_3, \ldots, c_\infty\}$. We use C to study persistence, because it directly answers the question of interest: 'How does a shock today affect the level of output in the short, medium, long, and very long run?' For example, with quarterly data, c_{40} is the impact of a unit shock on the level of output ten years hence. This approach is more informative than concentrating on c_∞, because the economic horizons of interest are typically much shorter than infinity. In the long-memory models that we consider below, the cumulative impulse response, even at quite long horizons, can differ substantially from c_∞.

---

[3] A more detailed discussion of alternative persistence measures and their interrelationships is contained in Diebold and Nerlove (1989).

3. Modeling the Permanent Component

The modeling of persistent processes is an issue closely related to the measurement of persistence; in particular, construction of the cumulative impulse-response sequence requires estimates of the parameters of the moving-average representation. A number of authors have recently addressed the issue of modeling persistence in real output, notably Campbell and Mankiw (1987a), who use unrestricted ARIMA representations. Fitting an ARIMA$(2, 1, 2)$ model to the logarithm of post-war quarterly real GNP, they obtain a c_∞ persistence estimate of 1.52, so that a unit innovation leads to a long-run response substantially *larger* than the initial innovation. This striking result of very strong shock persistence (and, in fact, shock magnification) runs counter to the findings of Watson (1986) and Clark (1987), who obtain smaller estimates of persistence ($c_\infty = 0.6$) with estimated unobserved components (UC) models.[4] They argue that the long-run behavioral implications of the unrestricted ARIMA models are misleading because such models concentrate on representations of the short-run dynamics. Both Watson and Clark note, however, that the UC model can be viewed as a special case of the more general ARIMA model: UC models are simply (nonlinearly) restricted ARIMA models.[5] Campbell and Mankiw (1987b) argue that the restrictions implied by the UC specification are unsupported.

We believe that there is some truth in both of these arguments. On the one hand, long-run properties of data series are likely to be difficult to determine in the context of an unrestricted ARIMA model. Mean reversion in economic time series depends crucially on correlations at long lags, which easily can be misspecified in simple ARIMA representations [see, e.g., Gagnon (1988)]. We shall provide implicit support for this thesis below. We assert, however, that what is required is not a specialization of the ARIMA model but a generalization, one that can capture a variety of long-run, low-frequency responses. Very high-order autoregressive models could capture such responses if degrees of freedom were plentiful; instead, we adopt a parsimonious model that achieves the same goal. Furthermore, our specification nests both the ARIMA and UC models.

---

[4] Like Campbell and Mankiw, of course, Watson obtains high persistence estimates ($c_\infty = 1.5$) from unrestricted ARIMA models.

[5] In particular, the restrictions implied by common UC representations *force* c_∞ to be less than unity.

Specifically, consider a generalization of the ARIMA(p, d, q) model to allow *fractional* integration,

$$\Phi(L)(1 - L)^d Y_t = \Theta(L)\varepsilon_t, \qquad \varepsilon_t \sim (0, \sigma_\varepsilon^2), \qquad (3)$$

where $\Phi(L) = 1 - \phi_1 L - \cdots - \phi_p L^p$, $\Theta(L) = 1 - \theta_1 L - \cdots - \theta_q L^q$, all roots of $\Phi(L)$ and $\Theta(L)$ lie outside the unit circle, and d is allowed to assume values in the real, as opposed to the integer, set of numbers.[6] Econometricians typically have considered only integer values of d; the leading special cases are the discrete options $d = 0$ (stationarity) and $d = 1$ (unit-root nonstationarity). Formally, however, an integer-d restriction in eq. (3) is arbitrary. We shall demonstrate that noninteger d values, i.e., fractional integration, provide for parsimonious yet flexible modeling of low-frequency variation; we denote such models as ARFIMA (AutoRegressive Fractionally Integrated Moving Average) models.

The ARFIMA model can be put in the moving-average form (2). First, write eq. (3) as

$$(1 - L)^d Y_t = B(L)\varepsilon_t, \qquad (4)$$

where $B(L) = \Phi^{-1}(L)\Theta(L)$. Extracting the factor $(1 - L)$ gives

$$(1 - L)^{d-1}(1 - L)Y_t = B(L)\varepsilon_t \qquad (5)$$

or

$$(1 - L)Y_t = A(L)\varepsilon_t, \qquad (6)$$

where $A(L) = (1 - L)^{1-d}B(L)$.[7] Operationally, a binomial expansion

---

[6] Stationarity and invertibility require $|d| < \frac{1}{2}$, which can always be achieved by taking a suitable number of differences. In what follows, we achieve a local generalization of unit root behavior by considering $\frac{1}{2} < d < \frac{3}{2}$; note that the first-differenced series then has an integration order less than $\frac{1}{2}$ in absolute value, so that stationarity and invertibility are achieved.

[7] More generally, we can allow for drift, $(1 - L)Y_t = \mu + A(L)\varepsilon_t$, as is done in the estimation reported below.

of the operator $(1 - L)^d$ is used,

$$(1 - L)^d = \sum_{j=0}^{\infty} \frac{\Gamma(j - d)L^j}{\Gamma(-d)\Gamma(j + 1)} \tag{7}$$

$$= 1 - dL + \frac{d(d - 1)}{2!}L^2 - \frac{d(d - 1)(d - 2)}{3!}L^3 + \cdots, \tag{8}$$

where $\Gamma(\cdot)$ denotes the gamma, or generalized factorial, function. Thus, the filter $(1 - L)^d$ provides an infinite-order lag-operator polynomial with slowly and monotonically declining weights.

The ARFIMA model (3) belongs to the class of long-memory processes, so named for their ability to display significant dependence between observations widely separated in time.[8] Standard ARMA processes are often labeled 'short-memory' processes because the dependence between observations τ periods apart decays rapidly as τ increases; indeed, it is well known that for large τ ARMA autocorrelations decay approximately geometrically,

$$\rho(\tau) \sim r^\tau,$$

where r is a constant such that $|r| < 1$. ARFIMA processes, however, have a slower hyperbolic autocorrelation decay; for large τ we have the approximation

$$\rho_Y(\tau) \sim \tau^{2d-1}, \qquad d < \frac{1}{2}, \qquad d \neq 0.$$

To see how the autocorrelations vary with fractional d, it is instructive to consider pure fractional noise, denoted ARFIMA$(0, d, 0)$, given by

$$(1 - L)^d Y_t = \varepsilon_t. \tag{9}$$

Table 11.1 provides a comparison of the τth-order autocorrelations of fractional noise with those of a first-order autoregression [AR(1)]. The two models are parameterized to provide the same first-order autocorrelations, but as the interval between observations increases, the autocor-

---

[8] Long-memory processes have their genesis in physics and in early hydrological work, such as Hurst (1951). Mandelbrot (1972) formalized many of the empirical insights about these processes and proposed R/S analysis, an early technique to characterize the extent of persistence. [For an application and generalization of R/S analysis, see Lo (1988).] Granger and Joyeux (1980) and Hosking (1981) independently proposed the use of fractionally integrated ARIMA procedures as long-memory models.

TABLE 11.1

Autocorrelation Functions for AR(1) and ARFIMA($0, d, 0$)

	\multicolumn{9}{c}{$Lag(\tau)$}								
	1	2	3	4	5	10	25	50	100
$(1 - 0.5L)Y_t = \varepsilon_t,$									
$\rho(\tau) =$	0.50	0.25	0.13	0.06	0.03	0.00	0.00	0.00	0.00
$(1 - L)^{0.3}Y_t = \varepsilon_t,$									
$\rho(\tau) =$	0.50	0.40	0.35	0.32	0.30	0.24	0.18	0.14	0.11

relations diverge. At lag 25, the AR(1) correlation is approximately 0.0, while the fractionally integrated series has a correlation of 0.18.

The intuition of long memory and the limitation of the integer-d restriction emerge clearly in the frequency domain. The series $\{Y_t\}$ displays long memory if its spectral density, f_Y, increases without limit as angular frequency tends to zero,

$$\lim_{\lambda \to 0} f_Y(\lambda) = \infty. \tag{10}$$

In fact, for an ARFIMA series, $f_Y(\lambda)$ behaves like λ^{-2d} as $\lambda \to 0$, so d parameterizes the low-frequency behavior. This is in contrast to the usual ARIMA model with $d = 1$, where the spectral density is forced to behave like λ^{-2} as $\lambda \to 0$. Thus, a rich range of spectral behavior near the origin becomes possible when the integer-d restriction is relaxed. The ARFIMA model, by allowing a variety of spectral shapes near the origin (corresponding to the continuum of possible d values), can provide superior approximations to the Wold representations of economic time series. Indeed, the "typical spectral shape" of economic variables [Nerlove (1964) and Granger (1966)], which has power that monotonically declines as frequency increases (except at seasonals), is well captured by the fractionally integrated process with d between zero and one. The fact that many economic time series in level form have spectra that appear to be infinite at the origin might suggest that a first difference is appropriate; however, after differencing, these time series often have no power at the origin, suggesting that a first difference is 'too much.' Such behavior is characteristic of a fractionally integrated process with d between zero and one [see Granger and Joyeux (1980)].

The potential macroeconomic relevance of the ARFIMA representation is also established by Granger (1980, 1988), who describes how fractional integration can be induced by aggregation. Specifically, if the underlying components of an aggregate series (e.g., individual firms' productions) follow AR(1) processes with parameters ρ_i and the ρ_i's are beta-distributed in the cross-section, then aggregation yields a fractionally integrated macroeconomic series. An example of a theoretical macroeconomic model producing fractionally integrated output is provided by Haubrich and Lo (1988), who exploit Granger's aggregation result in a real business cycle model with beta-distributed intrasectoral input–output coefficients to obtain fractionally integrated aggregate output.

4. Estimation of Fractionally Integrated Models

The long-memory aspects of fractionally integrated ARIMA models make their estimation more difficult than the usual ARIMA model with integer d. We use a two-step estimation procedure suggested by Geweke and Porter-Hudak (GPH) (1983). We first obtain a consistent and asymptotically normal estimate of d and transform the series by the expansion of $(1 - L)^d$. We then fit an ARMA model to the transformed series to obtain consistent estimates of the remaining model parameters Φ, Θ, and σ_ε^2.[9] Finally, these estimates are used to construct consistent estimates of the sequence of cumulative impulse responses.

The first-stage estimate of d is based on the order of the spectral density function near $\lambda = 0$. We start with the first difference of the relevant series, denoted $X_t = (1 - L)Y_t$; thus, we wish to estimate $\tilde{d}$ in the model

$$(1 - L)^{\tilde{d}} X_t = \Phi^{-1}(L)\Theta(L)\varepsilon_t \equiv u_t. \tag{11}$$

As d of the level series equals $1 + \tilde{d}$, a value of $\tilde{d}$ equal to zero corresponds to a unit root in Y_t.

The spectral density of X_t is given by

$$f_X(\lambda) = |1 - \exp(-i\lambda)|^{-2\tilde{d}} f_u(\lambda) = [2\sin(\lambda/2)]^{-2\tilde{d}} f_u(\lambda), \tag{12}$$

where $f_u(\lambda)$ is the spectral density of the stationary process u_t. Suppose that a sample of size T is available $\{X_t, t = 1, \ldots, T\}$; let $\lambda_j = 2\pi j/T$ $(j = 0, \ldots, T - 1)$ denote the harmonic ordinates of the sample. Taking logarithms of eq. (12), adding and subtracting $\ln\{f_u(0)\}$, and evaluating

---

[9] The possibility of maximum-likelihood estimation (MLE) has also received some attention, as in Brockwell and Davis (1987) and Sowell (1987). Both the two-step procedure and MLE have associated costs and benefits; however, the former has certain advantages that make it our method of choice for the present application, as discussed below.

at the harmonic ordinates, we obtain

$$\ln\{f_X(\lambda_j)\} = \ln\{f_u(0)\} - \tilde{d}\ln\{4\sin^2(\lambda_j/2)\} + \ln\{f_u(\lambda_j)/f_u(0)\}. \quad (13)$$

If we restrict consideration to the low-frequency ordinates near zero, say, λ_j, $j \le K \ll T$, the last term in (13) can be dropped as negligible. Let $I(\lambda_j)$ denote the periodogram at ordinate j, then add $\ln\{I(\lambda_j)\}$ to both sides of (13) and rearrange to obtain

$$\ln\{I(\lambda_j)\} = \ln\{f_u(0)\} - \tilde{d}\ln\{4\sin^2(\lambda_j/2)\} + \ln\{I(\lambda_j)/f_X(\lambda_j)\}. \quad (14)$$

The particular utility of this formation is its formal similarity to a simple linear regression equation,

$$\ln\{I(\lambda_j)\} = \beta_0 + \beta_1 \ln\{4\sin^2(\lambda_j/2)\} + \eta_j, \qquad j = 1,\ldots,K, \quad (15)$$

where β_0 is the constant $\ln\{f_u(0)\}$, and the η_j, equal to $\ln\{I(\lambda_j)/f_X(\lambda_j)\}$, are independently and identically distributed across the harmonic frequencies.

Now let the number of low-frequency ordinates used in the above spectral regression be a function of the sample size, i.e., $K = g(T)$. Then, under regularity conditions on $g(\cdot)$, the negative of the OLS estimate of the slope coefficient provides a consistent and asymptotically normal estimate of $\tilde{d}$.[10] This is true regardless of the orders and parameterizations of the Φ and Θ polynomials underlying the stationary process u_t. Furthermore, the variance of the estimate of b_1 is given by the usual OLS estimator, and the theoretical asymptotic variance of the regression error η_j is known to be equal to $\pi^2/6$, which can be imposed to increase efficiency. A formal statement of the Geweke and Porter-Hudak theorem appears in the appendix.

Given an estimate of $\tilde{d}$, we transform the series X_t by the long-memory filter (8), truncated at each point to the available sample. The transformed series is then modeled as an ARMA(p, q) process. Because the estimate of the order of fractional integration from the periodogram regression is consistent, the second-stage estimates of Φ and Θ are also consistent. Finally, consistent estimates of the sequence of cumulative impulse responses, C, are constructed.

---

[10] Based upon theoretical considerations and Monte Carlo simulations, Geweke and Porter-Hudak (1983), Brockwell and Davis (1987), and Shea (1989) recommend using $g(T) = T^\alpha$, and obtain good results with $\alpha = 0.5$. Thus, for example, in a sample of size 144, the first twelve periodogram ordinates would be used.

It is worth noting at this point the benefits of the semiparametric first-stage estimator of $\tilde{d}$ (and hence d); its asymptotic distribution does not depend on the infinite-dimensional nuisance parameter $\Phi^{-1}(L)\Theta(L)$. This is a desirable property in the present application, because the estimate of C turns out to depend largely on the estimated value of d, not on the estimates of the parameters in Φ and Θ. Thus, it is valuable to have an estimator of d whose properties do not depend on correct specification of Φ and Θ, the orders of which are typically unknown *a priori*. Alternative procedures such as simultaneous maximum-likelihood estimation of d, Φ, and Θ, which may have certain desirable properties under correct model specification, may be inconsistent under misspecification of Φ and Θ.

5. Empirical Results

In this section, we examine evidence for fractional integration in ten different measures of U.S. macroeconomic activity. These include post-war quarterly real GNP, which was used in Campbell and Mankiw (1987a,b), as well as post-war quarterly real GNP per capita. Real GNP is the most comprehensive measure of the macroeconomy; however, we will focus much of our attention on per capita GNP because movements induced in aggregate output by a varying population will be naturally persistent and may obscure the persistence intrinsic to the market economy, which is our main interest.

We also examine the Federal Reserve Board's index of industrial production on a quarterly basis. This provides a more specialized measure of real output, including just the manufacturing, mining, and utilities sectors (which account for roughly one-fourth to one-third of GNP), but over a substantially longer time range (1919–1987). In addition, we are able to control for seasonality and the effects of seasonal adjustment filters by examining both seasonally adjusted and nonseasonally adjusted (NSA) industrial production data.[11] Another specialized series examined is the quarterly average unemployment rate, which has cyclical movements closely related to those of aggregate output. The persistence of unemployment has been the focus of recent work on employment hysteresis, such as Blanchard and Summers (1986).

While real GNP is the most comprehensive macroeconomic indicator, on a quarterly basis it is only available from the *National Income and Product Accounts* (NIPA) for the last forty years. Annual GNP data,

---

[11] Ghysels (1987) argues that the smoothing effects of seasonal adjustment filters might lead to spurious unit-root-like behavior in seasonally adjusted series.

which have been constructed by a variety of researchers, provide a span of up to 120 years, and previous investigations using such long annual series have found less shock persistence than in the post-war quarterly data.[12] In light of this, we examine the long annual series of real net national product (NNP), as reported in Friedman and Schwartz (1982, table 4.8),[13] and real GNP, as reported in Romer (1989) and in Balke and Gordon (1989).[14] In addition, we examine two annual real output per capita series: real NNP per capita from Friedman and Schwartz (1982, table 4.8) and real GNP per capita from *Long-Term Economic Growth* (1973) spliced in 1929 to the annual NIPA record.

In summary, we examine a variety of real macroeconomic time series at quarterly and annual frequencies and in level and per capita terms. This range of combinations enables us to explore the robustness of our results. As a first step, we obtain estimates of the fractional-integration parameter d for each of the ten series. We then focus our attention on the leading case of post-war quarterly real GNP per capita and examine persistence through the sequence of cumulative impulse responses, C. The sensitivity of our results is then examined.

5.1. Estimation of d

Table 11.2 reports d estimates for all ten measures of aggregate economic activity along with asymptotic standard errors and the associated p values for the unit-root null hypothesis ($d = 1$). The asymptotic standard errors are constructed using the known theoretical GPH regression error variance of $\pi^2/6$ to increase efficiency.[15] The p values given the asymptotic probability, under the null hypothesis that $d = 1$, of obtaining the estimated d value; they are against the one-sided alternative $d < 1$. The number of low-frequency periodogram ordinates included in the GPH regression introduces a judgemental aspect; im-

---

[12] See, for example, Cochrane (1988). Recent annual data are also more accurate than the quarterly series, which interpolate a substantial portion of detail from annual surveys [see Carson (1987)]. However, important information contained in short-run, high-frequency fluctuations may be lost in the annual series.

[13] The Friedman and Schwartz series, which is net of a capital consumption allowance, is widely mislabeled as gross national product in the literature.

[14] As part of a debate that focuses primarily on cyclical volatility, Romer (1989) and Balke and Gordon (1989) have each constructed revised estimates of real GNP before 1929 based on reassessments of the sources and assumptions underlying previous estimates of early GNP.

[15] The Monte Carlo evidence presented by Geweke and Porter-Hudak (1983) and Diebold and Rudebusch (1989b) indicates that asymptotic normality is a good approximation for the sample sizes considered here.

TABLE 11.2
Estimates of d[a]

Data Series and Source	α		
	0.5	0.525	0.55
Annual Series			
Real NNP	0.67	0.61	0.61
1869–1975	(0.29)	(0.26)	(0.24)
[Friedman and Schwartz (1982)]	$p = 0.19$	$p = 0.07$	$p = 0.05$
Real GNP	0.59	0.70	0.65
1869–1987	(0.27)	(0.26)	(0.23)
[Romer (1989)]	$p = 0.06$	$p = 0.13$	$p = 0.06$
Real GNP	0.50	0.71	0.64
1869–1987	(0.27)	(0.26)	(0.23)
[Balke and Gordon (1989)]	$p = 0.03$	$p = 0.13$	$p = 0.06$
Real NNP, per capita	0.52	0.48	0.49
1869–1975	(0.29)	(0.26)	(0.24)
[Friedman and Schwartz (1982)]	$p = 0.05$	$p = 0.02$	$p = 0.02$
Real GNP, per capita	0.65	0.57	0.55
1900–1986	(0.32)	(0.29)	(0.26)
[*Long-Term Economic Growth*]	$p = 0.14$	$p = 0.07$	$p = 0.04$
Quarterly Series			
Real GNP	0.90	0.92	0.88
1947:Q1–1987:Q2	(0.24)	(0.23)	(0.21)
[NIPA]	$p = 0.34$	$p = 0.36$	$p = 0.28$
Real GNP, per capita	0.68	0.72	0.71
1947:Q1–1987:Q2	(0.24)	(0.23)	(0.21)
[NIPA]	$p = 0.09$	$p = 0.11$	$p = 0.08$
Industrial Production	0.85	0.86	0.81
1919:Q1–1987:Q2	(0.19)	(0.19)	(0.17)
[Federal Reserve Board]	$p = 0.21$	$p = 0.23$	$p = 0.13$
Industrial Production, NSA	0.84	0.86	0.80
1919:Q1–1987:Q2	(0.19)	(0.19)	(0.17)
[Federal Reserve Board]	$p = 0.20$	$p = 0.23$	$p = 0.12$
Civilian Unemployment Rate	0.72	0.65	0.71
1948:Q1–1987:Q2	(0.24)	(0.24)	(0.21)
[Bureau of Labor Statistics]	$p = 0.12$	$p = 0.06$	$p = 0.08$

[a] The sample size for the GPH spectral regression is T^{α}. All variables except the unemployment rate are in logarithms, and quarterly variables are seasonally adjusted except for Industrial Production, NSA. The standard errors given in parentheses are constructed imposing the known theoretical regression error variance of $\pi^{2}/6$. The p values for the unit-root null hypothesis ($d = 1$) are against the one-sided alternative $d < 1$.

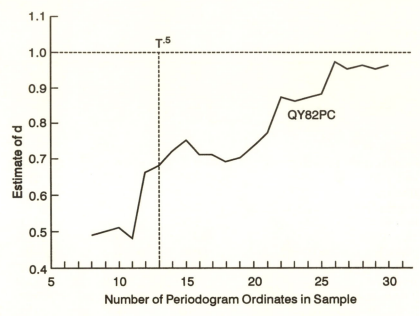

Fig. 11.1. Estimate of d for quarterly real GNP per capita from the GPH
spectral regression as a function of sample size.

proper inclusion of medium-frequency ordinates will contaminate the
estimate of d, while too small of a regression sample will lead to
imprecise estimates. Table 11.2 reports d estimates for each series for
three different regression sample sizes. The sample sizes are equal to
T^α, for $\alpha = 0.5, 0.525$, and 0.55. The estimates of the order of fractional
integration are quite robust across this variation.

While the d estimate for quarterly per capita GNP is about 0.7,
quarterly GNP yields a higher estimate of 0.9, suggesting, not surprisingly, more persistence.[16] The annual national output series, which span
more time, have smaller d estimates; ranging from 0.5 to 0.65, depending on the particular series. Romer's GNP series has an estimated
fractional-integration parameter very similar to those of the other
annual series. The estimated d for quarterly industrial production is
close to that for quarterly GNP, and seasonal adjustment makes virtually no difference. Finally, quarterly unemployment exhibits a fractional-integration parameter of about 0.70.

[16] For post-war quarterly per capita real GNP, fig. 11.1 provides the complete range of
estimates of d obtained for increasing numbers of periodogram ordinates included in the
GPH regression. The number of periodogram ordinates corresponding to the square root
of the sample size is indicated with a vertical dashed line.

The evidence from all of these series should be considered, as each provides a different perspective on the persistence of shocks to aggregate economic activity. The point estimates of d are quite striking, as *all* are less than unity, and some are very much less than unity; however, as we shall discuss below, the standard errors for these estimates are quite large. The results call for a deeper exploration of the nature of low-frequency economic dynamics.[17] In particular, the knife-edged parameterizations '$d = 1$' and '$d = 0$', which arise in standard ARIMA modeling and are the implicit subject of the unit-root literature, may be overly restrictive. In what follows, we focus on the leading case of interest, quarterly real GNP per capita. We first estimate the remaining ARFIMA model parameters; then, we proceed to construct persistence estimates and investigate their robustness.

5.2. Estimation of Cumulative Impulse Responses

Computation of the sequence of cumulative impulse responses requires estimation of all of the parameters of the ARFIMA(p, d, q) model. For quarterly per capita real GNP (denoted hereinafter as *QY82PC*), the GPH regression results suggest a fraction-integration parameter in the range of 0.7; thus, we transform the data by applying the filter $(1 - L)^{-0.3}$ to the first-differenced series. To capture the remaining short-run dynamics, we consider ARMA models with up to three autoregressive parameters and three moving-average parameters. We distinguish these models through the Akaike and Schwarz information criteria (AIC and SIC, respectively), which are differentiated by their degrees-of-freedom adjustment of the maximized log-likelihood function. Table 11.3 reports the selection criteria for the sixteen models under consideration, ranging from white noise to ARMA(3, 3). The Akaike criterion identifies an ARMA(1, 2), while the Schwarz criterion identifies a more parsimonious ARMA(1, 0). Like Campbell and Mankiw (1987a), we are not interested in selecting one 'best' model of short-run fluctuations in GNP; rather, we seek robust evidence from a variety of models on the effects of economic shocks and use the information criteria for guidance.

Table 11.4 provides the estimated cumulative impulse responses for all sixteen ARFIMA($p, 0.70, q$) models of *QY82PC*. These responses demonstrate the effect of a unit growth rate innovation on the level of output k periods hence, with k ranging from 1 to 400 quarters. The cumulative impulse responses are hump-shaped, with initial shock mag-

---

[17] Moreover, one might conjecture that standard unit-root tests, described in section 2, may have low power against fractional alternatives. This appears to be the case; see Diebold and Rudebusch (1989b).

TABLE 11.3
Model Selection Criteria, Log of Quarterly Real GNP per Capita ($QY82PC$).[a]
ARFIMA(p, d, q) model: $(1 - L)^{0.7}\Phi(L)QY82PC_t = \Theta(L)\varepsilon_t$

Number of AR	Number of MA Parameters (q)			
Parameters (p)	0	1	2	3
0	927.165	981.278	1008.250	1017.190
	924.083	975.115	999.007	1004.870
1	1016.720	1015.440	1018.520[c]	1017.550
	1010.560[b]	1006.190	1006.190	1002.140
2	1015.800	1013.740	1017.280	1015.790
	1006.550	1001.410	1001.870	997.299
3	1018.090	1016.230	1018.180	1016.340
	1005.770	1000.830	999.689	994.770

[a] For each model, we report the Akaike Information Criterion ($2 \ln L - 2k$) and, below that, the Schwartz Information Criterion ($2 \ln L - k \ln T$).
[b] Maximum SIC value.
[c] Maximum AIC value.

TABLE 11.4
Cumulative Impulse Responses, ARFIMA($p, 0.7, q$) Model, $QY82PC$.
$(1 - L)^{0.7}\Phi(L)QY82PC_t = \Theta(L)\varepsilon_t$

Model	Quarters							
p, q	1	2	4	8	16	50	100	400
0, 1	1.175	0.927	0.750	0.609	0.494	0.351	0.285	0.188
0, 2	1.260	1.372	1.024	0.815	0.657	0.464	0.377	0.248
0, 3	1.262	1.506	1.314	1.014	0.809	0.569	0.461	0.304
1, 0[a]	1.359	1.491	1.497	1.295	1.023	0.707	0.571	0.375
1, 1	1.324	1.472	1.529	1.377	1.099	0.753	0.608	0.399
1, 2[b]	1.304	1.591	1.563	1.280	1.003	0.697	0.564	0.371
1, 3	1.306	1.602	1.544	1.188	0.938	0.657	0.532	0.350
2, 0	1.306	1.468	1.544	1.411	1.133	0.774	0.624	0.410
2, 1	1.356	1.477	1.439	1.120	0.654	0.068	−0.564	−0.014
2, 2	1.307	1.605	1.538	1.149	0.912	0.640	0.518	0.341
2, 3	1.308	1.603	1.504	1.113	0.888	0.623	0.505	0.333
3, 0	1.319	1.591	1.556	1.209	0.943	0.660	0.535	0.352
3, 1	1.316	1.589	1.559	1.171	0.911	0.641	0.520	0.342
3, 2	1.316	1.600	1.543	1.280	0.990	0.687	0.556	0.365
3, 3	1.309	1.600	1.547	1.332	1.027	0.710	0.574	0.378

[a] Selected by the SIC.
[b] Selected by the AIC.

nification, followed by shock dissipation. The maximum c_k value occurs at less than 8 quarters; after 16 quarters the cumulative impulse response has fallen back to approximately unity. By fifty quarters out, the response has dropped to about 0.7, and after one hundred quarters, it is less than 0.6 and continues to decline. These results are robust to the particular values of p and q chosen.[18] It is interesting to note that our estimates of the long-run cumulative impulse response are closer to those obtained in other studies using UC models (although we do not impose their implicit restrictions), than to the shock magnification results obtained with ARIMA models. The short-run hump-shaped cumulative impulse-response pattern is very similar across all three classes of models; they differ, however, in their implied medium- and long-run dynamics.

Thus far, we have shown that the point estimates of the cumulative impulse responses are typically smaller than estimates obtained from ARIMA representations and are highly robust to the form of the second-stage ARMA model fitted. Also of interest is the sensitivity of the point estimates of the cumulative impulse responses to the first-stage estimate of d, obtained from the GPH regression, upon which we condition. The results of such a sensitivity analysis are contained in table 11.5 for quarterly per capita real GNP. For each d value, we report the estimates of c_{16}, c_{50}, and c_{400} for the ARFIMA$(2, d, 2)$ model and, if not redundant, two other ARFIMA models corresponding to those selected by the AIC and SIC. Recall the preferred d value as estimated via the GPH spectral regression is 0.70, and the associated cumulative impulse responses in table 11.5 summarize the persistence estimates given in table 11.4. The estimated cumulative impulse responses are highly dependent upon d; in particular, forcing a unit root on the data (i.e., imposing $d = 1$) leads to large long-run persistence estimates, on the order of 1.5, which is what Campbell and Mankiw (1987a) report. This inflates the preferred estimate of c_{400}, corresponding to $d = 0.7$, by a factor of four, and it inflates the preferred estimate of c_{50} by a factor of two.

The information provided by the point estimates of C obtained from ARFIMA models is useful in that it represents a 'best guess' at the shape of C, based upon a generalized approximation to the Wold representation. The results also indicate, however, that the *interval* estimates associated with the long-run response are wide. To approximate $k\%$ confidence intervals for the elements of C, we can vary d over

[18] The exception is the ARFIMA$(2, 0.7, 1)$, where the AR and MA polynomials have an approximate common factor of unity, which forces an estimated long-run cumulative response of zero. Both information criteria detect the redundancy and favor ARFIMA$(1, 0.7, 0)$ models. The unit moving-average root most likely reflects the 'pileup' problem [see Diebold and Nerlove (1989)].

TABLE 11.5
Shock Persistence in Estimated ARFIMA(p, d, q) Models, QY82PC[a]

Fractional Integration Parameter (d)	Stationary Model ARMA(p, q); AIC, SIC	Persistence Measures		
		c_{16}	c_{50}	c_{400}
1.0	(2, 2); 1018.28, 1002.87	1.50	1.50	1.50
	(1, 0); 1014.96, 1008.80	1.57	1.57	1.57
0.90	(2, 2); 1019.05, 1003.64	1.24	1.10	0.90
	(0, 3); 1019.68, 1007.35	1.40	1.24	1.01
	(1, 0); 1016.54, 1010.38	1.32	1.17	0.95
0.85	(2, 2); 1019.22, 1003.82	1.13	0.95	0.69
	(0, 3); 1018.42, 1003.01	1.23	1.03	0.76
	(1, 0); 1017.12, 1010.96	1.21	1.02	0.74
0.80	(2, 2); 1019.09, 1003.68	1.03	0.82	0.54
	(0, 3); 1020.24, 1007.91	1.08	0.85	0.56
	(1, 0); 1017.43, 1011.27	1.13	0.89	0.58
0.75	(2, 2); 1018.49, 1003.09	0.96	0.72	0.43
	(0, 3); 1019.38, 1007.05	0.94	0.70	0.41
	(1, 0); 1017.34, 1011.18	1.06	0.79	0.46
0.70	(2, 2); 1017.28, 1001.87	0.91	0.64	0.34
	(1, 2); 1018.52, 1006.19	1.00	0.70	0.37
	(1, 0); 1016.72, 1010.56	1.02	0.71	0.38
0.65	(2, 2); 1015.37, 999.97	0.90	0.59	0.28
	(1, 2); 1016.95, 1004.62	0.97	0.63	0.30
	(1, 0); 1015.50, 1009.34	1.02	0.66	0.31

[a] For each model, we report the AIC, $2\ln L - 2k$, and the SIC, $2\ln L - k\ln T$. The ARFIMA(p, d, q) model, $(1 - L)^d Y_t = $ ARMA(p, q), is estimated conditional on d. Up to three ARMA stationary models are reported for each d: the ARMA(2, 2) and those selected by the AIC and SIC. The measure of persistence, c_k, is the sum of the first k coefficients of the moving-average representation of the first-differenced series.

its $k\%$ confidence range (obtained by exploiting the asymptotic normal-ity of the first-stage GPH estimate) and condition upon estimated Φ and Θ values at each d value.[19] The sensitivity of the estimated cumulative impulse responses to the estimate of d, together with the standard errors of the d estimates reported in table 2, imply that interval estimates of the cumulative impulse responses will be quite wide. Clearly, varying the d estimate across just one standard error will encompass both long-run shock magnification as well as dissipation. The wide confidence intervals underscore a fundamental econometric real-

[19] Two implicit, and potentially offsetting, assumptions underlie this approximation. The first is that the elements of C are monotone in d, which is the case in table 11.5 but need not be true in general. Second, we ignore stochastic variation in the elements of C associated with variability of the second-stage Φ and Θ estimates.

ity: precise inference about low-frequency behavior is very difficult given the short time series available in macroeconomics. One hundred years of data can provide only one independent observation about the long-run response one hundred years hence.

6. Summary and Conclusions

We examine persistence in U.S. real output using a generalized approximation to the Wold representation. Our application of long-memory models, associated with *fractional* integration via the operator $(1 - L)^d$ and noninteger d, allows flexible modeling of low-frequency behavior, with important implications for the measurement of macroeconomic shock persistence. Evidence of long memory is found in all of the macroeconomic series studied, though it is not necessarily associated with a unit root, as estimated d values range from 0.5 to 0.90. Furthermore, the knife-edged cases of 'unit root' and 'no unit root', which correspond to $d = 1$ and $d = 0$, respectively, lose their exaggerated importance once d is allowed to vary on a continuum.

Post-war real GNP per capital is investigated in detail, and estimated long-run responses to a unit innovation are shown to depend crucially on d. Using d estimates obtained from a spectral regression procedure, an estimated 50-quarter cumulative impulse response of roughly 0.7 is obtained. For GNP at annual frequencies, the estimates of d suggest even less persistence. In short, the point estimates strongly suggest that aggregate shocks are partially dissipated, not magnified.

However, and most importantly, we argue that the confidence intervals associated with any univariate persistence estimates are likely to be quite wide.[20] Even when conducted on a common data sample as in Stock and Watson (1988), various modeling methodologies provide very different persistence estimates. The UC representations, which contain restrictions on low-frequency behavior, produce low estimates of macroeconomic persistence. When the UC restrictions are relaxed by using ARIMA models, larger persistence estimates are obtained. However, when the ARIMA restrictions are relaxed to consider fractional integration, persistence point estimates again fall. This is consistent

---

[20] In related work [Diebold and Rudebusch (1989a)], we show that the confidence intervals associated with the predicted response of consumption to income, under the permanent-income hypothesis, are also quite wide, which casts doubt on the existence of the 'Deaton Paradox.' In future work, it may prove beneficial (in terms of efficiency gains) to work with multivariate models; common trends may then manifest themselves in terms of fractional cointegration, in a fashion analogous to King, Plosser, Stock, and Watson (1987), who allow for 'integer' cointegration.

with misspecification in the unit-root models (UC or ARIMA). However, the confidence we can place in *any* estimate of the long-run response is low because there are so few independent observations on long-run behavior available in the data.

Appendix: The Geweke and Porter-Hudak (1983) Theorem

Suppose $\{Y_t\}$ is an ARFIMA(p, d, q) process, with $d < 0$. Let $I(\lambda_{j,T})$ denote the periodogram of $\{Y_t\}$ at the harmonic frequencies $\lambda_{j,T} = 2\pi j/T$ in a sample of size T. Let $b_{1,T}$ denote the OLS estimator of β_1 in the regression equation

$$\ln\{I(\lambda_{j,T})\} = \beta_0 + \beta_1 \ln\{4\sin^2(\lambda_{j,T}/2)\} + \mu_{j,T}, \qquad j = 1, \ldots, K.$$

Then there exists a function $g(T)$, which will have the properties $\lim_{T \to \infty} g(T) = \infty$, $\lim_{T \to \infty} g(T)/T = 0$, such that if $K = g(T)$, then plim $b_1 = -d$. If $\lim_{T \to \infty}(\ln(T))^2/g(T) = 0$, then $(b_1 + d)/\{\text{vâr}(b_1)\}^{1/2} \overset{d}{\to} N(0, 1)$, where $\text{vâr}(b_1)$ is the usual OLS estimator, i.e., the $(2, 2)$ entry of $s^2(X'X)^{-1}$. Furthermore, under the stated conditions, plim $s^2 = \pi^2/6$.

References

Balke, N. S. and R. J. Gordon, 1989, The estimation of prewar gross national product: Methodology and new evidence, *Journal of Political Economy* 97, 38–92.

Beveridge, S. and C. R. Nelson, 1981, A new approach to the decomposition of economic time series into permanent and transient components with particular attention to measurement of the business cycle, *Journal of Monetary Economics* 7, 151–174.

Blanchard, O. J. and L. H. Summers, 1986, Hysteresis and the European unemployment problem, in: S. Fischer, ed., NBER macroeconomics annual (MIT Press, Cambridge, MA).

Brockwell, P. J. and R. A. Davis, 1987, Time series: Theory and models (Springer-Verlag, New York, NY).

Campbell, J. Y. and A. Deaton, 1987, Is consumption too smooth?, NBER working paper no. 2134.

Campbell, J. Y. and N. G. Mankiw, 1987a, Are output fluctuations transitory?, *Quarterly Journal of Economics* 102, 857–880.

Campbell, J. Y. and N. G. Mankiw, 1987b, Permanent and transitory components in macroeconomic fluctuations, *American Economic Review* 77, 111–117.

Carson, C., 1987, GNP: An overview of source data and estimating methods, *Survey of Current Business* 67, 103–126.

Clark, P. K., 1987, The cyclical component of U.S. economic activity, *Quarterly Journal of Economics* 102, 798–814.

Cochrane, J. H., 1988, How big is the random walk in GNP?, *Journal of Political Economy* 96, 893–920.

Diebold, F. X. and M. Nerlove, 1989, Unit roots in economic time series: A selective survey, in: Thomas B. Fomby and George F. Rhodes, eds., Advances in econometrics: Co-integration, spurious regressions, and unit roots (JAI Press, Greenwich, CT).

Diebold, F. X. and G. D. Rudebusch, 1989a, Is consumption too smooth? Long memory and the Deaton paradox, Finance and economics discussion series no. 57 (Federal Reserve Board, Washington, DC).

Diebold, F. X. and G. D. Rudebusch, 1989b, Why unit root tests on macroeconomic variables may be misleading, Manuscript (Federal Reserve Board, Washington, DC).

Friedman, M. and A. J. Schwartz, 1982, Monetary trends in the United States and the United Kingdom (University of Chicago Press, Chicago, IL).

Fuller, Wayne A., 1976, Introduction to statistical time series (Wiley, New York, NY).

Gagnon, J. E., 1988, Short-run models and long-run forecasts, *Quarterly Journal of Economics* 103, 415–424.

Geweke, J. and S. Porter-Hudak, 1983, The estimation and application of long memory time series models, *Journal of Time Series Analysis* 4, 221–238.

Ghysels, E., 1987, Unit root tests and the statistical pitfalls of seasonal adjustment: The case of U.S. post-war real GNP, Working paper no. 2887 (University of Montreal, Montreal).

Granger, C. W. J., 1966, The typical spectral shape of an economic variable, *Econometrica* 34, 150–161.

Granger, C. W. J., 1980, Long memory relationships and the aggregation of dynamic models, *Journal of Econometrics* 14, 227–238.

Granger, C. W. J., 1988, Aggregation of time series variables: A survey, Discussion paper no. 1 (Institute for Empirical Macroeconomics, Federal Reserve Bank of Minneapolis and University of Minnesota, MN).

Granger, C. W. J. and R. Joyeux, 1980, An introduction to long-memory time series models and fractional differencing, *Journal of Time Series Analysis* 1, 15–39.

Haubrich, J. G. and A. W. Lo, 1989, The sources and nature of long-term memory in the business cycle, Rodney White Center working paper no. 5-89 (Wharton School, University of Pennsylvania, Philadelphia, PA).

Hosking, J. R. M., 1981, Fractional differencing, *Biometrika* 68, 165–176.

Hurst, H. E., 1951, Long-term storage capacity in reservoirs, Transactions of the American Society of Civil Engineers 116, 770–799.

King, R. G., C. I. Plosser, and S. T. Rebello, 1988, Production, growth and business cycles II: New directions, *Journal of Monetary Economics* 21, 309–341.

King, R. G., C. I. Plosser, J. H. Stock, and M. W. Watson, 1987, Stochastic trends and economic fluctuations, Center for Economic Research working paper no. 79 (University of Rochester, Rochester, NY).

Lo, A., 1988, Long-term memory in stock market prices, Manuscript (Sloan School of Management, Massachusetts Institute of Technology, Cambridge, MA).

Mandelbrot, B. B., 1972, Statistical methodology for nonperiodic cycles: From the covariance to R/S analysis, *Annals of Economic and Social Measurement* 1, 259–290.

Nelson, C. R. and C. I. Plosser, 1982, Trends and random walks in macroeconomic time series: Some evidence and implications, *Journal of Monetary Economics* 10, 139–162.

Nerlove, M., 1964, Spectral analysis of seasonal adjustment procedures, *Econometrica* 32, 241–286.

Perron, P. and P. C. B. Phillips, 1987, Does GNP have a unit root?, *Economics Letters* 23, 139–145.

Phillips, P. C. B., 1987, Time series regression with a unit root, *Econometrica* 55, 277–301.

Romer, C. D., 1989, The prewar business cycle reconsidered: New estimates of gross national product, 1869–1908, *Journal of Political Economy* 97, 1–37.

Schwert, G. W., 1987, Effects of model misspecification on tests for unit roots in macroeconomic data, *Journal of Monetary Economics* 20, 73–103.

Shea, G. S., 1989, Uncertainty and implied variance bounds in long-memory models of the interest rate term structure, Manuscript (Department of Finance, Penn State University, University Park, PA).

Sowell, F. B., 1987, Maximum-likelihood estimation of fractionally integrated time-series models, Research paper no. 87-07 (Institute of Statistics and Decision Sciences, Duke University, Durham, NC).

Stock, J. H. and M. W. Watson, 1986, Does GNP have a unit root?, *Economics Letters* 22, 147–151.

Stock, J. H. and M. W. Watson, 1988, Variable trends in economic time series, *Journal of Economic Perspectives* 2, 147–174.

U.S. Bureau of Economic Analysis, 1973, Long-term economic growth (Government Printing Office, Washington, DC).

Watson, M. W., 1986, Univariate detrending methods with stochastic trends, *Journal of Monetary Economics* 18, 49–75.

12

Is Consumption Too Smooth? Long Memory and the Deaton Paradox

FRANCIS X. DIEBOLD AND GLENN D. RUDEBUSCH*

1. Introduction

In the last decade, a large amount of macroeconomic research has been devoted to various aspects of the permanent income hypothesis (PIH) under rational expectations. While Euler equations from the simplest models (e.g., Hall (1978)) imply that consumption should follow an approximate random walk, it is generally agreed that the data instead indicate that variables other than lagged consumption appear to play a significant role in determining current consumption (i.e., consumption displays "excess sensitivity"). Moreover, recent work has stressed that, given the empirical result that income appears to be highly persistent, the PIH implies that changes in consumption should be larger than the innovations to income. This implication does not appear to accord with the data because movements in consumption are smaller than income innovations. This apparent excess smoothness of consumption, relative to PIH predictions with persistent income, has been labeled the "Deaton paradox."[1]

Numerous economic arguments have been advanced to explain the phenomena of excess sensitivity and excess smoothness. A partial listing of these explanations includes: liquidity constraints (Hall and Mishkin (1982)), nonconstant real interest rates (Michener (1984) and Hall

* We thank two referees and Fallow Sowell for useful comments, as well as seminar participants at the 1988 North American Winter Meetings of the Econometric Society, especially Ken West, and at the Board of Governors of the Federal Reserve System. Diebold gratefully acknowledges financial support from the National Science Foundation (Grant SES 89-21715) and the University of Pennsylvania Research Foundation (Grant 3-71441).

[1] Excess smoothness, first noted by Deaton (1987), is examined in Campbell and Deaton (1989), Campbell and Mankiw (1990), and West (1988), while excess sensitivity is discussed in Flavin (1981) and Campbell (1987). Some of the subtle connections between the two are considered in Campbell and Deaton (1989) and Flavin (1988).

(1988)), precautionary saving (Caballero (1990)), aggregation over time (Christiano, Eichenbaum, and Marshall (1987)), aggregation over agents (Deaton (1987)), transitory consumption (Flavin (1981, 1988)), divergence between the information sets of econometricians and economic agents (West (1988), Flavin (1988), and Quah (1990)), habit formation (Deaton 1987)), and non-separable utility functions (Campbell and Mankiw (1990)).

Many of the above research strategies are theoretical attempts to make the stylized PIH model more "realistic" by introducing various "real world" complications; however, none of these modifications has garnered wide support. Even more importantly, before introducing *economic* complications to the model in response to its alleged empirical failure, one should be sure that such empirical failure is not due to arbitrary *statistical* assumptions imposed when testing the model. In this vein, we investigate econometric issues related to the Deaton paradox.[2] Specifically, we examine the consequences of relaxing restrictions on the representation of the stochastic process generating income. We use a long-memory, fractionally integrated model that permits a wide range of low-frequency behavior and nests the ARIMA specification as a special case.

In section 2 we set forth the standard PIH model of consumption and describe the crucial role in the excess-smoothness paradox that is played by the long-run properties of the stochastic process generating income. The class of fractionally integrated models is introduced and issues related to time-series representations of income are discussed in section 3. Empirical results are contained in section 4, where the model with fractional integration highlights the uncertainty associated with estimates of the parameter linking income innovations to changes in consumption. Section 5 concludes.

2. The Permanent-Income Hypothesis

Suppose that an infinitely lived representative agent at time t must choose consumption in period t, C_t, in the face of a stream of stochastic future real labor income payments, Y_{t+i}, $i = 0, 1, \ldots, \infty$. The consumer assumes the real interest rate, r, will be constant over the infinite planning horizon and possesses an endowment of non-human wealth of W_t at the end of period t. We take the permanent income hypothesis to imply that the consumer will set consumption in period t equal to

---

[2] However, we do not attempt to explain the excess sensitivity of consumption or other inconsistencies between PIH predictions and the data.

contemporaneous ex ante permanent income, y_t^p, which is the annuity value of non-human wealth and expected human wealth; thus,

$$C_t = y_t^p \equiv [r/(1 + r)]\left[W_t + \sum_{i=0}^{\infty} \beta^i E_t Y_{t+i}\right] \tag{1}$$

where $\beta \equiv 1/(1 + r)$ and E_t is the operator for expectations formed at time t.[3] The evolution of wealth over time is given by

$$W_t = (1 + r)(W_{t-1} + Y_{t-1} - C_{t-1}). \tag{2}$$

Following Flavin (1981), the first difference of equation (1) can then be written

$$\Delta C_t = r \sum_{i-0}^{\infty} \beta^i [E_t Y_{t+i} - E_{t-1} Y_{t+i}], \tag{3}$$

so that changes in consumption are driven by revisions in conditional expectations of future labor income.

Under rational expectations, the nature of the process generating labor income determines the behavior of consumption.[4] The evaluation of PIH predictions of consumption behavior then hinges on the appropriate specification of the income process. Deaton (1987) formulated the excess smoothness paradox in conjunction with accumulating empirical evidence (e.g., Nelson and Plosser (1982)) that many macroeconomic variables are well characterized as having unit roots. Specifically, for the case of real labor income, Campbell (1987) is able to find no evidence against the unit root null hypothesis. Assuming a unit root, the generating process for real income can be written as

$$\Phi(L)\Delta Y_t = \gamma' + \Theta(L)\epsilon_t, \tag{4}$$

[3] Strictly, equation (1) is only true if the third and higher derivatives of the underlying utility function are equal to zero; otherwise, the uncertainty associated with future income flows may generate precautionary saving, so that consumption is less than permanent income. Caballero (1990) argues that such behavior could explain the excess smoothness phenomenon.

[4] We model the information set used by the consumer in projecting income to include only lags of income. As noted by West (1988), the effect of additional information could make consumption appear to be too smooth relative to the innovations of a univariate income process; however, his results indicate that this is unlikely to be the case. Campbell and Deaton (1989) reach a similar conclusion on this issue.

where

$$\Phi(L) = 1 - \phi_1 L - \phi_2 L^2 - \cdots - \phi_p L^p$$

$$\Theta(L) = 1 - \theta_1 L - \theta_2 L^2 - \cdots - \theta_q L^q,$$

and all roots of $\Phi(z)$ and $\Theta(z)$ are outside the unit circle.[5] Flavin (1981) and Hansen and Sargent (1981) provide the technology needed to compute the sequence of revisions in expected incomes,

$$\{E_t Y_{t+i} - E_{t-1} Y_{t+i}\}_{i=0}^{\infty},$$

and hence the change in consumption (3), following a shock ϵ_t to income. In fact, the change in consumption is proportional to the income shock,

$$\Delta C_t = \kappa \epsilon_t, \tag{5}$$

where

$$\kappa \equiv \frac{1 - \sum_{i=1}^{q} \beta^i \theta_i}{1 - \sum_{i-1}^{p} \beta^i \phi_i}. \tag{6}$$

This key relationship provides the link between the stochastic properties of income (4), as captured in κ and ϵ_t, and the stochastic properties of consumption.

It will prove useful to rewrite income in the (equivalent) moving-average form,

$$\Delta Y_t = \gamma + A(L) \epsilon_t, \tag{7}$$

where

$$A(L) = \Phi^{-1}(L) \Theta(L) \equiv 1 + a_1 L + a_2 L^2 \cdots$$

$$\gamma = \Phi^{-1}(1) \gamma'.$$

[5] It is not our intent here to address the "trends vs. unit roots" debate in the context of labor income, as in Christiano (1987), or, more generally, in Rudebusch (1990). Rather, as will be discussed subsequently, we work in a "stochastic trend" environment, but we explicitly broaden the analysis to include forms of long memory other than unit roots.

Then we have as well

$$\Delta C_t = \kappa \epsilon_t, \tag{8}$$

where

$$\kappa = \left(1 + \sum_{i=1}^{\infty} \beta^i a_i\right) \equiv c_\infty^\beta. \tag{9}$$

The multiplier c_∞^β, which relates income innovations to changes in consumption, is simply the infinite cumulative impulse response, $A(1)$, adjusted to reflect the discount factor β. In other words, c_∞^β is the discounted sum of income changes resulting from the shock ϵ_t. If $r = 0$, $c_\infty^\beta = c_\infty^1 \equiv A(1)$, but if $r > 0$, then c_∞^β can be greater or smaller than c_∞^1, depending on the entire shape of the cumulative impulse response function.

Taking the standard deviation of each side of the consumption response equation (8) yields

$$\mathrm{std}(\Delta C_t) = c_\infty^\beta \, \mathrm{std}(\epsilon_t). \tag{10}$$

Deaton (1987) and Campbell and Deaton (1989) show that a variety of ARIMA specifications for the real income process (together with reasonable assumptions regarding the real interest rate) lead to the same conclusion: c_∞^β is substantially above unity.[6] Thus, under the PIH, the variability of observed consumption changes should be greater than the variability of income innovations; in fact, the opposite is observed, as consumption appears to be too smooth. For example, Deaton (1987) finds that the standard deviation of the growth of consumption is only about half of the innovation standard deviation of an ARIMA $(1, 1, 0)$ process describing income.

In the PIH consumption model sketched so far, the underlying result is that changes in consumption depend upon the process generating income. The modeling of the income process is thus crucial for interpreting consumption behavior and evaluating the PIH. In the next section, we introduce a more general approximation to the Wold representation than those used previously, in order to more closely examine the low-frequency properties of income.

---

[6] It is not the unit root assumption per se that is responsible for this conclusion. Instead, the short memory dynamics that result for disposable income under the assumption of a unit root (that is, positive serial correlation in first differences) work to produce an impulse response that is greater than one.

3. Allowing for Fractionally Integrated Income

As in Diebold and Rudebusch (1989), we consider a generalization of
the standard ARIMA (p, d, q) model to allow fractional integration:

$$\Phi(L)(1 - L)^d Y_t = \Theta(L)\epsilon_t, \qquad \epsilon_t \sim (0, \sigma_\epsilon^2), \tag{11}$$

where

$$\Phi(L) = 1 - \phi_1 L - \cdots - \phi_p L^p,$$

$$\Theta(L) = 1 - \theta_1 L - \cdots - \theta_q L^q,$$

all roots of $\Phi(L)$ and $\Theta(L)$ lie outside the unit circle, and d is allowed
to assume values in the real, as opposed to the integer, set of numbers.[7]
Stationarity and invertibility require $|d| < 1/2$, which can always be
achieved by taking a suitable number of differences. Econometricians
typically have considered only integer values of d; the leading special
cases are the discrete options $d = 0$ and $d = 1$. However, allowance for
non-integer d values, that is, fractional integration, provides for parsimonious yet flexible modeling of low-frequency variation. Operationally,
a binomial pansion of the operator $(1 - L)^d$ is used:

$$(1 - L)^d = \sum_{j=0}^{\infty} \frac{\Gamma(j - d)L^j}{\Gamma(-d)\Gamma(j + 1)} \tag{12}$$

$$= 1 - dL + \frac{d(d - 1)}{2!}L^2$$

$$- \frac{d(d - 1)(d - 2)}{3!}L^3 + \cdots, \tag{13}$$

where $\Gamma(\cdot)$ denotes the gamma, or generalized factorial, integral. When
$d = 1$, this is just the usual first-differencing filter. For non-integer d,
the operator $(1 - L)^d$ provides an infinite-order lag-operator polynomial with coefficients that decline very slowly. We denote this general
representation, with potentially fractional d, as the ARFIMA (AutoRegressive Fractionally-Integrated Moving Average) model.

The ARFIMA model can be put in the moving-average form used
above to calculate the present discounted value of future income. First,

---

[7] Fractional integration allows a local generalization of the unit root hypothesis; rather
than forcing $d = 1$, we allow $1/2 < d < 3/2$.

write equation (11) as

$$(1 - L)^d Y_t = B(L)\epsilon_t, \tag{14}$$

where $B(L) = \Phi^{-1}(L)\Theta(L)$. Extracting the factor $(1 - L)$ gives

$$(1 - L)^{d-1}(1 - L)Y_t = B(L)\epsilon_t, \tag{15}$$

or

$$(1 - L)Y_t = A(L)\epsilon_t, \tag{16}$$

where $A(L) = (1 - L)^{1-d}B(L)$.[8]

The ARFIMA model (11) belongs to the class of long-memory processes, so-named for their ability to display significant dependence between observations widely separated in time.[9] Standard ARMA processes are short-memory because the autocorrelation (or dependence) between observations τ periods apart decays rapidly as τ increases. Indeed, the autocorrelations at lag τ decline exponentially:

$$\rho_Y(\tau) \sim r^\tau, \qquad 0 < r < 1, \tau \to \infty.$$

For ARFIMA processes, however, the autocorrelation function has a much slower hyperbolic decline:

$$\rho_Y(\tau) \sim \tau^{2d-1}, \qquad d < .5, \tau \to \infty.$$

The intuition of long memory and the limitation of the integer-d restriction emerge clearly in the frequency domain. The series $\{Y_t\}$ displays long memory if its spectral density, f_Y, increases without limit as angular frequency tends to zero:

$$\lim_{\lambda \to 0} f_Y(\lambda) = \infty. \tag{17}$$

In fact, for an ARFIMA series, $f_Y(\lambda)$ behaves like λ^{-2d} as $\lambda \to 0$, so d parameterizes the low-frequency behavior. This is in contrast to the usual ARIMA model, where the spectral density is forced to behave like λ^{-2} as $\lambda \to 0$. Thus, a rich range of spectral behavior near the origin

---

[8] As in section II, we can allow for drift, $(1 - L)Y_t = \gamma + A(L)\epsilon_t$, and do so in the estimation reported below.

[9] Granger and Joyeux (1980) and Hosking (1981) independently proposed the use of ARFIMA processes as flexible long-memory models. Further discussion of fractional integration can be found in Diebold and Nerlove (1990).

becomes possible when the integer-d restriction is relaxed. The "typical spectral shape" of economic variables (Granger (1966)), is monotonically declining with frequency, except for possible peaks at seasonals, with high power at low frequencies. This shape is well-captured by fractionally integrated processes. For example, while *levels* of economic data typically have high power at low frequencies, *differences* often have little power at low frequencies; this is characteristic of fractionally-integrated processes with $d < 1$.[10]

The ARFIMA model, by allowing a variety of spectral shapes near the origin (corresponding to the continuum of possible d values), can provide superior approximations to the Wold representations of economic time series. This is particularly important in the context of the Deaton paradox; as discussed in section II, an assessment of the excess smoothness of consumption depends critically on the estimates of the discounted sum of coefficients in a Wold representation.

4. Empirical Results

A. Estimation of d

We use a two-step procedure for the estimation of fractionally integrated models due to Geweke and Porter-Hudak (GPH) (1983). We first obtain a consistent and asymptotically normal estimate of d and transform the series by the expansion of $(1 - L)^d$. We then fit an ARMA model to the transformed series to obtain consistent estimates of the remaining model parameters Φ, Θ, and σ_ϵ^2. Finally, these estimates are used to construct consistent estimates of the discounted cumulative impulse response.

The first-stage estimate of d is based on the slope of the spectral density function near $\lambda = 0$. Denote the first difference of the relevant series, $X_t = (1 - L)Y_t$; we wish to estimate $\tilde{d}$ in the model

$$(1 - L)^{\tilde{d}} X_t = \Phi^{-1}(L)\Theta(L)\epsilon_t \equiv u_t. \tag{18}$$

As d of the level series equals $1 + \tilde{d}$, a value of $\tilde{d}$ equal to zero corresponds to a unit root in Y_t.

---

[10] Further intuition for the ARFIMA representation is provided by Granger (1980), who shows that fractional integration may be induced by aggregation. Specifically, if the underlying components of an aggregate series (e.g., firms' productions) follow AR(1) processes with parameters ρ_i, and the ρ_i's are beta-distributed in the cross section, then aggregation yields a fractionally integrated macroeconomic series.

The spectral density of X_t is given by

$$f_X(\lambda) = |1 - \exp(-i\lambda)|^{-2\tilde{d}} f_u(\lambda)$$

$$= [2\sin(\lambda/2)]^{-2\tilde{d}} f_u(\lambda) \tag{19}$$

where $f_u(\lambda)$ is the spectral density of the stationary process u_t. Suppose that a sample of size T is available $(X_t, t = 1, \ldots, T)$; let $\lambda_j = 2\pi j/T$ $(j = 0, \ldots, T - 1)$ denote the harmonic ordinates of the sample. Taking logarithms of equation (19), adding and subtracting $\ln\{f_u(0)\}$, and evaluating at the harmonic ordinates, we obtain

$$\ln\{f_X(\lambda_j)\} = \ln\{f_u(0)\} - \tilde{d}\ln\{4\sin^2(\lambda_j/2)\}$$

$$+ \ln\{f_u(\lambda_j)/f_u(0)\}. \tag{20}$$

If we restrict consideration to the low-frequency ordinates near zero, say, λ_j, $j \leq K \ll T$, the last term in (20) can be dropped as negligible. Let $I(\lambda_j)$ denote the periodogram at ordinate j, then add $\ln\{I(\lambda_j)\}$ to both sides of (20) and rearrange to obtain

$$\ln\{I(\lambda_j)\} = \ln\{f_u(0)\} - \tilde{d}\ln\{4\sin^2(\lambda_j/2)\}$$

$$+ \ln\{I(\lambda_j)/f_X(\lambda_j)\}. \tag{21}$$

The particular utility of this formulation is its formal similarity to a simple linear regression equation:

$$\ln\{I(\lambda_j)\} = \beta_0 + \beta_1 \ln\{4\sin^2(\lambda_j/2)\} + \eta_j, \qquad j = 1, \ldots, K \tag{22}$$

where β_0 is the constant $\ln\{f_u(0)\}$, and the η_j, equal to $\ln\{I(\lambda_j)/f_X(\lambda_j)\}$, are independently and identically distributed.

Now let the number of low-frequency ordinates used in the above spectral regression be a function of the sample size, i.e., $K = g(T)$. Then, under regularity conditions on $g(\cdot)$, essentially that $g(T)$ approach ∞ with T, but at a slower rate, the negative of the OLS estimate of the slope coefficient provides a consistent and asymptotically normal estimate of $\tilde{d}$. This is true regardless of the orders and parameterizations of the Φ and Θ polynomials underlying the stationary process u_t. Furthermore, the variance of the estimate of β_1 is given by the usual OLS estimator, and the theoretical asymptotic variance of the regression error η_j was shown by Geweke and Porter-Hudak (1983) to be equal to $\pi^2/6$, which can be imposed to increase efficiency.

The regularity conditions on $g(T)$ required for a consistent estimate of d do not uniquely determine $g(T)$ or K, the sample size for the GPH regression. However, since d parameterizes and is estimated from the long-run dynamics of the time series, economic considerations can suggest a reasonable definition of the long run and hence designate a reasonable GPH sample size. In particular, we exclude from the estimation of d the information contained in short-run business cycles, namely, cyclical movements with periods of five years or less.[11] This implies that periodogram ordinates at frequencies *lower* than the five-year frequency should be included in the GPH regression, which translates into a "cutoff frequency" for inclusion in the regression of $2\pi/5$ for annual data and $2\pi/20$ for quarterly data. In the time domain, this five-year cutoff criterion can be translated into a simple and intuitive rule: the number of periodogram ordinates included in the GPH regression (K) should equal the number of non-overlapping five-year intervals available in the data sample.[12] There is a trade-off involved in specifying the period of the shortest cycle included. A shorter cutoff period gives a larger GPH regression sample and hence smaller standard errors for the estimate of d; however, the shorter cutoff period also biases the estimate of d with high frequency information. Our results, however, were robust across a range of cutoff periods.

Table 12.1 provides GPH estimates of d for two income series: real disposable income, as reported in the National Income and Product Accounts (NIPA), and real labor income, as calculated by Blinder and Deaton (1985, table A-1).[13] The first series, although commonly used in testing the permanent income hypothesis, is somewhat too broad, as it includes all sources of income and not just income from labor. The Blinder and Deaton series, on the other hand, is an approximate labor income series equal to wages and salaries and a weighted sum of several other categories from the NIPA breakdown of personal income. In short, the two series have contrasting costs and benefits: the disposable income series is too broad but is directly measured, while the labor income series is conceptually more appropriate but judgmentally constructed. We therefore examine both; we estimate the fractional integration parameter for the per capita level of quarterly disposable income and labor income.[14] We also examine the NIPA annual dispos-

[11] According to the National Bureau of Economic Research's chronology of turning points, the average length of a U.S. business cycle is 52 months.

[12] Formally, let p denote the cutoff period, that is, the length of the shortest cycle to be included (expressed in units equivalent to the frequency of measurement of the series). Then the corresponding cutoff frequency is $2\pi/p$. Now, the Kth, or final, periodogram ordinate is at frequency $2\pi K/T$. Equating the two gives $2\pi K/T = 2\pi/p$, or $K = T/p$.

[13] Both data samples start in 1953:Q4 for conformity and to omit distortions during the Korean War.

[14] Campbell and Deaton (1989) have also formulated the Deaton paradox in the logarithm of income; we obtained similar d estimates with logs.

TABLE 12.1
Estimates of d from Geweke-Porter-Hudak Regression

Data Series and Source	$\hat{d}$
Quarterly disposable income 1953:Q4–1987:Q2 (NIPA)	1.10 (0.38)
Annual disposable income 1929–1987 (NIPA)	1.17 (0.26)
Quarterly labor income 1953:Q4–1984:Q4 (Blinder and Deaton (1985))	0.99 (0.43)

Notes: All variables are in constant dollars on a seasonally adjusted per capita basis. The standard errors given in parentheses are constructed imposing the known theoretical regression error variance of $\pi^2/6$. The sample size used in the GPH regression is $T/20$ for quarterly series and $T/5$ for annual series, rounded to the nearest integer, as discussed in the text.

able income series, for which a much longer time span of data (from 1929 through 1987) is available.

The point estimates of d in table 12.1 are all in the range of 1.0; however, it is important to note their large associated standard errors. Two standard deviations from the point estimates encompass the range from 0.5 to 1.5; thus, the confidence we can have in the estimates of d is quite low. Because of these results, we are wary of *conditioning* upon the assumption of a unit root and proceeding to estimate models based on first-differenced data.[15] Instead, we perform a full sensitivity analysis, explicitly acknowledging the uncertainty associated with any estimate of d. It has been suggested by others (e.g., Deaton (1987)) that the limited information in the available macroeconomic data precludes a determination of the long-run properties of labor income. We are able to provide explicit, formal support for this thesis below, as the discounted cumulative impulse response is seen to depend crucially upon the order of integration.

---

[15] This is particularly true in light of the low power of the usual unit root tests against fractionally integrated alternatives (Diebold and Rudebusch (1990)).

B. Estimation of κ

Computation of the discounted cumulative impulse response requires estimation of all of the parameters of the ARFIMA (p, d, q) model. In this section, we focus on quarterly real disposable income to compute this response and investigate its robustness to variations in the model.[16] We first transform the first difference of the level of disposable income by the long-memory filter (17) for a range of values of the fractional integration parameter. These transformed series are then modeled as ARMA (p, q) processes to capture the remaining short-run dynamics.[17] Finally, estimates of the discounted cumulative impulse response, conditional on a variety of assumed real interest rates, are constructed.

Tables 12.2 through 12.4 provide estimates of the discounted impulse response. The tables differ in their assumed discount factor β, with β equal to 1, 0.998, and 0.995 in tables 12.2, 12.3, and 12.4, respectively. These discount factors correspond to real interest rates ranging from 0% to 2% per year. In each table, the order of fractional integration is varied across 0.6, 0.8, 1.0, 1.2, and 1.4. For each d value, we estimate ARMA models with up to three autoregressive parameters and three moving-average parameters. We distinguish these models through the Akaike and Schwarz information criteria (AIC and SIC, respectively), which are differentiated by their degrees-of-freedom adjustment of the maximized log-likelihood function. The tables report the two optimal models according to the information criteria for each d value.[18] For each of the ten ARFIMA (p, d, q) models in each table, the discounted cumulative impulse responses at a variety of economic horizons are presented.

Strictly speaking, the stylized model of section 2 assumed the consumer had a relevant economic horizon of infinity. In richer models, shorter horizons are also of interest.[19] For a variety of reasons, the consumer may be myopic and may take into account the persistence of income, say, only over the next four years (c_{16}^{β}), ten years (c_{40}^{β}), twenty years (c_{80}^{β}), forty years (c_{160}^{β}), one hundred years (c_{400}^{β}), or one thou-

---

[16] We focus on quarterly disposable income to conserve space, however, our results were similar for the other income series.

[17] Although the long-memory filter is truncated at each point to the available sample, the estimate of d from the GPH regression and the second-stage estimates of Φ and Θ are all consistent.

[18] The two models reported for each d value are illustrative; not surprisingly, given d, the long-run response is similar across the sixteen ARMA models fitted.

[19] The infinite horizon may represent infinitely lived consumers or an operative bequest motive. In other models in which agents have finite but stochastic lifetimes or stochastic termination of generational linkages, the relevant horizon may be shorter.

TABLE 12.2
Discounted Impulse Response for Quarterly Disposable Income, $\beta = 1$

d	ARFIMA(p, d, q)(AIC) ARFIMA(p, d, q)(SIC)	c_{16}^{β}	c_{40}^{β}	c_{80}^{β}	c_{160}^{β}	c_{400}^{β}	c_{4000}^{β}
1.4	$(2, 1.4, 0)$	2.19	3.11	4.07	5.36	7.72	19.37
	$(2, 1.4, 0)$	2.19	3.11	4.07	5.36	7.72	19.37
1.2	$(3, 1.2, 0)$	1.70	2.03	2.33	2.68	3.22	5.10
	$(0, 1.2, 0)$	1.91	2.28	2.62	3.01	3.61	5.72
1.0	$(3, 1, 3)$	1.17	1.11	1.12	1.14	1.13	1.13
	$(0, 1, 0)$	1.00	1.00	1.00	1.00	1.00	1.00
0.8	$(3, .8, 3)$	1.17	0.91	0.80	0.71	0.58	0.37
	$(3, .8, 0)$	1.14	0.93	0.81	0.70	0.58	0.37
0.6	$(3, .6, 3)$	1.80	1.41	1.01	0.74	0.50	0.20
	$(1, .6, 1)$	1.70	1.43	1.03	0.74	0.50	0.20

Notes: For each d value, we report the models selected by the Akaike information criterion (AIC) and Schwartz information criterion (SIC). The ARFIMA (p, d, q) model, $(1 - L)^d Y_t = \text{ARMA}(p, q)$, is estimated conditional upon d. For each model, we report estimates of the discounted cumulative impulse response function, c_k^{β}, for $k = 16, 40, 80, 160, 400$ and 4000, as discussed in the text.

TABLE 12.3
Discounted Impulse Response for Quarterly Disposable Income, $\beta = .998$

d	ARFIMA(p, d, q)(AIC) ARFIMA(p, d, q)(SIC)	c_{16}^{β}	c_{40}^{β}	c_{80}^{β}	c_{160}^{β}	c_{400}^{β}	c_{4000}^{β}
1.4	$(2, 1.4, 0)$	2.17	3.04	3.90	4.92	6.30	7.49
	$(2, 1.4, 0)$	2.17	3.04	3.90	4.92	6.30	7.49
1.2	$(3, 1.2, 0)$	1.69	2.01	2.27	2.55	2.87	3.09
	$(0, 1.2, 0)$	1.90	2.26	2.55	2.86	3.22	3.47
1.0	$(3, 1, 3)$	1.16	1.11	1.12	1.13	1.13	1.13
	$(0, 1, 0)$	1.00	1.00	1.00	1.00	1.00	1.00
0.8	$(3, .8, 3)$	1.17	0.93	0.83	0.75	0.68	0.65
	$(3, .8, 0)$	1.14	0.95	0.83	0.75	0.68	0.65
0.6	$(3, .6, 3)$	1.80	1.42	1.07	0.86	0.71	0.66
	$(1, .6, 1)$	1.69	1.44	1.09	0.85	0.71	0.65

Notes: See notes to table 12.2.

sand years (c_{4000}^{β}). All of these horizons are reported in tables 12.2 through 12.4.

Let us focus on the results in table 12.3, which are based on a representative discount rate of $\beta = 0.998$. Assuming a one-hundred-year horizon, the estimated multiplier from income innovations to changes in consumption (i.e., $\kappa = c_{400}^{.998}$), ranges from 0.71 for $d = 0.6$ to 6.30 for

TABLE 12.4

Discounted Impulse Response for Quarterly Disposable Income, $\beta = .995$

d	$ARFIMA(p, d, q)(AIC)$ $ARFIMA(p, d, q)(SIC)$	c_{16}^{β}	c_{40}^{β}	c_{80}^{β}	c_{160}^{β}	c_{400}^{β}	c_{4000}^{β}
1.4	$(2, 1.4, 0)$	2.15	2.94	3.67	4.38	5.03	5.20
	$(2, 1.4, 0)$	2.15	2.94	3.67	4.38	5.03	5.20
1.2	$(3, 1.2, 0)$	1.68	1.97	2.19	2.39	2.54	2.57
	$(0, 1.2, 0)$	1.89	2.21	2.46	2.68	2.85	2.89
1.0	$(3, 1, 3)$	1.16	1.12	1.12	1.13	1.13	1.13
	$(0, 1, 0)$	1.00	1.00	1.00	1.00	1.00	1.00
0.8	$(3, .8, 3)$	1.18	0.95	0.86	0.81	0.78	0.77
	$(3, .8, 0)$	1.15	0.96	0.87	0.81	0.77	0.77
0.6	$(3, .6, 3)$	1.78	1.44	1.14	0.99	0.92	0.91
	$(1, .6, 1)$	1.68	1.45	1.15	0.99	0.92	0.91

Notes: See notes to table 12.2.

$d = 1.4$, which illustrates how wide the *interval* estimates are for the long-run response. To approximate $k\%$ confidence intervals for κ, we can vary d over its $k\%$ confidence range (obtained by exploiting the asymptotic normality of the first-stage GPH estimate) and condition upon estimated Φ and Θ values at each d value.[20] Clearly, varying the d estimate across two standard errors encompasses consumption volatility and smoothness relative to income innovations. As in Deaton (1987) and Campbell and Deaton (1989), the estimated income innovations from these fitted models appear to have a larger standard deviation than the standard deviation of changes in actual consumption. Unlike the previous work, however, we cannot reject such a response as a significant departure from the predictions of the PIH, that is, as *excess* smoothness of consumption, once the uncertainty associated with integration order is taken into account.

5. Conclusions

Under the permanent income hypothesis for consumption behavior, the long-run, or low-frequency, stochastic properties of income are decisive in determining the response of consumption to an innovation in income. Earlier ARIMA specifications have suggested that the response of

---

[20] This procedure provides a lower bound on the widths of the true confidence intervals, because it does not take into account the stochastic variation in the Φ and Θ estimates.

consumption to news about income should be much larger than appears to be true in the data. In this paper, we explicitly estimate the (generally fractional) degree of integration, rather than conditioning on a particular d estimate (as is implicitly done with ARIMA representations). More importantly, we are able to explicitly acknowledge the uncertainty associated with d and trace the effects of that uncertainty through to the cumulative impulse response function of income. We find that, while our point estimates are similar to those of others, our interval estimates for the multiplier linking changes in consumption to income innovations are quite wide, reflecting the (previously unacknowledged) uncertainty associated with d. The wide confidence intervals underscore a fundamental econometric reality: precise inference about low-frequency behavior is very difficult given the short span of income data available.

Finally, it is important to note that our arguments do not provide a complete reconciliation of data and theory. Specifically, while we have shown that violations of the PIH due to excess smoothness may not be as important as was previously believed, we have not addressed failures of the PIH due to excess sensitivity. The fact that consumption responds to anticipated changes in income is unaffected by the methods that we have employed and remains inconsistent with the theory.

References

Blinder, Alan S., and Angus Deaton, "The Time Series Consumption Function Revisited," *Brookings Papers on Economic Activity* (2, 1985), 465–511.

Cabellero, Ricardo, "Consumption Puzzles and Precautionary Savings," *Journal of Monetary Economics* 25 (1990), 113–136.

Campbell, John Y., "Does Saving Anticipate Declining Labor Income? An Alternative Test of the Permanent Income Hypothesis," *Econometrica* 55 (Nov. 1987), 1249–1274.

Campbell, John Y., and Angus Deaton, "Is Consumption Too Smooth?," *Review of Economic Studies* 56 (July 1989), 357–373.

Campbell, John Y., and N. Gregory Mankiw, "Permanent Income, Current Income, and Consumption," *Journal of Business and Economic Statistics* (July 1990), 265–279.

Christiano, Lawrence J., "Why Is Consumption Less Volatile than Income?," *Quarterly Review*, Federal Reserve Bank of Minneapolis (Fall 1987), 2–20.

Christiano, Lawrence J., Martin Eichenbaum, and D. Marshall, "The Permanent Income Hypothesis Revisited," Research Dept. Working Paper No. 335, Federal Reserve Bank of Minneapolis (1987); forthcoming *Econometrica* (1991).

Deaton, Angus, "Life Cycle Models of Consumption: Is the Evidence Consistent with the Theory?," in T. F. Bewley (ed.), *Advances in Econometrics, Fifth World Congress*, Volume II (Cambridge: Cambridge University Press, 1987), 121–146.

Diebold, Francis X., and Glenn D. Rudebusch, "Long Memory and Persistence in Aggregate Output," *Journal of Monetary Economics* 24 (Sept. 1989) 189–209.

——, "On the Power of Dickey-Fuller Tests against Fractional Alternatives," FEDS Working Paper 119, Board of Governors of the Federal Reserve System (1990); forthcoming *Economics Letters* (1991).

Diebold, Francis X., and Marc Nerlove, "Unit Roots in Economic Time Series: A Selective Survey," in Thomas B. Fomby and George F. Rhodes (eds.), *Advances in Econometrics: Co-Integration, Spurious Regressions, and Unit Roots* (Greenwich, Connecticut: JAI Press, 1990), 3–69.

Flavin, Marjorie A., "The Adjustment of Consumption to Changing Expectations About Future Income," *Journal of Political Economy* 89 (1981), 974–1009.

——, "The Excess Smoothness of Consumption: Identification and Interpretation," manuscript, Department of Economics, University of Virginia (1988).

Geweke, John, and Susan Porter-Hudak, "The Estimation and Application of Long Memory Time Series Models," *Journal of Time Series Analysis* 4 (1983), 221–238.

Granger, Clive W. J., "The Typical Spectral Shape of an Economic Variable," *Econometrica* 34 (1966), 150–161.

——, "Long Memory Relationships and the Aggregation of Dynamic Models," *Journal of Econometrics* 14 (1980), 227–238.

Granger, Clive W. J., and R. Joyeux, "An Introduction to Long-Memory Time Series Models and Fractional Differencing," *Journal of Time Series Analysis* 1 (1980), 15–39.

Hall, Robert E., "Stochastic Implications of the Life Cycle-Permanent Income Hypothesis: Theory and Evidence," *Journal of Political Economy* 86 (1978), 971–987.

——, "Intertemporal Substitution in Consumption," *Journal of Political Economy* (1988), 339–357.

Hall, Robert E., and Fredric S. Mishkin, "The Sensitivity of Consumption to Transitory Income: Evidence from Panel Data on Households," *Econometrica* 50 (1982), 461–481.

Hansen, Lars P., and Tom J. Sargent, "A Note on Weiner-Kolmogorov Prediction Formulas for Rational Expectation Models," *Economics Letters* 8 (1981), 266–260.

Hosking, J. R. M., "Fractional Differencing," *Biometrika* 68 (1981), 165–176.

Michener, R., "Permanent Income in General Equilibrium," *Journal of Monetary Economics* 13 (1984), 297–305.

Nelson, Charles R., and Charles I. Plosser, "Trends and Random Walks in Macroeconomic Time Series: Some Evidence and Implications," *Journal of Monetary Economics* 10 (1982), 139–162.

Quah, Danny, "Permanent and Transitory Movements in Labor Income: An Explanation for "Excess Smoothness" in Consumption," *Journal of Political Economy* 98 (June 1990), 449–475.

Rudebusch, Glenn D., "Trends and Random Walks in Macroeconomic Time Series: A Re-examination," Economic Activity Working Paper 105, Board of Governors of the Federal Reserve System (1990).

West, Kenneth D., "The Insensitivity of Consumption to News About Income," *Journal of Monetary Economics* 21 (1988), 17–33.

13

On the Power of Dickey–Fuller Tests against Fractional Alternatives

FRANCIS X. DIEBOLD AND GLENN D. RUDEBUSCH*

1. Fractional Integration versus Unit Roots

Nelson and Plosser (1982) and many other studies have failed to reject the null hypothesis of a single autoregressive unit root for many macroeconomic time series. Fractionally integrated models have received recent attention because of their ability to provide a natural and flexible characterization of persistent processes, while nesting the unit root hypothesis as a special, and potentially restrictive, case. Our analysis will consider whether common unit root tests when applied to fractionally integrated data are able to reject the unit root null hypothesis.

The general ARFIMA (henceforth, AutoRegressive Fractionally Integrated Moving Average) model can be written as

$$\Phi(L)(1 - L)^{d}X_{t} = \Theta(L)\epsilon_{t}, \tag{1}$$

where d is any real number. [As usual, $\Theta(L)$ and $\Theta(L)$ are the autoregressive and moving-average polynomials in the lag operator (with roots outside the unit circle), and $\epsilon_{t} \sim (0, \sigma_{\epsilon}^{2})$.] Operationally, the fractional difference operator $(1 - L)^{d}$ can be expressed by a binomial expansion. The process is stationary and invertible if $d \in (-1/2, 1/2)$, and one can always transform a fractionally integrated series of higher order ($d > 1/2$) into this range by taking a suitable number of integer differences.[1] with non-zero d, the ARFIMA model displays 'long memory', that is, substantial dependence between observations τ periods

---

* We thank the participants of the 1989 North American Winter meetings of the Econometric Society, especially Andy Rose, for useful comments. Diebold gratefully acknowledges financial support from the National Science Foundation (grant SES 89-2715) and the University of Pennsylvania Research Foundation (grant 3-71441).

[1] For a proof, see Hosking (1981). More extensive discussion and references may be found in Diebold and Rudebusch (1989a, 1989b) and Diebold and Nerlove (1990).

apart, even for large τ. Indeed, as τ increases, the ARFIMA autocorrelations decline at a very slow hyperbolic rate; in contrast, ARMA autocorrelations decline at a quite rapid geometric rate.

In our earlier work [Diebold and Rudebusch (1989a)], we obtained a point estimate of d equal to 0.68 for the level of U.S. postwar quarterly real GNP per capita (equivalently, the fractional order for the first difference of GNP is equal to -0.32). Thus, the level of real output appears to have long memory, in the sense that the d estimate is significantly greater than zero. However, the long memory may not be associated with a unit autoregressive root; notably the d estimate is substantially less than one, and the unit root hypothesis can be rejected at conventional significance levels. More generally, regardless of the significance of the difference of the d estimate from unity, the provocative point estimates suggest the following thought experiment: If a series *were* best characterized by a fractional process, would a researcher be able to detect that fact by rejecting the hypothesis of a unit root using conventional Dickey–Fuller [Fuller (1976)] tests? With this motivation, we proceed to examine the power of Dickey–Fuller tests when the true data-generating process is fractionally integrated.

2. Analytical Conjectures about Power

Consider a random walk

$$(1 - L)^d X_t = \epsilon_t, \qquad d = 1, \tag{2}$$

with white noise innovation, $\epsilon_t \sim (0, \sigma_\epsilon^2)$. In a classic paper, White (1958) characterized the distribution of the least-squares estimator $\hat{\beta}$ in the first-order autoregressive [henceforth, AR(1)] model,

$$X_t = \beta X_{t-1} + \epsilon_t, \tag{3}$$

under the unit-root null hypothesis that $\beta = 1$, i.e., when the true data-generating process is (2).

Consider the natural generalization of (2) to the case of a pure fractionally integrated process,

$$(1 - L)^d X_t = \epsilon_t, \qquad 1/2 < d < 3/2. \tag{4}$$

Or equivalently,

$$(1 - L) X_t = u_t, \quad \text{with } (1 - L)^{\tilde{d}} u_t = \epsilon_t, \tag{5}$$

where $\tilde{d} = d - 1$. Thus, $d \in (1/2, 3/2)$ corresponds to $\tilde{d} \in (-1/2, 1/2)$, and the natural analog of the White regression (3) is

$$X_t = \beta X_{t-1} + u_t, \quad \text{with } (1 - L)^{\tilde{d}} u_t = \epsilon_t, \tag{6}$$

where the unit root null hypothesis is again $\beta = 1$; however, although the regression innovation u_t is stationary and invertible, it is not white but rather fractionally integrated. White's results emerge for the special case of $\tilde{d} = 0$ ($d = 1$). In an important paper, Sowell (1990) shows that the asymptotic distribution theory depends crucially on $\tilde{d}$; in particular, the speed of convergence to the asymptotic distribution varies with $\tilde{d}$. As illustrated in fig. 13.1, if $\tilde{d} = 0$, the well-known [e.g., Fuller (1976)] result about convergence speed that $(\hat{\beta} - 1) = O(T^{-1})$ holds (where T is sample size), and this result *continues* to hold for $\tilde{d} \in (0, 1/2)$. Conversely, if $\tilde{d} \in (-1/2, 0)$, then $(\hat{\beta} - 1) = O(T^{-1-2\tilde{d}})$. Thus, convergence is faster or slower than $O(T^{1/2})$ as $\tilde{d}$ is greater or less than $-1/4$.

Sowell (1990) also shows that the asymptotic fractional unit root distribution theory may be severely misleading in all but *very* large samples. This is because the distribution of $\hat{\beta}$ depends on two underlying random variables, the convergence of one of which to its asymptotic distribution is very slow for plausible d values. The resulting finite-sample similarity of the integer unit root distribution and the fractional

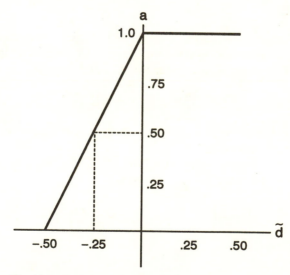

Fig. 13.1. Convergence speed, T^{-a}.

unit root distribution—in spite of their sharp asymptotic differences—leads Sowell to conjecture that conventional unit root tests may have low power against fractional alternatives.

3. A Monte Carlo Experiment

We consider two data-generating processes: fractional noise,

$$(1 - L)^d X_t = \epsilon_t, \tag{7}$$

with values of d equal to 0.3, 0.45, 0.6, 0.7, 0.8, 0.9, 1.0, 1.1, 1.2, and 1.3; and the AR(1),

$$(1 - bL)X_t = \epsilon_t, \tag{8}$$

with values of b equal to 0.7, 0.8, 0.9, 0.95, 0.98, 1.0, 1.02, 1.05, and 1.1. For both processes, parameter values equal to one correspond to the unit root null hypothesis. The innovation variance σ_ϵ^2 is held fixed at 1.0, and sample sizes (denoted by T) of 50, 100, and 250 are examined, with 5000 replications (denoted by N) performed for each sample size.

Samples for the ARFIMA$(0, d, 0)$ process (7) with $d = 0.3$ and $d = 0.45$ (stationary parameter configurations) are formed as follows. First, a vector, v, consisting of $TN(0, 1)$ deviates is generated using IMSL subroutine GGNML. Then the desired $T \times T$ data covariance matrix (Σ) is constructed. This is simply the Toeplitz matrix formed from the autocovariances, which are given by

$$\gamma_X(\tau) = [(\Gamma(1 - 2d)\Gamma(d + \tau))/(\Gamma(d)\Gamma(1 - d)\Gamma(1 - d + \tau))]\sigma_\epsilon^2, \tag{9}$$

where $\Gamma(\cdot)$ is the gamma function [see Hosking (1981)]. We next obtain the Choleski factorization of Σ, $\Sigma = PP'$, where P is lower triangular, using IMSL subroutine LUDECP. Finally the sample, x, is generated as $x = Pv$; clearly, $\text{cov}(x) = PP' = \Sigma$. Construction of x in this way eliminates dependence on pre-sample startup values, which can be particularly problematic with long-memory models. For the non-stationary parameter configurations $d = 0.6, 0.7, 0.8, 0.9, 1.0, 1.1, 1.2$ and 1.3, we generate fractional noise with a parameter $\bar{d} = d - 1$, as above, which yields observations on $(1 - L)x_t$. Then, taking $x_0 = 0$, we construct the sample $\{x_1, \ldots, x_T\}$ as cumulated sums.

For the stationary realizations of the AR(1) process (8), we generate $N(0, 1)$ variates and again transform by the Choleski factor of the covariance matrix. The Toeplitz covariance matrix Σ is formed from the autocovariances, which are given by

$$\gamma_X(\tau) = \left[\sigma_\epsilon^2/(1 - b^2)\right]b^\tau. \tag{10}$$

Data for the nonstationary parameter configurations corresponding to $b = 1.0$, 1.02, 1.05 and 1.1 are constructed directly from the recursion (8), using a startup value of $x_0 = 0$.

For each Monte Carlo replication $i = 1, \ldots, N$, we apply two unit root tests based on the regression,

$$X_t = \delta X_{t-1} + v_t. \tag{11}$$

We report the Dickey–Fuller t-statistic τ (for the null hypothesis that $\delta = 1$) and the Dickey–Fuller 'normalized bias' statistic ρ, which is equal to $T(\hat{\delta} - 1)$. All tests are two-sided and are performed at the 5 percent level using critical values from Fuller (1976).

The power estimates are computed as relative rejection frequencies and are presented in table 13.1 for ARFIMA$(0, d, 0)$ alternatives and in table 13.2 for AR(1) alternatives. Some similarities are apparent for both the ARFIMA and AR alternatives. First, for a fixed parameter value d or b, power increases monotonically with sample size, T. Second, for a fixed sample size, power increases monotonically with both $|d - 1|$ and $|b - 1|$. Third, for a fixed sample size, power is always asymmetric around the respective null hypotheses, $d = 1$ and $b = 1$, rising more quickly for parameter values greater than unity. Finally, for

TABLE 13.1
Monte-Carlo Power of Unit Root Tests ARFIMA$(0, d, 0)$ Alternative[a]

	d									
	0.3	0.45	0.6	0.7	0.8	0.9	1.0	1.1	1.2	1.3
$T = 50$										
τ	1.00	0.65	0.51	0.32	0.17	0.07	0.05	0.12	0.27	0.46
ρ	1.00	0.62	0.50	0.31	0.16	0.07	0.05	0.07	0.12	0.18
$T = 100$										
τ	1.00	0.88	0.71	0.48	0.25	0.09	0.04	0.14	0.33	0.54
ρ	1.00	0.87	0.71	0.48	0.25	0.09	0.04	0.08	0.15	0.21
$T = 250$										
τ	1.00	0.99	0.90	0.70	0.39	0.13	0.05	0.17	0.40	0.62
ρ	1.00	0.99	0.90	0.70	0.39	0.14	0.05	0.09	0.18	0.25

[a] All tests are two-sided and at the 5% level. Standard errors of the estimates vary, but all are less than 0.0071.

TABLE 13.2
Monte-Carlo Power of Unit Root Tests AR(1) Alternative[a]

	0.7	0.8	0.9	0.95	0.98	1.0	1.02	1.05	1.1
$T = 50$									
τ	0.90	0.58	0.18	0.08	0.04	0.05	0.21	0.70	0.97
ρ	0.89	0.55	0.17	0.07	0.04	0.05	0.12	0.70	0.97
$T = 100$									
τ	1.00	0.99	0.58	0.18	0.06	0.05	0.58	0.97	1.00
ρ	1.00	0.99	0.56	0.17	0.06	0.05	0.52	0.98	1.00
$T = 250$									
τ	1.00	1.00	1.00	0.75	0.17	0.05	0.97	1.00	1.00
ρ	1.00	1.00	1.00	0.75	0.17	0.05	0.98	1.00	1.00

The columns are headed by the value b.

[a] All tests are two-sided and at the 5% level. Standard errors of the estimates vary, but all are less than 0.0071.

a fixed sample size, the power of the τ and ρ tests is always approximately equal for $d < 1$ or $b < 1$, whereas divergences occur for other parameter configurations. Of great interest, however, is the *difference* across the alternatives: namely, power grows much more slowly with divergence of d from 1 than with divergence of b from 1.

4. Conclusion

Schwert (1989) has evaluated the ability of unit root tests to correctly determine the presence of an autoregressive unit root in a mixed ARIMA($p, 1, q$) process. His results suggest that the empirical size of these tests when applied to a mixed process is often greater than their nominal size. For example, in the presence of a first-order moving-average term, the unit root tests often lead to the incorrect conclusion that the time series under investigation is stationary. We focus on power rather than size, but our results lead to the complementary conclusion that the power of the conventional unit root tests against fractionally integrated alternatives is quite low. DeJong, Nankervis, Savin, and Whiteman (1989) and Rudebusch (1990) reach similar conclusions after examining the power functions of unit root tests against short-memory alternatives with dominant roots close (in the Euclidian sense) to unity. Here, we have effectively extended and amplified that argument by showing that fractional alternatives far (in the Euclidian sense) from the null are nevertheless close in terms of induced persistence, which translates into low power. Thus, the tests proposed by Dickey and Fuller can in the face of fractionally integrated processes lead to an incorrect conclusion that a time series has a unit root. We believe that our work, along with the other recent size and power studies, provide a joint condemnation of the widespread mechanical application of unit root tests. A more appropriate testing procedure would carefully consider the correct specification of the complete stochastic process before drawing conclusions about the presence of a unit root.

References

DeJong, D. N., J. C. Nankervis, N. E. Savin and C. H. Whiteman, 1989, Integration versus trend stationarity in macroeconomic time series, Working paper 89-31 (University of Iowa, Iowa City, IA).

Diebold, F. X. and M. Nerlove, 1990, Unit roots in economic time series: A selective survey, in: Thomas B. Fomby and George F. Rhodes, eds., Advances in econometrics: Co-Integration, spurious regressions, and unit roots (JAI Press, Greenwich, CT) 3–69.

Diebold, F. X. and G. D. Rudebusch, 1989a, Long memory and persistence in aggregate output, *Journal of Monetary Economics* 24, 189–209.

Diebold, F. X. and G. D. Rudebusch, 1989b, Is consumption too smooth? Long memory and the Deaton paradox, FED series no. 57 (Federal Reserve Board, Washington, DC) forthcoming in Review of Economics and Statistics.

Fuller, W. A., 1976, Introduction to statistical time series (Wiley, New York).

Hosking, J. R. M., 1981, Fractional differencing, *Biometrika* 68, 165–176.

Nelson, C. R. and C. I. Plosser, 1982, Trends and random walks in macroeconomic time series: Some evidence and implications, *Journal of Monetary Economics* 10, 139–162.

Rudebusch, G. D., 1990, Trends and random walks in macroeconomic time series: A re-examination, Economic Activity Working Paper 105 (Federal Reserve Board, Washington, DC).

Schwert, G. W., 1989, Tests for unit roots: A Monte Carlo investigation, *Journal of Business and Economic Statistics* 7, 147–159.

Sowell, F. B., 1990, Fractional unit root distribution, *Econometrica* 58, 495–506.

White, J. S., 1958, The limiting distribution of the serial correlation coefficient in the explosive case, *Annals of Mathematical Statistics* 29, 1188–1197.

Part IV

BUSINESS CYCLE FORECASTING

The papers in this final section consider issues in forecasting the economy. We begin with a general assessment of the past, present, and future of macroeconomic forecasting in chapter 14, and we provide more detailed discussions of specific topics in the remaining chapters. In chapters 15 through 17, we evaluate the predictive ability of the index of leading economic indicators; however, the methods used as well as the lessons learned are much broader in scope. For example, chapters 15 and 16 consider the general problem of forecasting of business cycle turning points, whereas chapter 17 uses the leading index in a more standard linear framework to forecast future output growth. In addition, as is made clear in chapters 16 and 17, it is crucial to judge "ex ante" forecasting ability, that is, the ability to forecast using the historically contemporaneous values. Chapter 18 shifts the focus to forecasting business fixed investment, whose volatility contributes so importantly to business fluctuations, and finds the ability of new models of investment —such as those based on Euler equations—to be much worse than that of traditional models of investment, such as those based on "accelerator" ideas. Finally, chapter 19 provides a general framework for comparing the accuracy of competing forecasts.

14

The Past, Present, and Future of Macroeconomic Forecasting

FRANCIS X. DIEBOLD*

THE REPORTS of the death of large-scale macroeconomic forecasting models are *not* exaggerated. But many observers interpret the failure of the early models as indicative of a bleak future for macroeconomic forecasting more generally. Such is not the case. Although the large-scale macroeconomic forecasting models didn't live up to their original promise, they nevertheless left a useful legacy of lasting contributions from which macroeconomic forecasting will continue to benefit: they spurred the development of powerful identification and estimation theory, computational and simulation techniques, comprehensive machine-readable macroeconomic databases, and much else. Moreover, past failures do not necessarily imply a bleak future: we learn from our mistakes. Just as macroeconomics has benefitted from rethinking since the 1970s, so too will macroeconomic forecasting.

Understanding the future of macroeconomic forecasting requires understanding the interplay between measurement and theory, and the corresponding evolution of the nonstructural and structural approaches to forecasting. Nonstructural macroeconomic forecasting methods attempt to exploit the reduced-form correlations in observed macroeconomic time series, with little reliance on economic theory. Structural models, in contrast, view and interpret economic data through the lens of a particular economic theory.

* Helpful input was provided by the panel members and audience at the American Economic Association's 1997 New Orleans roundtable, "Monetary and Fiscal Policy: The Role for Structural Macroeconomic Models," as well as participants at seminars at the Federal Reserve Bank of Atlanta, the International Monetary Fund, and the 1997 International Symposium on Forecasting. I am also grateful to Brad De Long, Robert Fildes, Lutz Kilian, Alan Krueger, Ben McCallum, Timothy Taylor, Ken Wolpin, Mike Woodford, and seminar participants at the Federal Reserve Bank of San Francisco, especially Tim Cogley, Ken Kasa, Glenn Rudebusch and Tom Sargent. I, however, bear full responsibility for all remaining flaws. The National Science Foundation, the Sloan Foundation and the University of Pennsylvania Research Foundation provided research support.

Structural econometric forecasting, because it is based on explicit theory, rises and falls with theory, typically with a lag. Structural Keynesian macroeconomic forecasting, based on postulated systems of decision rules, enjoyed a golden age in the 1950s and 1960s following the advances in Keynesian theory in the 1930s and 1940s, and the two then declined together in the 1970s and 1980s. The evolution of non-structural economic forecasting, in contrast, is less bound to fashions in economic theory; its origins long predate structural Keynesian macroeconomic forecasting and progress continues at a rapid pace.

One is naturally led to a number of important questions. What of the impressive advances in economic theory of the 1980s and 1990s? Should we not expect them to be followed by a new wave of structural macroeconomic forecasting, or has nonstructural forecasting permanently replaced structural forecasting? Is is necessary to choose between the structural and nonstructural approaches, or might the two be complements rather than substitutes? If a new structural forecasting *is* likely to emerge, in what ways will it resemble its ancestors? Our answers will take us on a whirlwind tour of the past, present and future of both structural and nonstructural forecasting. We'll begin by tracing the rise and fall of the structural Keynesian system-of-equations paradigm, and then we'll step back to assess the long-running and ongoing progress in the nonstructural tradition. Finally, we'll assess the rise of modern dynamic stochastic general equilibrium macroeconomic theory, its relationship to nonstructural methods, and its implications for a new structural macroeconomic forecasting.

The Rise and Fall of Keynesian Macroeconomic Theory and Structural Forecasting

Some important forecasting situations involve *conditional* forecasts; that is, forecasts of one or more variables conditional upon maintained assumptions regarding, for example, the behavior of policymakers. Conditional forecasts require structural models. Structural econometrics, and hence structural macroeconomic forecasting, makes use of macroeconomic theory, which implies that developments in structural forecasting naturally lag behind developments in theory. The first major wave of twentieth century macroeconomic theory was the Keynesian theory of the 1930s and 1940s, and it was followed by major advances in structural macroeconomic forecasting.

When Keynes's *General Theory* was published in 1936, theory was distinctly ahead of measurement. Measurement soon caught up, however, in the form of the systems of equations associated with Klein's

(1946) *Keynesian Revolution* and Klein and Goldberger's (1955) *Econometric Model of the United States: 1929–1952*. Indeed, the period following the publication of the *General Theory* was one of unprecedented and furious intellectual activity directed toward the construction, estimation and analysis of Keynesian structural econometric models. The statistics side of the structural econometrics research was fueled by the advances of Fisher, Neyman, Pearson, and many others earlier in the century. The economics side, of course, was driven by Keynes's landmark contribution, which spoke eloquently to the severe economic problems of the day and seemed to offer a workable solution.

The intellectual marriage of statistics and economic theory was reflected in the growth of the Econometric Society and its journal, *Econometrica*, and beautifully distilled in the work of the Cowles Commission for Research in Economics at the University of Chicago in the 1940s and early 1950s.[1] The intellectual focus and depth of talent assembled there were unprecedented in the history of economics: Cowles researchers included T. W. Anderson, K. Arrow, G. Debreu, T. Haavelmo, L. Hurwicz, L. R. Klein, T. Koopmans, H. Markowitz, J. Marshak, F. Modigliani, H. Simon, A. Wald, and many others. A central part (although by no means the only part) of the Cowles research program was identification and estimation of systems of stochastic difference equations designed to approximate the postulated decision rules of Keynesian macroeconomic theory.

Just as the blending of mathematical statistics and economics associated with the Cowles Commission was historically unprecedented, so too was the optimism about solving pressing macroeconomic problems. Early on, the macroeconomic system-of-equations research program appeared impressively successful, and structural econometric forecasting blossomed in the late 1950s and 1960s, the heyday of the large-scale Keynesian macroeconomic forecasting models. There was strong consensus regarding the general paradigm, even if there was disagreement on details such as the relative slopes of IS and LM curves, and the models were routinely used for forecasting and policy analysis in both academia and government.

But cracks in the foundation, which began with intellectual dissatisfaction with the underpinnings of Keynesian macroeconomic systems of equations, started to appear in the late 1960s and early 1970s. First, economists became dissatisfied with the lack of foundations for the disequilibrium nature of the Keynesian model. A new and still ongoing research program began which sought microfoundations for Keynesian

---

[1] For a concise history of the Chicago days of the Cowles Commission, see Hildreth (1986, ch. 1).

macroeconomic theory, particularly for the central tenets of sticky wages and prices. Many key early contributions appear in the classic Phelps et al. (1970) volume, and more recent contributions are collected in Mankiw and Romer (1991).

Second, just as macroeconomists became increasingly disenchanted with the ad hoc treatment of sticky prices in traditional models, they became similarly disenchanted with ad hoc treatment of expectations. Building on early work by Muth (1960, 1961), who introduced the idea of rational expectations and showed that schemes such as adaptive expectations were rational only in unlikely circumstances, the "rational expectations revolution" quickly took hold; Sargent and Wallace (1975) is an important and starkly simple early paper.

Third, and most generally, economists became dissatisfied not only with certain parts of the Keynesian macro-econometric program, such as the assumptions about price behavior and expectations formation, but rather with the overall modeling approach embodied in the program. The approach was dubbed the "system-of-equations" approach by Prescott (1986), in reference to the fact that it concentrated on the estimation of parameters of equation systems representing ad hoc postulated decision rules ("consumption functions," "investment functions," and so on) as opposed to more fundamental parameters of tastes and technology. Newly emerging macroeconomic work in the late 1960s and early 1970s, in contrast, was firmly grounded in tastes and technology; Lucas and Prescott (1971) and Lucas (1972) remain classic examples. Work in the tastes-and-technology tradition accelerated rapidly following Lucas's (1976) formal critique of the system-of-equations approach, based on the insight that analysis based on decision rules is a fundamentally defective paradigm for producing conditional forecasts, because the parameters of decision rules will generally change when policies change.

Finally, if the cracks in the foundation of Keynesian structural forecasting began as intellectual dissatisfaction, they were widened by the economic facts of the 1970s; in particular, the simultaneous presence of high inflation and unemployment, which naturally led economists to question the alleged inflation/unemployment tradeoff embedded in the Keynesian systems of equations. In addition, a series of studies published in the early 1970s revealed that simple statistical extrapolations, making no assumptions at all about economic structure, often forecasted macroeconomic activity just as well as large-scale Keynesian macroeconomic models; Nelson (1972) remains a classic. Keynesian macroeconomics soon declined, and Keynesian structural econometric forecasting followed suit.

Nonstructural Forecasting

By the late 1970s, it was clear that Keynesian structural macroeconomic forecasting, at least as traditionally implemented, was receding. One response was to augment the traditional system-of-equations econometrics in attempts to remedy its defects. Important work along those lines was undertaken by R. Fair and J. Taylor (for example, Fair, 1984, 1994; Taylor, 1993), who developed methods for incorporating rational expectations into econometric models, as well as methods for rigorous assessment of model fit and forecasting performance. Models in the Fair-Taylor spirit are now in use at a number of leading policy organizations, including the Federal Reserve Board and the International Monetary Fund, as described, for example, in Brayton et al. (1997). They are an important step forward, even if the theory on which they are built remains largely in the system-of-equations tradition.

Another response, involving a more radical change of direction, was to explore alternative, nonstructural forecasting methods. Many forecasting chores involve *unconditional*, rather than conditional, forecasts—that is, interest often centers on the likely future path of the economy when policy remains unchanged, so that the Lucas critique is not relevant—and unconditional forecasting does not require a structural model. That insight, together with the emerging discontent with Keynesian macroeconomic theory and the lack of a well-developed alternative, produced tremendous interest in nonstructural econometric forecasting in the 1970s. The title of an important paper by Sargent and Sims (1977), "Business Cycle Modeling Without Pretending to Have too Much a Priori Theory," nicely summarizes the spirit of the times.

The impressive intellectual development of nonstructural forecasting spans many decades; it predates the Keynesian episode and continues to the present. Macroeconomists and econometricians didn't pay much attention at first, in spite of the fact that key early contributions were made by economists; they were too busy with Keynesian theory and Keynesian structural econometrics. Nevertheless, rapid development took place in the hands of some of the most talented mathematicians, statisticians and engineers of the 20th century.

Let us begin our account in the 1920s, a period of fertile intellectual development in nonstructural modeling and forecasting. Many ideas were hatched and nurtured, and the groundwork was laid for the impressive technical advances of the ensuing decades. In particular, Slutsky (1927) and Yule (1927) argued that simple linear difference equations, driven by purely random stochastic shocks, provide a convenient and powerful framework for modeling and forecasting a variety of economic and financial time series. Such stochastic difference equations are called autoregressive processes, or autoregressions. They amount to regression models in which the current value of a variable is expressed as a weighted average of its own past values, plus a random shock. Autoregressive processes are closely related to moving average processes, also studied by Slutsky and Yule, in which the current value of a variable is expressed as a weighted average of current and lagged random shocks alone. In fact, under reasonable conditions, one can convert an autoregressive process to a moving average process, and conversely. Either way, the key insight is that system dynamics can convert random inputs into serially correlated outputs, a phenomenon often called the Slutsky-Yule effect. Frisch (1933) put the Slutsky-Yule insight to work in formulating the idea of "impulse" and "propagation" mechanisms in economic dynamics.

In the 1930s, the mathematician-turned-economist H. Wold made a stunning contribution, paving the way for later work by the mathematicians N. Wiener and A. Kolmogorov, and the engineer R. Kalman. Wold showed that, given sufficient stability of the underlying probabilistic mechanism generating a time series, its stochastic part can be represented as a model of the form studied by Slutsky and Yule. Thus, the Slutsky-Yule models are not only convenient and powerful, they are absolutely central—they're the only game in town. Wiener and Kolmogorov worked out the mathematical formulae for optimal forecasts from models of the type studied by Slutsky, Yule, and Wold. Kalman extended the theory in the last 1950s and early 1960s by relaxing some of the conditions that Wiener and Kolmogorov required; his forecasting formula, known as the Kalman filter, is designed to work with a powerful model representation known as state-space form and has a convenient recursive form amenable to real-time forecasting.[2] The Wold-Wiener-Kolmogorov-Kalman theory, which effectively represents the pinnacle of the Slutsky-Yule research program, is beautifully exposited in Whittle (1963, second edition 1983). Appropriately enough, a leading economist, T. Sargent, wrote the second edition's introduction, which catalogs the tremendous impact of the prediction theory on modern dynamic economics.

In part, the nonstructural econometric forecasting explosion of the 1970s was driven by econometricians absorbing the powerful earlier advances made by the likes of Wold, Wiener, Kolmogorov and Kalman. But there was a major additional push: in 1970, just as discontent with Keynesian structural econometric forecasting was beginning to emerge,

---

[2] See Harvey (1989) for extensive discussion of state space representations and the Kalman filter in relation to forecasting.

Box and Jenkins (1970; third edition, Box, Jenkins and Reinsel, 1994) published a landmark book on nonstructural time series analysis and forecasting.

Many of the Box-Jenkins insights started literatures that grew explosively. For example, prior to Box and Jenkins, trend was typically modeled as a simple linear deterministic function of time, whereas Box and Jenkins allowed trend to be driven by the cumulative effects of random shocks, resulting in "stochastic trend."[3] Stock and Watson (1988a) provide an insightful discussion of stochastic trend and its wide-ranging implications. Shocks to series with stochastic trend have permanent effects, an idea amplified in the empirical macroeconomics literature associated with Nelson and Plosser (1982) and Campbell and Mankiw (1987), among others. The direct implication for forecasting is that long-run forecasts fail to revert to any fixed trend; effectively, the underlying trend location is redefined each period, as emphasized, for example, in Diebold and Senhadji (1996).

The most important contribution of Box and Jenkins, however, is their sweeping vision, articulation, and illustration of an operational framework for applied nonstructural forecasting, consisting of iterative cycles of model formulation, estimation, diagnostic checking, and forecasting. Autoregressive moving average (ARMA) models are the centerpiece of the Box-Jenkins framework. ARMA models are combinations of the autoregressive and moving average models of Slutsky and Yule, and they have the potential to approximate dynamics more parsimoniously than purely autoregressive or moving average models.

An ongoing flood of work followed Box and Jenkins. Macroeconomics, in particular, is crucially concerned with cross-variable relationships, whereas the basic approach of Box and Jenkins uses only the past of a given economic variable to forecast its future. In other words, much of macroeconomics is concerned with multivariate relationships, whereas the basic Box-Jenkins models are univariate. Thus, many extensions of the Box-Jenkins program involve multivariate modeling and forecasting, and vector autoregressive models have emerged as the central multivariate model. Vector autoregressions were forcefully advocated in econometrics by Sims (1980) as a less restrictive alternative to traditional

---

[3] Processes with stochastic trend are also called integrated processes, or unit-root processes. The pioneering work of Dickey and Fuller (for example, Fuller, 1976) on unit root testing grew from a desire, motivated by Box and Jenkins, to determine whether various series displayed stochastic trend. The similarly pioneering work of Granger and Joyeux (1980) on "long memory," or "fractionally-integrated," processes grew from attempts to generalize the idea of integration on which Box and Jenkins relied so heavily; see Diebold and Rudebusch (1989) for a macroeconomic application of long memory models and Baillie (1996) for an insightful recent survey.

econometric systems-of-equations models, in which variables were arbitrarily labeled "endogenous" or "exogenous."[4] In vector autoregressions, in contrast, *all* variables are endogenous.

The mechanics of vector autoregressions are straightforward. Recall that we approximate dynamics with a univariate autoregression by regressing a variable on its own past values. In a vector autoregression, by way of logical extension, we regress each of a set of variables on past values of itself and past values of every other variable in the system. Cross-variable linkages are automatically incorporated because we include lags of all variables in each equation, and because we allow for correlations among the disturbances of the various equations. It turns out that one-equation-at-a-time least squares estimation of vector autoregressions is statistically efficient, in spite of the potential correlation of disturbances. Moreover, it is relatively simple and numerically stable, in contrast to the tedious numerical optimization required for estimation of multivariate ARMA models.

Many multivariate extensions of the Box-Jenkins paradigm are conveniently implemented in the vector autoregressive framework. Here we introduce a few to help convey a feel for the breadth of modern time-series econometrics and forecasting. The discussion is necessarily brief; for a more detailed introduction to modern time series forecasting, see Diebold (1998).

Granger (1969) and Sims (1972) made important early multivariate contributions, providing tools for exploring causal patterns in multivariate systems. The Granger-Sims causality notion is predictive; we say that x Granger-Sims causes y if the history of x is useful for forecasting y, over and above the history of y. We commonly use Granger-Sims causality tests to help identify and understand the patterns of cross-linkages and feedback in vector autoregressions.

The dynamic factor model of Sargent and Sims (1977) and Geweke (1977) is another important early multivariate contribution. The essential idea of dynamic factor models is that some economic shocks are common across sectors and others are idiosyncratic, so that large sets of variables may depend heavily on just a few common underlying sources of variation, a common feature of economic models and evidently also of economic data. The common shocks, or "factors," produce comovements and facilitate parsimonious modeling and forecasting of large numbers of variables. Dynamic factor models have proved particularly

---

[4] Ben McCallum notes in private communication that in an important sense, the situation was even worse: the endogenous-exogenous labeling was arguably not arbitrary, but rather *systematic*, with policy variables labeled as "exogenous" on the grounds that they *could have been* managed exogenously by policymakers if they had been unorthodox enough to do so.

useful with the emergence of macroeconomic panel datasets, including cross-country, cross-region, and cross-state data. Important recent contributions include Stock and Watson (1989), Quah and Sargent (1993), Forni and Reichlin (1997), and Stock and Watson (1997).

Granger (1981) and Engle and Granger (1987) develop the related idea of cointegration. We say that two series are cointegrated if each contains a stochastic trend, yet there exists a linear combination of the two trends that does not. Thus, for example, each of two series x and y may contain a stochastic trend, but the spread x-y may not. It is apparent that in such situations stochastic trends are shared, which makes the series move together. This is the essence of the Stock-Watson (1988b) "common trends" representation of cointegrated systems and is precisely the same idea as with the intimately related dynamic factor model: comovements may be due to dependence on common factors. Cointegration is also intimately connected to the idea of error-correction, pioneered by Sargan (1964) and long a cornerstone of "LSE econometrics," in which the current deviation of a system from equilibrium conveys information regarding its likely future course and is therefore useful for forecasting.[5] Indeed, there is a formal equivalence between cointegration and error correction, as established by Engle and Granger (1987).

All of the discussion thus far has been based on *linear* models. Nonlinear forecasting methods have also received increasing attention in recent years, as the Slutsky-Yale theory of linear modeling and forecasting has matured, and that trend will likely continue. Models of volatility dynamics, which permit volatility forecasting, are an important example; the literature began with Engle's (1982) seminal contribution, and recent surveys include Bollerslev, Chou and Kroner (1992) and Bollerslev, Engle and Nelson (1994). We will, however, avoid discussion of nonlinear methods here for the most part, because although they are clearly of value in areas such as finance, they are less useful in macroeconomics. There are two reasons. First, many of the nonlinear methods require large amounts of high-quality data for successful application, whereas in macroeconomics we typically have short samples of data contaminated by substantial measurement error. Second, many of the nonlinearities relevant in fields such as finance simply don't appear to be important in macroeconomics, perhaps because macroeconomic data are highly aggregated over both space and time. Early on, for example, models of time-varying volatility were fit to macroeconomic data, such as aggregate inflation, but those ventures were quickly

---

[5] For a good exposition of econometrics in the LSE tradition, see Hendry (1995).

abandoned as it became clear that volatility dynamics were much more important in high-frequency financial data.

One strand of nonlinear literature, however, is potentially relevant for macroeconomic forecasting—the idea that business cycle expansions and contractions might be usefully viewed as different regimes, which focuses attention on tracking the cycle, charting the timing of turning points, and constructing business cycle chronologies and associated indexes of leading, lagging and coincident indicators (Diebold and Rudebusch, 1996, 1998). Burns and Mitchell (1946) is a classic distillation of early work in the nonlinear tradition, much of which was done in the first four decades of the twentieth century, and which was extended in breadth and depth by G. Moore, V. Zarnowitz, and their colleagues at the National Bureau of Economic Research in the ensuing decades.[6]

Regime-switching models are a modern embodiment of certain aspects of the Burns-Mitchell nonlinear forecasting tradition. The idea of regime switching is implemented through threshold models, in which an indicator variable determines the current regime (say, expansion or contraction). In the observed indicator models of Tong (1990) and Granger and Teräsvirta (1993), the indicator variable is some aspect of the history of an observable variable. For example, the current regime may be determined by the sign of last period's growth rate. In contrast, Hamilton (1989) argues that models with *unobserved* regime indicators may be more appropriate in many business, economic and financial contexts. In Hamilton's widely applied model, sometimes called a "Markov-switching" or "hidden-Markov" model, the regime is governed by an unobserved indicator.

The future of nonstructural economic forecasting will be more of the same—steady progress—fueled by cheap, fast computing, massive storage, and increased sophistication of numerical and simulation techniques. Such techniques are rapidly allowing us to estimate complicated models not amenable to treatment with standard methods, and to dispense with the unrealistic assumptions often invoked in attempts to quantify forecast uncertainty. Efron and Tibshirani (1993) and Gourieroux and Monfort (1996), for example, provide good examples of recent developments. The future of nonstructural macroeconomic forecasting will likely also involve combining aspects of the linear and nonlinear traditions, as for example, with vector autoregressive models that allow for factor structure and regime switching (Diebold and Rudebusch, 1996; Kim and Nelson, 1998a,b).

---

[6] For overviews, see for example Moore (1983) and Zarnowitz (1992).

A New Wave of Macroeconomic Theory—
and Structural Forecasting

Nonstructural models are unrestricted reduced-form models. As such they are useful for producing unconditional forecasts in a variety of environments ranging from firm-level business forecasting to economy-wide macroeconomic forecasting. Again, however, in macroeconomics we often want to analyze scenarios that differ from the conditions presently prevailing, such as the effects of a change in a policy rule or a tax rate. Such conditional forecasts require structural models.

As we have seen, an early wave of structural econometrics followed the development of Keynesian theory. But the Keynesian theory was largely based on postulated decision rules, rather than the economic primitives of taste and technology; the system-of-equations approach to structural econometric forecasting inherited that defect and hence, wasn't really structural. Ultimately the system-of-equations approach to both theory and forecasting declined in the 1970s. Progress toward a new and truly structural macroeconomic forecasting had to await a new wave of powerful theory developed in the 1970s and 1980s. The new theory has its roots in the dissatisfaction, percolating in the late 1960s and early 1970s, with the system-of-equations approach. In many respects, the essence of the new approach is methodological and reflects a view of how macroeconomics should be done. Lucas (1972), in particular, paved the way for a new macroeconomics based on dynamic stochastic model economies with fully articulated preferences, technologies, and rules of the game. Hence the descriptively accurate name: dynamic stochastic general equilibrium (DSGE) modeling. The key innovation is that DSGE models are built on a foundation of fully specified stochastic dynamic optimization, as opposed to reduced-form decision rules, and are therefore not subject to the Lucas critique. But ultimately the "new" theory is neither new nor radical; rather, it is very much in the best tradition of neoclassical economics.

The new research program has sought from the outset to make clear that dynamic stochastic general equilibrium models can address practical, empirical questions. Early on, for example, Kydland and Prescott (1982) used DSGE models to argue that a neoclassical model driven purely by real technology shocks could explain a large fraction of U.S. business cycle fluctuations. Hence the early name "real business cycle" models. Later work, however, broadened the approach to allow for rich demographic structures, imperfect competition and sticky prices (and hence real effects of monetary shocks), and much else; the papers collected in Cooley (1995) offer a good overview. Ultimately, again, the essence of the new approach is not about whether the shocks that drive the cycle are real or monetary, whether prices are flexible or sticky, or whether competition is perfect or imperfect, but rather about the way macroeconomic questions should be approached.

The earliest and still rapidly developing strand of the dynamic stochastic general equilibrium literature makes use of simple "linear-quadratic" models, in which agents with quadratic preferences make optimizing decisions in environments with linear production technologies. Linear-quadratic models are surprisingly more flexible than a superficial assessment might indicate; they nest a variety of popular and useful preference and technology structures. Linear-quadratic models are also convenient, because a large literature provides powerful methods for solving, analyzing and forecasting with them. Moreover, it turns out that optimizing behavior within linear-quadratic economic models implies decision rules, such as those that govern consumption or investment behavior, that are stochastic *linear* functions of other variables. In particular, the decision rules conform to the great workhorse nonstructural model, the vector autoregression, subject to restrictions arising from theory. The result is a marvelous union of modern macroeconomic theory and nonstructural time-series econometrics, paving the way for a new structural econometrics.

Maximum likelihood methods are central to linear-quadratic DSGE modeling and trace to the important early work of Hansen and Sargent (1980); the modern approach is to construct and maximize the likelihood function using a state space representation in conjunction with the Kalman filter. Initially, maximum likelihood estimation was challenging in all but the simplest cases, but recent improvements in numerical algorithms and computing power have begun to make estimation and forecasting with linear-quadratic DSGE models workable for routine analysis and forecasting. Hansen and Sargent (1998) provide a powerful overview, synthesis, and extension of linear-quadratic DSGE modeling.

Kydland and Prescott (1982) started a distinct, but intimately related and equally important, strand of the DSGE literature. Two key features differentiate their product. First, Kydland and Prescott do not require that preferences be quadratic and technology be linear; instead, they use non-linear-quadratic models that are (arguably) more natural. Non-linear-quadratic models are challenging to solve, and the Kydland-Prescott program spurred a great deal of important research on numerical and computational aspects of model solutions.[7] One interesting outcome of that research is that, although non-linear-quadratic models

---

[7] See, for example, Rust (1996) and Judd (1998), who describe and contribute to the impressive advances being made for solving non-linear-quadratic stochastic dynamic programming problems.

don't have tidy vector-autoregressive systems of decision rules, they nevertheless often have decision rules that can be accurately *approximated* by vector autoregressions.

Second, Kydland and Prescott acknowledge from the outset that their models, like all models, are false, and they recognize that traditional econometric estimation procedures such as Gaussian maximum likelihood may lose some of their appeal in such situations.[8] Partly for that reason, and partly because of the sheer difficulty, non-linear-quadratic DSGE modelers often eschew formal estimation in favor of less structured "calibration" methods, as described in this journal in Kydland and Prescott (1996).[9] Calibration means different things to different people, but the central idea is learning about the properties of a complicated DSGE model and attempting to assess its agreement with the data, based on simulations of the model economy. The parameters underlying the simulated model economy are typically set informally, sometimes by statistical considerations such as generating realistic amounts of volatility in observed variables, sometimes by economic considerations such as producing "reasonable" steady state behavior, and sometimes by appealing to previous empirical studies.

Calibration is the natural response of economic theory to the computer age; hence the commonly used synonym "quantitative economic theory." Calibration, however, fails to provide a complete and probabilistic assessment of agreement between model and data and therefore, fails to deliver the goods necessary for forecasting with DSGE models. Econometric discontent based on recognition of that fact has been simmering for some time and is expressed forcefully by Sims (1996) in the Winter 1996 symposium in the *Journal of Economic Perspectives* on

[8] The reasoning is straightforward. Loosely speaking, under correct specification, Gaussian maximum likelihood estimates converge to the true parameter values as the sample size grows; hence the estimated model converges to the true model, which is the best model to use for any purpose. Under misspecification, however, the parameters can't converge to the "true" values, because an incorrect model has been fitted. Instead, the parameters converge to values that make the fitted model the best *approximation* to the data, where the measure of goodness of approximation is induced by the estimation procedure. The key insight is that, under misspecification, the best approximation for one purpose may differ from the best approximation for another purpose. The measure of goodness of approximation associated with Gaussian maximum likelihood estimation is 1-step-ahead mean squared error. Thus, if the model is to be used for 1-step-ahead forecasting, and if mean squared error is the relevant loss function, Gaussian maximum likelihood estimation is a logical choice. If, on the other hand, the model is to be used for another purpose, such as 4-step-ahead forecasting, Gaussian maximum likelihood estimation is less appealing.

[9] Important exceptions exist, however, such as McGrattan, Rogerson, and Wright (1997), who estimate non-linear-quadratic DSGE models by maximum likelihood methods.

calibration and econometrics.[10] The growing list of such symposia includes a special issue of *Journal of Applied Econometrics* (see the introduction by Pagan, 1994) and an *Economic Journal* "Controversy" section (see the introduction by Quah, 1995).

If dynamic stochastic general equilibrium models are to be used for forecasting, formal econometric analysis is desirable for at least two reasons. First, forecasting is intimately concerned with the quantification of the uncertainties that produce forecast errors. Accurate assessment of such uncertainties is key, for example, for producing credible forecast confidence intervals. Calibration methods, unlike probabilistic econometric methods, are ill-suited to the task.

Second, simply using a priori "reasonable" parameter values, although useful as a preliminary exercise to gauge agreement between model and data, is not likely to produce accurate forecasts. For example, it might be commonly agreed that technology shocks are likely to be serially correlated, and for purposes of a preliminary calibration exercise, we might adopt a simple first-order autoregressive scheme and set the serial correlation coefficient to an arbitrary but "reasonable" value, such as .95. But the first-order autoregressive process might be an oversimplification of reality, and even if adequate, the serial correlation coefficient that maximizes forecast accuracy might be, say, .73, not .95. Although such details might make little difference to a qualitative analysis of the model's properties, they are likely to make a major difference for forecast accuracy. In short, *accurate forecasting demands quantitative precision.*

The upshot is that for forecasting we need to take seriously the "fit" of DSGE models and search for best-fitting parameters. Moreover, we need estimation methods that are tractable, yet capable of delivering probabilistic inference, and we need to take misspecification seriously. Calibration and maximum likelihood estimation meet some, but not all, of those goals. Calibration is tractable and takes misspecification seriously, but it is not probabilistic. Maximum likelihood is probabilistic, but it is often challenging to implement and may not take misspecification seriously enough.[11]

---

[10] See also Hansen and Heckman (1996), in the same symposium, the lead paper in which is Kydland and Prescott (1996).

[11] Nevertheless, if calibration and Gaussian maximum likelihood estimation were the *only* strategies available for parameterizing a serious DSGE forecasting model, the choice would probably not be difficult: maximum likelihood estimation appears preferable, because: a) it enables probabilistic inference; b) recent improvements in computing and algorithms are making implementation less tedious, especially in the linear-quadratic case; and c) although the measure of goodness of approximation associated with Gaussian maximum likelihood estimation is 1-step-ahead mean squared forecast error, which may not be appropriate in all situations such as when interest centers on longer-horizon forecasts, short-horizon forecasts often *are* of interest.

The choice set, however, now includes a number of procedures other than calibration and maximum likelihood; in particular, new estimation procedures are being developed that attempt to find a middle ground. There are a variety of ways to proceed. Sims and his co-authors, including Leeper and Sims (1994), Leeper, Sims and Zha (1996), and Sims and Zha (1996), use a strategy based on examining the entire likelihood function, rather than just its maximum. Christiano and Eichenbaum (1992) match selected moments of real macroeconomic data and data simulated from a DSGE model. In similar fashion, Canova, Finn and Pagan (1994) match vector autoregressions, Rotemberg and Woodford (1997) match impulse-response functions, and Diebold, Ohanian and Berkowitz (1997) match spectra. Finally, Rotemberg and Woodford (1996) and Diebold and Kilian (1997) develop procedures that enable us to assess agreement between model and data predictability at various horizons of interest.

If structural modeling and forecasting have come a long way, they still have a long way to go; in closing this section, it is tempting to comment on a few aspects of their likely future development. DSGE theory will continue to improve and will begin to take certain aspects of reality, such as heterogeneity, more seriously. In particular, recent work (Geweke, 1985; Kirman, 1992; Altissimo, 1997) highlights the fact that aggregator functions may not be structural with respect to policy interventions, which suggests that current-vintage representative-agent DSGE models may not fully address the Lucas critique.[12]

The stochastic dynamics of driving variables, such as technology shocks, will be similarly enriched to reflect recent developments in nonstructural modeling, such as the possibility of regime switching, and to allow for multiple sources of uncertainty, including measurement error. The resulting models will have approximate representations as vector autoregressions with factor structure, possibly involving cointegration, as in King, Plosser, Stock and Watson (1991), and possibly with regime switching, as in Diebold and Rudebusch (1996) and Kim and Nelson (1998a, 1998b). Formal econometric procedures will be used to diagnose possible model inadequacies, as in Chow and Kwan (1997).

One might expect the scale of DSGE forecasting models to grow over time. That is likely to happen, and current models that determine, for example, three or four variables in equilibrium, are likely to evolve into richer models that determine, say, eight or ten variables in equilibrium.[13] But the expansion in scale is likely to stop there, for two reasons. First, the demise of the large-scale models heightened professional awareness

---

[12] See also Oliner, Rudebusch, and Sichel (1996), who document the instability of empirical Euler equations for investment.

[13] The work of Sims and his coauthors has already reached that point.

of the fact that bigger models are not necessary better, an idea memorably enshrined in Zellner's (1992) KISS principle: Keep It Sophisticatedly Simple. Second, in contrast to models in the system-of-equations tradition, which are typically estimated equation-by-equation and then assembled in modular fashion, the nature of DSGE models requires that their parameters be jointly estimated, which limits the complexity of the models that can be entertained.

Last and not least, *shrinkage* will likely emerge as a key component of estimation techniques for DSGE forecasting models. Shrinkage refers to the idea of coaxing, or "shrinking," parameter estimates in certain directions. Shrinkage can be implemented using Bayesian methods to coax parameter estimates away from the likelihood maximum and toward the prior mean. It seems obvious that shrinkage in a "correct" direction will likely improve forecast performance. Less obvious, but equally true, is the insight that even shrinkage in "incorrect" directions can improve forecast performance, by drastically reducing forecast error variance at the potentially low price of a small increase in bias.

Shrinkage has a long history of productive use in nonstructural modeling and forecasting. For example, it has long been known that vector autoregressions estimated using Bayesian shrinkage techniques produce forecasts drastically superior to those from unrestricted vector autoregressions. The "Minnesota prior," a simple vector random walk, remains widely used.[14] Shrinkage has an equally bright future in the new structural modeling and forecasting. Shrinkage is a potentially tailor-made device for estimating potentially misspecified DSGE forecasting models, because, as we have seen, DSGE theory essentially amounts to restrictions on vector autoregressions. At one extreme, we can ignore the theory and forecast with an estimated unrestricted vector autoregression: no shrinkage, loosely corresponding to a Bayesian analysis with a diffuse prior. At the other extreme, we can directly impose the theory and forecast with a restricted vector autoregression: complete shrinkage, loosely corresponding to a Bayesian analysis with a "spiked" prior. Intermediate cases, corresponding to forecasting with vector autoregressions estimated with various informative, but not spiked, priors are potentially more interesting. First, we may use statistically oriented priors, such as the familiar Minnesota prior, which shrinks toward a vector random walk. Second, we may use statistically oriented, but theory-inspired, priors, such as one corresponding to factor structure. Third, we may use DSGE theory-based priors, as in

---

[14] For an extensive discussion, see Doan, Litterman and Sims (1984). The Bayesian vector autoregressive tradition continues to progress, as for example with the work of Sims and Zha (1997), who develop methods applicable to large systems.

Ingram and Whiteman (1994), to coax the estimates in directions implied by an explicit economic theory.

Concluding Remarks

In a recent *New York Times* article entitled "The Model Was Too Rough: Why Economic Forecasting Became a Sideshow," economics writer Peter Passell noted: "Americans held unrealistic expectations for forecasting in the 1960s—as they did for so many other things in that optimistic age, from space exploration to big government." Our expectations for forecasting were quite appropriately revised downward in the 1970s and 1980s, and the ensuing era of humility has been good for all. The new humility, however, is not symptomatic of failure, just as the bravado of the 1960s was not symptomatic of success.

As the 1990s draw to a close, we find ourselves at a critical and newly optimistic juncture, with the futures of structural and nonstructural forecasting very much intertwined. The ongoing development of non-structural forecasting, together with the recent developments in dynamic stochastic general equilibrium theory and associated structural estimation methods, bode well for the future of macroeconomic forecasting. Only time will tell whether linear-quadratic or nonlinear-quadratic approximations to the macroeconomy are the best approach for practical macroeconomic forecasting, but regardless, the seeds have been sown for a new structural econometrics and structural econometric forecasting, a modern and thorough implementation of the Cowles vision. The new structural econometrics is emerging more slowly than did the earlier wave following Keynes, because the baby was almost thrown out with the 1970s bathwater; the flawed econometrics that Lucas criticized was taken in some circles as in indictment of *all* econometrics. It has taken some time to get on with macroeconometric work, but progress is evident.

The hallmark of macroeconomic forecasting over the next 20 years will be a marriage of the best of the nonstructural and structural approaches, facilitated by advances in numerical and simulation techniques that will help macroeconomists to solve, estimate, simulate, and yes, *forecast* with rich models. Moreover, related developments will occur in a variety of fields well beyond macroeconomics. It's already happening and in some cases, progress has been underway for years, as evidenced by example from the recent literatures in industrial organization (Ericson and Pakes, 1995), labor economics (Eckstein and Wolpin, 1989; Stock and Wise, 1990; Rust, 1994), public economics (Rios-Rull, 1995), agricultural economics (Rosen, Murphy and Scheinkman, 1994), health economics (Gilleskie, 1997), development economics (Rosenzweig and Wolpin, 1993), environmental economics (Rothwell and Rust, 1995), and international economics (Backus, Kehoe and Kydland, 1994).

References

Backus, D. K., P. J. Kehoe, and F. E. Kydland, "Dynamics of the Trade Balance and the Terms of Trade: The J-Curve?" *American Economic Review*, 1994, 84, 84–103.

Baillie, R. T., "Long Memory Processes and Fractional Integration in Econometrics," *Journal of Econometrics*, 1996, 73, 5–59.

Bollerslev, T., R. Y. Chou, and K. F. Kroner, "ARCH Modeling in Finance: A Selective Review of the Theory and Empirical Evidence," *Journal of Econometrics*, 1992, 52, 5–59.

Bollerslev, T., R. F. Engle, and D. B. Nelson, "ARCH Models." In R. Engle and D. McFadden, eds. *Handbook of Econometrics*, Vol. 4. Amsterdam: North-Holland, 1994.

Box, G. E. P., G. M. Jenkins, and G. C. Reinsel, *Time Series Analysis, Forecasting and Control*, Third Edition. Englewood Cliffs, NJ: Prentice Hall, 1994.

Brayton, F., A. Levin, R. Tryon, and J. C. Williams, "The Evolution of Macro Modeling at the Federal Reserve Board," Finance and Economics Discussion Series no. 1997-29, Federal Reserve Board, Washington, D.C., 1997.

Burns, A. F. and W. C. Mitchell, *Measuring Business Cycles*. New York: National Bureau of Economic Research, 1946.

Campbell, J. Y. and N. G. Mankiw, "Are Output Fluctuations Transitory?" *Quarterly Journal of Economics*, 1987, 102, 857–80.

Canova, F., M. Finn, and A. R. Pagan, "Evaluating a Real Business Cycle Model." In C. P. Hargreaves, ed. *Nonstationary Time Series and Cointegration*. Oxford: Oxford University Press, 1994.

Chow, G. C. and Y. K. Kwan, "How the Basic RBC Model Fails to Explain U.S. Time Series," *Journal of Monetary Economics*, 1997, forthcoming.

Christiano, L. J. and M. Eichenbaum, "Current Real Business Cycle Theories and Aggregate Labor Market Fluctuations," *American Economic Review*, 1992, 82, 430–50.

Cooley, T. F., ed., *Frontiers of Business Cycle Research*. Princeton: Princeton University Press, 1995.

Diebold, F. X., *Elements of Forecasting*. Cincinnati, Ohio: South-Western College Publishing, 1998.

Diebold, F. X. and L. Kilian, "Measuring Predictability: Theory and Macroeconomic Applications," Manuscript, Department of Economics, University of Pennsylvania, 1997.

Diebold, F. X., L. Ohanian, and J. Berkowitz, "Dynamic Equilibrium Economies: A Framework for Comparing Models and Data," *Review of Economic Studies*, forthcoming.

Diebold, F. X. and G. D. Rudebusch, "Long Memory and Persistence in Aggregate Output," *Journal of Monetary Economics*, 1989, 24, 189–209.

Diebold, F. X. and G. D. Rudebusch, "Measuring Business Cycles: A Modern Perspective," *Review of Economics and Statistics*, 1996, 78, 67–77.

Diebold, F. X. and G. D. Rudebusch, *Business Cycles: Durations, Dynamics, and Forecasting*. Princeton: Princeton University Press, 1998, forthcoming.

Diebold, F. X. and A. Senhadji, "The Uncertain Unit Root in U.S. GNP: Comment," *American Economic Review*, 1996, 86, 1291–98.

Doan, T., R. Litterman, and C. A. Sims, "Forecasting and Conditional Projection Using Realistic Prior Distributions," *Econometric Reviews*, 1984, 3, 1–144.

Eckstein, Z. and K. I. Wolpin, "The Specification and Estimation of Dynamic Stochastic Discrete Choice Models," *Journal of Human Resources*, 1989, 24, 562–98.

Efron, B. and R. J. Tibshirani, *An Introduction to the Bootstrap*. New York: Chapman and Hall, 1993.

Engle, R. F., "Autoregressive Conditional Heteroskedasticity with Estimates of the Variance of United Kingdom Inflation," *Econometrica*, 1982, 50, 987–1007.

Engle, R. F. and C. W. J. Granger, "Co-Integration and Error Correction: Representation, Estimation and Testing," *Econometrica*, 1987, 55, 251–76.

Ericson, R. and A. Pakes, "Markov-Perfect Industry Dynamics: A Framework for Empirical Work," *Review of Economic Studies*, 1995, 62, 53–82.

Fair, R. C., *Specification, Estimation, and Analysis of Macroeconometric Models*. Cambridge, Mass.: Harvard University Press, 1984.

Fair, R. C., *Testing Macroeconometric Models*. Cambridge, Mass.: Harvard University Press, 1994.

Forni, M. and L. Reichlin, "Let's Get Real: A Dynamic Factor Analytical Approach to Disaggregated Business Cycles," Manuscript, University of Modena and University of Bruxelles, 1997.

Frisch, R., "Propagation Problems and Impulse Problems in Dynamic Economics." In *Economic Essays in Honor of Gustav Cassel*. London: Allen and Unwin, 1933.

Fuller, W. A. *Introduction to Statistical Time Series*. New York: John Wiley and Sons, 1976.

Geweke, J., "The Dynamic Factor Analysis of Economic Time-Series Models." In D. J. Aigner and A. S. Goldberger, eds. *Latent Variables in Socioeconomic Models*. Amsterdam: North-Holland, 1977, 365–83.

Gilleskie, D., "A Dynamic Stochastic Model of Medical Care Use and Work Absence," *Econometrica*, 1997, forthcoming.

Gouieroux, C. and A. Monfort, *Simulation-Based Econometric Methods*. Oxford: Oxford University Press, 1996.

Granger, C. W. J., "Investigating Causal Relations by Econometric Models and Cross-Spectral Methods," *Econometrica*, 1969, 37, 424–38.

Granger, C. W. J., "Some Properties of Time Series Data and their Use in Econometric Model Specification," *Journal of Econometrics*, 1981, 16, 121–30.

Granger, C. W. J. and R. Joyeux, "An Introduction to Long-Memory Time Series Models and Fractional Differencing," *Journal of Time Series Analysis*, 1980, 1, 15–39.

Granger, C. W. J. and Y. Teräsvirta, *Modeling Nonlinear Economic Relationships*. Oxford: Oxford University Press, 1993.

Hamilton, J. D., "A New Approach to the Economic Analysis of Nonstationary Time Series and the Business Cycle," *Econometrica*, 1989, 57, 357–84.

Hansen, L. P. and J. J. Heckman, "The Empirical Foundations of Calibration," *Journal of Economic Perspectives*, 1996, 10, 87–104.

Hansen, L. P. and T. J. Sargent, "Formulating and Estimating Dynamic Linear Rational Expectations Models," *Journal of Economic Dynamics and Control*, 1980, 2, 7–46.

Hansen, L. P. and T. J. Sargent, *Recursive Models of Dynamic Linear Economies*. Princeton: Princeton University Press, 1998, forthcoming.

Harvey, A. C., *Forecasting, Structural Time Series Models and the Kalman Filter*. Cambridge: Cambridge University Press, 1989.

Hendry, D. F., *Dynamic Econometrics*. Oxford: Oxford University Press, 1995.

Hildreth, C., *The Cowles Commission in Chicago, 1939–1955*. New York: Springer-Verlag, 1986.

Ingram, B. and C. Whiteman, "Supplanting the 'Minnesota' Prior: Forecasting Macroeconomic Time Series Using Real Business Cycle Model Priors," *Journal of Monetary Economics*, 1994, 34, 497–510.

Judd, K., *Numerical Methods in Economics*. Cambridge, Mass.: MIT Press, 1998, forthcoming.

Kim, C.-J. and C. R. Nelson, "Business Cycle Turning Points, A New Coincident Index, and Tests of Duration Dependence Based on A Dynamic Factor Model with Regime-Switching," *Review of Economics and Statistics*, 1998a, forthcoming.

Kim, C.-J. and C. R. Nelson, *Dynamic Time Series Models and Markov Switching: Classical and Gibbs Sampling Approaches with Applications*. Manuscript, Department of Economics, University of Washington, 1998b.

King, R. G., C. I. Plosser, J. H. Stock, and M. W. Watson, "Stochastic Trends and Economic Fluctuations," *American Economic Review*, 1991, 81, 819–40.

Klein, L. R., *The Keynesian Revolution*. New York: MacMillan, 1946.

Klein, L. R. and A. S. Goldberger, *An Econometric Model of the United States: 1929–1952*. Amsterdam: North-Holland, 1955.

Kydland, F. E. and E. C. Prescott, "Time to Build and Aggregate Fluctuations," *Econometrica*, 1982, 50, 1345–71.

Kydland, F. E. and E. C. Prescott, "The Computational Experiment: An Econometric Tool," *Journal of Economic Perspectives*, 1996, 10, 69–86.

Leeper, E. M. and C. A. Sims, "Toward a Modern Macroeconomic Model Useable for Policy Analysis." In O. Blanchard and S. Fischer, eds. *NBER Macroeconomics Annual*. Cambridge, Mass.: MIT Press, 1994, 81–117.

Leeper, E. M., C. A. Sims, and T. Zha, "What Does Monetary Policy Do?," *Brookings Papers on Economic Activity*, 1996, 2, 1–78.

Lucas, R. E., "Expectations and the Neutrality of Money," *Journal of Economic Theory*, 1972, 4, 103–124.

Lucas, R. E., "Econometric Policy Evaluation: A Critique." In K. Brunner and A. Meltzer, eds. *The Phillips Curve and the Labor Market* (Carnegie-Rochester Conference Series, Volume 1). Amsterdam: North-Holland, 1976.

Lucas, R. E. and E. C. Prescott, "Investment Under Uncertainty," *Econometrica*, 1971, 39, 659–81.

Mankiw, N. G. and D. Romer, eds. *New Keynesian Economics*. Cambridge, Mass.: MIT Press, 1991.

McGrattan, E. R., R. Rogerson, and R. Wright, "An Equilibrium Model of the Business Cycle with Household Production and Fiscal Policy," *International Economic Review*, 1997, 38, 267–90.

Moore, G. H., *Business Cycles, Inflation, and Forecasting*. Cambridge, Mass.: Harper and Row, 1983.

Muth, J. F., "Optimal Properties of Exponentially Weighted Forecasts," *Journal of the American Statistical Association*, 1960, 55, 299–305.

Muth, J. F., "Rational Expectations and the Theory of Price Movements," *Econometrica*, 1961, 29, 315–35.

Nelson, C. R., "The Prediction Performance of the F.R.B.-M.I.T.-Penn Model of the U.S. Economy," *American Economic Review*, 1972, 62, 902–17.

Nelson, C. R. and C. I. Plosser, "Trends and Random Walks in Macroeconomic Time Series: Some Evidence and Implications," *Journal of Monetary Economics*, 1982, 10, 139–62.

Pagan, A., "Calibration and Econometric Research: An Overview." In A. Pagan, ed. *Calibration Techniques and Econometrics*, special issue of *Journal of Applied Econometrics*, 1994, 9, S1–S10.

Phelps, E. S., et al., *Microeconomic Foundations of Employment and Inflation Theory*. New York: W. W. Norton and Company, 1970.

Prescott, E. C., "Theory Ahead of Business Cycle Measurement," *Quarterly Review*, Federal Reserve Bank of Minneapolis, 1986, 9–33.

Quah, D. T., "Introduction." In D. Quah, Ed. *Business Cycle Empirics—Calibration and Estimation*, "Controversy" section of *Economic Journal*, 1995, 105, 1594–96.

Quah, D. and T. J. Sargent, "A Dynamic Index Model for Large Cross Sections." In J. H. Stock and M. W. Watson, eds., *Business Cycles, Indicators and Forecasting*. Chicago: University of Chicago Press for NBER, 1993, 285–310.

Rios-Rull, J.-V., "Models with Heterogeneous Agents." In T. F. Cooley, ed. *Frontiers of Business Cycle Research*. Princeton: Princeton University Press, 1995, 98–125.

Rosen, S., K. M. Murphy, and J. A. Scheinkman, "Cattle Cycles," *Journal of Political Economy*, 1994, 102, 468–92.

Rosenzweig, M. R. and K. I. Wolpin, "Credit Market Constraints, Consumption Smoothing, and the Accumulation of Durable Production Assets in Low-income Countries: Investments in Bullocks in India," *Journal of Political Economy*, 1993, 101, 223–44.

Rotemberg, J. J. and M. Woodford, "An Optimization-Based Econometric Framework for the Evaluation of Monetary Policy." In O. Blanchard and S.

Fischer, eds. *NBER Macroeconomics Annual*. Cambridge, Mass.: MIT Press, 1997.

Rotemberg, J. J. and M. Woodford, "Real Business-Cycle Models and the Forecastable Movements in Output, Hours, and Consumption," *American Economic Review*, 1996, 86, 71–89.

Rothwell, G. and J. Rust, "A Dynamic Programming Model of U.S. Nuclear Power Plant Operations," Manuscript, Department of Economics, University of Wisconsin, 1995.

Rust, J., "Structural Estimation of Markov Decision Processes." In R. Engle and D. McFadden, eds. *Handbook of Econometrics*, Vol. 4. Amsterdam: North-Holland, 1994.

Rust, J., "Numerical Dynamic Programming in Economics." Forthcoming in H. Amman, D. Kendrick and J. Rust, eds. *Handbook of Computational Economics*. Amsterdam: North-Holland, 1996.

Sargan, J. D., "Wages and Prices in the United Kingdom: A Study in Econometric Methodology." In P. E. Hart, G. Mills and J. N. Whitaker, eds. *Econometric Analysis for National Economic Planning*. London: Butterworths, 1964.

Sargent, T. J. and C. Sims, "Business Cycle Modeling Without Pretending to Have Too Much a Priori Theory." In C. Sims ed. *New Methods of Business Cycle Research*. Minneapolis: Federal Reserve Bank of Minneapolis, 1977.

Sargent, T. J. and N. Wallace, " 'Rational' Expectations, the Optimal Monetary Instrument, and the Optimal Money Supply Rule," *Journal of Political Economy*, 1975, 83, 241–54.

Sims, C. A., "Money, Income and Causality," *American Economic Review*, 1972, 62, 540–52.

Sims, C. A., "Macroeconomics and Reality," *Econometrica*, 1980, 48, 1–48.

Sims, C. A., "Macroeconomics and Methodology," *Journal of Economic Perspectives*, 1996, 10, 105–120.

Sims, C. A. and T. Zha, "Does Monetary Policy Cause Recessions?" Manuscript, Department of Economics, Yale University, 1996.

Sims, C. A. and T. Zha, "System Methods for Bayesian Forecasting Models," Manuscript, Yale University and Federal Reserve Bank of Atlanta, 1997.

Slutsky, E., "The Summation of Random Causes as the Source of Cyclic Processes," *Econometrica*, 1927, 5, 105–46.

Stock, J. H. and M. W. Watson, "Variable Trends in Economic Time Series," *Journal of Economic Perspectives*, 1988a, 2, 147–74.

Stock, J. H. and M. W. Watson, "Testing for Common Trends," *Journal of the American Statistical Association*, 1988b, 83, 1097–1107.

Stock, J. H. and M. W. Watson, "New Indexes of Coincident and Leading Economic Indicators." In O. Blanchard and S. Fischer, eds. *NBER Macroeconomics Annual*. Cambridge, Mass.: MIT Press, 351–94.

Stock, J. H. and M. W. Watson, "Adaptive Diffusion Indexes," Manuscript, Kennedy School, Harvard University, and Woodrow Wilson School, Princeton University, 1997.

Stock, J. H. and D. Wise, "Pensions, the Option Value of Work, and Retirement," *Econometrica*, 1990, 58, 1151–80.

Taylor, J., *Macroeconomic Policy in a World Economy*: *From Econometric Design to Practical Operation*. New York: Norton, 1993.

Tong, H., *Non-linear Time Series*. Oxford: Clarendon Press, 1990.

Whittle, P., *Prediction and Regulation by Linear Least-Square Methods*, Second Edition. Minneapolis: University of Minnesota Press, 1990.

Yule, G. U., "On a Method of Investigating Periodicities in Disturbed Series, with Special Reference to Wolfer's Sunspot Numbers," *Philosophical Transactions*, 1927, 226A.

Zarnowitz, V., *Business Cycles*: *Theory, History, Indicators, and Forecasting*. Chicago: University of Chicago Press, 1992.

Zellner, A. "Statistics, Science and Public Policy," *Journal of the American Statistical Association*, 1992, 87, 1–6.

15

Scoring the Leading Indicators

FRANCIS X. DIEBOLD AND GLENN D. RUDEBUSCH*

1. Introduction

To economic agents suffering through cycles of prosperity and depression, the prospect of a set of indicators that could provide advance warning of economic fluctuations is tantalizing. Leading cyclical indicators of U.S. aggregate economic activity have had continued popularity in the 50 years since their original development by Wesley Mitchell and Arthur Burns (1938).[1] The use of leading indicators has survived the criticism of "measurement without theory," first leveled by Koopmans (1947), as well as the rise (and partial decline) of the large-scale structural modeling approach to econometric forecasting. The release of the composite index of leading indicators is trumpeted each month by the popular and financial press, although the interpretation and significance that should be attached to the latest numbers are often unclear. This article provides a rigorous analysis of the predictive ability of the composite leading index in forecasting business cycle peaks and troughs. In particular, we apply formal probability-assessment scoring rules to the cyclical turning-point probabilities generated from the index of leading indicators via Neftci's (1982) sequential probability recursion.

The next section provides theoretical justification for the use of leading indicators in economic prediction, with a focus on the prediction of cyclical turning points. The informational content of a leading indicator can be evaluated only in the context of a given method of prediction, so various methods of translating leading signals into turning-point predictions are discussed. In Section 3, we consider standards for evaluating the predictive performance of the leading indicators

* We would like to thank Bill Nelson for research assistance, and Bill Cleveland, Milton Friedman, Jeff Fuhrer, Eric Ghysels, Kajal Lahiri, Salih Neftci, Paul Samuelson, Jim Stock, Peter Tinsley, Mark Watson, Roy Webb, Bill Wecker, Victor Zarnowitz, and an anonymous referee for useful comments.

[1] Paul Samuelson (1987) recalls an even earlier construction of leading indicators, the Harvard ABC curves, which were popular in the 1920s.

through a number of formal probability-assessment scoring rules that naturally complement the sequential probability recursion. The quadratic probability score, the probability-forecast analog of mean-squared prediction error, and additional measures of probability-forecast calibration and resolution are introduced. These scoring rules characterize the forecasting ability of the leading indicators in a number of dimensions.

The fourth and fifth sections contain empirical results. In Section 4, the probability forecasts are calculated, and several methodological innovations are introduced into the sequential probability recursion. These forecasts are scored in Section 5. The final section contains concluding remarks and suggests directions for future research.

2. Prediction with Leading Indicators

Leading economic indicators have long been used in the prediction of business cycle peaks and troughs. Many have argued that the composite leading index (CLI) is particularly useful in the analysis of business conditions if attention is placed on its ability to predict an economic event (a turning point), rather than to forecast future values of economic time series. This view contrasts with the regression-based approaches of Auerbach (1982) and Neftci (1979), who examine the predictive power of linear regressions of coincident variables on leading indicators.[2] It also contrasts with the work of Wecker (1979) and Kling (1987), which involves translating such linear projections into turning-point forecasts. Both have a foundation in the linear regression framework, where a prediction error of a given size carries the same weight, regardless of the point in the cycle at which it occurs. Consequently, a good fit at the turning points can be overwhelmed by a poor fit at the majority of data points between turning points.

In this article, we take an event-oriented, nonregression-based approach, motivated by the belief that the economy behaves differently in the downturn phase than in the upturn phase of the cycle and, in particular, that turning points delineate essential changes in the empirical relations among economic variables. Okun (1960), Hymans (1973), Zarnowitz and Moore (1982), Moore (1983), and others have noted that

---

[2] Auerbach (1982), for example, finds that the composite leading index is causally prior to unemployment and industrial production. This contrasts with Neftci (1979), who shows that the individual component indicators, taken one at a time, are less useful for predicting changes in cyclical variables. (Koch and Rasche [1988] report similar results.) This suggests that the benefits of "portfolio diversification" are one motivation for the use of a composite index.

the turning points of business cycles are special and that the composite index of leading indicators has been constructed so as to maximize the mount of *turning-point* information available.[3] Thus, the CLI as currently constructed may not be best suited for prediction and evaluation in the classical minimum mean-squared prediction error framework; the information content of the leading indicators has been focused on the occurrence of an economic event, the business cycle turning point, not on the value of an economic variable. Leading indicator information may be qualitative and event oriented, providing a signal of changes in economic regime.

Early writers on the business cycle paid close attention to the different mechanisms operating at peak and trough ("crisis and revival") and during expansion and contraction.[4] One difference is the apparent asymmetry of the business cycle: the long, gradual expansion versus the short, steep contraction, as discussed in Neftci (1984). Recent econometric work in the areas of switching and threshold models, nonlinear dynamical systems, and nonlinear filtering is in the same spirit.[5] Given different behavior of the macroeconomy during expansions and contractions, the dynamic optimization problems faced by agents imply the desirability of predicting turning points. In such a switching economy, there is an advantage in forecasting both the expected future value of an economic variable and its future probability structure, as delineated by turning points. For example, Neftci (1982) considers the case where Y_t is a stochastic variable representing major macroaggregates such as employment or production, and Y_t has two different probability distribution functions $G^u(Y_t)$ and $G^d(Y_t)$. The first represents probabilities associated with Y_t during the upswing or expansion regime; the second represents probabilities during the downswing or contraction regime. A turning point, peak or trough, is defined as the point in time when the probability distribution changes from $G^u(Y_t)$ to $G^d(Y_t)$ or vice versa. The prediction problem can then be separated into forecasting the period when the distributions switch and then obtaining forecasts of the future values of Y_t.

In general, when the relationships among the major macroaggregates change with the phase of the business cycle, a separate prediction of

[3] For example, in presenting a major redefinitional revision of the CLI, Zarnowitz and Boschen (1975) describe the most important selection criterion for choosing components of the index in terms of turning points: "The consistency of cyclical timing is crucially important for the principal use of the indicators: timely recognition (ideally, for the leading series, reasonably successful prediction) of business cycle turning points. Hence timing is accorded the highest weight."

[4] See, e.g., Haberler (1937) and Schumpeter (1939).

[5] See, e.g., Tong (1983); Hamilton (1987); and Brock and Sayers (1988).

turning points will be useful. For example, a businessman may project product sales based on a projection of aggregate gross national product (GNP). The relationship between sales and GNP may be very different when the economy is expanding from when it is contracting; thus, it is fruitful to predict not only the future values of GNP but also the regime. Moreover, regime-specific business-cycle behavior may be institutionalized, as are the federal budget deficit targets mandated by the Gramm-Rudman-Hollings legislation, which, by law, are suspended automatically during a recession.

Given a separate role for the prediction of turning points, there is now a place for a "leading indicator," a series that portends the downturn or upturn. In forecasting situations, a leading indicator is only as good as the rule used to interpret its movements, that is, the procedure that maps leading-indicator changes into turning-point predictions. The determination of rules that yield "early warnings" while minimizing "false alarms" is analogous to the construction of statistical tests with good properties in terms of type I and type II errors. The classic example of a turning-point filter associated with the CLI is the three-consecutive-declines rule for signaling a downturn. (See, e.g., Vaccara and Zarnowitz 1977.) More sophisticated rules have been studied by Okun (1960), Hymans (1973), and Zarnowitz and Moore (1982).

However, as described in Neftci (1982), a class of real-time sequential-analytic leading-indicator prediction rules can be rigorously formulated for the switching economy. Label the coincident indicator Y_t, which, as above, switches probability distribution at turning points. A leading indicator X_t also switches distribution (a turning point) but with some lead time over the turning point in Y_t. The forecaster tries to recognize the change in the probability distribution of X_t with enough lead time to fruitfully predict the turning point in Y_t. Let Z_X be an integer-valued random variable that represents the time-index date of the first period after the turning point in X_t. For example, in the prediction of a downturn,

$$X_t \sim F^u(X_t), \quad 1 \le t < Z_X,$$

$$X_t \sim F^d(X_t), \quad Z_X \le t,$$

where F^u and F^d are the respective upturn and downturn distributions. Time-sequential observations on the leading indicator are received, so at time t, there are $(t + 1)$ observations denoted $\bar{x}_t = (x_0, x_1, \ldots, x_t)$.

At time t, we calculate a probability for the event $Z_X \leq t$, that is, that by time t a turning point in X has occurred.

The probability of $Z_X \leq t$ after observing the data $\bar{x}_t$ at time t can be decomposed by Bayes's formula:

$$P(Z_X \leq t \mid \bar{x}_t) = \frac{P(\bar{x}_t \mid Z_X \leq t)P(Z_X \leq t)}{P(\bar{x}_t)}.$$

Define $\Pi_t = P(Z_X \leq t \mid \bar{x}_t)$ as the posterior probability of a turning point given the data available. As shown in Appendix A, we obtain a very convenient recursive formula for the posterior probability prediction of a downturn:

$$\Pi_t = [\Pi_{t-1} + \Gamma_t^u \cdot (1 - \Pi_{t-1})]f^d(x_t \mid \bar{x}_{t-1})/\{[\Pi_{t-1} + \Gamma_t^u$$

$$\cdot (1 - \Pi_{t-1})]f^d(x_t \mid \bar{x}_{t-1}) + (1 - \Pi_{t-1})f^u(x_t \mid \bar{x}_{t-1})(1 - \Gamma_t^u)\},$$

where $\Gamma_t^u = P(Z_X = t \mid Z_X \geq t)$, the probability of a turning point peak in period t given that one has not already occurred, and f^u and f^d are the probability densities of the latest (tth) observation if it came from, respectively, an upturn or downturn regime (in X_t) and conditional upon previous observations.[6] (To predict the probability of an upturn or trough, exchange f^u with f^d and use the transition probability Γ_t^d, the probability of a trough in t given a continuing contraction.) With this formula, the probability Π_t can be calculated sequentially by using the previous probability Π_{t-1}, a "prior" probability that $Z = t$ based solely on the distribution of previous turning points, and the likelihoods of the most recent observation x_t based on the distribution of X_t in upswings and downswings. Given Π_t, a probability forecast about the value of Z_X, the forecaster can then relate this to Z_Y, the occurrence of a turning point in Y_t. In practice, the probability of a turning point in X_t is mapped into the probability of an "imminent" turning point in Y_t over a fixed horizon.

The precise application of this formula to the problem of forecasting the business cycle is described in Section 4. The sequential turning-point probabilities supplied by the above formula have been applied by Neftci

---

[6] The conditional probability Γ_t^u is equivalent to the transition probability (expansion regime to contraction regime) in a Markov formulation.

(1982) and Palash and Redecki (1985) in a sequential-analytic optimal stopping-time framework, where a decision maker at each point in time faces the choice of whether to signal the occurrence of a recession or not to signal one and wait for more observations.[7] We instead examine these probabilities directly, treating them as forecasts in and of themselves, much like meteorological probability of precipitation forecasts. The next section describes statistics that directly assess the informational content of such probability forecasts generated with the CLI.

3. Evaluation of Probability Forecasts

On an ex post basis, one may simply examine turning points in the composite leading index and tabulate their lead times relative to reference cycle turning points. However, recognition of CLI turning points may be much more difficult in real time, so that truly objective evaluation requires ex ante real-time filtering rules, such as the sequential probability recursion (SPR), for detecting turning points in the CLI. In other words, while good ex post turning-point lead-time performance is a necessary characteristic of an ex ante useful CLI, it is not sufficient.

An evaluation of the CLI can only be conducted within a given methodology for translating CLI movements into forecasts; thus, any such evaluation is conditional on the methodology adopted. A systematic evaluation of the probability forecasts generated via the SPR has not yet appeared in the literature; here we perform such an evaluation by using a variety of techniques available for evaluating probability forecasts. We evaluate leading-indicator turning-point forecasts on a number of attributes, including accuracy, calibration, and resolution. Precise definitions of statistics measuring these attributes are given below, though not in their most general form where separate probabilities of many possible outcomes must be considered (see Diebold 1988). For our purposes, the universe consists of only two (mutually exclusive) events, the occurrence or nonoccurrence of a turning point, so the formulae simplify considerably.

Our first attribute for forecast evaluation is *accuracy*, which refers to the closeness, on average, of predicted probabilities and observed realizations, as measured by a zero-one dummy variable. Suppose we have time series of T probability forecasts $\{P_t\}_{t=1}^{T}$, where P_t is the probability of the occurrence of a turning point at date t (or, more

---

[7] In the optimal stopping-time framework, a turning point is deemed "imminent" if $\Pi_t > \Pi_t^*$, a critical value chosen to yield a small probability type I error, at which point "sampling" stops. We make direct use of all probabilities and never stop sampling.

generally, over a specific horizon H beyond date t). Similarly, let $\{R_t\}_{t=1}^T$ be the corresponding time series of realizations; R_t equals one if a turning point occurs in period t (or over the horizon H) and equals zero otherwise. The probability-forecast analog of mean squared error is Brier's (1950) quadratic probability score:[8]

$$ \text{QPS} = 1/T \sum_{t=1}^{T} 2(P_t - R_t)^2. $$

The QPS ranges from 0 to 2, with a score of 0 corresponding to perfect accuracy. Moreover, the QPS has the desirable property of being strictly proper, meaning that it achieves a strict minimum under truthful revelation of probabilities by the forecaster. In addition, it is the unique proper scoring rule that is a function only of the discrepancy between realizations and assessed probabilities, as shown by Winkler (1969).

We also consider another strictly proper accuracy-scoring rule, the log probability score (LPS), given by

$$ \text{LPS} = -1/T \sum_{t=1}^{T} [(1 - R_t)\ln(1 - P_t) + R_t \ln(P_t)]. $$

The LPS ranges from 0 to ∞, with a score of 0 corresponding to perfect accuracy. The LPS depends exclusively on the probability forecast of the event that actually occurred, assigning as a score the log of the assessed probability. In the two-event universe of this article, the LPS is a fully general scoring rule, because the probability forecast of a turning point (P_t) implicitly determines the probability forecast of a nonturning point ($1 - P_t$). The loss function associated with LPS differs from that corresponding to QPS, as large mistakes are penalized more heavily under LPS.

The *calibration* of a probability forecast refers to closeness of forecast probabilities and observed relative frequencies. Overall forecast calibration is measured by global squared bias: $\text{GSB} = 2(\bar{P} - \bar{R})^2$, where $\bar{P} = 1/T \sum_{t=1}^{T} P_t$ and $\bar{R} = 1/T \sum_{t=1}^{T} R_t$.

Clearly, $\text{GSB} \in [0, 2]$, with $\text{GSB} = 0$ corresponding to perfect global calibration, which occurs when the average probability forecast equals the average realization. One can also consider the calibration of sets of

---

[8] It is worth noting that use of such a quadratic loss function may not be appropriate in all contexts. In particular, loss, if symmetric, need not grow as the square of the error. It is also not clear that symmetric loss is appropriate. For example, if a forecaster is penalized more heavily for "missing a call" (i.e., making a type II error) than for "signaling a false alarm" (i.e., making a type I error), then the appropriate loss function is asymmetric.

probability forecasts. Partition the series of probability forecasts into $j = 1, \ldots, J$ cells with T^j forecasts in each cell ($\sum T^j = T$). Then, within-cell forecast calibration is measured by local squared bias:

$$\text{LSB} = 1/T \sum_{j=1}^{J} 2T^j(\bar{P}^j - \bar{R}^j)^2,$$

where $\bar{P}^j$ is the within-cell average probability and $\bar{R}_j$ is the average realization of turning points associated with these forecasts. Like GSB, LSB $\in [0, 2]$, and zero corresponds to perfect local calibration. While LSB $= 0$ implies GSB $= 0$, the converse is not true.

Resolution (RES) measures the extent to which different forecasts are in fact followed by different realizations. Formally,

$$\text{RES} = 1/T \sum_{j=1}^{J} 2T^j(\bar{R}^j - \bar{R})^2.$$

Thus, we measure resolution as a weighted average of squared deviations of cell realization means from the grand mean, where the weights are given by the number of probability forecasts falling within each cell. RES is simply a weighted variance of the $\bar{R}^j$ values (thus RES ≥ 0), and high resolution indicates that discriminating predictive information is available. To see this, consider the case in which all cell means are equal to the grand mean. Then the forecast has no resolution at all (RES $= 0$), the cell means being constant (at $\bar{R}$) regardless of the predicted probability values. Murphy (1973) has established the important decomposition:

$$\text{QPS} = \text{QPS}_{\text{const}} + \text{LSB} - \text{RES},$$

where $\text{QPS}_{\text{const}}$ is the QPS of the constant probability forecast $\bar{R}$.

We thus have three attributes on which to evaluate probability forecasts (given with their related scoring measures): accuracy (QPS, LPS), calibration (GSB, LSB), and resolution (RES). In Section 5, we shall use these measures to actually "score" the composite index of leading indicators in the prediction of cyclical turning points.

4. Empirical Analysis—Generation of Probabilities

To use the recursive formula of Section 2 to construct probability forecasts of business cycle turning points, we must obtain the transition probabilities $\{\Gamma_t^u\}$ and $\{\Gamma_t^d\}$, as well as the densities f^d and f^u, and an initial condition Π_0. The sequence of peak and trough conditional transition probabilities depends on the stochastic structure generating regime lengths. Neftci (1982) calculates transition probabilities (expansion to contraction regime) that increase with the age of the regime by using the relative frequencies of observed CLI turning points. It is not clear, however, that the probability of a turning point should increase as current regime continues, for example, that a long expansion is more likely to end than a short one. In other work, we have presented evidence that the expansions and contractions in the American business cycle, particularly in the postwar period, are not characterized by duration dependence; thus, the probability of a turning point is roughly independent of the age of the regime.[9] These results have been replicated for turning points in the CLI. Consequently, we provide sequential probability forecasts using these time-invariant transition probabilities (i.e., $\Gamma_t^u = \Gamma^u$ and $\Gamma_t^d = \Gamma^d$).

The sequential probability recursion also requires the probability density of the leading series given that the stochastic generating structure is expansion ($f^u(\cdot)$) and given that it is contraction ($f^d(\cdot)$). The leading series used in this paper is the percent change in the composite index of leading indicators. The division of the leading series into regimes depends on the underlying classification of economic activity. We have followed the *Business Conditions Digest* in denoting peaks and troughs of the CLI that correspond to the National Bureau of Economic Research (NBER) business cycle, and both chronologies are given in Appendix B. After grouping the leading indicator observations into two classes corresponding to upswing and downswing regimes, we estimate the relevant densities f^u and f^d. We have experimented with several procedures to obtain these densities, and following Neftci (1982), all are based on the assumption of a simple probability structure of X_t of the form

$$X_t = \begin{cases} \alpha^u + \epsilon_t^u & \text{in expansions,} \\ \alpha^d + \epsilon_t^d & \text{in contractions,} \end{cases}$$

where α^u and α^d are fixed and ϵ_t^u and ϵ_t^d are independently and identically distributed (iid) zero-mean random variables with variances

---

[9] See Diebold and Rudebusch (1988*b*, 1988*c*); see also McCulloch (1975).

σ_u^2 and σ_d^2, respectively. This extremely simple model may be viewed as providing an approximation to a switching density, conditional on regime.[10]

To estimate f^u and f^d, we fit a simple normal density function to observations in each regime. The procedure is easily replicated and provides a good approximation to the underlying data. A number of completely nonparametric density estimates, such as those of Terrel and Scott (1985), were also considered with no substantive effect on the results.

The final element in the sequential probability recursion is last period's posterior probability of a turning point. There are two corrections made to this probability in practice. First, at the start of a new regime, a start-up probability of zero is used as the previous period's probability. Also, as is clear from the formula, if the posterior probability reaches one at any point, it will force all remaining probability forecasts to be one in the regime. Thus, we put an upper bound of .95 on the previous posteriori probability as it enters the recursive probability formula.

An example of probabilities obtained from the SPR is given in figure 15.1. While a rigorous evaluation of these probabilities will be provided in the next section, it is helpful to first give some general discussion. In figure 15.1, the probabilities are obtained by using fitted normal densities $f^u(x_t)$ and $f^d(x_t)$ and a uniform transition prior: $\Gamma_t^u = .02$ during expansions and $\Gamma_t^d = .10$ during contractions, for all t. The dates of NBER peaks and troughs are denoted by vertical dashed lines. The turning point probabilities start in December 1948 and continue to August 1986. Those preceding a peak (trough) refer to the probability of the beginning of a recession (expansion). (In the figure, the probabilities are reported for 5 months past the turning point, but these late probabilities will not be scored.) The probabilities in figure 15.1 provide a signal for the onset of every recession except the very sudden downturn of 1981; however, the lead times of these signals are variable and, in particular, too long in 1957. Four false signals of recession are given: two major ones in 1951 and 1966, two minor ones in 1962 and 1984. It is instructive to compare these SPR probability signals with those produced by alternative rules, such as three consecutive declines

---

[10] Extensions to time-varying intraregime conditional densities are straightforward conceptually but quite tedious in practice, as can be inferred from App. A. In particular, convenient analytic recursions, such as the SPR given above, are not available in the more general case. To the extent that superior approximations could be obtained from more sophisticated nonlinear models, our results provide a *lower bound* on the predictive performance of the CLI.

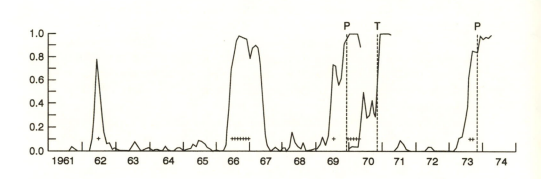

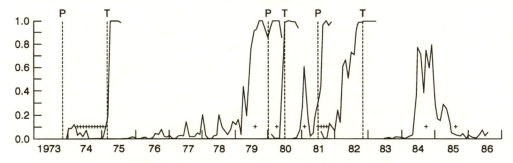

Fig. 15.1. Sequential probabilities of a turning point.

in the CLI. The plus signs (+) in figure 15.1 denote the third month in each string of three consecutive declines in the CLI. There is, in general, a correspondence between the triple decline signal and high probabilities of recession. The probability measure, however, gives more information, and it is *sustained* information of a quantitative type.[11] The

---

[11] The three-consecutive-declines rule ignores the *magnitude* of the fall in the CLI; it does not distinguish, e.g., between three 1% declines and three 0.1% declines.

probability measure, for example, clearly distinguishes the triple CLI decline in 1962 as a false signal within 2 months while sustaining the recession signal in 1969. In addition, this quantitative information is often given with a greater lead time as in 1979, where the probability of imminent recession reaches 80 percent in the month before the third decline. The probabilities in figure 15.1 preceding a trough give the likelihood of an imminent upturn. There is no simple rule of thumb that signals troughs available for comparison, so we will defer further evaluation to Section 5.

Before scoring these probabilities, several qualifications and caveats should be noted. The probability estimates, while sequential and real time in spirit, are not completely ex ante, out-of-sample forecasts. First, they make use of some quantities, in particular the f^u and f^d densities, which are estimated over the entire sample. Second, the numbers used for the CLI are of a final revised form, whereas, in real-time forecasting, only preliminary and partially revised data are available. In addition, the components of the CLI are often changed and reweighted ex post to improve performance over the sample. Thus, for instance, the 1971 CLI data that we use was not available in 1971 but is the most recent (1987) formulation of the CLI reconstructed for 1971. Completely ex ante forecasts would involve both a rolling sample construction of densities based on previous data and the use of the preliminary and first-revision original construction CLI data that was available in real time.[12]

While the above two qualifications would tend to induce an overestimation of the performance of the CLI, there are also a number of lines of reasoning that suggest an underestimation of the performance of the CLI based on an incorrect assessment of false signals. First, note that we evaluate and score the CLI on how well it predicts NBER business-cycle turning points. Insofar as the CLI portends mere economic slow-downs and growth-cycle turning points and insofar as a policymaker is interested in an early warning of such near recessions, then the scoring of the CLI probability forecasts only with respect to business cycles may be misleading. (See J. Shiskin's comments following Hymans [1973].) A second and more subtle point is that if the leading indicators have been used in the formation of effective countercyclical policy, then they will be evaluated as less effective than they really are. For example, in 1966 the CLI signaled a forthcoming recession, and if policymakers

---

[12] Hymans (1973) examines, in the context of a simple forecasting rule, the effect of using original CLI data in forecasting and finds a negligible effect, while Zarnowitz and Moore (1982) find a somewhat larger effect. For further discussion of the properties of revisions in the leading indicators, see Diebold and Rudebusch (1988a). For a completely ex ante analysis, see Diebold and Rudebusch (1988b).

took that signal and avoided a recession, then the signal, although a proper one, would be labeled, ex post, as false.

With these qualifications of potential over- and underassessment of the CLI noted, we now provide a detailed analysis of the turning-point forecasts.

5. Empirical Analysis—Scoring of Probabilities

In this section, we analyze the sequential turning-point probability forecasts generated in the previous section. A comparison of the scores of SPR forecasts with other probability forecasts, including constant-probability forecasts and variants of the CLI three-consecutive-declines rule, allows us to provide a joint characterization of the usefulness of the SPR and the information content of the CLI. Tables 15.1–15.6 present scoring attributes for probability forecasts of peaks and troughs generated by this variety of methods. Given differences in the dynamics of upswings and downswings, we might expect differences in predictive performance of the composite index of leading indicators when forecasting peaks versus troughs. This suggests that the actual *scoring* calculations (rather than just choice of the transition probabilities Γ^u and Γ^d in the generation stage) should be performed separately on probabilities generated in expansions and contractions.

Let us first evaluate the forecasts in terms of accuracy. Tables 15.1 and 15.2 present the Quadratic Probability Score (QPS) and the Log Probability Score (LPS) for each forecasting technique. While both statistics measure accuracy, the implicit loss functions differ. The forecasting methods include a no-change, NAIVE forecast, which amounts to a constant zero probability forecast, $P_t = 0$, of a downturn or upturn. This is the probability forecast analog of a random walk (in this case, $QPS = 2\bar{R}$). More generally, one can search in the zero-one interval for the number that is the most accurate as a probability prediction of turning points. Such optimal, CONSTANT probability forecasts are of the form $P_t = \kappa^u$ during expansions and $P_t = \kappa^d$ during contractions, where the constants are chosen to minimize QPS or LPS. In the second row of table 15.1, for example, at a forecast horizon of 5 months, a 10% probability forecast of a downturn ($\kappa^u = .10$, given in parentheses below the score) is the most accurate constant-probability forecast. These optimal constant-probability forecasts are a natural first choice for the prior probabilities used in the generation of posterior turning-point probabilities via the SPR (i.e., $\Gamma^u = \kappa^u$ and $\Gamma^d = \kappa^d$ in the rows labeled SPR). An alternative constant prior could be chosen by searching the zero-one interval for the constant prior that provides the most

TABLE 15.1
QPS as a Function of Horizon, Various Forecasting Methods

Method	Forecast Horizon					
	1	3	5	7	9	13
Prediction of peaks:						
NAIVE	.04	.12	.19	.27	.35	.52
CONSTANT	.04	.11	.18	.24	.29	.38
(κ^u)	(.02)	(.06)	(.10)	(.14)	(.18)	(.26)
SPR	.29	.35	.38	.38	.41	.49
(Γ^u)	(.02)	(.06)	(.10)	(.14)	(.18)	(.26)
SPR*	.04	.12	.19	.23	.28	.39
(Γ^u)	(10^{-7})	(.0001)	(.001)	(.005)	(.01)	(.03)
3CD	.19	.23	.26	.28	.34	.50
3CDa	.24	.23	.23	.24	.29	.45
Prediction of troughs:						
NAIVE	.18	.55	.91	1.25	1.55	1.88
CONSTANT	.17	.40	.50	.47	.35	.13
(κ^d)	(.09)	(.27)	(.45)	(.63)	(.78)	(.93)
SPR	.27	.41	.45	.48	.42	.17
(Γ^d)	(.09)	(.27)	(.45)	(.63)	(.78)	(.93)
SPR*	.15	.29	.39	.43	.37	.15
(Γ^d)	(.005)	(.07)	(.23)	(.39)	(.95)	(.97)

Note: The CONSTANT probability forecast is a constant (given in parentheses) that minimizes the QPS. The SPR probabilities use this constant probability as a prior (Γ^u or Γ^d, given in parentheses). The SPR* probabilities are generated with the prior transition probabilities (given in parentheses) that minimize the QPS. The forecast horizon is given in months, and the scoring sample is from December 1948 to December 1986.

accurate probabilities generated via the SPR. Such probabilities (scored in rows SPR*) are the best that can be generated from the CLI by the SPR. Finally, two variants on the "three-consecutive-declines" theme for the prediction of downturns were evaluated. The simplest rule of three, denoted 3CD, produces probability forecasts of zero or one, depending on whether the most recent three observations have been negative. A number of methods were used, in an attempt to enhance these probability forecasts, with some success. In particular, a linear decay method is also scored (3CDa) where generated forecasts of unity are followed by .8, .6, .4, .2, 0.0 (unless, of course, three more consecutive declines occur, at which time the probability immediately returns to 1.0).

A number of interesting features emerge from tables 15.1 and 15.2. All methods score best at short horizons (1–3 months), and predictive

TABLE 15.2
LPS as a Function of Horizon, Various Forecasting Methods

Method	Forecast Horizon					
	1	3	5	7	9	13
Prediction of peaks:						
NAIVE	.27	.80	1.34	1.89	2.44	3.53
CONSTANT	.10	.22	.32	.40	.47	.57
	(.02)	(.06)	(.10)	(.14)	(.18)	(.26)
SPR	.49	.60	.66	.66	.69	.85
	(.02)	(.06)	(.10)	(.14)	(.18)	(.26)
SPR*	.13	.24	.35	.40	.48	.70
	(10^{-5})	(.0003)	(.002)	(.005)	(.02)	(.05)
3CD	1.33	1.56	1.80	1.89	2.37	3.45
3CDa	1.26	1.27	1.30	1.38	1.73	2.81
Prediction of troughs:						
NAIVE	1.26	3.77	6.28	8.63	10.68	12.87
CONSTANT	.30	.59	.69	.66	.54	.25
	(.09)	(.27)	(.45)	(.63)	(.78)	(.93)
SPR	.56	.64	.73	.75	.64	.41
	(.09)	(.27)	(.45)	(.63)	(.78)	(.93)
SPR*	.35	.48	.66	.70	.63	.41
	(.005)	(.09)	(.26)	(.50)	(.72)	(.94)

Note: The CONSTANT probability forecast is a constant (given in parentheses) that minimizes the LPS. The SPR probabilities use this constant probability as a prior (Γ^u or Γ^d, given in parentheses). The SPR* probabilities are generated with the prior transition probabilities (given in parentheses) that minimize the LPS. The forecast horizon is given in months, and the scoring sample is from December 1948 to December 1986.

performance deteriorates with horizon.[13] In addition, as alluded to earlier, the predictive performance of all techniques differs sharply between expansions and contractions. In particular, troughs are harder to predict than are peaks. At a 3-month horizon, for example, SPR* has a QPS of .12 for peak prediction and a QPS of .29 for trough prediction.

These accuracy scores shed light on two important additional issues: first, the performance of the SPR forecasts relative to other rules for interpreting movements in the CLI and, second, the performance of the CLI-based forecasts relative to benchmark naive and constant-probabil-

---

[13] This is consistent with the results of other studies on average lead time. While the performance of trough forecasts appears to improve at very long horizons (9–12 months), this is merely a manifestation of the fact that contractions typically are short, so that, given a long enough horizon, one can always obtain accurate, though useless, trough predictions by forecasting a turning point with probability one.

ity forecasts. To address the first issue, compare the SPR* scores to those obtained from applying the three-consecutive-decline rules (3CD and 3CDa).[14] These rules are in general outperformed by the SPR at all horizons; note, in particular, the poor log-probability scores obtained by the simple rules. With regard to the second issue, the information content of the CLI, we compare the SPR, SPR*, NAIVE, and CONSTANT forecast rows. While SPR* performs much better than the naive, no-change forecast, its comparative advantage relative to the optimal constant probability forecast (CONSTANT) is less pronounced. Relative performance differs significantly over expansions and contractions: in the prediction of troughs, SPR* is generally superior to CONSTANT, while the two methods produce similar results in the prediction of peaks. This holds true regardless of whether the QPS or LPS loss function is used.

We can characterize the performance of the probability forecasts in greater detail by examining other scores. The extent of bias in the forecasts for various horizons is given in a global sense (GSB) over upswing and downswing observations in table 15.3. All forecasts except the naive, no-change forecast and the SPR forecast are well calibrated, that is, correct on average. The direction of the bias of the NAIVE forecast is, of course, one of underprediction of returning-point probabilities. For the SPR (where $\Gamma^u = \kappa^u$, $\Gamma^d = \kappa^d$), however, the bias is one of overprediction of the probabilities of turning points.[15]

The weighted average of the biases associated with particular forecasts (e.g., the 25% probability forecast of recession compared with the associated realized relative frequency), or local squared bias (LSB), is given in table 15.4.[16] Again, the overprediction bias of the SPR is evident. The local calibration of the SPR* forecasts is elucidated further by examining the relationship between the individual probability forecasts and resulting relative frequency of realizations (table 15.5). The actual frequency distribution of probability forecast values is also shown. Taken together, the entries in the table enable us to examine the joint distribution of forecasts and realizations, as factored into the distribution of realizations conditional on forecasts and the marginal

[14] An evaluation in which the predictive power of monetary and financial variables is explored and lead times are the sole evaluation criterion is provided in Palash and Radecki (1985) and favors the SPR.

[15] This is clear since the unbiased SPR* requires lower priors and hence involves lower posteriors. Since these optimal priors, which are natural ones to use, are unbiased, the overprediction or false alarm bias of the posterior SPR probabilities reflects either deficiencies in the CLI or in our application of the forecasting methodology.

[16] Following standard practice, our continuous probability forecasts were discretized by mapping [0, .1) into .05, [.1, .2) into .15, etc. This LSB discretization is responsible for the slight differences in GSB and LSB for the NAIVE and CONSTANT forecasts.

TABLE 15.3
GSB as a Function of Horizon, Various Forecasting Methods

Method	*Forecast Horizon*					
	1	*3*	*5*	*7*	*9*	*13*
Prediction of peaks:						
NAIVE	.00	.01	.02	.04	.06	.13
CONSTANT	.00	.00	.00	.00	.00	.00
	(.02)	(.06)	(.10)	(.14)	(.18)	(.26)
SPR	.08	.11	.12	.12	.11	.10
	(.02)	(.06)	(.10)	(.14)	(.18)	(.26)
SPR*	.00	.00	.00	.00	.00	.00
	(10^{-7})	(.0001)	(.001)	(.005)	(.01)	(.03)
3CD	.01	.00	.00	.00	.02	.05
3CD*a*	.03	.02	.00	.00	.00	.02
Prediction of troughs:						
NAIVE	.02	.15	.41	.78	1.19	1.74
CONSTANT	.00	.00	.00	.00	.00	.00
	(.09)	(.27)	(.45)	(.63)	(.78)	(.93)
SPR	.07	.06	.02	.00	.00	.00
	(.09)	(.27)	(.45)	(.63)	(.78)	(.93)
SPR*	.00	.00	.00	.02	.05	.00
	(.005)	(.07)	(.23)	(.39)	(.95)	(.97)

Note: The CONSTANT probability forecast is a constant (given in parentheses) that minimizes the QPS. The SPR probabilities use this constant probability as a prior (Γ^u or Γ^d, given in parentheses). The SPR* probabilities are generated with the prior transition probabilities (given in parentheses) that minimizes the QPS. The forecast horizon is given in months, and the scoring sample is from December 1948 to December 1986.

distribution of the forecasts. For illustrative purposes, we constructed table 15.5 using a horizon of 12 for expansions and a horizon of 6 for contractions, with optimal transition probabilities of .03 and .23, respectively. The feature of note (for both expansions and contractions) is the local bias associated with both very small probability forecasts and very large probability forecasts, which illustrates the problem of false alarms and missed calls. The mid-range probability forecasts, however, display little systematic bias.

The resolution (RES) scores, given in table 15.6, provide insight into the value of SPR and SPR* forecasts and the information which they transmit as they range through the [0, 1] interval. Resolution is high if, on average, different forecasts tend to be followed by different realizations, so that movements in forecast probabilities convey meaningful information. First, compare the NAIVE and CONST forecasts, which,

TABLE 15.4
LSB as a Function of Horizon, Various Forecasting Methods

Method	Forecast Horizon					
	1	3	5	7	9	13
Prediction of peaks:						
NAIVE	.00	.00	.00	.02	.03	.08
CONSTANT	.00	.00	.00	.00	.00	.00
	(.02)	(.06)	(.10)	(.14)	(.18)	(.26)
SPR	.25	.26	.23	.20	.19	.19
	(.02)	(.06)	(.10)	(.14)	(.18)	(.26)
SPR*	.00	.03	.05	.05	.06	.06
	(10^{-7})	(.0001)	(.001)	(.005)	(.01)	(.03)
3CD	.14	.10	.07	.05	.05	.09
3CDa	.20	.14	.08	.05	.04	.07
Prediction of troughs:						
NAIVE	.00	.10	.33	.66	4.04	1.56
CONSTANT	.00	.00	.00	.00	.00	.00
	(.09)	(.27)	(.45)	(.63)	(.78)	(.93)
SPR	.14	.13	.12	.19	.13	.07
	(.09)	(.27)	(.45)	(.63)	(.78)	(.93)
SPR*	.04	.03	.09	.12	.06	.04
	(.005)	(.07)	(.23)	(.39)	(.95)	(.97)

Note: The CONSTANT probability forecast is a constant (given in parentheses) that minimizes the QPS. The SPR probabilities use this constant probability as a prior (Γ^u or Γ^d, given in parentheses). The SPR* probabilities are generated with the prior transition probabilities (given in parentheses) that minimize the QPS. The forecast horizon is given in months, and the scoring sample is from December 1948 to December 1986.

by definition, have zero resolution.[17] 3CD and 3CDa fare somewhat better, but the restrictive nature of the forecasts generated by these methods (e.g., probabilities of only 0.0 or 1.0 for 3CD) results in low RES. The RES is highest for the SPR and SPR* forecasts, reflecting the fact that different forecasts *do* tend to be followed by different realizations, so that movements in the generated probabilities through the [0, 1] interval contain useful information. In addition, RES is highest in contractions. Were it not for this fact, SPR and SPR* trough prediction performance in terms of QPS and LPS would be substantially worsened.

[17] For a constant forecast, the grand realization mean is equal to the mean realization in the one cell in which all forecasts lie.

TABLE 15.5
Reliability Analysis of SPR* Forecasts

P_j	$\bar{R}_j$	$P_j - \bar{R}_j$	No. of Forecasts	% of Forecasts
Prediction of peaks:				
.05	.11	.06	201	57
.15	.29	.14	28	8
.25	.25	.00	14	4
.35	.40	.05	15	4
.45	.46	.01	6	2
.55	.57	.02	9	3
.65	.22	.33	9	3
.75	.50	.25	10	3
.85	.45	.40	19	5
.95	.62	.33	42	12
Prediction of troughs:				
.05	.24	.19	29	33
.15	.14	.01	7	8
.25	.14	.11	7	8
.35	.40	.05	5	6
.45	.40	.05	5	6
.55	.75	.20	4	5
.65	1.00	.35	4	5
.75	.50	.25	6	7
.85	.33	.52	6	7
.95	1.00	.05	15	17

Note: For expansions H = 12 and Γ = .03; for contractions H = 5 and Γ = .23.

6. Concluding Remarks

We have examined the performance of a Bayesian sequential probability forecasting recursion, with the Composite Index of Leading Indicators. Performance was evaluated in a number of dimensions, including accuracy, calibration, and resolution. One clear result for good forecast performance, as well as proper forecast evaluation, was the need for prior transition probabilities, densities, horizons, and scorings that separated expansions and contractions. Furthermore, this suggests that leading economic indicators might usefully be specialized during expansions for the prediction of peaks and during contractions for the prediction of troughs. In other words, the use of two indexes, an "expansion index" and a "contraction index," constructed with different components and component weights, could enhance predictive performance.

TABLE 15.6
RES as a Function of Horizon, Various Forecasting Methods

Method	Forecast Horizon					
	1	3	5	7	9	13
Prediction of peaks:						
NAIVE	.00	.00	.00	.00	.00	.00
CONSTANT	.00	.00	.00	.00	.00	.00
	(.02)	(.06)	(.10)	(.14)	(.18)	(.26)
SPR	.00	.02	.04	.06	.07	.08
	(.02)	(.06)	(.10)	(.14)	(.18)	(.26)
SPR*	.00	.01	.03	.06	.07	.07
	(10^{-7})	(.0001)	(.001)	(.005)	(.01)	(.03)
3CD	.00	.00	.01	.02	.02	.02
3CDa	.00	.02	.04	.06	.06	.04
Prediction of troughs:						
NAIVE	.00	.00	.00	.00	.00	.00
CONSTANT	.00	.00	.00	.00	.00	.00
	(.09)	(.27)	(.45)	(.63)	(.78)	(.93)
SPR	.04	.12	.17	.17	.05	.03
	(.09)	(.27)	(.45)	(.63)	(.78)	(.93)
SPR*	.06	.14	.20	.16	.05	.02
	(.005)	(.07)	(.23)	(.39)	(.95)	(.97)

Note: The CONSTANT probability forecast is a constant (given in parentheses) that minimizes the QPS. The SPR probabilities use this constant probability as a prior (Γ^u or Γ^d, given in parentheses). The SPR* probabilities are generated with the prior transaction probabilities (given in parentheses) that minimize the QPS. The forecast horizon is given in months, and the scoring sample is from December 1948 to December 1986.

The sequential probability recursion was the best method of those considered for forecasting turning points, especially given its firm grounding in probability theory and its ability to forecast both peaks and troughs. The *absolute* performance of the sequential probability recursion in terms of accuracy, like all the other forecasting methods, was worse in contractions. Its performance *relative* to other methods, however, was best in contractions. We also examined forecast calibration and resolution, the underlying determinants of accuracy. The calibration analysis showed that most bias could be traced to those probability forecasts near zero or one, illustrating the unavoidable possibilities of "false alarms" and "missed calls." The sequential probability recursion performed best in terms of resolution, which indicates that useful information is conveyed by movements in its probability forecasts.

Whether the increased resolution afforded by use of the sequential probability recursion in forecasting with the CLI is sufficient to make it the forecasting method of choice depends on the loss function used for accuracy evaluation. Recall, for example, that the QPS may be decomposed into the QPS of a particular constant probability forecast, plus LSB, less RES. More generally, however, one can imagine less restrictive loss functions such as

$$L = f[f(\overline{R}), \text{LSB}, \text{RES}].$$

Even if a linear form is adopted, for example, we need not impose the weights of 1, 1 and -1 which correspond to QPS. To the extent that the partial derivative of L with respect to RES is negative and sufficiently large (in absolute value), the sequential probability recursion can be expected to perform well. Moreover, loss functions that place relatively high (in absolute value) weight on RES may be a good approximation to those of many forecasters and policymakers. To see this, look at figure 15.1 and ask yourself, "Which would be more useful to *me*, the SPR forecasts shown in the figure, or, for example, a constant-probability forecast (that would appear in the figure as horizontal lines in expansions and contractions)?" Many, for better or for worse, would probably choose the former.

Appendix A: Derivation of the Sequential Probability Recursion

In this appendix, we provide a proof of the sequential probability recursion along the lines of Neftci (1980). Let Z be an integer-valued random variable denoting the value of the time index in the first period after the turning point in the leading series X. (That is, if $Z = 10$, then the turning point has occurred between periods 9 and 10.) At time t we calculate a probability for the event $Z \le t$, that is, that by time t the turning point has occurred. We have an a priori probability (at time t) denoted $P(Z \le t)$. We also receive sequential observations on X, and at time t, we have $t + 1$ observations, denoted $(x_0, x_1, \ldots, x_t) \equiv \overline{x}_t$.

The posterior probability of $Z \le t$ at time t is given immediately by Bayes's rule, as in the text. This can be rewritten as

$$P(Z \le t \mid \overline{x}_t)$$

$$= \frac{\displaystyle\sum_{i=0}^{t} P(\overline{x}_t \mid Z = i) P(Z = i)}{\left[\displaystyle\sum_{i=0}^{t} P(\overline{x}_t \mid Z = i) P(Z = i)\right] + P(\overline{x}_t \mid Z > t) P(Z > t)}. \quad \text{(A1)}$$

Consider first the numerator, which we denote by A_t:

$$A_t = P(x_0, \ldots, x_t \mid Z = 0)P(Z = 0)$$

$$+ \sum_{i=1}^{t} P(x_0, \ldots, x_t \mid Z = i)P(Z = i). \tag{A2}$$

Recalling that, if $Z = i$, then $(x_0, \ldots, x_{i-1})$ and $(x_i, \ldots, x_t)$ have different (and independent) distributions, we rewrite this as

$$A_t = P(x_0, \ldots, x_t \mid Z = 0)P(Z = 0)$$

$$+ \sum_{i=1}^{t} [P(x_0, \ldots, x_{i-1} \mid Z = i)P(x_i, \ldots, x_t \mid Z = i)P(Z = i)].$$

$$\tag{A3}$$

In period $(t + 1)$, we have (A4):

$$A_{t+1} = P(x_0, \ldots, x_{t+1} \mid Z = 0)P(Z = 0)$$

$$+ \sum_{i=1}^{t} [P(x_0, \ldots, x_{i-1} \mid Z + i)$$

$$\times P(x_i, \ldots, x_{t+1} \mid Z = i)P(Z = i)]$$

$$+ P(x_0, \ldots, x_{t+1} \mid Z = t + 1)P(Z = t + 1). \tag{A4}$$

Making use of the usual factorization, we obtain

$$A_{t+1} = P(x_0, \ldots, x_t \mid Z = 0)P(x_{t+1} \mid Z = 0, x_0, \ldots, x_t)P(Z = 0)$$

$$+ \sum_{i=1}^{t} [P(x_0, \ldots, x_{i-1} \mid Z = i)P(x_i, \ldots, x_t \mid Z = i)$$

$$\times P(Z = i)P(x_{t+1} \mid Z = i, x_i, \ldots, x_t)]$$

$$+ [P(x_0, \ldots, x_t \mid Z = t + 1)P(x_{t+1} \mid Z = t + 1, x_0, \ldots, x_t)$$

$$\times P(Z = t + 1)]. \tag{A5}$$

Thus,

$$A_{t+1} = A_t P(x_{t+1} \mid Z = t + 1, x_0, \ldots, x_t)$$

$$+ P(Z = t + 1)P(x_0, \ldots, x_t \mid Z = t + 1)$$

$$\times P(x_{t+1} \mid Z = t + 1, x_0, \ldots, x_t). \tag{A6}$$

Now if we write

$$\Pi_t = \frac{A_t}{A_t + B_t}, \tag{A7}$$

so that

$$B_t = P(x_0, \ldots, x_t \mid Z > t)P(Z > t), \tag{A8}$$

then we immediately obtain the recursion

$$B_{t+1} = B_t P(x_{t+1} \mid x_0, \ldots, x_t, Z > t + 1)\frac{P(Z > t + 1)}{P(Z > t)}. \tag{A9}$$

Now note that

$$\Pi_{t+1} = \frac{B_{t+1}}{A_{t+1} + B_{t+1}}, \tag{A10}$$

and substitute (A6) and (A9) to get

$$\Pi_{t+1} = \frac{C}{C + D}, \tag{A11}$$

where $C = [\Pi_t + P(Z = t + 1 \mid Z > t)(1 - \Pi_t)][P(x_{t+1} \mid x_0, \ldots, x_t, Z = t + 1)]$, and $D = (1 - \Pi_t)P(x_{t+1} \mid x_0, \ldots, x_t, Z > t + 1)[1 - P(Z = t + 1 \mid Z > t)]$, after applying (A7) and (A8) and some tedious algebra.

To work the proof for continuous X, we realize that we have implicitly been working with the sample space partition

$$\Delta_t = \{\omega \in \Omega: x_0 < X_0 < x_0 + h, \ldots, x_t < X_t < x_t + h\}.$$

Letting $h \to 0$, we again obtain (A11), except that now the conditional *probabilities*

$$P(x_{t+1} \mid x_0, \ldots, x_t, Z = t + 1)$$

and

$$P(x_{t+1} \mid x_0, \ldots, x_t, Z > t + 1)$$

are replaced by the equivalent conditional *densities*

$$f(x_{t+1} \mid x_0, \ldots, x_t, Z \le t + 1)$$

and

$$f(x_{t+1} \mid x_0, \ldots, x_t, Z > t + 1).$$

These are, respectively, the densities

$$f^d(x_{t+1} \mid \bar{x})$$

and

$$f^u(x_{t+1} \mid \bar{x})$$

given in the text, shifted forward one period.

Appendix B: Business Cycle Chronologies

The NBER dating, year and month, of the postwar business cycles is given in the right-hand column in table 15.B1. The chronology of turning points in the composite index of leading indicators (taken from the *Business Conditions Digest*, chart 1A) is given in the left-hand column. Peaks and troughs are considered to be members of the "old" regime; thus, a peak (trough) is the last observation in an expansion (recession).

TABLE 15.B1

	CLI *Turning Points*	NBER *Turning Points*
Trough	1949:6	1949:10
Peak	1953:3	1953:7
Trough	1953:11	1954:5
Peak	1955:9	1957:8
Trough	1958:2	1958:4
Peak	1959:5	1960:4
Trough	1960:12	1961:2
Peak	1969:4	1969:12
Trough	1970:10	1970:11
Peak	1973:3	1973:11
Trough	1975:2	1975:3
Peak	1979:3	1980:1
Trough	1980:5	1980:7
Peak	1981:4	1981:7
Trough	1982:3	1982:11

References

Auerbach, A. J. 1982. The index of leading indicators: "Measurement without theory" thirty-five years later. *Review of Economics and Statistics* 64 (November): 589–95.

Brier, G. W. 1950. Verification of forecasts expressed in terms of probability. *Monthly Weather Review* 75 (January): 1–3.

Brock, W. A., and Sayers, C. L. 1988. Is the business cycle characterized by deterministic chaos? *Journal of Monetary Economics* 22 (July): 71–90.

Diebold, F. X. 1988. An application of operational-subjective statistical methods to rational expectations: Comment. *Journal of Business and Economic Statistics* 6 (October): 470–72.

Diebold, F. X., and Rudebusch, G. D. 1988a. Stochastic properties of revisions in the index of leading indicators. *Proceedings of the American Statistical Association, Business and Economic Statistics Section*, pp. 712–17. Washington, D.C.: American Statistical Association.

Diebold, F. X., and Rudebusch, G. D. 1988b. A nonparametric investigation of duration dependence in the American business cycle. Economic Activity Working Paper no. 91. Federal Reserve Board.

Diebold, F. X., and Rudebusch, G. D. 1988c. Ex ante forecasting with the leading indicators. Finance and Economics Discussion Series no. 40, Federal Reserve Board. Forthcoming in K. Lahiri and G. H. Moore (eds.), *Leading Economic Indicators: New Approaches and Forecasting Records*. Cambridge: Cambridge University Press.

Haberler, G. 1937. *Prosperity and Depression*. Geneva: League of Nations.

Hamilton, J. D. 1987. A new approach to the economic analysis of nonstationary time series and the business cycle. Discussion Paper no. 171. University of Virginia, Department of Economics. Forthcoming in *Econometrica*, vol. 57.

Hymans, S. H. 1973. On the use of leading indicators to predict cyclical turning points. *Brookings Papers on Economic Activity* 2:339–84.

Kling, J. L. 1987. Predicting the turning points of business and economic time series. *Journal of Business* 60 (April): 201–38.

Koch, P. D., and Rasche, R. H. 1988. An examination of the Commerce Department leading-indicator approach. *Journal of Business and Economic Statistics* 6 (April): 167–87.

Koopmans, T. C. 1947. Measurement without theory. *Review of Economics and Statistics* 27 (August): 161–72.

McCulloch, J. H. 1975. The Monte-Carlo cycle in business activity. *Economic Inquiry* 13 (September): 303–21.

Mitchell, W. C., and Burns, A. F. 1938. *Statistical Indicators of Cyclical Revivals*. New York: National Bureau of Economic Research.

Moore, G. H. 1983. *Business Cycles, Inflation, and Forecasting*. 2d ed. Cambridge, Mass.: Ballinger.

Murphy, A. H. 1973. A new vector partition of the probability score. *Journal of Applied Meteorology* 12 (September): 595–600.

Neftci, S. N. 1979. Lead-lag relations, exogeneity, and prediction of economic time-series. *Econometrica*, 47 (January): 101–13.

Neftci, S. N. 1980. Optimal prediction of cyclical downturns. Working paper. George Washington University, Department of Economics.

Neftci, S. N. 1982. Optimal prediction of cyclical downturns. *Journal of Economic Dynamics and Control* 4 (August): 225–41.

Neftci, S. N. 1984. Are economic time series asymmetric over the business cycle? *Journal of Political Economy* 92 (April): 307–28.

Okun, A. M. 1960. On the appraisal of cyclical turning point predictors. *Journal of Business* 33 (April): 101–20.

Palash, C. J., and Radecki, L. J. 1985. Using monetary and financial variables to predict cyclical downturns. *Federal Reserve Bank of New York Review* 10 (Summer): 36–45.

Samuelson, P. A. 1987. Paradise lost and refound: The Harvard ABC barometers. *Journal of Portfolio Management* 4 (Spring): 4–9.

Schumpeter, J. A. 1939. *Business Cycles*. 2 vols. New York: McGraw-Hill.

Terrel, G. R., and Scott, D. W. 1985. Oversmoothed nonparametric density estimates. *Journal of the American Statistical Association* 80 (March): 209–14.

Tong, H. 1983. *Threshold Models in Nonlinear Time Series Analysis*. New York: Springer-Verlag.

Vaccara, B., and Zarnowitz, V. 1977. How good are the leading indicators? *Proceedings of the American Statistical Association, Business and Economic Statistics Section*. Washington, D.C.: American Statistical Association.

Wecker, W. E. 1979. Predicting the turning points of a time series. *Journal of Business* 52 (January): 35–50.

Winkler, R. L. 1969. Scoring rules and the evaluation of probability assessors. *Journal of the American Statistical Association* 64 (September): 1073–78.

Zarnowitz, V., and Boschan, C. 1975. Cyclical indicators: An evaluation and new leading indexes. *Business Conditions Digest* (May), pp. v–xxii.

Zarnowitz, V., and Moore, G. 1982. Sequential signals of recession and recovery. *Journal of Business* 55 (January): 57–85.

16

Turning Point Prediction with the Composite Leading Index: An Ex Ante Analysis

FRANCIS X. DIEBOLD AND GLENN D. RUDEBUSCH*

ON THE DAY of its release, the preliminary estimate of the Department of Commerce composite index of leading indicators (CLI) is widely reported in the popular and financial press. Although declines in the composite leading index are often regarded as a potential signal of the onset of a recession, evaluations of the ability of the CLI to predict turning points have been limited in most previous studies by the use of final, revised CLI data. However, the composite leading index is extensively revised after each preliminary estimate; not only are revisions made as more complete historical data become available for the components, but ex post, the statistical weights are updated and components are added or eliminated to improve leading performance. Forecasts constructed with an ex post, recomputed CLI may differ from real-time forecasts based on the contemporaneous, original construction CLI. In this chapter, we perform a completely ex ante, or real-time, evaluation of the ability of the CLI to predict turning points by using the original preliminary estimates and revisions as they became available in real time.

In section 1, we describe revisions in the CLI and our procedure for generating ex ante turning point probability forecasts from the CLI. The methodology is the Bayesian procedure described in Diebold and Rudebusch (1989a), adapted to a newly constructed ex ante dataset. This new dataset, which has over 70,000 elements, contains every preliminary, provisionally revised, and final estimate of the CLI since the inception of the index in 1968. This allows us to reproduce the precise information content in the CLI available to forecasters at any point in time. Our implementation also incorporates results on the nature of duration

* We would like to thank Bill Nelson, Suzanne Nace, and Gerhard Fries for research assistance, and Barry Beckman, Frank de Leeuw, Jim Hamilton, Kajal Lahiri, Johannes Ledolter, Geoffrey Moore, Jim Stock, Mark Watson, and Victor Zarnowitz for useful comments at various stages of this research program.

dependence in U.S. expansions and contractions. While these results, which are examined in an appendix, are of independent interest to students of the business cycle, they also provide requisite inputs for the turning point probability forecasts.

In section 2, we evaluate the ex ante forecasts in terms of Brier's (1950) quadratic probability score (QPS), the probability-forecast analog of mean squared error. We also examine an informative factorization of the joint density of forecasts and realizations. The performance of the ex ante Bayesian probability forecast is compared with that of a range of alternatives, including a naive "no change" forecast, the optimal constant probability forecast, and the well-known rule of three consecutive declines.

In section 3, to facilitate interpretation of the results, we describe the stochastic properties of the preliminary CLI release and subsequent revisions, both within and across definitional regimes. Particular attention is paid to the information content of the preliminary estimate relative to the final revised value. A characterization of the statistical properties of the revisions is given relative to the polar cases of efficient forecast error and classical measurement error.

1. Ex Ante CLI Probability Forecasts

While the information content of preliminary estimates is a consideration in any real-time forecasting situation, it is especially important when evaluating the performance of the composite index of leading indicators. The CLI is extensively revised from its preliminary estimate to its final form, undergoing both statistical and definitional revisions. Toward the end of each month, the Bureau of Economic Analysis (BEA) produces a preliminary estimate of the previous month's composite leading index on the basis of incomplete and preliminary source data, and it may also revise the index for any or all of the preceding eleven months. Thus, each initial estimate is subject to up to eleven revisions within the first year. These *statistical* revisions in the CLI occur because of statistical revisions in the component indicators (due to larger and/or more representative samples as time passes, etc.) and also because of late-arriving data that are included, for example, in the first revision but not in the preliminary estimate.

However, the currently available CLI data are not only of a revised statistical form, but the components have also been reweighted and reselected ex post to improve the performance of the index over the sample. These *definitional* revisions in the composite leading index have several different forms:

    1. Compositional changes due to changes in data availability, data timing, or cyclical lead performance

    2. Changes in weights assigned to component indicators due to statistical updating as more data become available

    3. Definitional changes in component indicators, which may be due to changes in component definitions or coverage, and so on.

A substantial number, about one every two years, of these definitional revisions have occurred since the first presentation of the index of leading indicators in the November 1968 *Business Conditions Digest* (*BCD*). Compositional changes in the CLI occurred in August 1969, April 1975, February 1979, January 1982, January 1983, and January 1987. For example, a major revision occurred in January of 1983 when the BEA updated statistical factors, incorporated historical revisions in the component data, and replaced two of the components (crude materials price inflation and the change in liquid assets) with series that were broadly similar but produced a more consistent ex post leading performance.

    Given these extensive revisions, it is of interest to recreate a real-time forecasting environment for predictive evaluation. For forecasting cyclical turning points, a leading index is only as good as the rule used to interpret its movements and map these movements into turning point predictions.[1] The classic example of a turning point filter associated with the CLI is the "three consecutive declines" rule for signaling a downturn (e.g., Vaccara and Zarnowitz, 1977), but many other methods have been proposed (e.g., Hymans, 1973; Wecker, 1979; Zarnowitz and Moore, 1982). More recently, a class of sequential-analytic event-oriented leading indicator prediction rules has gained popularity. The approach originates in Neftci's (1982) ingenious application of Shiryayev's (1978) results on optimal detection of changes in the probability generating process. Neftci uses this technique in a business cycle context to forecast turning points, that is, the dates of transition between "expansion" and "contraction" regimes. This approach, which we denote as the sequential probability recursion (SPR), has been refined recently by Diebold and Rudebusch (1989a) and Hamilton (1989). Evaluation of real-time turning point forecasts produced via the SPR methodology, as well as various other simpler methodologies, is the subject of this chapter.

---

[1] For an ex ante analysis that considers the standard problem of forecasting the level of an economic series, such as aggregate output, see Diebold and Rudebusch (1989b).

Assume that the behavior of the economy differs during expansions and contractions. Given this nonlinearity, it is advantageous to forecast both the expected future value of an economic variable and the form of its future probability structure as delineated by turning points (see Neftci, 1982; Diebold and Rudebusch, 1989a). To formalize this forecasting procedure, let Y_t be a coincident time-series that moves with general economic activity and switches probability distribution at turning points, and let X_t be a leading time-series with turning points (i.e., changes in distribution) that occur before the turning points in the coincident series. Let Z be an integer-valued random variable that represents the time index date of the first period after the turning point in X_t. For example, in the prediction of a downturn:

$$X_t \sim F_t^u(X_t) \qquad 1 \le t < Z$$
$$X_t \sim F_t^d(X_t) \qquad Z \le t \tag{1}$$

where F_t^u and F_t^d are the respective upturn and downturn distributions. Time-sequential observations on the leading indicator are received, so at time t, there are $(t + 1)$ observations denoted $\bar{x}_t = (x_0, x_1, \ldots, x_t)$. At time t, we calculate a probability for the event $Z \le t$, that is, that by time t a turning point in X has occurred.

The probability of $Z \le t$ after observing the data $\bar{x}_t$ at time t can be decomposed by Bayes's formula:

$$P(Z \le t \mid \bar{x}_t) = \frac{P(\bar{x}_t \mid Z \le t)P(Z \le t)}{P(\bar{x}_t)} \tag{2}$$

Define $\Pi_t = P(Z \le t \mid \bar{x}_t)$ as the posterior probability of a turning point given the data available. Then, as shown in Diebold and Rudebusch (1989a), a very convenient recursive formula for the posterior probability of a downturn is available:

$$\Pi_t = \frac{[\Pi_{t-1} + \Gamma_t^u(1 - \Pi_{t-1})]f_t^d(\bar{x}_t)}{\{[\Pi_{t-1} + \Gamma_t^u(1 - \Pi_{t-1})]f_t^d(\bar{x}_t) + (1 - \Pi_{t-1})f_t^u(\bar{x}_t)(1 - \Gamma_t^u)\}} \tag{3}$$

where $\Gamma_t^u = P(Z = t \mid z \ge t)$, the probability of a peak in period t given that one has not already occurred, and f_t^u and f_t^d are the probability densities of the latest (tth) observation if it came from, respectively, an upswing or downswing regime (in X_t). (To use this formula in the prediction of troughs, exchange f_t^u with f_t^d and use the transition probability Γ_t^d, the probability of a trough in t given a continuing contraction.) With this formula, the probability Π_t can be calculated sequentially by using the previous probability Π_{t-1}, the "prior" (independent of $\bar{x}_t$) turning point probability that $Z = t$ (i.e., Γ_t^u or Γ_t^u), and the likelihoods of the most recent observation x_t based on the distribution of X_t in upswings and downswings. Given Π_t, a probability forecast about the value of Z, the forecaster maps this into the occurrence of a turning point in Y_t. In practice, the probability of a turning point in X_t is related to the probability of an imminent turning point in Y_t over a fixed horizon decided upon by the investigator.

To apply the above sequential probability recursion, we must first estimate the densities f_t^d and f_t^u, as well as the turning point transition probabilities Γ_t^u and Γ_t^d, and we must specify an initial condition Π_0. The specification of these elements has been explored to some degree in Diebold and Rudebusch (1989a), and we adopt their final specification with one crucial modification: we consider an ex ante forecasting exercise with rolling creation of the CLI upswing and downswing densities based only on observations that would have been available in historical time.

The sequential probability formula requires the probability densities of the leading series conditional on an expansion regime and conditional on a contraction regime. The leading series is assumed to have two stochastic generating structures, expansion and contraction, and this division of the leading series into regimes depends upon the underlying classification of economic activity. We have followed the *Business Conditions Digest* (see chart A in various issues) in denoting peaks and troughs of the CLI that correspond to the NBER business cycle. The procedure used to construct f_t^u and f_t^d involved fitting a normal density function to previous observations in each regime. In particular, if $\bar{x}_t = (x_0, x_1, \ldots, x_t)$ is the vector of sequential observations on the leading indicator observed up to time t, let $\bar{x}_t^u$ be the vector of those observations from the upswing regime and $\bar{x}_t^d$ be those observations from the downswing regime. Then f_t^u is a normal density with mean and variance equal to the sample mean and variance of $\bar{x}_t^u$, and f_t^d is a normal density with mean and variance equal to the sample mean and variance of the elements of $\bar{x}_t^d$. The composite leading index was first reported in the *BCD* in 1968 and was reported ex post back to 1948. Our scoring sample runs from December 1968 to December 1986, and for each month a new set of densities is computed based on previous data back to 1948. A twelve-month data lag is also built in, so that the last twelve observations are not used in constructing the densities. This is to allow a real-time forecaster sufficient time to recognize regime changes and classify observations.[2]

The appendix provides evidence that, for the postwar period, the probability of a peak or a trough does not change significantly as the current regime progresses [also see the more sophisticated analysis in Diebold and Rudebusch (1990)]. For example, a long expansion is no more likely to end than a short one. Thus, we limit ourselves to time-invariant specifications of the transition conditional probabilities, that is, $\Gamma_t^u = \Gamma^u$ and $\Gamma_t^d = \Gamma^d$.

The final element in the recursive probability formula is last period's posterior probability of a turning point. There are two corrections made to this probability in practice. First, at the start of a new regime, a startup probability of zero is used as the previous period's probability. Also, as is clear from the formula, if the posterior probability reaches one at any point, it will force all remaining probability forecasts to be one in the regime. Thus, we put an upper bound of 0.95 on the previous posterior probability as it enters the recursive probability formula.

Examples of turning point probability forecasts based on ex ante and ex post CLI data are given in Figures 16.1 and 16.2. (The forecasts shown use constant prior transition probabilities that are optimal in an average accuracy sense, to be defined rigorously in the next section, at a forecast horizon of seven months for expansions and three months for contractions.) The ex post probability forecasts perform quite well. Using an arbitrary critical probability of 0.9 [as advocated in Neftci (1982)] to signal turning points, the ex post forecasts would have signaled in advance three of the four peaks (missing the very sudden 1981 peak) and two of the four troughs with no false alarms. Using the real-time data, only one of the peaks is predicted and two of the troughs, again with no false alarms. While these results are indicative, they depend upon the critical probability value (.9) chosen. In the next section, we consider a more rigorous evaluation procedure that makes use of the information contained in the entire range of probability forecasts.

---

[2] For general references to the use of preliminary data in forecasting, see Howrey (1978). Three exceptions to the use of final, revised data in CLI evaluation are Stekler and Schepsman (1973) and Zarnowitz and Moore (1982), who find that the use of preliminary data increases false signals, and Hymans (1973), who finds little difference.

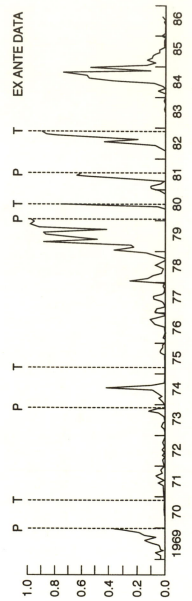

Fig. 16.1. Ex ante CLI recession probabilities.

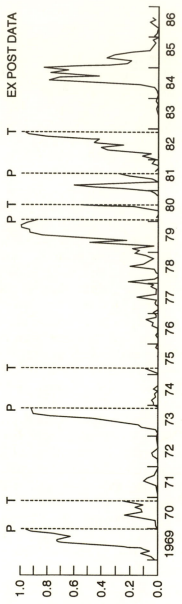

Fig. 16.2. Ex post CLI recession probabilities.

2. Evaluation of the Probability Forecasts

Accuracy refers to the closeness, on average, of predicted probabilities and observed relative frequencies. Consider a time-series of T probability forecasts $\{\Pi_t\}_{t=1}^{T}$, where Π_t is the time-t probability forecast of a turning point over horizon H. Let $\{R_t\}_{t=1}^{T}$ be the corresponding time-series of realizations; R_t equals one if a turning point occurs within the horizon (i.e., between times t and $t + H$) and equals zero otherwise. The quadratic probability score (Brier, 1950) is given by:

$$\text{QPS} = 1/T \sum_{t=1}^{T} 2(\Pi_t - R_t)^2 \tag{4}$$

The QPS ranges from 0 to 2, with a score of 0 corresponding to perfect accuracy. The QPS is the unique strictly proper scoring rule that is a function of the divergence between predictions and realizations; extended discussion and motivation, as well as consideration of alternative loss functions and evaluation measures, may be found in Diebold and Rudebusch (1989a).

The quadratic probability scores for a variety of probability forecasting methods are presented in Table 16.1. The forecasts are scored separately in the prediction of peaks and troughs, and scoring horizons range from one to thirteen months. Three different applications of the SPR are scored. Two are produced with the final, revised CLI data as of January 1987: SPR^u uses upswing and downswing CLI densities formed with the complete sample of data, while SPR^b rolls through the final data sample and creates densities only with data temporally prior to the forecast. The third SPR forecast, SPR^c, is truly ex ante and is formed with precisely the information set that would have been available to a real-time forecaster. At each horizon, we present the QPS of these SPR forecasts optimized with respect to the constant transition probabilities. Thus, the forecasts are completely ex ante, conditional upon Γ^u and Γ^d.

Other non-leading-indicator turning point probability forecasts are also scored. The forecasting methods include a no-change, NAIVE forecast, which amounts to a constant zero probability forecast, $\Pi_t = 0$, of a downturn or upturn. This is the probability forecast analog of a random walk (in this case, $\text{QPS} = 2\bar{R}$). More generally, one can search in the zero–one interval for the number that is the most accurate as a probability prediction of turning points. Such optimal, CONSTANT probability forecasts are of the form $\Pi_t = \kappa^u$ during expansions and

TABLE 16.1

QPS as a Function of Horizon for Various Forecasting

Method	Forecast Horizon (in months)						
	1	3	5	7	9	11	13
Prediction of peaks							
SPR[a]	.05	.09	.12	.14	.22	.29	.36
(Γ^u)	(.00001)	(.003)	(.007)	(.02)	(.03)	(.04)	(.11)
SPR[b]	.05	.08	.12	.14	.21	.29	.36
(Γ^u)	(.00001)	(.002)	(.006)	(.02)	(.03)	(.04)	(.10)
SPR[c]	.04	.11	.19	.25	.31	.37	.42
(Γ^u)	(.00002)	(.0005)	(.003)	(.01)	(.03)	(.04)	(.05)
NAIVE	.05	.15	.25	.35	.45	.56	.66
CONSTANT	.05	.14	.22	.29	.35	.40	.44
(κ^u)	(.02)	(.07)	(.12)	(.18)	(.23)	(.28)	(.33)
3CD[b]	.14	.13	.08	.11	.21	.32	.41
3CD[c]	.11	.17	.24	.29	.39	.47	.55
Prediction of troughs							
SPR[a]	.10	.30	.45	.49	.56		
(Γ^d)	(.005)	(.05)	(.18)	(.29)	(.42)		
SPR[b]	.10	.30	.46	.48	.52		
(Γ^d)	(.005)	(.05)	(.21)	(.33)	(.51)		
SPR[c]	.10	.35	.60	.71	.57		
(Γ^d)	(.0001)	(.001)	(.005)	(.34)	(.61)		
NAIVE	.16	.49	.82	1.10	1.35		
CONSTANT	.15	.37	.48	.50	.44		
(κ^d)	(.08)	(.25)	(.41)	(.55)	(.67)		

Note: The scoring sample is Dec. 1968–Dec. 1986. For each CONSTANT and SPR score, the associated constant prior transition probability is given beneath in parentheses. Superscripts on the forecasting methodologies refer to: (a) Based on the final revised CLI data as of January 1987, with SPR densities formed from final revised data. (b) Based on the final revised CLI data as of January 1987, with rolling SPR densities. (c) Based on ex ante real-time CLI data, with rolling SPR densities.

$\Pi_t = \kappa^d$ during contractions, where the constants are chosen to minimize QPS. In the fifth row of Table 16.1, for example, at a forecast horizon of five months, a 12 percent probability forecast of a downturn ($K^u = .12$, given in parentheses below the score) is the most accurate constant probability forecast. Finally, two variants on the "three consecutive declines" theme for the prediction of downturns were evaluated for expansions. A recession signaling rule of three consecutive declines (3CD) was applied that translates three declines in the CLI into successive probability forecasts of 1.0, .8, .6, .4, .2, and 0.0 (unless, of course, three more consecutive declines occur, at which time the probability forecast returns to 1.0). This was applied to both the final data (3CD[b]) and the real-time data (3CD[c]). We attach no particular importance to this "rule-of-three," but rather take it to be indicative of various rules of thumb that have appeared in the literature. No similar rule of thumb for the prediction of troughs appears in the literature; we therefore construct and score this forecast only for expansions. The linear decay that we adopt prevents abrupt dropoffs of Π_t from 1.0 to 0.0 and improves the performance of the "raw" rule of three at most horizons.

The results in Table 16.1 indicate that there is clearly information in the final revised CLI data for the prediction of both peaks and troughs. Both the simple 3CD rule-of-thumb and the more rigorous SPR substantially outperform, in an average accuracy sense, the naive and constant probability forecasts at a variety of horizons. The use of rolling densities formed from the ex post data in the construction of SPR forecasts (SPR[b]) does not change this result.

The situation shifts dramatically, however, when the CLI data contemporaneous to the forecast are used in forming forecasts (SPR[c] and 3CD[c]). With preliminary data, the simple rule-of-thumb 3CD[c] never outperforms the constant probability forecast. The SPR[c] does improve upon the constant probability forecast, though the enhancement at most horizons is not as great as for the ex post forecast SPR[b]. Furthermore, during downswings, SPR[c] performance is worse than CONSTANT at the longer forecasting horizons.

The deterioration of the SPR forecasts from ex post to ex ante can be decomposed into (a) that due to different ex ante and ex post densities f^u and f^d characterizing upswings and downswings, and (b) that due to different preliminary and revised CLI values. Comparing the SPR[a], SPR[b], and SPR[c] rows of Table 16.1, we conclude that use of ex ante CLI data, as opposed to real-time density estimates, is responsible for most of the forecast divergence.

3. Characterization of Revisions in the CLI

It was noted earlier that differences in ex ante and ex post turning point forecasting performance can be traced to one or both of the following: use of real-time CLI data and use of real-time estimated densities in the SPR. We saw that the first of these, not the second, was responsible for most of the difference; as such, we now study the properties of both intra- and inter-definitional revisions in the CLI.

We first consider the nature of revisions across definitional and compositional changes. The size of revisions to the CLI provides an indication of the information content of the preliminary estimates. Over the entire sample from December 1968 to January 1987, the standard deviation of the revision from the preliminary estimate of the CLI percentage change to the final estimate as given in January 1987 is .86 percentage points. Thus, for example, if the preliminary increase is 1.0 percent, one can only be 80 percent confident that the final estimate will be greater than $-.10$ and less than 2.10 percent (assuming normality). Within the most recent subsample of January 1983 to February 1986 (this allows for a final, eleventh revision through January of 1987), where definitional revisions are not a factor, the standard deviation from the preliminary estimate to eleventh revision is .49, and the corresponding 80 percent confidence interval is $\pm.63$ percent.

We now examine statistical revisions *within* two recent definitional regimes, in particular, the periods February 1979 to December 1981 and January 1983 to January 1987. These represent timely and comparatively long regimes, and they provide an interesting contrast in terms of aggregate economic activity. For each date in each sample, we have twelve estimates available, which we denote Y1, Y2, ..., Y12, where Y1 is the preliminary number and Y12 is the final revised number. We therefore have eleven non-overlapping revisions for each calendar date, defined by Y2Y1 = Y2 − Y1, ..., Y12Y11 = Y12 − Y11.

It may be useful to classify the stochastic properties of revisions relative to the polar cases of classical measurement error and efficient forecast error, as in Mankiw, Runkle, and Shapiro (1984) and Mankiw and Shapiro (1986). The intuition behind the dichotomy is simple: If a provisional estimate differs from the revised value by only measurement error, then the revision is uncorrelated with the revised value but correlated with the provisional information set. On the other hand, if a provisional estimate represents an efficient forecast (i.e., rational, or minimum mean squared error conditional on available information), then the revision is correlated with the revised value but uncorrelated with the provisional information set. By determining where the CLI revisions lie within this spectrum, we can gain insight into the potential for achieving improvement in the preliminary numbers. If the intra-definitional-regime revisions behave as efficient forecast errors, then they are optimal estimates of the final, revised numbers. To the extent that the final numbers produce the better forecasts, then, efficient forecast error revisions are desirable.

We consider first the January 1983–January 1987 sample. Descriptive statistics, for varying degrees of revision collapse, are shown in Table 16.2. Note that the standard deviations of Y1, ..., Y12 are all in the

TABLE 16.2
Revisions in the Composite Leading Index, 1983–7

Variable	N	Mean	SD	T Ratio
Y1	49	0.52	0.86	4.26
Y2	48	0.60	0.92	4.48
Y3	47	0.55	0.83	4.57
Y4	46	0.54	0.85	4.34
Y5	45	0.54	0.85	4.27
Y6	44	0.55	0.86	4.23
Y7	43	0.57	0.88	4.26
Y8	42	0.57	0.88	4.16
Y9	41	0.60	0.87	4.41
Y10	40	0.60	0.89	4.28
Y11	39	0.58	0.88	4.12
Y12	38	0.56	0.88	3.92
Y3Y1	47	0.03	0.45	0.49
Y5Y3	45	0.00	0.16	0.00
Y7Y5	43	0.01	0.16	0.29
Y9Y7	41	0.01	0.09	0.70
Y12Y9	38	−0.03	0.13	−1.46
Y5Y1	45	0.04	0.48	0.53
Y9Y5	41	0.02	0.18	0.86
Y12Y9	38	−0.03	0.13	−1.46
Y6Y1	44	0.04	0.47	0.58
Y12Y6	38	−0.01	0.16	−0.21
Y12Y1	38	0.07	0.49	0.82

Note: YmYn denotes the revision from the nth estimate to the mth estimate of the percent change in the CLI.

neighborhood of .86 percent, whereas the standard deviations of the revisions begin around .5 (for the earliest revisions) and eventually decrease to around .1 (for the last revisions). Thus, the standard deviation of the revisions (particularly the early revisions) is quite large relative to the standard deviation of the percent-change CLI estimates. This implies that all of the CLI growth rate estimates, and particularly that of Y1, have large associated confidence intervals. The *t*-tests detect no bias in any of the revisions.

If revisions are efficient forecast errors, then the variances of Y1 through Y12 should be monotonically increasing, because an efficient forecast is necessarily smoother than the series being forecast. Conversely, if revisions are measurement errors, then the variances of Y1,..., Y12 should be decreasing. The data do not distinguish these two cases, as the estimated standard deviations of Y1, ..., Y12 display little variation.

Correlations between levels and three broad revisions are given in Table 16.3. Under the null of efficient forecast errors, the above-diagonal entries should be significant, while the below-diagonal entries should be insignificant. The table appears roughly consistent with the rational forecast error scenario; in particular, the entries of the first above-diagonal row of the table are significant at the 10 percent level and large in absolute value; for a more detailed analysis, see Diebold and Rudebusch (1988). The other above-diagonal entries are insignificant, perhaps because revisions after the fourth estimate contain little information, and the correlations cannot be estimated with precision.

The results for the earlier sample (1979–81) are quite different. There is a dropoff in variance as we move from Y1 to Y2 (Table 16.4) that is not consistent with forecast efficiency, and the correlations reported in Table 16.5 indicate a measurement error component, as evidenced by the lack of significant above-diagonal correlations as well as a highly significant below-diagonal correlation.

We interpret these results as indicating that the definitional change implemented in January 1983 significantly enhanced the statistical properties of the CLI revisions. One obvious source of measurement error in the preliminary estimate is that it is based on incomplete data, for not all component indicators are included in the preliminary (and sometimes even the second and third) releases. To the extent that better forecasts for the missing component indicators can be found, an element of measurement error is immediately introduced into the revisions. In the 1979–81 sample, two components, net business formation

TABLE 16.3

Revisions and Revised Values: Correlations and P-Values, 1983–7

	Y1	Y5	Y9	Y12
Y5Y1	−0.23	0.33	0.28	0.28
	0.12	0.03	0.08	0.09
Y9Y5	0.00	−0.11	0.09	0.07
	0.98	0.48	0.56	0.69
Y12Y9	−0.06	−0.09	−0.15	−0.01
	0.72	0.60	0.35	0.97

Note: Y*m*Y*n* denotes the revision from the *n*th estimate to the *m*th estimate of the percent change in the CLI.

TABLE 16.4
Revisions in the Composite Leading Index, 1979–81

Variable	N	Mean	SD	T Ratio
Y1	35	−.32	1.77	−1.07
Y2	34	−.24	1.55	−.88
Y3	33	−.26	1.57	−.96
Y4	32	−.23	1.56	−.84
Y5	31	−.15	1.57	−.53
Y6	30	−.17	1.60	−.58
Y7	29	−.20	1.62	−.68
Y8	28	−.20	1.61	−.64
Y9	27	−.14	1.64	−.44
Y10	26	−.14	1.61	−.45
Y11	25	−.16	1.61	−.48
Y12	24	−.21	1.64	−.63
Y3Y1	33	.08	.59	.79
Y5Y3	31	.01	.24	.15
Y7Y5	29	−.07	.13	−2.68
Y9Y7	27	−.01	.14	−.41
Y12Y9	24	.01	.21	.19
Y5Y1	31	.07	.57	.73
Y9Y5	27	−.08	.19	−2.03
Y12Y9	24	.01	.21	.19
Y6Y1	30	.04	.57	.42
Y12Y6	24	−.03	.27	−.61
Y12Y1	24	−.02	.74	−.14

Note: Y*m*Y*n* denotes the revision from the *n*th estimate to the *m*th estimate of the percent change in the CLI.

TABLE 16.5
Revisions and Revised Values: Correlations and P-Values, 1979–81

	Y1	*Y5*	*Y9*	*Y12*
Y5Y1	−0.54	−0.25	−0.25	−0.23
	0.00	0.17	0.20	0.28
Y9Y5	−0.12	−0.13	−0.01	−0.03
	0.55	0.53	0.97	0.88
Y12Y9	−0.39	−0.37	−0.37	−0.26
	0.06	0.08	0.07	0.22

Note: Y*m*Y*n* denotes the revision from the *n*th estimate to the *m*th estimate of the percent change in the CLI.

and the change in inventories, were not available for any of the preliminary numbers, and inventory change was also omitted from twenty-six of thirty-five first revisions and from one second revision. For the more recent sample from 1983–7, only the preliminary numbers suffer from omitted components.[3]

4. Summary and Conclusions

We have used a Bayesian algorithm to produce ex ante probability forecasts of peaks and troughs from the CLI. Most notably, the forecasts were constructed using the original preliminary data and revisions as they became available in real time. The forecasts were evaluated, and compared with ex post forecasts and forecasts generated by alternative methods, using proper probability forecast scoring rules. Finally, in order to better understand the differences between ex ante and ex post forecast performance, we characterized the properties of CLI revisions. Our main findings include the following:

1. A deterioration in turning point forecasting performance occurs when ex ante data are used, regardless of the forecasting method adopted. In the prediction of peaks, the real-time SPR maintains a small margin of superiority over its competitors. The deterioration in ex ante SPR forecast performance is relatively more severe for the prediction of troughs, leading to mixed results for comparative predictive ability, depending on the forecast horizon. The real-time SPR appears to maintain slight superiority at short horizons, but fares slightly worse than less sophisticated methods at longer horizons. This may be due simply to the short lengths of most contractions, so that good forecasting at long horizons is trivially simple (but not useful) merely by setting Π to a large enough value.

2. Deterioration in SPR forecast performance is due mostly to the move to ex ante data, as opposed to the use of rolling probability densities in the SPR. Examination reveals that the size and volatility of CLI revisions, both within and across definitional regimes, are high relative to the magnitude of the revised percentage change in the CLI. Moreover, the CLI revisions appear to contain a measurement error component, which may be partially explained by the missing indicators

---

[3] After the most recent compositional redefinition of the CLI (see Hertzberg and Beckman, 1989), only components that will be available for the preliminary estimate were included in the newly reconstructed CLI.

in the preliminary CLI estimate. The measurement error component does not appear to be too severe in practice, however, and may be becoming less pronounced over time, due to beneficial definitional revisions.

3. There is no indication that turning point probabilities increase with the age of an expansion or contraction, in the period since World War II. Overall, postwar expansions and contractions show only weak, if any, duration dependence. This means that the transition probabilities used in the SPR, Γ_t^u and Γ_d^t, may be taken as approximately constant.

Appendix: Duration Dependence in U.S. Business Cycles

Key elements of the SPR procedure for forecasting peaks and troughs are the probabilities of a turning point conditional only upon the expansion or contraction length-to-date. These probabilities, denoted by Γ_t^u during upswings and Γ_t^d during downswings, are the prior probabilities for the Bayesian recursion. Figure 16A.1 shows two examples of the possible relationship between the probability that an ongoing expansion will reach a peak and the age of that expansion.[4] The linear upward

---

[4] This same duration analysis applies to the probability of a trough and the age of the preceding contraction. However, the slope and position of the lines will differ across expansions and contractions to reflect different average regime lengths.

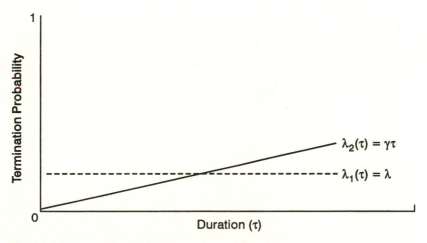

Fig. 16.A1. Increasing and constant hazard functions.

sloping hazard function (solid line, λ_2), which corresponds to a process with positive duration dependence, indicates that as an expansion progresses, the probability of a peak increases. The horizontal hazard (dashed line, λ_1), on the other hand, for which the transition probability is constant, corresponds to an absence of duration dependence. The resulting distributions of lengths of expansions and contractions are illustrated in Figure 16A.2. The duration distribution associated with the constant hazard is exponential. In discrete time, the distribution is geometric, with the probability of a regime of duration τ given by:

$$P(\text{duration} = \tau) = (1 - p)^{\tau - 1} p \qquad (0 < p < 1) \qquad \text{(A1)}$$

where the probability p of a turning point is a constant. This is shown as the monotonically declining dashed line in Figure 16A.2. The duration

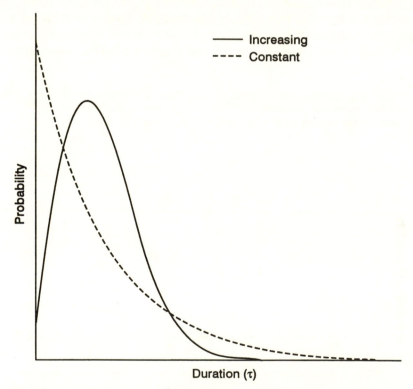

Fig. 16.A2. Duration distributions associated with increasing and constant hazards.

distribution corresponding to the increasing hazard, on the other hand, is non-geometric; its explicit shape will depend on the explicit nature of the hazard. In general, however, its probability mass will be more concentrated than that of the geometric, an implication of the turning point probability rising with duration length.[5] Consider, for example, the case of $p_\tau = \tau/100$; then the resulting density is

$$P(\text{duration} = \tau) = (1 - p_\tau)^{\tau - 1} p_\tau \qquad (A2)$$

which was used to generate the solid curve in Figure 16A.2. The hazard probability begins at .01 and rises by steps of .01 per period, leading to regime durations clustered around an intrinsic period.

We examine directly whether a histogram of historical duration lengths conforms to a geometric distribution, as it must under the non-periodic null hypothesis of constant turning point probabilities. Similar tests have been applied by McCulloch (1975), Savin (1977), and de Leeuw (1987). These studies are limited by the choice of a particular set of assumptions used in the construction of the histograms for the tests, which may account for the somewhat conflicting results obtained. We provide a sensitivity analysis exploring the whole range of possible assumptions.

We proceed as follows. For any given vector of expansion or contraction durations x, the data are first transformed by a minimum duration factor t_0 as $x^* = x - (t_0 - 1)$, which shifts the origin to reflect the length of the shortest possible regime. Minimum allowable expansion and contraction durations arise from definitional aspects of the NBER reference cycle dating procedure. Moore and Zarnowitz (1986), for example, indicate that expansions and contractions of less than six months would be very unlikely to qualify. (Note that under the geometric null, the unconditional distribution of τ is the same as the distribution of τ conditional on τ taking on a value greater than or equal to t_0.) Given the number of histogram bins K to be used, the bin width W is defined by $(x^*_{\max} - x^*_{\min})/K$, where $x^*_{\max}$ and $x^*_{\min}$ are the largest and smallest elements of the observed duration sequence x^*. The element, x^*_i, is grouped in bin n if $(x^*_{\min} + (n - 1)W) \leq x^*_i < (x^*_{\min} + nW)$. The histogram bin heights are computed by dividing the number of bin members by $N \cdot W$, that is, the duration sample size multiplied by the bin width.

---

[5] This insight provides a link between the concepts of duration dependence and periodicity. See Diebold and Rudebusch (1990) for detailed discussion.

We also compute exact finite sample confidence intervals under the geometric null. The maximum likelihood estimate of the hazard parameter of the best-fitting geometric distribution is $\hat{\lambda} = 1/\bar{x}^*$, where $\bar{x}^* = \sum_{i=1}^{N} x_i^*/N$ is the sample mean. A sample of N pseudorandom deviates is drawn from this geometric distribution, and the histogram with cell boundaries identical to the original is computed. (Generated deviates falling below x_{min}^* or above x_{max}^* are classified as members of bin 1 or bin K, respectively.) This procedure is replicated 5,000 times. This allows construction of confidence intervals around individual bin heights. The goodness-of-fit test statistic also can be calculated as

$$S = \sum_{i=1}^{K} \left[(O_i - E_i)^2/E_i \right] \tag{A3}$$

where O_i is the observed number of elements of bin i and E_i is the expected number of elements of bin i under the geometric null (the average across simulations). Using the 5,000 simulated samples as observations allows construction of the exact distribution of the test statistic, which for our small sample sizes typically deviates from its asymptotic χ^2 distribution.

The lengths of expansions and contractions (in months) are derived from the business cycle turning dates as designated by the National Bureau of Economic Research. The entire sample of thirty-one expansions and thirty contractions, every business cycle since 1854, is given in Table 16A.1. Nine different subsamples are considered, including pre- and post-World War II expansions and contractions, as well as peacetime expansions. We generally favor the entire expansion and contraction samples since, as pointed out by Romer (1986), the evidence of structural shift between the pre- and postwar economies is not completely convincing. The choice of a proper sample depends upon which cycles are considered part of the intrinsic structure of the economy and which are attributed to special non-cyclical events (e.g., wars). We also consider the sensitivity of our results to the number of histogram cells (K), two through five. Statistical theory provides some guide in the construction of a histogram as to the correct number of cells to be distinguished. Terrell and Scott (1985) show that the minimum number of cells required for an optimal histogram is[6]

$$K^* = \{(2N)^{1/3}\} \tag{A4}$$

---

[6] The optimality is in terms of minimum deviation [in the Kullback-Liebler (1951) sense] of the estimated histogram cell heights from the true, but unknown, values of the probability distribution.

TABLE 16.A1
NBER Business Cycle Reference Dates and Durations

Trough	Peak	Contraction	Expansion
December 1854	June 1857	NA	30
December 1858	October 1860	18	22
June 1861	April 1865	8	46
December 1867	June 1869	32	<u>18</u>
December 1870	October 1873	18	34
March 1879	March 1882	65	36
May 1885	March 1887	38	22
April 1888	July 1890	13	27
May 1891	January 1893	10	20
June 1894	December 1895	17	18
June 1897	June 1899	18	24
December 1900	September 1902	18	21
August 1904	May 1907	23	33
June 1908	January 1910	13	19
January 1912	January 1913	24	12
December 1914	August 1918	23	<u>44</u>
March 1919	January 1920	7	<u>10</u>
July 1921	May 1923	18	<u>22</u>
July 1924	October 1926	14	27
November 1927	August 1929	13	21
March 1933	May 1937	43	50
June 1938	February 1945	13	<u>80</u>
October 1945	November 1948	8	<u>37</u>
October 1949	July 1953	11	<u>45</u>
May 1954	August 1957	10	<u>39</u>
April 1958	April 1960	8	24
February 1961	December 1969	10	<u>106</u>
November 1970	November 1973	11	36
March 1975	January 1980	16	58
July 1980	July 1981	6	12
November 1982	?	16	72[a]

[a] The 72-month duration of the expansion beginning in November of 1982 is intended as a conservative estimate, implying that it ended in November 1988.

Note: Wartime expansions are underlined.

where the special brackets indicate rounding up to the nearest integer.[7] Histograms formed with this optimal minimum cell number have been shown to perform very well in practice. Finally, we consider a variety of

---

[7] The choice of cell number is important; too coarse a partition yields an uninformative distribution estimate, while too fine a partition yields a very jagged (and hence equally uninformative) estimate.

TABLE 16.A2
Business Cycle Subsamples Investigated, with Associated Size

Sample	Sample Size
Expansions	
E1. Entire sample	31
E2. Entire sample, excluding wars	26
E3. Post-World War II	9
E4. Post-World War II, excluding wars	7
E5. Pre-World War II	21
E6. Pre-World War II, excluding wars	19
Contractions	
C1. Entire sample	30
C2. Pre-World War II	21
C3. Post-World War II	9

minimum duration values. For each subsample, t_0 values up to the shortest expansion or contraction duration in that subsample are considered; in this way, we ensure that all values of x^* remain positive.

Probability-values (p-values) for the goodness-of-fit test statistic based on nonparametric distribution estimates are shown in Table 16A.3, and selected corresponding histograms are shown in Figures 16A.3, 16A.4, and 16A.5. The p-values represent the likelihood of obtaining the value of the test statistic actually obtained, under the geometric null of no duration dependence; large p-values therefore imply that the transition probabilities Γ^u and Γ^d should be invariant to the age of the ongoing regime. The range of samples investigated, denoted E1 through E6 and C1 through C3 for expansions and contractions, respectively, is identified in Table 16A.2.

In Table 16A.3 our choice for a single preferred p-value for each sample is underlined, though our conclusions based on these preferred probabilities will always be tempered by their sensitivity to the number of histogram cells (K) used to characterize the distribution and the minimum duration values (t_0).[8] A reasonable choice for t_0 is the actual shortest observed duration, which is six months for contractions, the length of the 1980 contraction, and ten months for expansions. Our preferred cell number is the Terrell-Scott optimal bin number. Setting

[8] Previous researchers, such as McCulloch, Savin, or de Leeuw, have essentially focused on only a few of the entries in Table 16A.3, without an examination of the sensitivity of the results to their assumptions.

TABLE 16.A3

Goodness-of-Fit Tests, Expansion, and Contraction Samples
(Probability Values under the Geometric Null)

		Sample								
K	t_0	E1	E2	E3	E4	E5	E6	C1	C2	C3
2	4	.47	.17	.47	.71	.82	.80	.77	.49	.77
2	5	.47	.15	.47	.70	.82	.80	.76	.51	.76
2	6	.47	.14	.46	.70	.82	.79	.77	.51	.75
2	7	.62	.13	.47	.70	.82	.80	NA	NA	.77
2	8	.61	.21	.46	.71	.82	.80	NA	NA	NA
2	9	.62	.21	.72	.70	.82	.80	NA	NA	NA
2	10	.80	.21	.71	.69	.64	.79	NA	NA	NA
2	11	NA	NA	.72	.69	NA	NA	NA	NA	NA
2	12	NA	NA	.71	.69	NA	NA	NA	NA	NA
3	4	.78	.40	.60	.25	.14	.03	.48	.04	.63
3	5	.78	.48	.60	.25	.17	.06	.59	.06	.65
3	6	.85	.49	.64	.25	.26	.07	.63	.20	.64
3	7	.85	.58	.66	.33	.27	.09	NA	NA	.74
3	8	.91	.62	.66	.33	.35	.14	NA	NA	NA
3	9	.91	.65	.65	.38	.46	.14	NA	NA	NA
3	10	.96	.75	.73	.37	.50	.21	NA	NA	NA
3	11	NA	NA	.72	.37	NA	NA	NA	NA	NA
3	12	NA	NA	.74	.41	NA	NA	NA	NA	NA
4	4	.55	.15	.05	.23	.01	.00	.82	.60	.98
4	5	.61	.18	.05	.25	.01	.00	.84	.79	.98
4	6	.68	.22	.08	.28	.02	.01	.77	.91	.96
4	7	.72	.27	.09	.30	.03	.01	NA	NA	.96
4	8	.75	.32	.10	.33	.05	.02	NA	NA	NA
4	9	.79	.38	.11	.35	.09	.03	NA	NA	NA
4	10	.85	.44	.13	.40	.13	.04	NA	NA	NA
4	11	NA	NA	.13	.47	NA	NA	NA	NA	NA
4	12	NA	NA	.14	.45	NA	NA	NA	NA	NA
5	4	.45	.59	.34	.09	.00	.00	.95	.01	.93
5	5	.51	.67	.39	.10	.00	.00	.97	.04	.92
5	6	.58	.72	.43	.13	.00	.00	.97	.11	.92
5	7	.64	.79	.45	.15	.00	.00	NA	NA	.87
5	8	.69	.85	.51	.18	.01	.00	NA	NA	NA
5	9	.74	.90	.55	.18	.02	.01	NA	NA	NA
5	10	.80	.95	.59	.21	.04	.02	NA	NA	NA
5	11	NA	NA	.67	.23	NA	NA	NA	NA	NA
5	12	NA	NA	.70	.26	NA	NA	NA	NA	NA

Note: The definition of samples and sample key is given in Table 16.A2. Our preferred (K, t_0) combination for each sample is underlined. NA = not applicable.

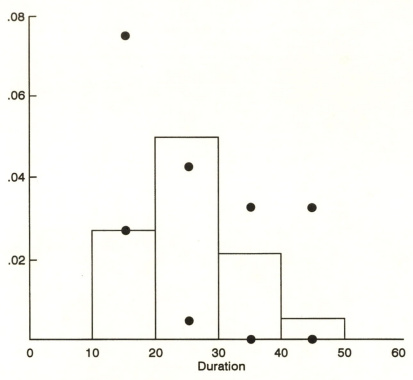

Fig. 16.A3. Pre-World War II, peacetime expansions (E6).

$K = K^*$ for our samples implies that observations should be grouped into four cells for all samples except the postwar ones, where three cells should be used.

Of the underlined p-values for the nine samples investigated in Table 16A.3, only one indicates significant duration dependence at the 5 percent level. This is sample E6, the set of all prewar, peacetime expansions. However, for the sample of all prewar expansions, duration dependence is also significant at the 5 percent level when a slightly smaller t_0 value is used or when observations are placed into five cells. The nonparametric duration distribution estimate for sample E6 is shown in Figure 16A.3 (where $K = 4$ and $t_0 = 10$). For each histogram cell, the high and low points of the 95 percent confidence interval for that individual cell height under the geometric null are indicated by asterisks (*). The distribution of prewar, peacetime expansions shows a clear peak, representing a clustering of durations, unlike a steadily declining geometric distribution. In contrast, for the sample of all expansions, shown in Figure 16A.4, the cell heights are not significantly different from their values under the geometric null, as suggested by the

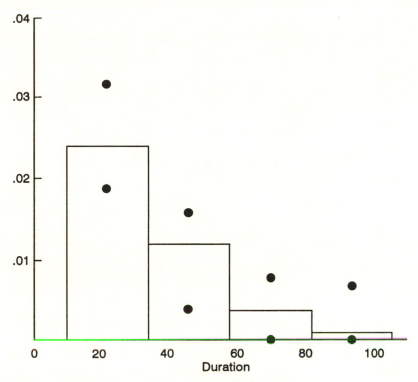

Fig. 16.A4. Expansions, complete sample (E1).

associated p-value of .81; a similar distributional shape is found for the sample of all contractions (not shown). The p-value for postwar contractions is rather small, especially for slightly smaller t_0 values, although the null is not rejected at conventional significance levels. The nonparametric distribution estimate for this sample (with $K = 3$, $t_0 = 6$), given in Figure 16A.5 shows a small, insignificant peak, though our ability to discriminate between alternatives is limited by the small sample.

The sample period that is relevant for our forecasting evaluation is the postwar period, and there is little evidence of duration dependence in postwar expansions and contractions.[9] Obviously, our failure to reject the geometric null hypothesis does not imply its acceptance; nevertheless, if duration dependence is present, it would appear to be a very weak phenomenon.

[9] This result does not necessarily imply, however, that business fluctuations amount to "Monte Carlo cycles," as claimed by McCulloch. In particular, entire business cycles (peak-to-peak or trough-to-trough) may display strong duration dependence even though expansions and contractions do not. See Diebold and Rudebusch (1990) and Zarnowitz (1987).

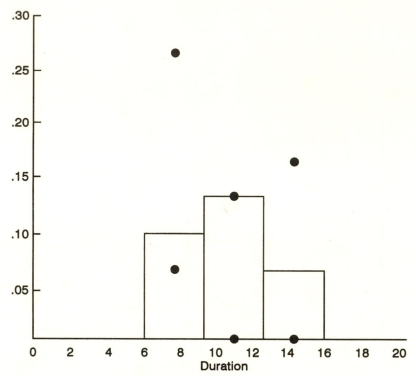

Fig. 16.A5. Post-World War II contractions (C2).

References

Brier, G. W. (1950), "Verification of Forecasts Expressed in Terms of Probability," *Monthly Weather Review*, 75, 1–3.

de Leeuw, F. (1987), "Do Expansions Have Memory?," Discussion Paper No. 16, U.S. Department of Commerce, Bureau of Economic Analysis.

Diebold, F. X. and G. D. Rudebusch (1988), "Stochastic Properties of Revisions in the Index of Leading Indicators," In *Papers and Proceedings of the American Statistical Association, Business and Economic Statistics Section, 1987*. Washington, D.C.: American Statistical Association.

—— (1989a), "Scoring the Leading Indicators," *Journal of Business*, 62, 369–91.

—— (1989b), "Forecasting Output with the Composite Leading Index: An Ex Ante Analysis," FEDS Working Paper, Federal Reserve Board.

—— (1990), "A Nonparametric Investigation of Duration Dependence in the American Business Cycle," *Journal of Political Economy* 98, 596–616.

Hamilton, J. D. (1989), "A New Approach to the Economic Analysis of Nonstationary Time Series and the Business Cycle," *Econometrica*, 57, 357–84.

Hertzberg, M. P., and B. A. Beckman (1989), "Business Cycle Indicators: Revised Composite Indexes," *Business Conditions Digest*, 29, 97–102.

Howrey, E. P. (1978), "The Use of Preliminary Data in Econometric Forecasting," *Review of Economics and Statistics*, 60, 193–200.

Hymans, S. H. (1973), "On the use of Leading Indicators to Predict Cyclical Turning Points," *Brookings Papers on Economic Activity*, 2, 339–84.

Kullback, S., and R. A. Liebler (1951), "On Information and Sufficiency," *Annals of Mathematical Statistics*, 22, 79–86.

Mankiw, N. G., D. E. Runkle, and M. D. Shapiro (1984), "Are Preliminary Estimates of the Money Stock Rational Forecasts?," *Journal of Monetary Economics*, 14, 15–27.

Mankiw, N. G., and M. D. Shapiro (1986), "News or Noise? An Analysis of GNP Revisions," *Survey of Current Business*, May.

McCulloch, J. H. (1975), "The Monte Carlo-Cycle in Business Activity," *Economic Inquiry*, 13, 303–21.

Moore, G. H., and V. Zarnowitz (1986), "The Development and Role of the National Bureau of Economic Research's Business Cycle Chronologies," in R. J. Gordon, ed., *The American Business Cycle*. Chicago: University of Chicago Press.

Neftci, S. N. (1982), "Optimal Prediction of Cyclical Downturns," *Journal of Economic Dynamics and Control*, 4, 225–41.

Romer, C. D. (1986), "Is the Stabilization of the Postwar Economy a Figment of the Data?," *American Economic Review*, 76, 314–34.

Savin, N. E. (1977), "A Test of the Monte Carlo Hypothesis: Comment," *Economic Inquiry*, 15, 613–17.

Shiryayev, A. N. (1978), *Optimal Stopping Rules*. New York: Springer-Verlag.

Stekler, H. O., and M. Schepsman (1973), "Forecasting with an Index of Leading Series," *Journal of the American Statistical Association*, 68, 291–6.

Terrell, G. R., and D. W. Scott (1985), "Oversmoothed Nonparametric Density Estimates," *Journal of the American Statistical Association*, 80, 209–14.

Vaccara, B., and V. Zarnowitz (1977), "How Good are the Leading Indicators?," *Proceedings of the American Statistical Association, Business and Economic Statistics Section, 1976*. Washington, D.C.: American Statistical Association.

Wecker, W. E. (1979), "Predicting the Turning Points of a Time Series," *Journal of Business*, 52, 35–50.

Zarnowitz, V. (1987), "The Regularity of Business Cycles." National Bureau of Economic Research Working Paper No. 2381.

Zarnowitz, V., and G. H. Moore (1982), "Sequential Signals of Recession and Recovery," *Journal of Business*, 55, 57–85.

17

Forecasting Output with the Composite Leading Index: A Real-Time Analysis

FRANCIS X. DIEBOLD AND GLENN D. RUDEBUSCH*

> The Governor's best-known tool for economic forecasting—the index of leading indicators—will undergo a major revision by the end of the year.
> *New York Times* (May 29, 1987)

1. Introduction

The prediction of aggregate economic activity with the composite leading index (CLI) has enjoyed widespread popularity for several decades. Some empirical justification for this popularity has been provided by a number of recent formal evaluations of the forecasting ability of the CLI, which have found that the CLI *does* contain useful information for the prediction of aggregate economic activity. For example, Auerbach (1982) and Koch and Rasche (1988), in analyses of bivariate causality, found strong evidence that the CLI is useful in linear prediction of industrial production even after conditioning on lagged values of production and even in out-of-sample forecasts. In a multivariate context, Braun and Zarnowitz (1989) provided confirmatory evidence showing that inclusion of the CLI in commonly estimated vector autoregressive representations leads to a reduction of in-sample residual variance.

As in most examinations of predictive performance, the aforementioned studies evaluate either or both of two types of forecast errors: (1)

* Diebold gratefully acknowledges financial support from the National Science Foundation (Grant SES 89-2715), the University of Pennsylvania Research Foundation (Grant 3-71441), and the Institute for Empirical Macroeconomics. The authors thank the editor, associate editor, and two anonymous referees, as well as Alan Auerbach, Neil Ericsson, Lawrence Klein, Doug McManus, Andy Rose, Mark Rush, Herman Stekler, Peter Tinsley, and Ken West for useful comments. Bill Nelson and Roberto Sella provided outstanding research assistance.

the residual errors from a model fit to the entire sample of data, and (2) the out-of-sample forecast errors from a model fit to just a portion of the data set. Many have noted that these two types of errors may have very different characteristics. In particular, the out-of-sample forecast errors for a given model are usually much larger than its in-sample residual errors [for example, see Makridakis and Winkler (1989)]. This difference can often be traced to the overfitting of the (misspecified) model, which reduces the in-sample errors but does not improve forecast performance [e.g., Hendry (1980)]. In our analysis, we highlight a little-recognized limitation of forecast evaluations that examine either in-sample residuals or out-of-sample forecast errors, namely, that they are conducted with final revised values of the data. In contrast, actual real-time forecasting must rely on preliminary and partially revised data. In this article we introduce a third category of forecast errors that directly confronts this issue. We evaluate the *real-time* predictive performance of the CLI by not only examining out-of-sample forecasts but also by using the preliminary and partially revised CLI data that would have been available at the historical date of each forecast. Essentially, we are able to reproduce the CLI information set of a real-time forecaster.

The use of final revised CLI data in previous analyses of the predictive ability of the CLI would not be a critical flaw if the CLI were subject to only small revisions. Unfortunately, the CLI is extensively revised from its preliminary estimate to its final value. Not only are statistical revisions incorporated as more complete historical data become available for the components, but components are often added and eliminated, ex post, to improve the leading index's performance retrospectively. The existence of such revisions, especially the definitional ones, suggests the possibility that the good performance of the CLI in previous forecasting exercises may be spurious, in the sense that the CLI data actually available in real time were substantially less helpful in forecasting changes in real activity than the evaluations that use final CLI data suggest.

In Section 2 we discuss the nature of statistical and definitional revisions in the CLI and provide details of the CLI data matrix that was constructed for our analysis. Section 3 describes our prediction methodology, which proceeds in a number of stages as the forecaster's information set is progressively restricted from an ex post to a real-time, or ex ante, analysis. The empirical results are contained in Section 4, and Section 5 discusses the robustness of those results. Concluding remarks are offered in Section 6.

2. Revisions in the Leading Index

Although the information content of preliminary and partially revised data is a consideration in any real-time forecasting situation, it is especially important when evaluating the performance of the composite index of leading indicators. The CLI is extensively revised from its preliminary estimate to its final form, undergoing both statistical and definitional revisions. This section describes the nature of these revisions. For descriptions of the components and the methodology used to construct the CLI, see Auerbach (1982) and Hertzberg and Beckman (1989).

Toward the end of each month during our sample, the Bureau of Economic Analysis (BEA) issued a *Business Conditions Digest* (BCD), which contained a preliminary estimate of the previous month's value of the CLI on the basis of incomplete and preliminary source data. For example, the October 1988 issue of the BCD contained the initial estimate of the September 1988 value of the leading index. Each month, the BCD also provided revisions in the index for any or all of the preceding 11 months. These *statistical* revisions to the CLI occurred because of statistical revisions in the component indicators (reflecting the collection of larger, more representative source data samples as time passes) and because some components were released too late to be included in the preliminary estimate and could only be included in the first or second revision of the index.

Statistical revisions, of course, plague the real-time interpretation of most economic time series; in the case of the CLI, however, the final data have not only undergone these statistical revisions but, in addition, the components that make up the index have been reselected and reweighted ex post. These *definitional* revisions in the CLI involve a retrospective reevaluation of the CLI's performance over the enlarged historical sample and are attempts to improve the lead-time performance of the index during the historical sample. Major changes in the definition of the CLI are fairly frequent, occurring in August 1969, April 1975, February 1979, January 1982, January 1983, January 1987, and January 1989—about once every two years since the introduction of the CLI in the November 1968 issue of the BCD. As a typical example, in the 1983 revision, the BEA recalculated component weights and standardization factors (on the basis of additional data) and replaced two of the components (crude materials price inflation and the change in liquid assets) with series that were broadly similar but produced a more consistent cyclical lead performance retrospectively. [A complete chronology and description of all compositional changes is provided in Diebold and Rudebusch (1988).] Clearly, such ex post definitional changes make inference about the real-time forecasting ability of the CLI very difficult.

In other work (Diebold and Rudebusch 1988), we have examined the magnitude of both statistical and definitional revisions to the CLI. From December 1969 through January 1986, the standard deviation of the revision from the preliminary estimate of the percent change in the CLI to the final estimate (as of December 1987) is .86%. This is large relative to the standard deviation of the percent change in the final estimate of the CLI over that same period, which is 1.11%; the signal-to-noise ratio is about 1.3. Within definitional regimes, when definitional revisions are not a factor, the standard deviations of revisions are smaller but still substantial. Such large revisions imply that the ex ante, real-time forecasting performance of the CLI may be much worse than the ex post evaluations conducted with final, revised data suggest.

In this article, we examine precisely how much of a deterioration in the forecasting performance of the CLI occurs from using real-time CLI data. For this purpose we have collected all preliminary and partially revised values of the CLI as published sequentially in issues of the BCD from November 1968 through December 1988. The data matrix containing all of these values is illustrated schematically in Table 17.1. Each row of the matrix provides the value of the CLI for a particular month, ranging from 1948:1 to 1988:11 (491 months). The entries of a given row vary across the columns as the value of the CLI for that month is revised. Each column of the matrix provides the data given in one issue of the BCD; the leftmost column is from the November 1968 issue, which first introduced the CLI and presented historical CLI data from January 1948 through October 1968, the next column is from December 1968, and so forth, across the 242 issues. A zero value in the i, j entry indicates that data for the ith month (the row) were not yet released in the jth month (the column). Moving through real time across the columns, each additional month adds one more nonzero observation to the column (denoted by superscript p for preliminary) and changes any or all of the previous, nonzero entries. Every statistical and definitional revision in the CLI is thus represented. Statistical revisions change only the last few nonzero entries in the preceding column, whereas definitional revisions usually will change all of them. This data matrix, which contains about 90,000 nontrivial entries, allows us to reproduce the precise information content in the CLI available to forecasters at any point in time.

TABLE 17.1
Schematic of CLI Data Matrix

Data for This Month	Data Released in This Month (BCD Issue Date)					
	$j = 1968{:}11$	$j = 1968{:}12$	$\cdots$	$j = t$	$\cdots$	$j = 1988{:}11$	$j = 1988{:}12$
$i = 1948{:}1$	$\mathrm{CLI}(i)_j$	$\mathrm{CLI}(i)_j$	$\cdots$	$\mathrm{CLI}(i)_j$	$\cdots$	$\mathrm{CLI}(i)_j$	$\mathrm{CLI}(i)_j$
$i = 1948{:}2$	$\mathrm{CLI}(i)_j$	$\mathrm{CLI}(i)_j$	$\cdots$	$\mathrm{CLI}(i)_j$	$\cdots$	$\mathrm{CLI}(i)_j$	$\mathrm{CLI}(i)_j$
$i = 1948{:}3$	$\mathrm{CLI}(i)_j$	$\mathrm{CLI}(i)_j$	$\cdots$	$\mathrm{CLI}(i)_j$	$\cdots$	$\mathrm{CLI}(i)_j$	$\mathrm{CLI}(i)_j$
$\vdots$							
$i = 1968{:}10$	$\mathrm{CLI}(i)^p$	$\mathrm{CLI}(i)_j$	$\cdots$	$\mathrm{CLI}(i)_j$	$\cdots$	$\mathrm{CLI}(i)_j$	$\mathrm{CLI}(i)_j$
$i = 1968{:}11$	0	$\mathrm{CLI}(i)_j^p$	$\cdots$	$\mathrm{CLI}(i)_j$	$\cdots$	$\mathrm{CLI}(i)_j$	$\mathrm{CLI}(i)_j$
$i = 1968{:}12$	0	0	$\cdots$	$\mathrm{CLI}(i)_j$	$\cdots$	$\mathrm{CLI}(i)_j$	$\mathrm{CLI}(i)_j$
$\vdots$							
$i = t - 1$	0	0	$\cdots$	$\mathrm{CLI}(i)_j^p$	$\cdots$	$\mathrm{CLI}(i)_j$	$\mathrm{CLI}(i)_j$
$i = t$	0	0	$\cdots$	0	$\cdots$	$\mathrm{CLI}(i)_j$	$\mathrm{CLI}(i)_j$
$\vdots$							
$i = 1988{:}10$	0	0	$\cdots$	0	$\cdots$	$\mathrm{CLI}(i)^p$	$\mathrm{CLI}(i)_j$
$i = 1988{:}11$	0	0	$\cdots$	0	$\cdots$	0	$\mathrm{CLI}(i)_j^p$

Note: The CLI data matrix is 491×242. The entry $\mathrm{CLI}(i)_j$ denotes the value of the leading index in the ith month that was available and current as of the jth month; a zero entry indicates that no CLI data had been released for that month. A superscript p denotes the preliminary (initial) estimate for a given month. Moving across the columns from left to right yields varying nonzero entries (from revisions) and a progressively larger sample as history unfolds.

3. Methodology

We shall consider the usefulness of the CLI for predicting industrial production (IP) in a linear forecasting framework. In particular, we examine the marginal predictive information content of the CLI beyond that embodied in lags of industrial production. There are five basic forecasting scenarios that we consider, each differing by the inclusion or exclusion of CLI lags and by the degree to which they mimic an actual real-time forecasting environment. The first two scenarios involve in-sample residuals and constitute the usual ex post Granger causality test. The second two are partially ex ante exercises that use recursive estimates of forecasting models, that is, the sample is enlarged by one observation at a time and the model is reestimated with each new observation and used to produce out-of-sample forecasts. Finally, the last scenario produces real-time forecasts with the CLI by using recursive estimates and by using the preliminary and partially revised estimates of the CLI that were historically available.

The first two forecasting scenarios are based on the entire sample of final revised data. The first of these estimates the regression,

$$IP_t = \beta_0 + \sum_{i=1}^{p} \beta_i \, IP_{t-i-k+1} + \varepsilon_t, \qquad (1)$$

where IP is the log of the level of industrial production. The forecasting equation for this scenario will be referred to as the FF1 regression (for *F*ull sample, *F*inal data, and lags of *1* variable on the right side, namely, IP). The number of months ahead the prediction is being made (k) is varied over 1, 4, 8, and 12. The lag length of the estimated regression (p) is also varied over 1, 4, 8, and 12. (The sample of IP data used on the left side of FF1, and FF2 later, always ranges from 1950:1 to 1988:12. Of course, depending on p and k, the ranges of the right side IP data and, in FF2, of the CLI data vary.)

The second ex post regression includes on the right side lagged values of the final revised CLI. (In terms of the earlier-discussed CLI data matrix, the CLI data used are from the rightmost column.) Specifically, we estimate (from 1950:1 to 1988:12) the regression:

$$IP_t = \beta_0 + \sum_{i=1}^{p} \beta_i \, IP_{t-i-k+1} + \sum_{i=1}^{p} \gamma_i \, CLI_{t-i-k+1} + \varepsilon_t, \qquad (2)$$

where CLI is the log of the level of the composite leading index, and again we let $k = 1, 4, 8, 12$ and $p = 1, 4, 8, 12$. We denote this as the

FF2 regression (*F*ull sample, *F*inal data, and lags of 2 variables on the right side, namely, IP and CLI).

From the FF1 and FF2 regressions, we save the 231 residuals from 1969:10 to 1988:12. (This sample of residuals is used for comparison with the later recursively estimated regressions. Given November 1968 as the first historical release date of the CLI, the first possible 12-step-ahead, real-time forecast was for the 1969:10 value of IP.) The causality test of Granger (1969), which was employed in this context by Auerbach (1982), provides a formal comparison of the sums of squares of these residuals. The FF1 regression provides the predictive content of only own-lags of IP, and the FF2 regression gives predictions enhanced with the marginal contribution from the CLI. In terms of subsequent results, it will prove useful to think of the fitted values from the FF1 and FF2 regressions as "forecasts"; clearly, however, these "forecasts" are completely ex post, as the estimation uses the *full* sample of *final revised* data. As noted in the introduction, the "forecast errors" in these two ex post scenarios are merely in-sample regression residuals. These errors are used to construct an associated mean squared prediction error (MSPE) and mean absolute prediction error (MAPE) from each regression. The MSPE is simply a normalized restricted sum of squares (in the FF1 case) and a normalized unrestricted sum of squares (in the FF2 case).

In the second pair of forecasting scenarios, the ex post nature of FF1 and FF2 is partially relaxed via recursive estimation of the equations to mimic real-time forecasting (which is affected by subsample sampling variability in coefficient estimates); however, the final revised CLI data are still used. In this out-of-sample forecasting exercise, Equations (1) and (2) are denoted by RF1 and RF2 (for *R*ecursive, *F*inal data regressions). An example will make the procedure clear. Consider the estimation of RF2, and suppose that $p = k = 4$. Then, we first estimate, over the period 1950:1 through 1969:6,

$$\text{IP}_t = \beta_0 + \sum_{i=1}^{4} \beta_i \, \text{IP}_{t-i-4+1} + \sum_{i=1}^{4} \gamma_i \, \text{CLI}_{t-i-4+1} + \varepsilon_t, \qquad (3)$$

where the CLI is the final revised series (1988:12 definition). The four-step-ahead forecast of $\text{IP}_{1969:10}$ (which is made with the final data through 1969:6) is then constructed from the estimated coefficients as

$$\hat{\text{IP}}_{1969:10} = \hat{\beta}_0 + \sum_{i=1}^{4} \hat{\beta}_i \, \text{IP}_{1969:10-i-4+1} + \sum_{i=1}^{4} \hat{\gamma}_i \, \text{CLI}_{1969:10-i-4+1}. \quad (4)$$

The regression is then reestimated with one more observation using data from 1950:1 through 1969:7, the forecast for 1969:11 is constructed, and so forth. We progress recursively through the sample in this fashion—continually reestimating and reforecasting—until the forecast for 1988:12 is constructed, at which point the sample is exhausted. For RF1 and RF2 and for each combination of k and p, we obtain a 231-element vector of out-of-sample forecasts. An MSPE and an MAPE are calculated for each of the associated vectors of prediction errors.

In the recursive regression RF2, each "forecast" is completely out-of-sample with regard to parameter estimation but, as should be clear from the earlier discussion of definitional revisions in the CLI, these "forecasts" may incorporate subtle ex post information through retrospective reconstruction of the CLI by the BEA. To eliminate this ex post information, our final scenario constructs real-time ex ante forecasts with the CLI by recursively estimating (2), but at each month in which the k-step-ahead forecast is made using only the preliminary and partially revised CLI data that were actually available in that month. Thus, as a new regression is estimated for each month, the CLI data vector used for the regression changes. For each new month, the CLI data vector will have one more element for the latest preliminary number, but the 11 previous elements, in the case of statistical revisions, or perhaps all previous elements, in the case of definitional revisions, may have changed. We shall denote this real-time ex ante forecasting regression by RP2 (Recursive, Preliminary CLI data forecasts). The MSPE and MAPE of this regression can be compared with RF2, determining the forecast deterioration due to provisional data, and with RF1, providing a real-time ex ante causality test analog. [The CLI data vector used in RP2 corresponds to a particular column of the real-time data matrix, moving from the leftmost column to the rightmost column as time passes. In terms of Eq. (3) (with $p = k = 4$), the four-step-ahead forecast for 1969:10 is made with the CLI data matrix column that contains the preliminary number for 1969:6. If we took into account the one-month lags in releasing the CLI and IP data, the real-time forecast dates would be advanced one month, but the data used and the forecasts obtained would not change.]

In the next section, we analyze the forecast errors that result from application of the aforementioned procedures. We also have explored, as shall be described in Section 5, several variations and extensions of these methods to assess the robustness of our results.

4. Empirical Analysis

The methodology outlined previously produces 80 vectors of forecast errors, corresponding to all combinations of steps ahead forecasted ($k = 1, 4, 8,$ and 12) and number of lags included ($p = 1, 4, 8,$ and 12) for each regression strategy FF1, FF2, RF1, RF2, and RP2. Each vector of errors has 231 elements, corresponding to forecasts for 1969:10 through 1988:12. For each vector the MSPE and the MAPE were calculated; these are presented in Tables 17.2 and 17.3, respectively.

Let us first consider the MSPE results in Table 17.2. There are four separate comparisons that are of particular interest. The first is the ex post Granger causality test, which compares the MSPE for the in-sample residuals from the FF1 regression [denoted by MSPE (FF1)] with the MSPE for the in-sample residuals from the FF2 regression [denoted by MSPE (FF2)]. For all p and k combinations, a consistent pattern emerges:

$$MSPE(FF2) < MSPE(FF1). \qquad \text{(Result A)}$$

This confirms the bivariate causality results of Auerbach (1981); that is, the CLI has marginal predictive content, ex post.

The second comparison of interest extends the Granger causality methods to out-of-sample forecasts from regressions estimated recursively with the final data. In this case,

$$MSPE(RF2) < MSPE(RF1). \qquad \text{(Result B)}$$

TABLE 17.2
Mean Squared Prediction Error, Industrial Production

Steps Ahead (k)	Lags Included (p)	Forecast Scenario				
		FF1	FF2	RF1	RF2	RP2
1	1	.87	.63	.88	.70	1.08
1	4	.64	.50	.65	.54	.65
1	8	.64	.47	.66	.54	.66
1	12	.64	.47	.67	.56	.66
4	1	7.66	4.68	8.11	5.89	11.85
4	4	6.29	3.47	6.74	4.42	7.64
4	8	6.29	3.16	6.80	4.09	7.21
4	12	6.47	3.24	7.24	4.55	7.89
8	1	20.55	12.92	22.87	16.90	34.15
8	4	18.69	9.21	20.96	12.22	25.54
8	8	19.10	8.99	21.89	12.82	26.08
8	12	19.28	9.21	22.80	14.50	28.31
12	1	34.77	24.57	40.13	31.26	56.09
12	4	33.38	18.63	39.41	24.61	48.69
12	8	33.83	18.51	41.12	27.02	50.52
12	12	33.14	18.06	41.56	28.59	52.36

Note: Entries are MSPE × 10,000.

TABLE 17.3
Mean Absolute Prediction Error, Industrial Production

Steps Ahead (k)	Lags Included (p)	Forecast Scenario				
		FF1	FF2	RF1	RF2	RP2
1	1	.68	.61	.69	.66	.78
1	4	.58	.53	.58	.57	.62
1	8	.58	.52	.59	.56	.61
1	12	.59	.62	.60	.58	.62
4	1	2.00	1.68	2.13	1.92	2.51
4	4	1.80	1.47	1.91	1.66	2.09
4	8	1.80	1.39	1.93	1.56	1.99
4	12	1.79	1.40	1.93	1.63	2.06
8	1	3.51	2.88	3.80	3.23	4.14
8	4	3.30	2.36	3.60	2.71	3.52
8	8	3.32	2.30	3.67	2.69	3.51
8	12	3.34	2.34	3.73	2.86	3.72
12	1	4.78	4.04	5.20	4.58	5.39
12	4	4.67	3.40	5.15	3.93	5.02
12	8	4.68	3.48	5.23	4.12	5.11
12	12	4.65	3.44	5.25	4.18	5.24

Note: Entries are MAPE $\times$ 100.

Thus this out-of-sample analog to the Granger test also indicates that the CLI has marginal predictive power beyond own-lags of IP.

It is also interesting to note the deterioration in performance of the out-of-sample forecasts compared with the in-sample residuals. For all p and k, MSPE(FF1) < MSPE(RF1) and MSPE(FF2) < MSPE(RF2).

Finally, we consider real-time forecast comparisons that involve the preliminary CLI data. Our third result compares the recursive forecasting regression using the final CLI data with the recursive forecasting regression using the preliminary CLI data and finds that

$$\text{MSPE(RF2)} < \text{MSPE(RP2)}. \qquad \text{(Result C)}$$

This indicates that the final revised CLI data are more helpful in forecasting IP than the preliminary data; thus statistical and definitional revisions clearly improve the CLI's predictive power. Our final comparison considers whether the preliminary CLI data have any marginal predictive power over one-lags of IP. Here, we summarize our findings as

$$\text{MSPE(RP2)} \approx \text{MSPE(RF1)} \qquad \text{(Result D)}$$

to indicate that, in general, the MSPE of these scenarios are quite close and there is no clear ranking across all combinations of p and k for these two MSPE's. Thus inclusion of the CLI in real time does not improve and, often, *worsens* predictive performance relative to simply forecasting with an IP autoregression. None of these results change when MSPE is replaced by MAPE (Table 17.3).

The MSPE and MAPE results are illustrated in Figure 17.1 for the case of four-step-ahead forecasts ($k = 4$) using eight lags ($p = 8$). The sawtooth pattern suggested by Results A–D is clearly evident. MSPE falls from FF1 to FF2 with inclusion of final CLI data. It rises again to an even higher level in the recursive RF1 but falls with the addition of revised CLI data in RF2. Finally, however, the MSPE rises when the preliminary CLI data are included in RP2.

Although the foregoing rankings are indicative, it is important to examine formally the statistical significance of the comparisons. A test for significance of the MSPE difference between two unbiased forecasts is readily available. Let e_1 denote a given forecast error, and let e_2 denote a second comparison forecast error. Then the difference in the MSPE's, which reduces to the difference in variances, by unbiasedness, is simply the covariance of $(e_1 + e_2)$ and $(e_1 - e_2)$. That is,

$$E[(e_1 + e_2)(e_1 - e_2)] = \sigma_1^2 - \sigma_2^2. \tag{5}$$

Thus testing for significance of $\sigma_1^2 - \sigma_2^2$ is equivalent to testing significance of $\text{cov}[(e_1 + e_2), (e_1 - e_2)]$. [See Granger and Newbold (1986), who noted that this test is uniformly most powerful invariant.]

We estimate this covariance and test its significance using methods robust to serial correlation of unknown form; such an approach is particularly important for $k > 1$, because multiple-step-ahead forecast errors are generally serially correlated. Define $x = e_1 + e_2$ and $y = e_1 - e_2$. We proceed by noting that the covariance (5) is just the cross-covariance of x and y at a displacement of 0, that is, $\gamma_{xy}(0)$, which can be consistently estimated in the usual manner. It is well known that under standard assumptions [see Priestley (1980, pp. 692–693)] the variance of the sample covariance is

$$\text{var}(\hat{\gamma}_{xy}(0)) \approx \frac{1}{T} \sum_{\tau=-\infty}^{\infty} \left[\gamma_{xx}(\tau)\gamma_{yy}(\tau) + \gamma_{xy}(\tau)\gamma_{yx}(\tau) \right],$$

a consistent estimate of which requires consistent estimates of $\gamma_{xx}(\tau)$, $\gamma_{yy}(\tau)$, $\gamma_{xy}(\tau)$, and $\gamma_{yx}(\tau)$, which can be obtained in the usual manner. One remaining issue is the truncation of the doubly infinite sum. We explored a range of truncation points; the empirical results, which are

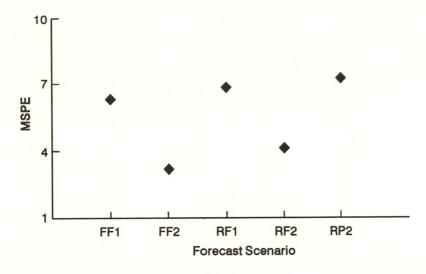

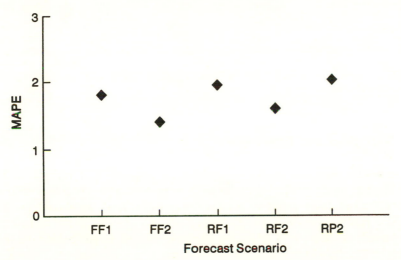

Fig. 17.1. Performance of IP forecasts: four-step-ahead forecast with eight lags ($k = 4$, $p = 8$).

contained in Table 17.4, use a truncation at lag 25, but the estimates were robust to other choices. The MSPE differences associated with Results A, B, and C are almost uniformly significant at all steps ahead and for all lags included. The MSPE differences associated with Result D, conversely, are insignificant. We conclude that, subject to the qualifications and caveats noted below, inclusion of the CLI in real-time forecasting equations is of little value.

TABLE 17.4
Tests for Significance of MSPE Differences

Steps Ahead (k)	Lags Included (p)	Result A, FF1–FF2	Result B, RF1–RF2	Result C, RF2–RP2	Result D, RF1–RP2
1	1	.021	.033	.018	.266
1	4	.000	.005	.040	.451
1	8	.000	.002	.025	.426
1	12	.000	.006	.037	.378
4	1	.035	.066	.020	.202
4	4	.004	.018	.021	.393
4	8	.001	.010	.016	.480
4	12	.001	.008	.009	.459
8	1	.057	.108	.019	.173
8	4	.014	.038	.008	.295
8	8	.013	.039	.009	.338
8	12	.012	.038	.007	.320
12	1	.085	.142	.027	.183
12	4	.043	.071	.014	.269
12	8	.048	.079	.020	.333
12	12	.044	.078	.017	.325

Note: Entries are marginal significance levels (p values) for the null hypothesis that the true MSPE difference is 0.

5. Variations and Extensions

The results reported above are robust to a number of variations. In particular, qualitatively similar results were obtained when first differences rather than levels of all variables were used, as shown in the MSPE comparisons in Table 17.5. Qualitatively similar results were also obtained, as shown in Table 17.6, after eliminating from the sample the pre-1960 data, which are of lower quality.

From the perspective of those who originally developed the leading indexes of economic activity, a potential objection to our results is that we evaluate the CLI using a questionable criterion, namely, the ability to forecast movements in IP. Instead, they might argue that the CLI is designed to signal broad changes in business conditions and, particularly, business recessions. One response to this would be to consider a more comprehensive indicator of aggregate economic activity. (IP includes roughly one-third of total output.) With this in mind, we also conducted the analysis of Section 4 after replacing IP with the composite index of coincident economic indicators, a much broader monthly

TABLE 17.5
Mean Squared Prediction Error, Growth in Industrial Production

Steps Ahead (k)	Lags Included (p)	Forecast Scenario				
		FF1	FF2	RF1	RF2	RP2
1	1	6.48	5.85	6.57	5.95	6.51
1	4	6.39	5.19	6.52	5.41	5.85
1	8	6.42	4.89	6.60	5.42	5.75
1	12	6.44	4.90	6.79	5.77	6.48
4	1	8.48	7.30	8.72	7.55	8.82
4	4	8.53	6.72	8.83	7.17	8.71
4	8	8.58	6.44	9.05	7.33	9.16
4	12	8.53	6.59	9.36	8.02	9.94
8	1	8.73	8.28	8.99	8.51	9.47
8	4	8.78	7.98	9.17	8.44	9.70
8	8	8.78	8.22	9.50	9.19	19.58
8	12	8.72	8.16	9.49	9.45	10.88
12	1	9.05	8.82	9.55	9.33	9.31
12	4	8.95	8.75	9.65	9.54	9.79
12	8	8.89	8.50	9.64	9.45	10.05
12	12	8.74	8.46	9.60	9.66	9.94

Note: Entries are MSPE $\times$ 100,000.

measure of economic conditions. Little difference was found. As shown in Table 17.7, there is an obvious sawtooth pattern for the MSPE for forecasting the composite coincident index that accords with the earlier results.

More fundamentally, however, there is some evidence that those who originally constructed the leading index intended to use it for the prediction of business cycle turning points rather than for forecasting changes in the level of aggregate economic activity over the entire cycle. In this view attention is placed on the ability of the leading index to predict an economic event (a turning point) rather than its ability to forecast future values of economic time series. We have some sympathy for this view; indeed, in Diebold and Rudebusch (1989), we employed a turning point filter that translated movements in the CLI (using final revised data) into probabilities of an imminent recession. However, in Diebold and Rudebusch (1991), a companion article to this one, we showed that the ability of the CLI to forecast turning points on a real-time basis (using the data matrix of Table 17.1) is substantially worse than its ability on an ex post basis using final revised data. Thus we believe that our qualitative conclusions are robust to use of an evaluation criterion of turning point prediction. To provide further

TABLE 17.6
Mean Squared Prediction Error, Post-1960 Industrial Production

Steps Ahead (k)	Lags Included (p)	Forecast Scenario				
		FF1	FF2	RF1	RF2	RP2
1	1	.87	.61	.89	.66	.88
1	4	.64	.49	.71	.59	.67
1	8	.64	.46	.74	.59	.69
1	12	.64	.44	.77	.61	.72
4	1	7.70	4.30	8.40	5.39	8.69
4	4	6.20	3.26	7.10	4.39	6.35
4	8	6.19	2.97	7.46	4.18	6.35
4	12	6.10	2.77	8.03	4.30	6.58
8	1	20.69	11.85	24.40	16.06	26.75
8	4	18.42	8.67	22.30	12.93	22.19
8	8	18.39	7.81	24.50	13.29	24.45
8	12	18.04	7.64	25.14	14.67	26.39
12	1	35.01	22.98	43.79	32.57	51.23
12	4	32.27	17.80	42.07	28.94	48.04
12	8	32.09	17.32	43.36	31.97	52.18
12	12	31.01	16.85	43.41	35.23	55.50

Note: Entries are MSPE $\times$ 10,000.

evidence more directly in line with the present investigation, we examined regressions where IP on the left side was replaced in each scenario by a dummy variable signaling expansion or recession. The relative ranking of prediction errors followed that in Section 4. [Further evidence is provided by three earlier studies—Stekler and Schepsman (1973), Hymans (1973), and Zarnowitz and Moore (1982)—that have employed preliminary CLI data along with simple turning point filters, for example, the use of three consecutive declines as a recessionary signal. These studies have also found that use of preliminary data reduces the usefulness of the CLI in turning point forecasting.]

One could also accord much more statistical expertise to the real-time forecaster than we have done; in particular, there are real-time prediction procedures that are more sophisticated in extracting information from preliminary data than the regression RP2. As discussed by Howrey (1978, 1984), one could model and forecast future data revisions in a real-time, recursive procedure and incorporate these expected revisions into forecasts (via the Kalman filter). Given the frequency of the unforecastable definitional CLI revisions (and the resulting change in the properties of revisions as components are replaced), however, this

TABLE 17.7
Mean Squared Prediction Error, Composite Coincident Index

Steps Ahead (k)	Lags Included (p)	Forecast Scenario				
		FF1	FF2	RF1	RF2	RP2
1	1	.66	.48	.66	.48	.67
1	4	.49	.41	.50	.42	.48
1	8	.49	.39	.51	.43	.49
1	12	.49	.37	.52	.43	.50
4	1	5.80	3.25	6.16	3.49	6.16
4	4	4.42	2.64	4.73	2.87	4.26
4	8	4.44	2.46	4.86	2.84	4.30
4	12	4.34	2.36	4.94	2.89	4.52
8	1	16.46	8.64	18.61	9.87	18.26
8	4	13.66	7.14	15.53	8.08	14.77
8	8	14.04	6.93	16.32	8.29	15.31
8	12	13.66	6.96	16.40	8.63	15.51
12	1	29.87	16.68	35.28	19.85	31.75
12	4	26.63	13.87	32.13	16.15	29.49
12	8	27.10	13.95	33.51	16.77	30.03
12	12	26.50	14.02	33.97	17.45	30.29

Note: Entries are MSPE $\times$ 10,000.

procedure would appear to be of little practical use for forecasting with the CLI.

Finally, we note that the IP data used throughout this article are always of final revised form (as of May 1, 1989). We took such an approach, in part, because our intent is to measure the differences in forecast performance when using the preliminary as opposed to revised CLI *while holding other factors constant*. The alternative, of course, would be to use the preliminary and partially revised IP data as they were available contemporaneously. This choice emerges for both the left side and the right side of the forecasting equations.

First, consider the use of final IP on the left side. We use final rather than contemporaneous IP as the regressand because we are interested in evaluating the ability of the CLI to forecast truth, which is taken to be the final IP value. An alternative approach might examine the accuracy of predictions of the initial estimate (or kth revision, $k = 1, 2, 3, \ldots$) of each month's IP. It is conceivable that the CLI is better at predicting early releases of IP than at predicting final values of IP (in part, perhaps, because the former use labor input data to infer physical output data released subsequently). To reiterate, however, we are interested in prediction of the best, that is, final, estimate of movements in aggregate output.

Second, consider the use of final IP on the right side. The alternative would involve constructing a matrix of preliminary and partially revised IP data, similar to the CLI matrix illustrated in Table 17.1, and using each column sequentially in forecasting regressions. This would provide a completely real-time analysis. Clearly, the outcome of this exercise would depend on the nature and size of revisions in the IP index. First, we note that definitional revisions of IP, which would cause conceptual complications if important, do occur but are of negligible importance during our sample. The three relevant revisions, which occurred in 1971, 1975, and 1985, primarily affected the industry-level classification scheme with only very small effects on the monthly movements in the aggregate IP index. [See Hosley and Kennedy (1985) and Federal Reserve Board (1986) for details.] Statistical revisions were also very small relative to those in the CLI, with a signal-to-noise ratio for the initial estimate of IP of about 2.8, twice as large as for the CLI [see Kennedy (1990)]. It is conceivable that adding this small amount of noise to the right side IP lags in RF1 and RP2 could increase the forecast errors relatively more in RF1, thus overturning our Result D. In such a (truly) real-time scenario, the uncertainty about recent movements in IP would allow the CLI to aid in prediction. Although we recognize such a possibility, we would argue that it is in some sense inconsequential. Such a result would provide a justification for use of the CLI that is quite different from the one adduced in the earlier ex post studies described in the introduction. Namely, the CLI would have little intrinsic leading ability but could possibly supplant the inadequacies of other data series.

6. Summary and Concluding Remarks

We have analyzed the value of the CLI of economic indicators in linear prediction of IP. We found that the CLI performed admirably in an ex post evaluation, confirming the results of others. By constructing a series of scenarios that progressively approached a real-time analysis (i.e., by contracting the forecaster's CLI information set until it matched that available in real time), however, we were able to chart a severe deterioration in the CLI's predictive performance. In forecasting frameworks with squared error loss and absolute error loss, we found that inclusion of the CLI in real-time forecasting equations generally failed to improve forecast performance.

Do our cumulative results indicate that the CLI is of no value as a forecasting tool? Perhaps, but not necessarily. In addition to the reservations expressed in Section 5, there are two general qualifications to such a conclusion. First, our evaluation, like previous evaluations, involved straightforward application of the linear model. It is possible that seasoned and skilled users can use their expert knowledge to extract useful predictive information from the CLI via more sophisticated procedures. Second, it is possible that the "mistakes" in the selection of components made in the early history of the construction of the CLI were part of a process of learning about cyclical behavior and statistical indexes that will not be repeated. In this interpretation, future definitional revisions in the CLI would be minor, and the CLI might perform much better on an ex ante basis. [Here, perhaps, the research of Stock and Watson (1989) may prove fruitful.] On balance, however, our results should be interpreted as sounding a strong cautionary note on forecasting with the CLI as presently constructed by the BEA.

Finally, from a methodological point of view, it is worth noting that our general approach may have wide applicability for questions of model selection and inference. In particular, the examination of out-of-sample or real-time causality using tests for MSPE equality on *recursive* residuals from restricted and unrestricted models may provide a more powerful tool to discriminate between models than conventional causality tests.

References

Auerbach, A. J. (1982), "The Index of Leading Indicators: 'Measurement Without Theory' Thirty-Five Years Later," *Review of Economics and Statistics*, 64, 589–595.

Braun, P., and Zarnowitz, V. (1989), "Major Macroeconomic Variables and Leading Indexes: Some Estimates of Their Interrelations, 1886–1982," NBER Working Paper 2812.

Diebold, F. X., and Rudebusch, G. D. (1988), "Stochastic Properties of Revisions in the Index of Leading Indicators," in *Proceedings of the Business and Economic Statistics Section, American Statistical Association*, pp. 712–717.

—— (1989), "Scoring the Leading Indicators," *Journal of Business*, 64, 369–391.

—— (1991), "Turning Point Prediction With the Composite Leading Index: An Ex Ante Analysis," in *Leading Economic Indicators: New Approaches and Forecasting Records*, eds. K. Lahiri and G. H. Moore, Cambridge, U.K.: Cambridge University Press, pp. 231–256.

Federal Reserve Board (1986), *Industrial Production, 1986 Version*, Washington, DC: Author.

Granger, C. W. J. (1969), "Investigating Causal Relations by Econometric Models and Cross-Spectral Methods," *Econometrica*, 37, 424–428.

Granger, C. W. J., and Newbold, P. (1986), *Forecasting Economic Time Series* (2nd ed.), New York: Academic Press.

Hendry, D. F. (1980), "Predictive Failure and Econometric Modelling in Macroeconomics: The Transactions Demand for Money," in *Economic Modelling*, ed. P. Ormerod, London: Heinemann Educational Books, pp. 217–242.

Hertzberg, M. P., and Beckman, B. A. (1989), "Business Cycle Indicators: Revised Composite Indexes," *Business Conditions Digest*, 29, 97–102.

Hosley, J. D., and Kennedy, J. E. (1985), "A Revision of the Index of Industrial Production," *Federal Reserve Bulletin*, 71, 487–501.

Howrey, E. P. (1978), "The Use of Preliminary Data in Econometric Forecasting," *Review of Economics and Statistics*, 60, 193–200.

—— (1984), "Data Revision, Reconstruction, and Prediction: An Application to Inventory Investment," *Review of Economics and Statistics*, 66, 386–393.

Hymans, S. H. (1973), "On the Use of Leading Indicators to Predict Cyclical Turning Points," *Brookings Papers on Economic Activity*, 2, 339–384.

Kennedy, J. E. (1990), "An Analysis of Revisions to the Industrial Production Index," Federal Reserve Board, Economic Activity Section Working Paper 109.

Koch, P. D., and Rasche, R. H. (1988), "An Examination of the Commerce Department Leading-Indicator Approach," *Journal of Business & Economic Statistics*, 6, 167–187.

Makridakis, S., and Winkler, R. L. (1989), "Sampling Distributions of Post-sample Forecasting Errors," *Applied Statistics*, 38, 331–342.

Priestley, M. B. (1980), *Spectral Analysis and Time Series*, New York: Academic Press.

Stekler, H. O., and Schepsman, M. (1973), "Forecasting With an Index of Leading Series," *Journal of the American Statistical Association*, 68, 291–296.

Stock, J. H., and Watson, M. W. (1989), "New Indexes of Coincident and Leading Economic Indicators," in *NBER Macroeconomics Annual, 1989*, eds. O. J. Blanchard and S. Fischer, Cambridge, MA: MIT Press, pp. 351–394.

Zarnowitz, V., and Moore, G. (1982), "Sequential Signals of Recession and Recovery," *Journal of Business*, 55, 57–85.

18

New and Old Models of Business Investment: A Comparison of Forecasting Performance

STEPHEN D. OLINER, GLENN D. RUDEBUSCH,
AND DANIEL E. SICHEL*

RECENT empirical research on investment has focused on the estimation of the stochastic first-order conditions, or Euler equations, from dynamic models derived under rational expectations. Because these models have an explicit structural interpretation, they are theoretically more appealing than traditional models of investment. However, the empirical performance of Euler-equation models has not been tested against the traditional models. This paper performs such a test by adding two Euler equations to the usual group of traditional investment models examined in previous studies—namely, the accelerator, neoclassical, modified neoclassical, and Q-theory models.[1]

The first of our two Euler equations is a "canonical" model that typifies the equations estimated in recent years.[2] Despite its popularity, this canonical model has a restrictive dynamic structure that is unlikely to capture the time lags inherent in the investment process. In contrast, our second Euler equation explicitly accounts for the lag between the start of an investment project and the later date at which the new

* The authors thank two anonymous referees for helpful comments and Tom Brennan, Greg Brown, Sam Coffin, and Gretchen Weinbach for excellent research assistance. This paper is a condensed version of Oliner, Rudebusch, and Sichel (1993).

[1] Earlier evaluations of investment models include Bernanke, Bohn, and Reiss (1988), Kopcke (1985, 1993), Clark (1979), Elliott (1973), Bischoff (1971), Jorgenson, Hunter, and Nadiri (1970a, b), and Jorgenson and Siebert (1968).

[2] To our knowledge, Abel (1980) was the first to estimate an investment Euler equation under rational expectations. For later work within this literature, see Pindyck and Rotemberg (1983), Shapiro (1986a, b), Gilchrist (1990), Gertler, Hubbard, and Kashyap (1991), Hubbard and Kashyap (1992), Whited (1992), Carpenter (1992), and Ng and Schaller (1993).

capital begins to contribute to the firm's production. By embedding such "time-to-build" lags, which were emphasized by Kydland and Prescott (1982), this equation has a richer structure than most previous investment Euler equations.[3]

This paper focuses on the ability of the various models to forecast investment in equipment and in nonresidential structures. From a practical standpoint, such out-of-sample tests are needed to determine which models have the most value as forecasting tools. Moreover, beyond this practical objective, out-of-sample performance is a powerful test of model specification (see, for example, Hendry 1979). We conduct two sets of tests. The first set of tests examines the size, bias, and serial correlation of the models' one-step-ahead forecast errors, similar to the out-of-sample tests performed by Kopcke (1985) and Clark (1979). In addition, we compare the information content of model forecasts by regressing actual investment on predictions from pairs of models. Fair and Shiller (1990) have argued that such regressions provide a powerful test of alternative models.

To summarize the results, we find that the Euler equations produce extremely poor forecasts of investment for both equipment and nonresidential structures. The time-to-build version of the Euler equation outperforms the basic Euler equation in our tests, but the improvement is modest. All the Euler equations have mean squared forecast errors many times larger than those of the traditional models. Moreover, the Fair-Shiller tests suggest that, as a group, the traditional models for equipment dominate the Euler equations; for nonresidential structures, the Fair-Shiller tests show that neither the Euler equations nor the traditional models have any forecasting ability.

The paper is organized as follows. The next section describes the models in our horse race, while section 2 briefly discusses our data set. Section 3 presents full-sample estimates of each model, in order to gain some initial information on their relative fit. Section 4 documents that the Euler equations produce relatively poor forecasts, and section 5 attempts to explain why this is so, arguing that the standard assumptions that underlie these equations could be to blame. Section 6 concludes the paper and suggests areas for future research.

---

[3] Relatively few researchers have estimated structural time-to-build models of investment. This work appears to be limited to Chirinko and Schiantarelli (1991), Altug (1989), Rossi (1988), and Park (1984). For recent theoretical work on time-to-build models, see Altug (1993).

1. The Investment Models

A. Two Investment Euler Equations

To derive our Euler equations of investment spending, we adopt several assumptions that are fairly standard in the literature:

- The firm's production function is Cobb-Douglas with constant returns to scale:

$$Y_t = F(K_{t-1}, L_t) = AK_{t-1}^\theta L_t^{(1-\theta)}, \tag{1}$$

where Y_t and L_t are output and employment during period t, and K_{t-1} is the capital stock at the end of period $t-1$. The marginal product of capital is

$$F_{K_t} \equiv \partial Y_{t+1}/\partial K_t = \theta Y_{t+1}/K_t. \tag{2}$$

- Capital is a quasi-fixed factor subject to the usual quadratic adjustment costs, while employment is assumed to be a variable factor. Let I_t denote gross investment during period t. Then, the adjustment cost function is

$$C(I_t, K_{t-1}) = \left[\alpha_0(I_t/K_{t-1}) + (\alpha_1/2)(I_t/K_{t-1})^2 \right] K_{t-1}.^4 \tag{3}$$

The partial derivatives of $C(I_t, K_{t-1})$ are

$$C_{I_t} = \alpha_0 + \alpha_1 IK_t \quad \text{and} \quad C_{K_{t-1}} = -(\alpha_1/2)IK_t^2, \tag{4}$$

where $IK_t \equiv I_t/K_{t-1}$. For the firm's investment decision to be well defined, C_I must be increasing with the level of investment; that is, $\partial C_{I_t}/\partial I_t = \alpha_1/K_{t-1}$ must be greater than zero, implying that $\alpha_1 > 0$. We have no prior on the sign of α_0.

- All markets are perfectly competitive, implying that the price of output, the price of capital goods, and the wage rate are exogenous. We normalize both input prices by the price of output (p_t) and denote the resulting real price of capital goods and real wage by p_t^I and w_t, respectively.[5]

---

[4] If, instead, we were to specify a more general adjustment cost function that included interactions between fixed capital and employment, the investment Euler equations would include terms for the change in employment. However, these terms would introduce information into the Euler equations that is absent from the traditional models, undercutting our aim to compare limited-information models of investment.

[5] The assumption of perfect competition in output markets could be relaxed—and indeed has been in other work on investment Euler equations. However, because the neoclassical and Q models that we estimate assume perfect competition, we make this assumption when deriving the Euler equation to enforce a degree of consistency across models.

- The firm's discount rate is exogenous, so that financing decisions are irrelevant for the optimal investment path. We denote the firm's time-varying discount rate by r_t and the corresponding discount factor by $\beta_t = 1/(1 + r_t)$.
- There is only one type of capital, with a constant depreciation rate of δ. As discussed below, we relax this assumption in our empirical work by estimating separate equations for equipment and nonresidential structures.[6]
- Investment projects are subject to time-to-build lags, where our specification of these lags follows Taylor (1982). Let S_t denote the value of projects started in period t. All projects take τ periods to complete, so that additions to the capital stock in period t equal project starts in period $t - \tau$. The equation of motion for the capital stock is then

$$K_t = (1 - \delta)K_{t-1} + S_{t-\tau}. \tag{5}$$

Further, let ϕ_i denote the proportion of the project's total value that is put in place i periods after the start, with $\phi_0, \ldots, \phi_\tau \geq 0$ and $\Sigma_{i=0}^\tau \phi_i = 1$. Thus, I_t equals the value put in place during period t from all projects underway at that time:

$$I_t = \sum_{i=0}^{\tau} \phi_i S_{t-i}. \tag{6}$$

Given this setup, we assume that the firm maximizes the expected present value of real future profits,

$$V_t = E_t\left(\sum_{s=t}^{\infty} \beta_{t,s}^* \pi_s \right) \tag{7}$$

where $\beta_{t,s}^* = \Pi_{j=t+1}^s \beta_j$ is the discount factor from period s back to period t and

$$\pi_s = F(K_{s-1}, L_s) - C\left(\sum_{i=0}^{\tau} \phi_i S_{s-i}, K_{s-1} \right) - w_s L_s - p_s^I\left(\sum_{i=0}^{\tau} \phi_i S_{s-i} \right) \tag{8}$$

(using equation (6) to represent I_s). Real profits equal revenue minus adjustment costs, labor costs, and the cost of purchasing new capital.

---

[6] To simplify the notation, we also ignore the role of taxes in this section. However, corporate tax provisions are incorporated in our empirical measure of the price of capital goods.

Firms maximize (7) by choosing S_s, K_s, and L_s for all $s \geq t$, subject to equation (5), the capital-stock constraint. To carry out this maximization, we define the Lagrangian

$$\mathcal{L}_t = E_t \left[\sum_{s=t}^{\infty} \beta_{t,s}^* (\pi_s - \lambda_s (K_s - (1 - \delta) K_{s-1} - S_{s-\tau})) \right]. \quad (9)$$

Setting $\partial \mathcal{L}_t / \partial x_s =$ for all s, with $x_s = (S_s, K_s, L_s)$, yields a set of first-order conditions for each value of s. The two conditions needed to derive the Euler equation are

$$S_t : \sum_{i=0}^{\tau} \phi_i E_t \left(\beta_{t,t+i}^* (p_{t+i}^I + C_{I_{t+i}}) \right) = E_t (\beta_{t,t+\tau}^* \lambda_{t+\tau}) \quad (10)$$

$$K_{t+\tau} : E_t \left(\beta_{t,t+\tau+1}^* (F_{K_{t+\tau}} - C_{K_{t+\tau}}) \right)$$

$$= E_t (\beta_{t,t+\tau}^* \lambda_{t+\tau} - (1 - \delta) \beta_{t,t+\tau+1}^* \lambda_{t+\tau+1}). \quad (11)$$

At the optimal level of starts, equation (10) says that the expected cost of acquiring and installing capital goods over the next τ periods ($p_{t+i}^I + C_{I_{t+i}}$, for $i = 0, \ldots, \tau$) equals the expected shadow value of the marginal addition to the capital stock when the project comes on line ($\lambda_{t+\tau}$). Both the cost of the project and its shadow value are discounted back to period t in this comparison. Equation (11) relates the shadow value of capital to its expected marginal return net of adjustment costs ($F_K - C_K$).

To derive the Euler equation, combine equations (10) and (11) to eliminate the terms in λ:

$$E_t \left(\beta_{t,t+\tau+1}^* (F_{K_{t+\tau}} - C_{K_{t+\tau}}) \right) - \sum_{i=0}^{\tau} \phi_i E_t \left(\beta_{t,t+i}^* (p_{t+i}^I + C_{I_{t+i}}) \right)$$

$$+ \sum_{i=0}^{\tau} (1 - \delta) \phi_i E_t \left(\beta_{t,t+i+1}^* (p_{t+i+1}^I + C_{I_{t+i+1}}) \right) = 0. \quad (12)$$

Now, assume that expectations are rational and let ϵ_{t+i} represent the expectational error for the terms in (12) dated at period $t + i$, with $E_t(\epsilon_{t+i}) = 0$. In addition, substitute the expressions for F_K, C_I, and C_K

from equations (2) and (4) into (12). Then, after some rearrangement, we obtain

$$\sum_{i=0}^{\tau} \phi_i\left(\tilde{\Delta} p^I_{t+i+1}\right) + \sum_{i=0}^{\tau} \alpha_0 \phi_i\left(\tilde{\Delta} \beta^*_{t,t+i+1}\right) + \alpha_1\left(\beta^*_{t,t+\tau+1} IK^2_{t+\tau+1}/2\right)$$

$$+ \sum_{i=0}^{\tau} \alpha_1 \phi_i\left(\tilde{\Delta} IK_{t+i+1}\right) + \theta\left(\beta^*_{t,t+\tau+1}\frac{Y_{t+\tau+1}}{K_{t+\tau}}\right) = \sum_{i=1}^{\tau+1} \epsilon_{t+i} \quad (13)$$

where

$$\tilde{\Delta} p^I_{t+i+1} \equiv (1-\delta)\beta^*_{t,t+i+1} p^I_{t+i+1} - \beta^*_{t,t+i} p^I_{t+i}$$

$$\tilde{\Delta} \beta^*_{t,t+i+1} \equiv (1-\delta)\beta^*_{t,t+i+1} - \beta^*_{t,t+i}$$

$$\tilde{\Delta} IK_{t+i+1} \equiv (1-\delta)\beta^*_{t,t+i+1} IK_{t+i+1} - \beta^*_{t,t+i} IK_{t+i}.$$

Most variables enter the Euler equation in the quasi-differenced form indicated by the $\tilde{\Delta}$ symbol. Because we treat δ and the β^* terms as data, all expressions in parentheses in (13) can be computed prior to estimation. This leaves $\tau + 3$ structural parameters to be estimated: α_0 and α_1 from the adjustment cost function, θ from the production function, and $\phi_0, \ldots, \phi_{\tau-1}$ to account for time-to-build lags (we restrict ϕ_τ to equal $1 - \sum_{i=0}^{\tau-1} \phi_i$).

The above Euler equation with time-to-build lags has a richer dynamic structure than is usually found in formal models of investment. The more typical specification arises as a special case of equation (13) when the time-to-build lag is zero: $\tau = 0$, $\phi_0 = 1$, and $\phi_i = 0$ for $i > 0$. In this case, (13) reduces to a simpler and more familiar equation:

$$\left(\tilde{\Delta} p^I_{t+1}\right) + \alpha_0\left((1-\delta)\beta_{t+1} - 1\right) + \alpha_1\left(\frac{\beta_{t+1}}{2} IK^2_{t+1} + \tilde{\Delta} IK_{t+1}\right)$$

$$+ \theta\left(\beta_{t+1}\frac{Y_{t+1}}{K_t}\right) = \epsilon_{t+1} \quad (14)$$

where we have used the facts that $\beta^*_{t,t+1} = \beta_{t+1}$ and $\beta^*_{t,t} = 1$. As shown, (14) is a linear equation in three structural parameters: α_0, α_1, and θ. We examine the forecast performance of both the Euler equation with time-to-build lags [equation (13)] and the simpler version that omits time-to-build [equation (14)].

B. Four Traditional Models of Investment

Several well-known models of investment predate the Euler-equation approach: The Q model, the accelerator model, Jorgenson's neoclassical model, and the modified neoclassical model. Each of these models was analyzed in the comparative studies done by Clark (1979) and Bernanke, Bohn, and Reiss (1988). Our specification of each model is the same as in Clark (1979), except that we scale investment by the capital stock rather than by potential output.

Our traditional Q model takes the form:

$$IK_t = \psi + \sum_{s=0}^{N} \omega_s Q_{t-s}^A, \tag{15}$$

where Q^A is average Q, the ratio of the firm's market value to the replacement cost of its capital stock. Equation (15), although often estimated in the literature, is not a structural model. If we ignore time-to-build lags, the structural Q equation implied by our framework is

$$IK_t = -\alpha_0/\alpha_1 + (1/\alpha_1)(\lambda_t - p_t^I) = -\alpha_0/\alpha_1 + (1/\alpha_1)Q_t^A, \tag{16}$$

where the second equality replaces marginal $Q(\lambda_t - p_t^I)$ with average Q.[7] As can be seen from (16), the structural Q equation from a standard dynamic framework admits no role for lags of Q^A. These lags have been included by empirical researchers simply to improve the fit of the equation. The structural Q equation that emerges when we take into account time-to-build bears even less resemblance to equation (15).[8] Thus, we regard (15) as a reduced-form equation relating investment to prices in financial markets.

For both the accelerator model and Jorgenson's neoclassical model, the investment equation has the form:

$$I_t = \psi + \sum_{s=0}^{N} \bar{\omega}_s \Delta K_{t-s}^* + \delta K_{t-1}, \tag{17}$$

where K_t^* is the firm's desired capital stock. In the accelerator model, the desired capital stock K_t^* is assumed proportional to output Y_t, so

---

[7] To derive the first equality in (16), set $\tau = 0$ and $\phi_0 = 1$ in equation (10) and use (4) to substitute for C_t. The second equality follows from Hayashi (1982), who showed that average Q equals marginal Q under constant returns to scale and competitive markets.

[8] See Oliner, Rudebusch, and Sichel (1993) for details.

that $\Delta K_t^* = \zeta \Delta Y_t$. If we make this substitution for ΔK^* in equation (17), scale both sides of (17) by K_{t-1}, and add the random error u_t, we obtain:

$$IK_t = \delta + \frac{\psi}{K_{t-1}} + \sum_{s=0}^{N} \omega_s \frac{\Delta Y_{t-s}}{K_{t-1}} + u_t. \tag{18}$$

In contrast, Jorgenson's neoclassical model sets the marginal product of capital in a Cobb-Douglas technology equal to its real one-period rental price (c), so that $K_t^* = \theta(Y/c)_t$, and

$$IK_t = \delta + \frac{\psi}{K_{t-1}} + \sum_{s=0}^{N} \omega_s \frac{\Delta (Y/c)_{t-s}}{K_{t-1}} + u_t. \tag{19}$$

Finally, the modified neoclassical model, originated by Bischoff (1971), relaxes the symmetric treatment of output and the rental price in the neoclassical model. Bischoff assumed that capital is "putty-clay": Firms can choose the factor proportions for each new vintage of capital, but this choice is irreversible once the vintage has been installed. As discussed more fully in Oliner, Rudebusch, and Sichel (1993), the putty-clay assumption implies the following investment equation:

$$IK_t = \frac{\psi}{K_{t-1}} + \sum_{s=0}^{N} \left[\omega_{1s} \frac{(1/c)_{t-s-1} Y_{t-s}}{K_{t-1}} + \omega_{2s} \frac{(Y/c)_{t-s-1}}{K_{t-1}} \right] + u_t. \tag{20}$$

The ω_{2s} coefficients in equation (20) are expected to be negative, while ω_{1s} and the distributed lag coefficients for the other traditional models are expected to be positive.

2. Data

We estimate equations (13), (14), (15), (18), (19), and (20) with quarterly data for the aggregate private business sector in the United States. These data cover the period 1952:1 to 1992:4. To estimate the traditional models, we require series for gross investment (I), capital stock (K), output (Y), the real user cost of capital (c), and average Q (Q^A). To estimate the Euler equations, we employ the same constant-dollar series for I, K, and Y, along with series for the real after-tax price of investment goods (p^I) and the discount factor (β), and an assumed value for the depreciation rate (δ). Here, we briefly describe the data, while the appendix in Oliner, Rudebusch, and Sichel (1993) fully documents each series.

Our constant-dollar series for output and gross investment are from the National Income and Product Accounts; because we estimate separate equations for producers' durable equipment and nonresidential structures, the investment data are disaggregated into these two categories. For each investment series, the corresponding capital stock is the annual constant-dollar net stock from the Bureau of Economic Analysis, which we interpolate to a quarterly frequency. To construct the real user cost of capital (c) and the real after-tax purchase price of investment goods (p^I), we follow the methodology in the Federal Reserve Board's Quarterly Econometric Model. Our measure of average Q is based on the tax-adjusted formulation in Bernanke, Bohn, and Reiss (1988). The quarterly discount factor for the Euler equations is $\beta = 1/(1 + r)$, where r is an unweighted average of the real interest rate on three-month Treasury bills and the real return on equity; we use a short-term interest rate to conform with the definition of β as a discount factor between adjacent quarters. Finally, to estimate the Euler equations and to construct the user cost of capital for the traditional models, we set the quarterly depreciation rate (δ) to 0.03784 for equipment and 0.01412 for nonresidential structures, the values employed by Bernanke, Bohn, and Reiss (1988).

3. Full-Sample Estimates of the Investment Models

A. The Traditional Models

Table 18.1 shows full-sample parameter estimates for the traditional investment models described in section 1. Each equation is estimated by ordinary least squares over the period 1955:2 to 1992:4, with all distributed lags allowed to be twelve quarters in length; we estimate these lags without constraints.[9]

Except for the Q model, the coefficients on the distributed lag terms in the equipment equations are strongly significant and of the expected sign, tracing out a hump-shaped distribution with a modal lag of three to four quarters. In contrast, in the Q model, the only significant

---

[9] Our use of OLS departs from the usual method of estimating the traditional investment models with a correction for AR(1) errors. If these models actually captured the dynamics driving investment, the errors would be white noise and an AR(1) correction would not be needed. The AR(1) correction, therefore, should be viewed as a "fix-up" for these models, which should be omitted from a fair horserace with the Euler equations. Given our use of OLS, we calculate standard errors by the Newey-West (1987) procedure that is robust to heteroskedasticity and autocorrelation of unknown form.

TABLE 18.1
OLS Estimates of the Traditional Investment Models

Variables	Accelerator		Neoclassical		Q	
	PDE	NRS	PDE	NRS	PDE	NRS
Constant	4.04**	1.63**	4.18**	1.72**	3.91**	1.96**
	(.072)	(.123)	(.101)	(.104)	(.112)	(.071)
$1/K_{t-1}$	−497.4**	391.5**	−322.8**	475.1**		
	(79.1)	(87.3)	(88.2)	(136.9)		
X_t	.69	−3.31	−.068	−.048	−.569**	−.122
	(2.73)	(4.63)	(.064)	(.032)	(.245)	(.109)
X_{t-1}	10.97**	1.72	.070	−.039	.216	−.007
	(2.04)	(2.98)	(.069)	(.029)	(.217)	(.070)
X_{t-2}	15.97**	3.97	.190**	−.034	.297	.091
	(2.24)	(3.10)	(.069)	(.028)	(.186)	(.060)
X_{t-3}	17.71**	6.32**	.243**	−.015	.209	.111
	(2.64)	(2.77)	(.076)	(.030)	(.173)	(.069)
X_{t-4}	13.44**	5.38	.293**	.003	.188	.043
	(1.92)	(2.92)	(.075)	(.027)	(.159)	(.064)
X_{t-5}	15.11**	7.67**	.276**	.003	.004	.060
	(1.92)	(2.98)	(.082)	(.027)	(.162)	(.064)
X_{t-6}	14.12**	6.97**	.254**	−.005	−.023	.060
	(2.51)	(3.15)	(.064)	(.028)	(.150)	(.064)
X_{t-7}	12.12**	7.84**	.242**	.001	.038	−.023
	(2.39)	(3.08)	(.062)	(.028)	(.160)	(.066)
X_{t-8}	6.07**	4.55	.196**	.009	−.021	.039
	(2.76)	(3.38)	(.071)	(.032)	(.151)	(.077)
X_{t-9}	7.11**	3.43	.210**	.011	.036	−.001
	(3.14)	(2.94)	(.066)	(.029)	(.146)	(.076)
X_{t-10}	11.01**	3.87	.193**	.005	−.099	.027
	(2.34)	(2.95)	(.060)	(.029)	(.153)	(.079)
X_{t-11}	13.12**	5.25	.249**	−.006	−.052	−.195
	(3.45)	(3.76)	(.077)	(.028)	(.204)	(.103)
$\bar{R}^2$	.723	.401	.436	.218	.111	.042
DW	.300	.093	.204	.079	.134	.061

coefficient on the lags of Q^A is negative, contrary to our expectation. More generally, the Durbin-Watson statistic in each equipment equation is below 0.5, a sign of highly autocorrelated errors. Clearly, these models all fail to capture some persistent determinants of equipment investment.

For nonresidential structures, the performance of the traditional models is even less satisfactory. Although the coefficients in the accelerator and modified neoclassical models have the expected signs, fewer of the lags are significant than was the case for equipment. Moreover, the distributed lags in the neoclassical and Q models are uniformly in-

TABLE 18.1
(*Continued*)

Variables	Modified Neoclassical PDE	Modified Neoclassical NRS	Variables	Modified Neoclassical PDE	Modified Neoclassical NRS
Constant	3.00** (.252)	1.95** (.265)			
$1/K_{t-1}$	-585.2** (93.4)	608.2** (195.0)			
X_t	$-.066$ (.201)	$-.029$ (.133)	W_t	.080 (.271)	$-.020$ (.162)
X_{t-1}	.515** (.192)	.139 (.102)	W_{t-1}	$-.418$** (.210)	$-.141$ (.110)
X_{t-2}	.643** (.245)	.259 (.139)	W_{t-2}	$-.665$** (.231)	$-.257$ (.146)
X_{t-3}	.735** (.210)	.276** (.114)	W_{t-3}	$-.679$** (.231)	$-.266$** (.117)
X_{t-4}	.527** (.185)	.208** (.105)	W_{t-4}	$-.566$** (.185)	$-.222$** (.112)
X_{t-5}	.633** (.192)	.278** (.116)	W_{t-5}	$-.617$** (.209)	$-.291$** (.115)
X_{t-6}	.624** (.187)	.313** (.117)	W_{t-6}	$-.619$** (.185)	$-.318$** (.120)
X_{t-7}	.491** (.154)	.325** (.101)	W_{t-7}	$-.524$** (.178)	$-.326$** (.118)
X_{t-8}	.265 (.169)	.225 (.122)	W_{t-8}	$-.254$ (.174)	$-.240$ (.135)
X_{t-9}	.309 (.198)	.218 (.150)	W_{t-9}	$-.319$ (.202)	$-.224$ (.154)
X_{t-10}	.559** (.168)	.245 (.131)	W_{t-10}	$-.545$** (.190)	$-.269$ (.140)
X_{t-11}	.532** (.243)	.256 (.173)	W_{t-11}	$-.508$** (.188)	$-.185$ (.144)
$\bar{R}^2$	.815	.480			
DW	.436	.174			

Notes: All models were estimated over 1955:2–1992:4, with I_t/K_{t-1} as the dependent variable. To reduce the number of leading zeroes, all reported coefficients and standard errors have been multiplied by 100. The standard errors were calculated with the Newey-West (1987) correction for heteroskedasticity and autocorrelation and are in parentheses.

$$X_{t-i} = \begin{cases} \Delta Y_{t-i}/K_{t-1} & \text{for accelerator model} \\ \Delta(Y/c)_{t-i}/K_{t-1} & \text{for neoclassical model} \\ (1/c)_{t-i-1}Y_{t-i}/K_{t-1} & \text{for modified neoclassical model} \\ Q_{t-i}^A & \text{for } Q \text{ model.} \end{cases}$$

For the modified neoclassical model, $W_{t-i} = (Y/c)_{t-i-1}/K_{t-1}$.
PDE = Producers' durable equipment.
NRS = Nonresidential structures.
DW = Durbin-Watson statistic.
** = significant at the 5 percent level.

significant, and the Durbin-Watson statistic for each model is even smaller than its counterpart for equipment. The structures models may perform relatively poorly for a simple reason: Roughly half of the structures aggregate consists of public utilities, oil and gas wells, private schools, churches, and hospitals, which have a diverse set of determinants excluded from our models.

B. The Euler Equations

We estimate the Euler equations using the Generalized Method of Moments (GMM) procedure described by Hansen and Singleton (1982). As with the traditional models, we use the Newey-West (1987) method to obtain a covariance matrix for the GMM parameter estimates that is robust to heteroskedasticity and serial correlation.

For GMM to yield consistent parameter estimates, the instruments must be uncorrelated with the error term, ϵ. If the error term were purely an expectational error, rational expectations implies that any variable in the firm's information set during period t would be uncorrelated with ϵ_{t+i} $(i = 1, \ldots, \tau)$. In this case, all variables dated $t - 1$ and earlier would be valid instruments, as would endogenous variables chosen in period t. We take a more conservative stance, restricting our instruments to variables dated $t - 2$ and earlier. This decision reflects our concern about the potential for measurement error among the variables in the Euler equations.[10] Because our Euler equations include variables dated as early as $t - 1$ $(IK_t \equiv I_t/K_{t-1})$, ϵ_{t-1} could well include the error component of $t - 1$ dated variables. If so, any endogenous variable would have to be dated $t - 2$ or earlier to be a valid instrument. Accordingly, the instrument set for the basic Euler equation includes a constant and the second and third lags of p_t^I, IK_t, IK_t^2, Y_t/K_{t-1}, and β_t, while the instrument set for the Euler equation with time-to-build also includes the fourth and fifth lags of these variables.[11]

To estimate the time-to-build equation, we must specify τ, the length of time between project starts and completions. The previous estimates of structural time-to-build models with quarterly data, Park (1984) and

----

[10] In particular, measurement error almost certainly afflicts the price series p^I, given the problem of measuring quality change in capital goods. This error then contaminates the series for real investment and capital stock that BEA constructs from p^I.

[11] As a test of robustness, we also estimated the Euler equations with an instrument set that included the first lag of each instrument. The results were not materially different from those reported below. We should note that the exclusion of instruments dated $t - 1$ will not ensure consistent estimates if the measurement errors are autocorrelated. In that case, all lagged endogenous variables will be correlated with the Euler equation's error term. Implicitly, we are assuming that any measurement errors are not strongly autocorrelated.

Altug (1989), set τ to be three and four quarters, respectively. These values of τ likely are appropriate for equipment investment, but are too small to encompass some construction projects. However, with a time-to-build lag much longer than four quarters, the large number of free parameters (the ϕs) probably cannot be estimated with any precision. Therefore, we opted to follow the earlier work and set $\tau = 3$, which allows the investment project to be spread over four quarters. We estimate ($\phi_0, \phi_1, \phi_2, \phi_3$), restricting the ϕ_is to sum to one.

The basic Euler equation without time-to-build is estimated from 1955:2 to 1992:3 (the final period in the sample, 1992:4, provides data for the variables dated $t + 1$). Similarly, the Euler equation with time-to-build is estimated from 1955:2 to 1991:4. The estimates for both equations are shown in Table 18.2. As can be seen in column 1, the signs of $\hat{\theta}$ and $\hat{\alpha}_1$ in the basic model for equipment are positive, consistent with our expectation. However, neither coefficient is significantly different from zero, and $\hat{\theta}$ is quite small given its interpretation in our model as the share of income accruing to equipment. In addition, the omission of time-to-build from the basic equation appears inconsistent with the data. As shown by the estimates for the time-to-build model in column 2, $\hat{\phi}_0 = 0.278$, indicating that only 27.8 percent of equipment spending occurs during the quarter of the project start; the bulk of investment is estimated to take place two and three quarters after the start. Thus, the Euler equation with time-to-build captures the dynamics of equipment investment better than does the basic equation. Moreover, the addition of time-to-build increases $\hat{\alpha}_1$ by enough to make that coefficient significantly greater than zero. Still, the time-to-build model does not alleviate all the problems with the basic equation, as $\hat{\theta}$ is still very low.

The results for the Euler equations for structures are worse than those for equipment, paralleling our results for the traditional models. As shown in columns 3 and 4, $\hat{\theta}$ and $\hat{\alpha}_1$ are significantly negative for both Euler equations, violating our theoretical priors. Given these nonsensical parameter estimates, the time-to-build model for structures cannot be viewed as a success, even though the ϕs are uniformly positive and significant.

Despite the problems with the Euler equation estimates, the only specification test typically reported for Euler equations—the J statistic—does not reject any of the models at even the 20 percent level.[12] This result illustrates the weakness of the J statistic as an overall test of

---

[12] The J statistic tests the null hypothesis that the instruments are orthogonal to the error term, as required for consistent estimation. This statistic equals the number of observations multiplied by the minimized value of the objective function used in GMM estimation. It is asymptotically distributed $\chi^2(\mathrm{df})$, with df equal to the number of instruments minus the number of parameters.

TABLE 18.2
GMM Estimates of Investment Euler Equations

Parameters	Equipment		Structures	
	Basic Model (1)	Time-to-Build (2)	Basic Model (3)	Time-to-Build (4)
Production function				
θ	.020	.021	−.193**	−.151**
	(.017)	(.015)	(.048)	(.033)
Adjustment costs				
α_0	−.962**	−1.006**	−4.235**	−3.537**
	(.185)	(.163)	(.822)	(.558)
α_1	1.590	3.965**	−18.334**	−20.735**
	(1.469)	(1.560)	(8.926)	(5.353)
Time-to-build				
ϕ_0		.278**		.174**
		(.090)		(.040)
ϕ_1		.066		.242**
		(.092)		(.044)
ϕ_2		.303**		.270**
		(.114)		(.052)
ϕ_3		.353**		.315**
		(.094)		(.059)
J Statistic	10.33	15.84	7.78	11.46
p-value	.24	.39	.46	.72

Notes: Basic model was estimated over 1955:2–1992:3, while the time-to-build model was estimated over 1955:2–1991:4. The standard errors are in parentheses and were calculated with the Newey-West (1987) correction for heteroskedasticity and autocorrelation. Estimation of the time-to-build model was done subject to the restriction that $\phi_0 + \phi_1 + \phi_2 + \phi_3 = 1$.
** = significant at the 5 percent level.

model specification. Further evidence of the inadequacy of the J statistic can be found in Oliner, Rudebusch, and Sichel (1996), where we show that the estimated parameters of an investment Euler equation appear to be unstable even though the J statistic fails to reject the model.

4. Out-of-Sample Performance of the Investment Models

A. Generating Out-of-Sample Forecasts

For each traditional model, the forecast of IK_{t+1} is $\hat{\gamma}_t \mathbf{Z}_{t+1}$, where $\hat{\gamma}_t$ denotes the vector of OLS parameter estimates based on data through period t and $\mathbf{Z}_{t+1}$ denotes the vector of actual values for the explanatory variables in period $t + 1$. We generate a sequence of these one-step-ahead forecasts by extending the sample one period at a time and recalculating $\hat{\gamma}_t \mathbf{Z}_{t+1}$ for each sample. These forecasts are "out-of-sample" in that all coefficients are estimated from data prior to the forecast date. The forecasts, however, are "ex post" because they use the actual values of the explanatory variables at time $t + 1$ in the forecast of investment at time $t + 1$. In real-time forecasting, such values are not available and must be replaced by projections. We analyze ex post forecasts because our interest centers on the adequacy of the investment equations themselves, not the ease of forecasting the explanatory variables.[13]

We apply an analogous procedure to the Euler equations to generate one-step-ahead, ex post forecasts of IK. The specifics of our procedure can be described most easily for the basic Euler equation that omits time-to-build [equation (14)]. First, equation (14) is estimated by GMM using data through period t. Next, we solve the Euler equation for IK_{t+1}. Given the parameter estimates ($\hat{\alpha}_0$, $\hat{\alpha}_1$, $\hat{\theta}$), the assumed value for δ, and the actual values for all variables in the equation other than IK_{t+1}, equation (14) defines a quadratic equation in IK_{t+1}:

$$\left(\frac{\hat{\alpha}_1 \beta_{t+1}}{2} \right) IK_{t+1}^2 + (\hat{\alpha}_1(1 - \delta)\beta_{t+1}) IK_{t+1} + \hat{W}_{t+1} = 0, \quad (21)$$

where

$$\hat{W}_{t+1} = \left(\tilde{\Delta} p_{t+1}^I \right) + \hat{\alpha}_0((1 - \delta)\beta_{t+1} - 1) - \hat{\alpha}_1 IK_t + \hat{\theta} \left(\beta_{t+} \frac{Y_{t+1}}{K_t} \right)$$

and we have set the expectational error ϵ_{t+1} to zero. Solving equation (21) yields

$$IK_{t+1} = -(1 - \delta) \pm \left((1 - \delta)^2 - 2\hat{W}_{t+1}/(\hat{\alpha}_1 \beta_{t+1}) \right)^{1/2}, \quad (22)$$

as the forecasting equation for IK_{t+1}. We use the positive branch of equation (22). By extending the sample one period at a time and then repeating this procedure, we obtain the desired sequence of one-step-ahead, ex post forecasts.

---

[13] However, we did compute ex ante forecasts from the traditional models using univariate autoregressions to generate one-step-ahead forecasts for the explanatory variables. The ex ante forecast errors were almost the same as the ex post errors, as one might expect given the generally small coefficients reported in Table 18.1 for the contemporaneous explanatory variables.

The same method yields a forecasting rule for the Euler equation with time-to-build, equation (13). Given GMM estimates of α_0, α_1, θ, and the ϕs, equation (13) can be written as a quadratic in $IK_{t+\tau+1}$:

$$\left(\frac{\hat{\alpha}_1 \beta^*_{t,t+\tau+1}}{2}\right) IK^2_{t+\tau+1} + \left(\hat{\alpha}_1 \hat{\phi}_\tau (1-\delta) \beta^*_{t,t+\tau+1}\right) IK_{t+\tau+1}$$

$$+ \hat{W}_{t+\tau+1} = 0, \tag{23}$$

where

$$\hat{W}_{t+\tau+1}$$

$$= \sum_{i=0}^{\tau} \hat{\phi}_i \left(\tilde{\Delta} p^I_{t+i+1}\right) + \hat{\alpha}_0 \sum_{i=0}^{\tau} \hat{\phi}_i \left(\tilde{\Delta} \beta^*_{t,t+i+1}\right) + \hat{\theta} \left(\beta^*_{t,t+\tau+1} \frac{Y_{t+\tau+1}}{K_{t+\tau}}\right)$$

$$+ \hat{\alpha}_1 \sum_{i=0}^{\tau-1} \phi_i \left(\tilde{\Delta} IK_{t+i+1}\right) - \hat{\alpha}_1 \hat{\phi}_\tau \beta^*_{t,t+\tau} IK_{t+\tau}.$$

To make the time subscripts consistent with those in the basic Euler equation, we lag each term in equation (23) by τ periods and then solve (23) for IK_{t+1}:

$$IK_{t+1} = -\hat{\phi}_\tau (1-\delta) \pm \left(\hat{\phi}_\tau^2 (1-\delta)^2 - 2\hat{W}_{t+1} / (\hat{\alpha}_1 \beta^*_{t-\tau,t+1})\right)^{1/2}. \tag{24}$$

The positive branch of equation (24) generates our ex post forecast of IK_{t+1} for the time-to-build model, based on the actual values for the right-hand side variables and GMM estimates of the parameters computed with data through period t.[14]

---

[14] Equations (22) and (24) are nonlinear functions of estimated parameters. Following Kennedy (1983), we also computed forecasts from equation (22) with a correction for the possible bias from this nonlinearity. The correction made virtually no difference and is not used below. We tried one other sensitivity test for the Euler equation forecasts from equation (22). Rather than using the actual values for right-hand-side variables dated at period $t + 1$, we used the projections of these variables on our instrument set. Strictly speaking, this procedure is more congruent with the rational expectations assumption built into the Euler equations. However, the use of projections rather than actual period $t + 1$ values had no material effect on the Euler equation forecasts.

B. Out-of-Sample Forecast Errors

Table 18.3 summarizes the out-of-sample forecast performance of the equipment models over the period 1964:1 through 1992:4. The first column shows the root mean squared error (RMSE) of the one-step-ahead forecasts, multiplied by 100 to remove leading zeroes. The next two columns present statistics derived from a regression of the forecast errors on a constant. Column 2 shows the estimated coefficient from this regression, which equals the mean forecast error, a measure of the forecast's bias. The Durbin-Watson statistic from the regression, shown in the third column, characterizes the extent of first-order autocorrelation in the forecast errors.

Column 1 shows that both Euler equations produce far less accurate forecasts of equipment investment than do the traditional models. The RMSE of the basic Euler equation is roughly twenty-five times larger

TABLE 18.3
Summary Statistics for Equipment Forecast Errors

Model	100*RMSE	100*(Forecast Error) Regressed on a Constant		N
		Bias	DW	
Accelerator	.228	− .022 (.51)	.234	116
Neoclassical	.336	.045 (.73)	.233	116
Modified Neoclassical	.227	− .105** (2.92)	.431	116
Q	.396	− .231** (3.75)	.137	116
Basic Euler Equation	9.720	− .078 (.13)	2.431	116
Time-to-Build Euler Eqn.[1]	2.224	.376 (1.18)	.676	113

Notes: As described in the text, errors are calculated from rolling, one-quarter-ahead forecasts for 1964:1 to 1992:4. All forecasts are out-of-sample, ex post forecasts. Absolute value of t statistics are in parentheses and are calculated from Newey-West (1987) standard errors.
[1] Excludes forecasts for three periods for which the model failed to generate a real-valued solution.
RMSE = Root mean square error.
DW = Durbin-Watson statistic.
N = Number of forecast errors.
** = significant at the 5 percent level.

than that of the worst traditional model, the Q equation. The addition of time-to-build lags markedly improves the forecast performance of the Euler equation, but the RMSE of the time-to-build equation is still well above those of the traditional models. The RMSEs of the traditional models as a group lie in a fairly narrow range, with the accelerator and modified neoclassical models at the low end.

The relatively small RMSEs of the traditional models should not be interpreted as an endorsement of their forecasting ability. The low Durbin-Watson (DW) statistics indicate that the traditional models all make persistent forecast errors. Moreover, the forecasts from the modified neoclassical and Q models have a significant downward bias. The traditional models look good only relative to the performance of the Euler equations.

Table 18.4 documents the forecast performance of the structures models. As in Table 18.3, the RMSEs for both Euler equations are many times larger than those of the traditional models. However, in contrast to the results for equipment, the inclusion of time-to-build lags does not greatly reduce the RMSE of the Euler equation. Another difference from Table 18.3 is the absence of bias in the forecasts from

TABLE 18.4
Summary Statistics for Structures Forecast Errors

Model	100*RMSE	100*(Forecast Error) Regressed on a Constant		N
		Bias	DW	
Accelerator	.213	.039 (.94)	.081	116
Neoclassical	.241	.077 (1.73)	.079	116
Modified Neoclassical	.205	.008 (.21)	.117	116
Q	.258	.067 (1.37)	.065	116
Basic Euler Equation	8.735	.525 (.72)	2.331	116
Time-to-Build Euler Eqn.[1]	7.244	1.161 (1.78)	.871	112

Notes: See Table 18.3.
[1] Excludes forecasts for four periods for which the model failed to generate a real-valued solution.
RMSE = Root mean square error.
DW = Durbin-Watson statistic.
N = Number of forecast errors.

the traditional models. Still, the forecast errors from these models are highly autocorrelated, with the largest DW statistic at 0.117, suggesting the omission of important explanatory variables.

C. Pairwise Forecast Comparisons

The inability of the Euler equations to forecast out of sample also is evident in pairwise model comparisons. These comparisons are made, following Fair and Shiller (1990), in regressions of the form

$$IK_{t+1} - IK_t = a + \Omega_E(IK^f_{E,t+1} - IK_t) + \Omega_T(IK^f_{T,t+1} - IK_t) + u_t$$

$$(25)$$

where $IK^f_{E,t+1}$ and $IK^f_{T,t+1}$ are the one-step-ahead forecasts of IK_{t+1} from a Euler equation and a traditional model. Equation (25) regresses the actual change in IK on the predicted change from the two models. If $\Omega_E = 0$, the forecasts from the Euler equation contain no predictive information beyond that in the constant or the traditional model. Conversely, if $\Omega_T = 0$, the forecasts from the traditional model contain no relevant information beyond that in the constant or the Euler equation. If neither model can predict changes in IK, the estimates of both Ω_E and Ω_T should be zero; if both models have predictive power, both Ω_E and Ω_T should be nonzero.

Table 18.5 displays the pairwise forecast comparisons for the models of equipment investment. The estimates of Ω_E and Ω_T appear in the first two columns, along with t statistics calculated from Newey-West standard errors. The top part of the table compares the basic Euler equation to the traditional models. As shown, the estimates of Ω_E are uniformly insignificant. That is, forecasts from the basic Euler equation have no significant information over and above that provided by the traditional models. In contrast, two of the traditional models—the accelerator and the modified neoclassical models—do have information not conveyed by the Euler equation. However, the relatively low values for $\bar{R}^2$ caution against relying too heavily on any of the models.

The bottom part of Table 18.5 compares the Euler equation with time-to-build lags to the traditional models. The accelerator and the modified neoclassical models provide information not in the time-to-build Euler equation, similar to the results in the top panel. However, Ω_E is now statistically significant in the comparison with each traditional model. Apparently, the addition of time-to-build lags yields a Euler equation forecast with information not found in the traditional

TABLE 18.5
Fair-Shiller Regressions for Equipment

	Ω_E	Ω_T	Traditional Model	$\bar{R}^2$	N
Basic Euler Equation					
1.	−.0006	.187**	Accelerator	.132	116
	(.74)	(2.64)			
2.	−.0007	.068	Neoclassical	.021	116
	(.94)	(1.49)			
3.	−.0004	.233**	Modified Neoclassical	.175	116
	(.62)	(3.64)			
4.	−.0007	.069	Q	.019	116
	(.88)	(1.45)			
Time-to-Build Euler Equation					
5.	.011**	.200**	Accelerator	.170	113
	(4.04)	(2.80)			
6.	.009**	.065	Neoclassical	.037	113
	(3.03)	(1.40)			
7.	.009**	.235**	Modified Neoclassical	.200	113
	(3.77)	(3.69)			
8.	.008**	.073	Q	.043	113
	(2.37)	(1.48)			

Notes: Each row reports the OLS estimates of Ω_E and Ω_T from the regression

$$IK_t - IK_{t-1} = a + \Omega_E(IK_{E,t}^f - IK_{t-1}) + \Omega_T(IK_{T,t}^f - IK_{t-1}) + u_t,$$

estimated over 1964:1–1992:4. $IK_{E,t}^f$ and $IK_{T,t}^f$ are the one-step-ahead forecasts of IK_t from an Euler equation and a traditional model, respectively. Absolute values of t statistics are in parentheses and are calculated from Newey-West (1987) standard errors. ** = significant at the 5 percent level.

models. Nonetheless, we do not interpret this result as particularly favorable to the Euler equation. First, Ω_E is estimated to be extremely small, suggesting that the Euler equation should get little weight when pooled with the traditional models. Second, despite the significance of Ω_E, the predictive power of the Euler equation is extremely limited. If we omit the traditional model from the Fair-Shiller regression, the $\bar{R}^2$ drops to 0.013. Thus, the Euler equation with time-to-build lags explains only 1.3 percent of the variation in $IK_{t+1} - IK_t$ over the full sample.

Table 18.6 presents the analogous pairwise comparisons for the models of structures investment. As can be seen, none of the structures models can predict changes in IK. The estimates of Ω_E and Ω_T are uniformly insignificant at the 5 percent level. Moreover, the values of $\bar{R}^2$ cluster around zero, with the largest value being only 0.016.

TABLE 18.6
Fair-Shiller Regressions for Structures

	Ω_E	Ω_T	*Traditional Model*	$\bar{R}^2$	N
Basic Euler Equation					
1.	−.0009	.022	Accelerator	.010	116
	(1.62)	(.65)			
2.	−.001	−.0004	Neoclassical	.004	116
	(1.52)	(.01)			
3.	−.0009	.013	Modified Neoclassical	.006	116
	(1.59)	(.42)			
4.	−.001	−.012	Q	.007	116
	(1.46)	(.50)			
Time-to-Build Euler Equation					
5.	.0009	.047	Accelerator	.016	112
	(1.61)	(1.30)			
6.	.0007	.009	Neoclassical	−.009	112
	(1.41)	(.28)			
7.	.0009	.036	Modified Neoclassical	.005	112
	(1.53)	(1.08)			
8.	.0007	−.005	Q	−.009	112
	(1.35)	(.17)			

Notes: See Table 18.5.

5. Why Do the Euler Equations Perform So Badly?

Several factors could account for the Euler equations' inaccurate forecasts of investment spending. One possibility is that the GMM estimator has poor finite-sample properties [see West and Wilcox (1994) and Fuhrer, Moore, and Schuh (1995) for discussions of this problem in the context of inventory models]. Another possible shortcoming is the use of aggregate data to estimate Euler equations that apply at the firm level. In this section, however, we argue that the Euler equations may well forecast poorly because they impose an invalid dynamic structure on the data.

Consider equation (22), which generates the forecasts of IK_{t+1} for the basic Euler equation, expressed (after some algebra) in the form:

$$ IK_{t+1} = -(1 - \delta) + \left[(1 - \delta)^2 + 2 \left(\frac{IK_t}{\beta_{t+1}} - \frac{MPK_t - c_t}{\hat{\alpha}_1} \right) \right]^{1/2}, \quad (26) $$

where $MPK_t = \hat{\theta} Y_{t+1}/K_t$ is the marginal product of capital, and c_t

represents the discrete-time version of Jorgenson's user cost of capital.[15] Equation (26) shows that the forecast of IK_{t+1} depends on its own value in period t and on the difference between the marginal product and the cost of capital. The relative importance of each factor reflects the magnitude of marginal adjustment costs, $\hat{\alpha}_1$. If $\hat{\alpha}_1$ is large, then adjusting the rate of investment is quite costly, and IK_{t+1} will deviate relatively little from IK_t, regardless of the difference between MPK_t and c_t. In contrast, as $\hat{\alpha}_1$ approaches zero, $MPK_t - c_t$ becomes the dominant influence on IK_{t+1}. Intuitively, when marginal adjustment costs are very small, the firm quickly adjusts the capital stock to arbitrage away differences between the marginal product of capital and the user cost.[16] Accordingly, the Euler equation will forecast IK_{t+1} to deviate sharply from IK_t whenever $(MPK_t - c_t)/\hat{\alpha}_1$ is large. Given the smoothness of the actual data for IK, the forecasts in such cases will be inaccurate.

The previous section showed that adding time-to-build lags does not remedy the problems with the basic Euler equation, and equation (26) provides the key for understanding this result. In particular, the version of equation (26) for the time-to-build model would replace IK_t and $MPK_t - c_t$ with four-quarter moving averages of these variables that run from period $t - 3$ to period t. Thus, whenever $\hat{\alpha}_1$ is small or a wide gap exists between MPK and c for several quarters, the time-to-build model will forecast big changes in investment. In 1986, for example, the time-to-build model for equipment produced terrible forecasts. The collapse in oil prices that year sharply reduced the price deflator for aggregate output relative to the deflator for equipment alone, driving up real equipment prices (p^I). The resulting capital gain for owners of equipment lowered the user cost, c_t, relative to MPK_t. Accordingly, the time-to-build Euler equation expected equipment outlays to be accelerated in order to take advantage of the low user cost, implying a dramatic decline in IK_{t+1} from its level in period t. In reality, no such intertemporal shift occurred.

As a general matter, the actual series for IK does not display the high degree of time shifting expected by either Euler equation in response to changes in relative prices and interest rates. This problem could well reflect some unrealistic assumptions that underlie both Euler equations. First, the equations embed the "putty-putty" technology of the original neoclassical model. That is, the Euler equations do not distinguish

---

[15] Specifically, $c_t = (p_t^I + \alpha_0)(r_{t+1} + \delta) - (1 - \delta)(p_{t+1}^I - p_t^I)$.

[16] Note that IK_{t+1} is *negatively* related to $MPK_t - c_t$. That is, $MPK_t > c_t$ implies a low value of IK_{t+1} relative to IK_t. The intuition is simply that the firm shifts investment from period $t + 1$ to period t to capture the profits from the high marginal product of capital.

between already-installed capital and capital still to be purchased. These equations expect the capital-output ratio for the entire installed capital stock to adjust to a change in relative prices or interest rates. Such an adjustment, even if done slowly, could induce a large shift in investment outlays. In contrast, a putty-clay model would not allow firms to alter the capital intensity of their existing production facilities.

In addition, the Euler equations assume that investment is fully reversible. Under the more reasonable assumption of irreversibility, Pindyck (1991) and others have shown that investment spending will adjust sluggishly to price changes that generate increased uncertainty about the economic environment.

Finally, the maintained assumption of convex adjustment costs—which generates the investment dynamics in our Euler equations—may be unfounded. Although convex adjustment costs are a convenient assumption, the case for convexity is weak, especially when the adjustments costs are internal to the firm. Convexity implies that the installation of new capital goods should be progressively less costly when dragged out over longer and longer periods. There is no inherent reason why this should be so, a point made originally by Rothschild (1971) and forcefully restated by Nickell (1978), but ignored in most empirical models of investment.

6. Conclusion

This paper extends earlier "horse race" comparisons of empirical investment models by adding two Euler equations to the usual stable of traditional—but largely nonstructural—models and by focusing on out-of-sample performance. The basic Euler equation used in the comparisons is a "canonical" Euler equation representative of those found in the applied investment literature. In addition, we use a richer Euler equation with time-to-build lags. Our results indicate that the forecast performance of both Euler equations is substantially worse than that of the traditional models. Although the time-to-build equation performs slightly better than the basic Euler equation, both Euler equations produce forecasts of investment spending that are much too volatile.

Our results have the following implications. First, and most important, the inability of the Euler equations to forecast investment spending even one quarter ahead suggests that these models are misspecified.[17]

---

[17] See Oliner, Rudebusch, and Sichel (1996) for further evidence of misspecification. In that paper, we formally test for parameter constancy in an investment Euler equation similar to those estimated here. We find significant evidence of instability in each parameter.

Investment Euler equations based on simple adjustment cost functions have become a fixture in applied work, but researchers should not assume that these equations are valid structural models. We argued that better models of investment might be provided by Euler equations that embed irreversibility or a putty-clay technology, in order to produce more sluggish adjustments in investment.

Second, none of the models we evaluated could forecast investment in nonresidential structures. This aggregate has a very diverse set of components, and no single model is likely to capture the determinants for all these types of structures. It would be interesting to know whether the traditional models or Euler equations can forecast investment for a single component of the aggregate, such as industrial or commercial buildings.

References

Abel, Andrew B. "Empirical Investment Equations: An Integrative Framework." In *On the State of Macroeconomics*, edited by Karl Brunner and Allan H. Meltzer, pp. 39–91. Carnegie-Rochester Conference Series on Public Policy 12, Spring 1980.

Altug, Sumru. "Time-to-Build and Aggregate Fluctuations: Some New Evidence." *International Economic Review* 30 (November 1989), 889–920.

——. "Time-to-Build, Delivery Lags, and the Equilibrium Pricing of Capital Goods." *Journal of Money, Credit, and Banking* 25 (August 1993, Part 1), 301–19.

Bernanke, Ben, Henning Bohn, and Peter C. Reiss. "Alternative Non-Nested Specification Tests of Time-Series Investment Models." *Journal of Econometrics* 37 (March 1988), 293–326.

Bischoff, Charles W. "The Effect of Alternative Lag Distributions." In *Tax Incentives and Capital Spending*, edited by Gary Fromm, pp. 61–130. Washington, D.C.: Brookings Institution, 1971.

Carpenter, Robert E. "An Empirical Investigation of the Financial Hierarchy Hypothesis: Evidence from Panel Data." Washington University Working Paper Series, no. 164, 1992.

Chirinko, Robert S., and Fabio Schiantarelli. "Delivery Lags, Adjustment Costs, and Econometric Investment Models." New York University, C. V. Starr Center for Applied Economics, Research Report no. 91-41, August 1991.

Clark, Peter K. "Investment in the 1970s: Theory, Performance, and Prediction." *Brookings Papers on Economic Activity* (1979:1), 73–113.

Elliott, J. W. "Theories of Corporate Investment Behavior Revisited." *American Economic Review* 63 (March 1973), 195–207.

Fair, Ray C., and Robert J. Shiller. "Comparing Information in Forecasts from Econometric Models." *American Economic Review* 80 (June 1990), 375–89.

Fuhrer, Jeffrey, George Moore, and Scott Schuh. "Estimating the Linear-Quadratic Inventory Model: Maximum Likelihood versus Generalized Method of Moments." *Journal of Monetary Economics* 35 (February 1995), 115–58.

Gertler, Mark, R. Glenn Hubbard, and Anil K. Kashyap. "Interest Rate Spreads, Credit Constraints, and Investment Fluctuations: An Empirical Investigation." In *Financial Markets and Financial Crises*, edited by R. Glenn Hubbard, pp. 11–31. Chicago: University of Chicago Press, 1991.

Gilchrist, Simon. "An Empirical Analysis of Corporate Investment and Financing Hierarchies Using Firm Level Panel Data." Mimeo, 1990.

Hansen, Lars P., and Kenneth J. Singleton. "Generalized Instrumental Variables Estimation of Nonlinear Rational Expectations Models." *Econometrica* 50 (September 1982), 1269–86.

Hayashi, Fumio. "Tobin's Marginal q and Average q: A Neoclassical Interpretation." *Econometrica* 50 (January 1982), 213–24.

Hendry, D. F. "Predictive Failure and Econometric Modelling in Macroeconomics: The Transactions Demand for Money." In *Economic Modelling*, edited by P. Ormerod, pp. 217–42. London: Heinemann Education Books, 1979.

Hubbard, R. Glenn, and Anil K. Kashyap. "Internal Net Worth and the Investment Process: An Application to U.S. Agriculture." *Journal of Political Economy* 100 (June 1992), 506–34.

Jorgenson, Dale W., Jerald Hunter, and M. Ishaq Nadiri. "A Comparison of Alternative Econometric Models of Quarterly Investment Behavior." *Econometrica* 38 (March 1970), 187–212 (a).

——. "The Predictive Performance of Econometric Models of Quarterly Investment Behavior." *Econometrica* 38 (March 1970), 213–24 (b).

Jorgenson, Dale W., and Calvin D. Siebert. "A Comparison of Alternative Theories of Corporate Investment Behavior." *American Economic Review* 58 (September 1968), 681–712.

Kennedy, Peter E. "Logarithmic Dependent Variables and Prediction Bias." *Oxford Bulletin of Economics and Statistics* 45 (1983), 389–92.

Kopcke, Richard W. "The Determinants of Investment Spending." *New England Economic Review* (July/August 1985), 19–35.

——. "The Determinants of Business Investment: Has Capital Spending Been Surprisingly Low?" *New England Economic Review* (January/February 1993), 3–31.

Kydland, Finn E., and Edward C. Prescott. "Time to Build and Aggregate Fluctuations." *Econometrica* 50 (November 1982), 1345–70.

Newey, Whitney K., and Kenneth West. "A Simple, Positive Semi-Definite, Heteroskedasticity and Autocorrelation Consistent Covariance Matrix." *Econometrica* 55 (May 1987), 703–8.

Nickell, S. J. *The Investment Decisions of Firms*. Welwyn, England: James Nisbet and Company, Ltd. and Cambridge University Press, 1978.

Ng, Serena, and Huntley Schaller. "The Risky Spread, Investment, and Monetary Policy Transmission: Evidence on the Role of Asymmetric Information." Carleton University, Economics Papers no. 93-07, 1993.

Oliner, Stephen, Glenn Rudebusch, and Daniel Sichel. "New and Old Models of Business Investment: A Comparison of Forecasting Performance." Economic Activity Section Working Paper no. 141, Board of Governors of the Federal Reserve System, 1993.

———. "The Lucas Critique Revisited: Assessing the Stability of Empirical Euler Equations for Investment." *Journal of Econometrics* 70 (1996), 291–316.

Park, Jong Ahn. "Gestation Lags with Variable Plans: An Empirical Study of Aggregate Investment." Ph.D. dissertation, Carnegie-Mellon University, Graduate School of Industrial Administration, 1984.

Pindyck, Robert S. "Irreversibility, Uncertainty, and Investment." *Journal of Economic Literature* 29 (September 1991), 1110–48.

Pindyck, Robert S., and Julio Rotemberg. "Dynamic Factor Demands under Rational Expectations." *Scandinavian Journal of Economics* 85, no. 2 (1983), 223–38.

Rossi, Peter E. "Comparison of Dynamic Factor Demand Models." In *Dynamic Econometric Modeling*, edited by William A. Barnett, Ernst R. Berndt, and Halbert White, pp. 357–76. Cambridge, England: Cambridge University Press, 1988.

Rothschild, Michael. "On the Cost of Adjustment." *Quarterly Journal of Economics* 85 (November 1971), 605–22.

Shapiro, Matthew D. "The Dynamic Demand for Capital and Labor." *Quarterly Journal of Economics* 103 (August 1986), 513–42 (a).

———. "Capital Utilization and Capital Accumulation: Theory and Evidence." *Journal of Applied Econometrics* 1 (1986), 211–34 (b).

Taylor, John B. "The Swedish Investment Funds System as a Stabilization Policy Rule." *Brookings Papers on Economic Activity* (1982:1), 57–99.

West, Kenneth D., and David W. Wilcox. "Some Evidence on Finite Sample Distributions of Instrumental Variables Estimators of the Linear Quadratic Inventory Model." In *Inventory Cycles and Monetary Policy*, edited by Ricardo Fiorito, pp. 253–82. New York: Springer-Verlag, 1994.

Whited, Toni. "Debt, Liquidity Constraints, and Corporate Investment: Evidence from Panel Data." *Journal of Finance* 47 (September 1992), 1425–60.

19

Comparing Predictive Accuracy

FRANCIS X. DIEBOLD AND ROBERTO S. MARIANO*

PREDICTION is of fundamental importance in all of the sciences, including economics. Forecast accuracy is of obvious importance to users of forecasts because forecasts are used to guide decisions. Forecast accuracy is also of obvious importance to producers of forecasts, whose reputations (and fortunes) rise and fall with forecast accuracy. Comparisons of forecast accuracy are also of importance to economists more generally who are interested in discriminating among competing economic hypotheses (models). Predictive performance and model adequacy are inextricably linked—predictive failure implies model inadequacy.

Given the obvious desirability of a formal statistical procedure for forecast-accuracy comparisons, one is struck by the casual manner in which such comparisons are typically carried out. The literature contains literally thousands of forecast-accuracy comparisons; almost without exception, point estimates of forecast accuracy are examined, with no attempt to assess their sampling uncertainty. On reflection, the reason for the casual approach is clear: Correlation of forecast errors across space and time, as well as several additional complications, makes formal comparison of forecast accuracy difficult. Dhrymes et al. (1972) and Howrey, Klein, and McCarthy (1974), for example, offered pessimistic assessments of the possibilities for formal testing.

In this article we propose widely applicable tests of the null hypothesis of no difference in the accuracy of two competing forecasts. Our approach is similar in spirit to that of Vuong (1989) in the sense that we

* Seminar participants at Chicago, Cornell, the Federal Reserve Board, London School of Economics, Maryland, the Model Comparison Seminar, Oxford, Pennsylvania, Pittsburgh, and Santa Cruz provided helpful input, as did Rob Engle, Jim Hamilton, Hashem Pesaran, Ingmar Prucha, Peter Robinson, and Ken West, but all errors are ours alone. Portions of this article were written while the first author visited the Financial Markets Group at the London School of Economics, whose hospitality is gratefully acknowledged. Financial support from the National Science Foundation, the Sloan Foundation, and the University of Pennsylvania Research Foundation is gratefully acknowledged. Ralph Bradley, José A. Lopez, and Gretchen Weinbach provided research assistance.

propose methods for measuring and assessing the significance of divergences between models and data. Our approach, however, is based directly on predictive performance, and we entertain a wide class of accuracy measures that users can tailor to particular decision-making situations. This is important because, as is well known, realistic economic loss functions frequently do not conform to stylized textbook favorites like mean squared prediction error (MSPE). [For example, Leitch and Tanner (1991) and Chinn and Meese (1991) stressed direction of change, Cumby and Modest (1987) stressed market and country timing, McCulloch and Rossi (1990), and West, Edison, and Cho (1993) stressed utility-based criteria, and Clements and Hendry (1993) proposed a new accuracy measure, the generalized forecast-error second moment.] Moreover, we allow for forecast errors that are potentially non-Gaussian, nonzero mean, serially correlated, and contemporaneously correlated.

We proceed by detailing our test procedures in Section 1. Then, in Section 2, we review the small extant literature to provide necessary background for the finite-sample evaluation of our tests in Section 3. In Section 4 we provide an illustrative application, and in Section 5 we offer conclusions and directions for future research.

1. Testing Equality of Forecast Accuracy

Consider two forecasts, $\{\hat{y}_{it}\}_{t=1}^{T}$ and $\{\hat{y}_{jt}\}_{t=1}^{T}$, of the time series $\{y_t\}_{t=1}^{T}$. Let the associated forecast errors be $\{e_{it}\}_{t=1}^{T}$ and $\{e_{jt}\}_{t=1}^{T}$. We wish to assess the expected loss associated with each of the forecasts (or its negative, accuracy). Of great importance, and almost always ignored, is the fact that the *economic* loss associated with a forecast may be poorly assessed by the usual *statistical* metrics. That is, forecasts are used to guide decisions, and the loss associated with a forecast error of a particular sign and size is induced directly by the nature of the decision problem at hand. When one considers the variety of decisions undertaken by economic agents guided by forecasts (e.g., risk-hedging decisions, inventory-stocking decisions, policy decisions, advertising-expenditure decisions, public-utility rate-setting decisions, etc.), it is clear that the loss associated with a particular forecast error is in general an asymmetric function of the error and, even if symmetric, certainly need not conform to stylized textbook examples like MSPE.

Thus, we allow the time-t loss associated with a forecast (say i) to be an arbitrary function of the realization and prediction, $g(y_t, \hat{y}_{it})$. In many applications, the loss function will be a direct function of the forecast error; that is, $g(y_t, \hat{y}_{it}) = g(e_{it})$. To economize on notation, we write $g(e_{it})$ from this point on, recognizing that certain loss functions (like direction-of-change) do not collapse to $g(e_{it})$ form, in which case the full $g(y_t, \hat{y}_{it})$ form would be used. The null hypothesis of equal forecast accuracy for two forecasts is $E[g(e_{it})] = E[g(e_{jt})]$, or $E[d_t] = 0$, where $d_t \equiv [g(e_{it}) - g(e_{jt})]$ is the loss differential. Thus, the "equal accuracy" null hypothesis is equivalent to the null hypothesis that the population mean of the loss-differential series is 0.

1.1. An Asymptotic Test

Consider a sample path $\{d_t\}_{t=1}^T$ of a loss-differential series. If the loss-differential series is covariance stationary and short memory, then standard results may be used to deduce the asymptotic distribution of the sample mean loss differential. We have

$$\sqrt{T}(\bar{d} - \mu) \xrightarrow{d} N(0, 2\pi f_d(0)),$$

where

$$\bar{d} = \frac{1}{T} \sum_{t=1}^T \left[g(e_{it}) - g(e_{jt}) \right]$$

is the sample mean loss differential,

$$f_d(0) = \frac{1}{2\pi} \sum_{\tau=-\infty}^{\infty} \gamma_d(\tau)$$

is the spectral density of the loss differential at frequency 0, $\gamma_d(\tau) = E[(d_t - \mu)(d_{t-\tau} - \mu)]$ is the autocovariance of the loss differential at displacement τ, and μ is the population mean loss differential. The formula for $f_d(0)$ shows that the correction for serial correlation can be substantial, even if the loss differential is only weakly serially correlated, due to cumulation of the autocovariance terms.

Because in large samples the sample mean loss differential $\bar{d}$ is approximately normally distributed with mean μ and variance $2\pi f_d(0)/T$, the obvious large-sample $N(0, 1)$ statistic for testing the null hypothesis of equal forecast accuracy is

$$S_1 = \frac{\bar{d}}{\sqrt{\dfrac{2\pi\hat{f}_d(0)}{T}}},$$

where $\hat{f}_d(0)$ is a consistent estimate of $f_d(0)$.

Following standard practice, we obtain a consistent estimate of $2\pi f_d(0)$ by taking a *weighted* sum of the available sample autocovariances,

$$2\pi\hat{f}_d(0) = \sum_{\tau=-(T-1)}^{(T-1)} 1\left(\frac{\tau}{S(T)}\right)\hat{\gamma}_d(\tau),$$

where

$$\hat{\gamma}_d(\tau) = \frac{1}{T}\sum_{t=|\tau|+1}^{T} (d_t - \bar{d})(d_{t-|\tau|} - \bar{d}),$$

$1(\tau/S(T))$ is the lag window, and $S(T)$ is the truncation lag.

To motivate a choice of lag window and truncation lag that we have often found useful in practice, recall the familiar result that optimal k-step-ahead forecast errors are at most $(k - 1)$-dependent. In practical applications, of course, $(k - 1)$-dependence may be violated for a variety of reasons. Nevertheless, it seems reasonable to take $(k - 1)$-dependence as a reasonable benchmark for a k-step-ahead forecast error (and the assumption may be readily assessed empirically). This suggests the attractiveness of the uniform, or rectangular, lag window, defined by

$$1\left(\frac{\tau}{S(T)}\right) = 1 \quad \text{for } \left|\frac{\tau}{S(T)}\right| \le 1$$

$$= 0 \quad \text{otherwise.}$$

$(k - 1)$-dependence implies that *only* $(k - 1)$ sample autocovariances need be used in the estimation of $f_d(0)$ because all the others are 0, so $S(T) = (k - 1)$. This is legitimate (i.e., the estimator is consistent) under $(k - 1)$-dependence so long as a uniform window is used because the uniform window assigns unit weight to all included autocovariances.

Because the Dirichlet spectral window associated with the rectangular lag window dips below 0 at certain locations, the resulting estimator of the spectral density function is not guaranteed to be positive semidefinite. The large positive weight near the origin associated with the Dirichlet kernel, however, makes it unlikely to obtain a negative estimate of $f_d(0)$. In applications, in the rare event that a negative estimate arises, we treat it as 0 and automatically reject the null hypothesis of equal forecast accuracy. If it is viewed as particularly important to impose nonnegativity of the estimated spectral density, it may be enforced by using a Bartlett lag window, with corresponding nonnegative Fejer spectral window, as in the work of Newey and West (1987), at the cost of having to increase the truncation lag "appropriately" with sample size. Other lag windows and truncation lag selection procedures are of course possible as well. Andrews (1991), for example, suggested using a quadratic spectral lag window, together with a "plug-in" automatic bandwidth selection procedure.

1.2. Exact Finite-Sample Tests

Sometimes only a few forecast-error observations are available in practice. One approach in such situations is to bootstrap our asymptotic test statistic, as done by Mark (1995). Ashley's (1994) work is also very much in that spirit. Little is known about the first-order asymptotic validity of the bootstrap in this situation, however, let alone higher-order asymptotics or actual finite-sample performance. Therefore, it is useful to have available exact finite-sample tests of predictive accuracy, to complement the asymptotic test presented previously. Two powerful such tests are based on the observed loss differentials (the sign test) or their ranks (Wilcoxon's signed-rank test). [These tests are standard, so our discussion is terse. See, for example, Lehmann (1975) for details.]

THE SIGN TEST

The null hypothesis is a zero-median loss differential: $\text{med}(g(e_{it}) - g(e_{jt})) = 0$. Note that the null of a zero-median loss differential is not the same as the null of zero difference between median losses; that is, $\text{med}(g(e_{it}) - g(e_{jt})) \neq \text{med}(g(e_{it})) - \text{med}(g(e_{jt}))$. For that reason, the null differs slightly in spirit from that associated with our earlier discussed asymptotic test statistic S_1, but it nevertheless has an intuitive and meaningful interpretation—namely, that $P(g(e_{it}) > g(e_{jt})) = P(g(e_{it}) < g(e_{jt}))$.

If, however, the loss differential is symmetrically distributed, then the null hypothesis of a zero-median loss differential corresponds precisely to the earlier null because in that case the median and mean are equal. Symmetry of the loss differential will obtain, for example, if the distributions of $g(e_{it})$ and $g(e_{jt})$ are the same up to a location shift. Symmetry is ultimately an empirical matter and may be assessed using standard procedures. We have found roughly symmetric loss-differential series to be quite common in practice.

The construction and intuition of a test statistic are straightforward. Assuming that the loss-differential series is iid (and we shall relax that assumption shortly), the number of positive loss-differential observations in a sample of size T has the binomial distribution with parameters T and $\frac{1}{2}$ under the null hypothesis. The test statistic is therefore simply

$$S_2 = \sum_{t=1}^{T} I_+(d_t),$$

where

$$I_+(d_t) = 1 \quad \text{if } d_t > 0$$

$$= 0 \quad \text{otherwise.}$$

Significance may be assessed using a table of the cumulative binomial distribution. In large samples, the studentized version of the sign-test statistic is standard normal:

$$S_{2a} = \frac{S_2 - .5T}{\sqrt{.25T}} \overset{a}{\sim} N(0, 1).$$

WILCOXON'S SIGNED-RANK TEST

A related distribution-free procedure that *requires* symmetry of the loss differential (but can be more powerful than the sign test in that case) is Wilcoxon's signed-rank test. We again assume for the moment that the loss-differential series is iid. The test statistic is

$$S_3 = \sum_{t=1}^{T} I_+(d_t) \text{rank}(|d_t|),$$

the sum of the ranks of the absolute values of the positive observations. The exact finite-sample critical values of the test statistic are invariant to the distribution of the loss differential—it need be only zero-mean and symmetric—and have been tabulated. Moreover, its studentized version is asymptotically standard normal,

$$S_{3a} = \frac{S_3 - \dfrac{T(T+1)}{4}}{\sqrt{\dfrac{T(T+1)(2T+1)}{24}}} \overset{a}{\sim} N(0,1).$$

1.3. Discussion

Here we highlight some of the virtues and limitations of our tests. First, as we have stressed repeatedly, our tests are valid for a very wide class of loss functions. In particular, the loss function need not be quadratic and need not even be symmetric of continuous.

Second, a variety of realistic features of forecast errors are readily accommodated. The forecast errors can be nonzero-mean, non-Gaussian, and contemporaneously correlated. Allowance for contemporaneous correlation, in particular, is important because the forecasts being compared are forecasts of the *same* economic time series and because the information sets of forecasters are largely overlapping so that forecast errors tend to be strongly contemporaneously correlated.

Moreover, the asymptotic test statistic S_1 can of course handle a *serially* correlated loss differential. This is potentially important because, as discussed earlier, even optimal forecast errors are serially correlated in general. Serial correlation presents more of a problem for the exact finite-sample test statistics S_2 and S_3 and their asymptotic counterparts S_{2a} and S_{3a} because the elements of the set of all possible rearrangements of the sample loss differential series are *not* equally likely when the data are serially correlated, which violates the assumptions on which such randomization tests are based. Nevertheless, serial correlation may be handled via Bonferroni bounds, as suggested in a different context by Campbell and Ghysels (1995). Under the assumption that the forecast errors and hence the loss differential are $(k-1)$-dependent, each of the following k sets of loss differentials will be free of serial correlation: $\{d_{ij,1}, d_{ij,1+k}, d_{ij,1+2k}, \ldots\}$, $\{d_{ij,2}, d_{ij,2+k},$ $d_{ij,2+2k}, \ldots\}, \ldots, \{d_{ij,k}, d_{ij,2k}, d_{ij,3k}, \ldots\}$. Thus, a test with size bounded by α can be obtained by performing k tests, each of size α/k, on each of the k loss-differential sequences and rejecting the null hypothesis if the null is rejected for *any* of the k samples. Finally, it is interesting to note that, in multistep forecast comparisons, forecast-error serial correlation may be a "common feature," in the terminology of Engle and Kozicki (1993), because it is induced largely by the fact that the forecast horizon is longer than the interval at which the data are sampled and may therefore not be present in loss *differentials* even if present in the forecast errors themselves. This possibility can of course be checked empirically.

2. Extant Tests

In this section we provide a brief description of three existing tests of forecast accuracy that have appeared in the literature and will be used in our subsequent Monte Carlo comparison.

2.1. The Simple F Test: A Naive Benchmark

If (1) loss is quadratic and (2) the forecast errors are (a) zero mean, (b) Gaussian, (c) serially uncorrelated, or (d) contemporaneously uncorrelated, then the null hypothesis of equal forecast accuracy corresponds to equal forecast error variances [by (1) and (2a)], and by (2b)–(2d), the ratio of sample variances has the usual F distribution under the null hypothesis. More precisely, the test statistic

$$F = \frac{\dfrac{e_j' e_i}{T}}{\dfrac{e_j' e_j}{T}} = \frac{e_i' e_i}{e_j' e_j}$$

is distributed as $F(T, T)$, where the forecast error series have been stacked into the $(T \times 1)$ vectors e_i and e_j.

Test statistic F is of little use in practice, however, because the conditions required to obtain its distribution are too restrictive. Assumption (2d) is particularly unpalatable for reasons discussed earlier. Its violation produces correlation between the numerator and denominator of F, which will not then have the F distribution.

2.2. The Morgan–Granger–Newbold Test

The contemporaneous correlation problem led Granger and Newbold (1977) to apply an orthogonalizing transformation due to Morgan (1939–1940) that enables relaxation of Assumption (2d). Let $x_t = (e_{it} + e_{jt})$ and $z_t = (e_{it} - e_{jt})$, and let $x = (e_i + e_j)$ and $z = (e_i - e_j)$. Then, under the maintained Assumptions (1) and (2a)–(2c), the null hypothesis of equal forecast accuracy is equivalent to zero correlation between x and z (i.e., $\rho_{xz} = 0$) and the test statistic

$$\text{MGN} = \frac{\hat{\rho}_{xz}}{\sqrt{\dfrac{1 - \hat{\rho}_{xz}^2}{T - 1}}}$$

is distributed as Student's t with $T - 1$ df, where

$$\hat{\rho}_{xz} = \frac{x'z}{\sqrt{(x'x)(z'z)}}$$

(e.g., see Hogg and Craig 1978, pp. 300–303).

Let us now consider relaxing the Assumptions (1) and (2a)–(2c) underlying the Morgan–Granger–Newbold (MGN) test. It is clear that the entire framework depends crucially on the assumption of quadratic loss (1), which cannot be relaxed. The remaining assumptions, however, can be weakened in varying degrees; we shall consider them in turn.

First, it is not difficult to relax the unbiasedness Assumption (2a), while maintaining Assumptions (1), (2b), and (2c). Second, the normality Assumption (2b) may be relaxed, while maintaining (1), (2a), and (2c), at the cost of substantial tedium involved with accounting for the higher-order moments that then enter the distribution of the sample correlation coefficient (e.g., see Kendall and Stuart 1979, chap. 26). Finally, the no-serial-correlation Assumption (2c) may be relaxed in addition to the no-contemporaneous-correlation Assumption (2d) while maintaining (1), (2a), and (2b), as discussed in Subsection 2.3.

2.3. The Meese–Rogoff Test

Under Assumptions (1), (2a), and (2b), Meese and Rogoff (1988) showed that

$$\sqrt{T}\,\hat{\gamma}_{xz} \xrightarrow{d} N(0, \Sigma),$$

where $\hat{\gamma}_{xz} = x'z/T$, $\Sigma = \sum_{\tau=-\infty}^{\infty}[\gamma_{xx}(\tau)\gamma_{zz}(\tau) + \gamma_{xz}(\tau)\gamma_{zx}(\tau)]$, $\gamma_{xz}(\tau) = \text{cov}(x_t, z_{t-\tau})$, $\gamma_{zx}(\tau) = \text{cov}(z_t, x_{t-\tau})$, $\gamma_{xx}(\tau) = \text{cov}(x_t, x_{t-\tau})$, and $\gamma_{zz}(\tau) = \text{cov}(z_t, z_{t-\tau})$. This is a well-known result (e.g., Priestley 1981, pp. 692–693) for the distribution of the sample cross-covariance function, $\text{cov}(\hat{\gamma}_{xz}(s), \hat{\gamma}_{xz}(u))$, specialized to a displacement of 0.

A consistent estimator of Σ is

$$\hat{\Sigma} = \sum_{\tau=-S(T)}^{S(T)} \left[1 - \frac{|\tau|}{T} \right] [\hat{\gamma}_{xx}(\tau)\hat{\gamma}_{zz}(\tau) + \hat{\gamma}_{xz}(\tau)\hat{\gamma}_{zx}(\tau)],$$

where

$$\hat{\gamma}_{xz}(\tau) = \frac{1}{T} \sum_{t=\tau+1}^{T} x_t z_{t-\tau}, \qquad \tau \geq 0$$

$$= \hat{\gamma}_{zx}(-\tau) \quad \text{otherwise,}$$

$$\hat{\gamma}_{zx}(\tau) = \frac{1}{T} \sum_{t=\tau+1}^{T} z_t x_{t-\tau}, \qquad \tau \geq 0$$

$$= \hat{\gamma}_{xz}(-\tau) \quad \text{otherwise,}$$

$$\hat{\gamma}_{xx}(\tau) = \frac{1}{T} \sum_{t=\tau+1}^{T} x_t x_{t-\tau},$$

$$\hat{\gamma}_{zz}(\tau) = \frac{1}{T} \sum_{t=\tau+1}^{T} z_t z_{t-\tau},$$

and the truncation lag $S(T)$ grows with the sample size but at a slower rate. Alternatively, following Diebold and Rudebusch (1991), one may use the closely related covariance matrix estimator,

$$\hat{\Sigma}^* = \sum_{\tau=-S(T)}^{S(T)} [\hat{\gamma}_{xx}(\tau)\hat{\gamma}_{zz}(\tau) + \hat{\gamma}_{xz}(\tau)\hat{\gamma}_{zx}(\tau)].$$

Either way, the test statistic is

$$\text{MR} = \frac{\hat{\gamma}_{xz}}{\sqrt{\hat{\Sigma}/T}}.$$

Under the null hypothesis and the maintained Assumptions (1), (2a), and (2b), MR (Meese–Rogoff) is asymptotically distributed as standard normal.

It is easy to show that, if the null hypothesis and Assumptions (1), (2a), (2b), and (2c) are satisfied, then all terms in Σ are 0 except $\gamma_{xx}(0)$ and $\gamma_{zz}(0)$ so that MR coincides asymptotically with MGN. It is interesting to note also that reformulation of the test in terms of correlation rather than covariance would have enabled Meese and Rogoff to dispense with the normality assumption because the sample autocorrelations are asymptotically normal even for non-Gaussian time series (e.g., Brockwell and Davis 1992, pp. 221–222).

2.4. Additional Extensions

In Subsection 2.3, we considered relaxation of Assumptions (2a)–(2c), one at a time, while consistently maintaining Assumption (1) and consistently relaxing Assumption (2d). Simultaneous relaxation of multiple assumptions is possible within the MGN orthogonalizing transformation framework but much more tedious. The distribution theory required for joint relaxation of (2b) and (2c), for example, is complicated by the presence of fourth-order cumulants in the distribution of the sample autocovariances, as shown, for example, by Hannan (1970, p. 209) and Mizrach (1991). More importantly, however, *any* procedure based on the MGN orthogonalizing transformation is inextricably wed to the assumption of quadratic loss.

3. Monte Carlo Analysis

3.1. Experimental Design

We evaluate the finite-sample size of test statistics F, MGN, MR, S_1, S_2, S_{2a}, S_3, and S_{3a} under the null hypothesis and various of the maintained assumptions. The design includes a variety of specifications of forecast-error contemporaneous correlation, forecast-error serial correlation, and forecast-error distributions. To maintain applicability of all test statistics for comparison purposes, we use quadratic loss; that is, the null hypothesis is an equality of MSPE's. We emphasize again, however, that an important advantage of test statistics S_1, S_2, S_{2a}, S_3, and S_{3a} in substantive economic applications—and one not shared by the others—is their direct applicability to analyses with nonquadratic loss functions.

Consider first the case of Gaussian forecast errors. We draw realizations of the bivariate forecast-error process, $\{e_{it}, e_{jt}\}_{t=1}^{T}$, with varying degrees of contemporaneous and serial correlation in the generated forecast errors. This is achieved in two steps. First, we build in the desired degree of contemporaneous correlation by drawing a (2×1) forecast error innovation vector u_t from a bivariate standard normal distribution, $u_t \sim N(0_2, I_2)$, and then premultiplying by the Choleski factor of the desired contemporaneous innovation correlation matrix. Let the desired correlation matrix be

$$\mathbf{R} = \begin{bmatrix} 1 & \rho \\ \rho & 1 \end{bmatrix}, \qquad \rho \in [0, 1).$$

Then the Choleski factor is

$$\mathbf{P} = \begin{bmatrix} 1 & 0 \\ \rho & \sqrt{1 - \rho^2} \end{bmatrix}.$$

Thus, the transformed (2×1) vector $v_t = Pu_t \sim N(0_2, \mathbf{R})$. This operation is repeated T times, yielding $\{v_{it}, v_{jt}\}_{t=1}^{T}$.

Second, (moving average) MA(1) serial correlation (with parameter θ) is introduced by taking

$$\begin{bmatrix} e_{it} \\ e_{jt} \end{bmatrix} = \begin{bmatrix} \dfrac{1 + \theta L}{\sqrt{1 + \theta^2}} & 0 \\ 0 & \dfrac{1 + \theta L}{\sqrt{1 + \theta^2}} \end{bmatrix} \begin{bmatrix} v_{it} \\ v_{jt} \end{bmatrix}, \qquad t = 1, \ldots, T.$$

We use $v_0 = 0$. Multiplication by $(1 + \theta^2)^{-1/2}$ is done to keep the unconditional variance normalized to 1.

We consider sample sizes of $T = 8$, 16, 32, 64, 128, 256, and 512, contemporaneous correlation parameters of $\rho = 0$, .5, and .9, and MA parameters of $\theta = 0$, .5, .9. Simple calculations reveal that ρ is not only the correlation between v_i and v_j, but also the correlation between the forecast errors e_i and e_j so that varying the correlation of v_i and v_j through $[0, .9]$ effectively varies the correlation of the observed forecast errors through the same range.

We also consider non-Gaussian forecast errors. The design is the same as for the Gaussian case described previously but driven by fat-tailed variates $(u_{it}^*, u_{jt}^*)'$ [rather than $(u_{it}, u_{jt})'$], which are independent standardized t random variables with 6 df. The variance of a $t(6)$ random variable is $3/2$. Thus, standardization amounts to dividing the $t(6)$ random variable by $\sqrt{3/2}$.

Throughout, we perform tests at the $\alpha = .1$ level. When using the exact sign and signed-rank tests, restriction of nominal size to precisely 10% is impossible (without introducing randomization), so we use the obtainable exact size closest to 10%, as specified in the tables. We perform at least 5,000 Monte Carlo replications. The truncation lag is set at 1, reflecting the fact that the experiment is designed to mimic the comparison of two-step-ahead forecast errors, with associated MA(1) structure.

3.2. Results

Results appear in Tables 19.1–19.6, which show the empirical size of the various test statistics in cases of Gaussian and non-Gaussian forecast errors as the degree of contemporaneous correlation, the degree of serial correlation, and sample size are varied.

Let us first discuss the case of Gaussian forecast errors. The results may be summarized as follows:

1. F is correctly sized in the absence of both contemporaneous and serial correlation but is missized in the presence of either contemporaneous or serial correlation. Serial correlation pushes empirical size above nominal size, but contemporaneous correlation pushes empirical size *drastically* below nominal size. In combination, and particularly for large ρ and θ, contemporaneous correlation dominates and F is undersized.

2. MGN is designed to remain unaffected by contemporaneous correlation and therefore remains correctly sized so long as $\theta = 0$. Serial correlation, however, pushes empirical size above nominal size.

3. As expected, MR is robust to contemporaneous and serial correlation in large samples, but it is oversized in small samples in the presence of serial correlation. The asymptotic distribution obtains rather quickly, however, resulting in approximately correct size for $T > 64$.

4. The behavior of S_1 is similar to that of MR. S_1 is robust to contemporaneous and serial correlation in large samples, but it is oversized in small samples, with nominal and empirical size converging a bit more slowly than for MR.

5. The Bonferroni bounds associated with S_2 and S_3 work well, with nominal and empirical size in close agreement throughout. Moreover, the asymptotics on which S_{2a} and S_{3a} depend obtain quickly.

Now consider the case of non-Gaussian forecast errors. The striking and readily apparent result is that F, MGN, and MR are drastically missized in large as well as small samples. S_1, S_{2a}, and S_{3a}, on the other hand, maintain approximately correct size for all but the very small sample sizes. In those cases, S_2 and S_3 continue to perform well. The results are well summarized by Figure 19.1, which charts the dependence of F, MGN, MR, and S_1 on T for the non-Gaussian case with $\rho = \theta = .5$.

TABLE 19.1
Empirical Size under Quadratic Loss, Test Statistic F

T	ρ	Gaussian $\theta = .0$	$\theta = .5$	$\theta = .9$	Fat-Tailed $\theta = .0$	$\theta = .5$	$\theta = .9$
8	.0	9.85	12.14	14.10	14.28	15.76	17.21
8	.5	7.02	9.49	11.42	9.61	11.64	13.02
8	.9	.58	1.26	1.86	.57	1.13	1.79
16	.0	9.83	12.97	14.85	16.47	18.59	19.78
16	.5	7.30	10.11	11.89	11.14	13.55	14.94
16	.9	.47	.99	1.55	.34	.70	1.13
32	.0	9.88	12.68	14.34	18.06	19.55	20.35
32	.5	6.98	9.50	11.22	21.30	21.00	21.37
32	.9	.23	.55	1.00	.01	.07	.23
64	.0	9.71	13.05	14.62	29.84	29.72	29.96
64	.5	6.48	9.25	10.62	23.48	23.93	24.15
64	.9	.16	.47	.79	.02	.12	.29
128	.0	10.30	13.41	14.99	30.34	30.95	31.26
128	.5	7.01	10.13	11.64	24.89	25.01	25.16
128	.9	.16	.50	.74	.11	.44	.73
256	.0	10.01	13.05	14.65	31.07	31.12	31.24
256	.5	7.37	10.31	11.78	25.48	25.45	25.70
256	.9	.19	.51	.80	.51	1.13	1.44
512	.0	10.22	13.51	15.25	31.45	32.38	32.60
512	.5	7.53	10.16	11.49	26.35	26.92	16.95
512	.9	.18	.50	.85	.81	1.58	2.06

Note: T is sample size, ρ is the contemporaneous correlation between the innovations underlying the forecast errors, and θ is the coefficient of the MA(1) forecast error. All tests are at the 10% level. 10,000 Monte Carlo replications are performed.

4. An Empirical Example

We shall illustrate the practical use of the tests with an application to exchange-rate forecasting. The series to be forecast, measured monthly, is the three-month change in the nominal dollar/Dutch guilder end-of-

TABLE 19.2
Empirical Size under Quadratic Loss, Test Statistic MGN

T	ρ	Gaussian			Fat-Tailed		
		$\theta = .0$	$\theta = .5$	$\theta = .9$	$\theta = .0$	$\theta = .5$	$\theta = .9$
8	.0	10.19	14.14	17.94	18.10	21.89	25.65
8	.5	9.96	14.66	18.61	16.00	20.51	24.19
8	.9	9.75	14.53	18.67	11.76	16.31	20.00
16	.0	10.07	14.34	17.54	20.33	24.54	27.08
16	.5	9.56	14.37	17.95	37.15	36.18	25.66
16	.9	10.02	14.70	18.20	12.01	16.76	19.81
32	.0	9.89	15.04	18.00	22.94	26.32	28.72
32	.5	10.08	15.11	17.95	20.23	23.76	26.20
32	.9	9.59	15.32	18.25	12.75	17.78	20.54
64	.0	10.09	15.37	17.99	24.56	28.15	30.00
64	.5	9.95	15.18	18.15	21.10	25.18	27.28
64	.9	10.26	15.67	18.49	12.98	18.09	20.53
128	.0	9.96	15.09	17.59	26.47	29.50	30.94
128	.5	10.23	15.07	17.48	23.62	26.82	28.51
128	.9	10.11	15.05	18.05	14.34	18.89	21.56
256	.0	10.28	15.62	18.37	27.39	30.74	32.46
256	.5	10.60	16.02	18.44	23.81	28.38	30.31
256	.9	10.11	15.48	17.91	14.15	19.43	22.03
512	.0	10.12	15.34	17.68	27.64	30.55	32.14
512	.5	10.05	14.96	17.66	24.10	27.40	29.28
512	.9	9.90	15.09	17.53	14.78	19.16	21.49

Note: T is sample size, ρ is the contemporaneous correlation between the innovations underlying the forecast errors, and θ is the coefficient of the MA(1) forecast error. All tests are at the 10% level. 10,000 Monte Carlo replications are performed.

month spot exchange rate (in U.S. cents, noon, New York interbank), from 1977.01 to 1991.12. We assess two forecasts, the "no change" (0) forecast associated with a random-walk model and the forecast implicit in the three-month forward rate (the difference between the three-month forward rate and the spot rate).

TABLE 19.3
Empirical Size under Quadratic Loss, Test Statistic MR

		Gaussian			Fat-Tailed		
T	ρ	$\theta = .0$	$\theta = .5$	$\theta = .9$	$\theta = .0$	$\theta = .5$	$\theta = .9$
8	.0	9.67	19.33	22.45	16.16	25.26	27.62
8	.5	9.50	19.00	22.07	14.81	24.50	26.99
8	.9	9.66	19.51	22.85	11.23	21.28	24.14
16	.0	9.62	13.92	14.72	19.94	22.56	23.06
16	.5	10.02	13.88	14.96	17.70	21.04	21.26
16	.9	10.04	13.82	14.94	11.76	15.68	16.70
32	.0	9.96	10.98	11.12	22.78	22.86	21.72
32	.5	9.68	11.46	11.66	19.78	20.32	20.14
32	.9	9.86	11.62	11.96	12.42	13.54	13.46
64	.0	10.32	11.02	11.04	24.50	22.60	21.58
64	.5	9.84	10.56	10.64	21.44	19.48	18.84
64	.9	9.58	10.58	10.34	13.38	13.38	13.20
128	.0	9.78	10.54	10.44	25.86	22.90	21.54
128	.5	10.02	11.04	11.18	22.76	20.26	19.44
128	.9	10.76	11.28	11.38	13.44	13.52	12.92
256	.0	10.04	9.90	9.58	27.16	23.74	22.70
256	.5	10.32	9.92	9.82	24.00	20.50	19.18
256	.9	9.92	10.16	10.34	13.38	12.70	12.24
512	.0	9.94	10.48	10.56	26.92	23.40	21.78
512	.5	9.52	10.56	10.48	23.56	20.52	19.36
512	.9	9.80	9.82	9.88	13.96	12.98	12.74

Note: T is sample size, ρ is the contemporaneous correlation between the innovations underlying the forecast errors, and θ is the coefficient of the MA(1) forecast error. All tests are at the 10% level. At least 5,000 Monte Carlo replications are performed.

The actual and predicted changes are shown in Figure 19.2. The random-walk forecast, of course, is just constant at 0, whereas the forward market forecast moves over time. The movements in both forecasts, however, are dwarfed by the realized movements in exchange rates.

TABLE 19.4

Empirical Size under Quadratic Loss, Test Statistic S_1

T	ρ	Gaussian			Fat-Tailed		
		$\theta = .0$	$\theta = .5$	$\theta = .9$	$\theta = .0$	$\theta = .5$	$\theta = .9$
8	.0	31.39	31.10	31.03	31.62	29.51	29.07
8	.5	31.37	30.39	29.93	31.21	29.71	29.36
8	.9	31.08	30.19	30.18	31.18	30.12	29.75
16	.0	20.39	19.11	18.94	19.26	18.50	18.32
16	.5	20.43	19.52	18.86	19.57	17.67	17.63
16	.9	20.90	19.55	19.59	20.15	18.38	18.16
32	.0	12.42	12.28	12.18	11.30	11.64	11.56
32	.5	13.32	13.22	12.94	11.54	10.66	10.84
32	.9	12.60	13.38	13.22	11.16	11.22	11.50
64	.0	12.47	12.11	11.94	12.44	11.62	11.36
64	.5	12.76	12.49	12.35	12.10	12.26	12.10
64	.9	12.21	12.23	12.03	13.00	12.36	12.16
128	.0	11.72	11.94	12.04	11.48	10.72	10.28
128	.5	11.44	11.72	11.60	10.84	10.96	10.96
128	.9	11.76	11.26	11.34	11.50	10.66	10.86
256	.0	11.11	10.65	10.66	12.06	11.67	11.79
256	.5	10.90	10.39	10.48	12.16	11.46	11.60
256	.9	10.69	10.79	10.75	11.51	11.59	11.16
512	.0	11.15	10.67	10.63	10.06	9.46	9.62
512	.5	10.90	10.39	10.49	9.94	9.66	9.76
512	.9	10.31	10.09	10.05	10.12	10.12	10.06

Note: T is sample size, ρ is the contemporaneous correlation between the innovations underlying the forecast errors, and θ is the coefficient of the MA(1) forecast error. All tests are at the 10% level. At least 5,000 Monte Carlo replications are performed.

We shall assess the forecasts' accuracy under absolute error loss. In terms of point estimates, the random-walk forecast is more accurate. The mean absolute error of the random-walk forecast is 1.42, as opposed to 1.53 for the forward market forecast; as one hears so often, "The random walk wins." The loss-differential series is shown in Figure 19.3, in which no obvious nonstationarities are visually apparently.

TABLE 19.5
Empirical Size under Quadratic Loss, Test Statistics S_2 and S_{2a}

T	ρ	Gaussian			Fat-Tailed		
		$\theta = .0$	$\theta = .5$	$\theta = .9$	$\theta = .0$	$\theta = .5$	$\theta = .9$
		S_2, nominal size = 25%					
8	.0	22.24	22.48	22.38	23.94	23.46	23.34
8	.5	22.14	23.46	22.16	23.08	24.80	23.06
8	.9	22.24	23.02	22.66	22.92	23.26	22.86
		S_2, nominal size = 14.08%					
16	.0	13.46	13.26	13.14	13.62	13.06	13.76
16	.5	14.22	13.46	12.92	13.70	13.24	13.62
16	.9	13.08	13.84	13.28	12.86	13.06	13.20
		S_2, nominal size = 15.36%					
32	.0	14.36	14.52	14.28	14.54	14.32	14.30
32	.5	14.36	14.06	13.94	15.08	14.36	15.02
32	.9	14.68	14.62	13.46	14.94	14.76	14.52
		S_{2a}, nominal size = 10%					
64	.0	9.72	9.92	9.42	9.68	10.36	10.44
64	.5	9.66	10.34	9.68	9.52	10.06	10.00
64	.9	10.84	9.46	10.34	9.40	8.98	10.02
		S_{2a}, nominal size = 10%					
128	.0	11.62	11.62	11.84	12.22	12.20	11.42
128	.5	11.66	11.62	11.90	12.06	11.94	11.44
128	.9	11.22	11.72	11.28	12.06	10.76	11.40

Note: T is sample size, ρ is the contemporaneous correlation between the innovations underlying the forecast errors, and θ is the coefficient of the MA(1) forecast error. At least 5,000 Monte Carlo replications are performed.

Approximate stationarity is also supported by the sample autocorrelation function of the loss differential, shown in Figure 19.4, which decays quickly.

Because the forecasts are three-step-ahead, our earlier arguments suggest the need to allow for at least two-dependent forecast errors, which may translate into a two-dependent loss differential. This intuition is confirmed by the sample autocorrelation function of the loss differential, in which sizable and significant sample autocorrelations appear at lags 1 and 2 and nowhere else. The Box–Pierce χ^2 test of

TABLE 19.6
Empirical Size under Quadratic Loss, Test Statistics S_3 and S_{3a}

T	ρ	Gaussian			Fat-Tailed		
		$\theta = .0$	$\theta = .5$	$\theta = .9$	$\theta = .0$	$\theta = .5$	$\theta = .9$
		S_3, nominal size = 25%					
8	.0	22.50	22.92	22.90	23.26	23.34	21.96
8	.5	22.98	22.26	23.06	23.42	23.86	22.88
8	.9	23.16	22.36	24.24	24.26	23.32	23.34
		S_3, nominal size = 10.92%					
16	.0	10.62	10.06	10.40	10.16	10.42	9.84
16	.5	10.38	10.92	10.32	10.54	10.94	10.34
16	.9	10.64	10.18	9.62	10.58	10.96	10.64
		S_3, nominal size = 10.12%					
32	.0	10.72	10.28	9.30	9.90	10.00	9.98
32	.5	10.56	10.00	10.02	10.40	10.64	10.30
32	.9	10.92	10.44	10.30	10.46	9.96	10.70
		S_{3a}, nominal size = 10%					
64	.0	9.38	9.54	9.16	9.64	9.24	8.84
64	.5	9.80	10.02	9.66	9.58	8.82	8.78
64	.9	9.90	9.24	9.68	9.92	9.78	10.00
		S_{3a}, nominal size = 10%					
128	.0	9.94	9.70	9.12	9.82	9.04	8.46
128	.5	9.52	10.00	9.32	10.08	9.24	9.20
128	.9	9.46	9.64	9.42	9.28	9.22	9.26

Note: T is sample size, ρ is the contemporaneous correlation between the innovations underlying the forecast errors, and θ is the coefficient of the MA(1) forecast error. At least 5,000 Monte Carlo replications are performed.

jointly zero autocorrelations at lags 1 through 15 is 51.12, which is highly significant relative to its asymptotic null distribution of χ^2_{15}. Conversely, the Box–Pierce χ^2 test of jointly zero autocorrelations at lags 3 through 15 is 12.79, which is insignificant relative to its null distribution of χ^2_{13}.

We now proceed to test the null of equal expected loss. F, MGN, and MR are inapplicable because one or more of their maintained assumptions are explicitly violated. We therefore focus on our test statistic S_1, setting the truncation lag at two in light of the preceding discussion. We

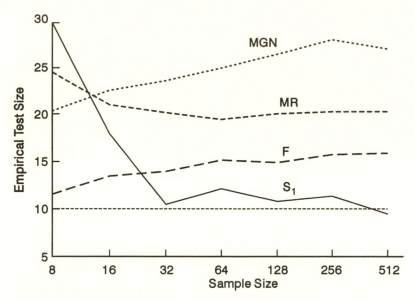

Fig. 19.1. Empirical size, four test statistics: fat-tailed case; theta = rho = .5.

obtain $S_1 = -1.3$, implying a p value of .19. Thus, for the sample at hand, we do not reject at conventional levels the hypothesis of equal expected absolute error—the forward rate is not a statistically significantly worse predictor of the future spot rate than is the current spot rate.

5. Conclusions and Directions for Future Research

We have proposed several tests of the null hypothesis of equal forecast accuracy. We allow the forecast errors to be non-Gaussian, nonzero mean, serially correlated, and contemporaneously correlated. Perhaps most importantly, our tests are applicable under a very wide variety of loss structures.

We hasten to add that comparison of forecast accuracy is but one of many diagnostics that should be examined when comparing models. Moreover, the superiority of a particular model in terms of forecast accuracy does not necessarily imply that forecasts from other models contain no additional information. That, of course, is the well-known message of the forecast combination and encompassing literatures; see,

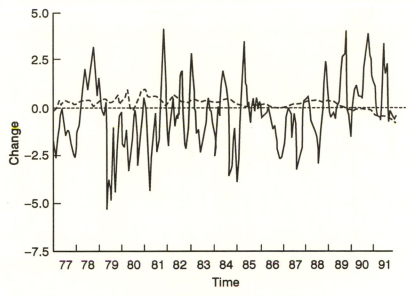

Fig. 19.2. Actual and Predicted Exchange-Rate Changes. The solid line is the actual exchange-rate change. The short dashed line is the predicted change from the random-walk model, and the long dashed line is the predicted change implied by the forward rate.

for example, Clemen (1989), Chong and Hendry (1986), and Fair and Shiller (1990).

Several extensions of the results presented here appear to be promising directions for future research. Some are obvious, such as generalization to comparison of more than two forecasts or, perhaps most generally, multiple forecasts for each of multiple variables. Others are less obvious and more interesting. We shall list just a few:

    1. Our framework may be broadened to examine not only whether forecast loss differentials have nonzero mean but also whether other variables may explain loss differentials. For example, one could regress the loss differential not only on a constant but also on a "stage of the business cycle" indicator to assess the extent to which relative predictive performance differs over the cycle.

    2. The ability to formally compare predictive accuracy afforded by our tests may prove useful as a model-specification diagnostic, as well as a means to test both nested and nonnested hypotheses under nonstandard conditions, in the tradition of Ashley, Granger, and Schmalensee (1980) and Mariano and Brown (1983).

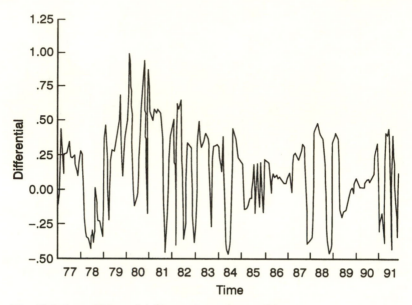

Fig. 19.3. Loss differential (forward–random walk).

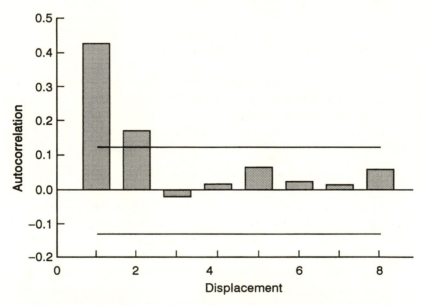

Fig. 19.4. Loss Differential Autocorrelations. The first eight sample autocorrelations are graphed, together with Bartlett's approximate 95% confidence interval.

3. Explicit account may be taken of the effects of uncertainty associated with estimated model parameters on the behavior of the test statistics, as shown by West (1994).

Let us provide some examples of the ideas sketched in 2. First, consider the development of a test of exclusion restrictions in time series regression that is valid *regardless* of whether the data are stationary or cointegrated. The desirability of such a test is apparent from works like those of Stock and Watson (1989), Christiano and Eichenbaum (1990), Rudebusch (1993), and Toda and Phillips (1993), in which it is simultaneously apparent that (a) it is difficult to determine reliably the integration status of macroeconomic time series and (b) the conclusions of macroeconometric studies are often critically dependent on the integration status of the relevant time series. One may proceed by noting that tests of exclusion restrictions amount to comparisons of restricted and unrestricted sums of squares. This suggests estimating the restricted and unrestricted models using part of the available data and then using our test of equality of the mean squared errors of the respective one-step-ahead forecasts.

As a second example, it would appear that our test is applicable in nonstandard testing situations, such as when a nuisance parameter is not identified under the null. This occurs, for example, when testing for the appropriate number of states in Hamilton's (1989) Markov-switching model. In spite of the fact that standard tests are inapplicable, certainly the null and alternative models may be estimated and their out-of-sample forecasting performance compared rigorously, as shown by Engel (1994).

In closing, we note that this article is part of a larger research program aimed at doing model selection, estimation, prediction, and evaluation using the relevant loss function, whatever that loss function may be. This article has addressed evaluation. Granger (1969) and Christoffersen and Diebold (1994) addressed prediction. These results, together with those of Weiss and Andersen (1984) and Weiss (1991, 1994) on estimation under the relevant loss function will make feasible recursive, real-time, prediction-based model selection under the relevant loss function.

References

Andrews, D. W. K. (1991), "Heteroskedasticity and Autocorrelation Consistent Covariance Matrix Estimation," *Econometrica*, 59, 817–858.

Ashley, R. (1994), "Postsample Model Validation and Inference Made Feasible," unpublished manuscript, Virginia Polytechnic Institute, Dept. of Economics.

Ashley, R., Granger, C. W. J., and Schmalensee, R. (1980), "Advertising and Aggregate Consumption: An Analysis of Causality," *Econometrica*, 48, 1149–1167.

Brockwell, P. J., and Davis, R. A. (1992), *Time Series: Theory and Methods* (2nd ed.), New York: Springer-Verlag.

Campbell, B., and Ghysels, E. (1995), "Is the Outcome of the Federal Budget Process Unbiased and Efficient? A Nonparametric Assessment," *Review of Economics and Statistics*, 77, 17–31.

Chinn, M., and Meese, R. A. (1991), "Banking on Currency Forecasts: Is Change in Money Predictable?" unpublished manuscript, University of California, Berkeley, Graduate School of Business.

Chong, Y. Y., and Hendry, D. F. (1986), "Econometric Evaluation of Linear Macroeconomic Models," *Review of Economic Studies*, 53, 671–690.

Christiano, L., and Eichenbaum, M. (1990), "Unit Roots in Real GNP: Do We Know, and Do We Care?" *Carnegie-Rochester Conference Series on Public Policy*, 32, 7–61.

Christoffersen, P., and Diebold, F. X. (1994), "Optimal Prediction Under Asymmetric Loss," Technical Working Paper 167, National Bureau of Economic Research, Cambridge, MA.

Clemen, R. T. (1989), "Combining Forecasts: A Review and Annotated Bibliography" (with discussion), *International Journal of Forecasting*, 5, 559–583.

Clements, M. P., and Hendry, D. T. (1993), "On the Limitations of Comparing Mean Square Forecast Errors" (with discussion), *Journal of Forecasting*, 12, 617–676.

Cumby, R. E., and Modest, D. M. (1987), "Testing for Market Timing Ability: A Framework for Forecast Evaluation," *Journal of Financial Economics*, 19, 169–189.

Diebold, F. X., and Rudebusch, G. D. (1991), "Forecasting Output with the Composite Leading Index: An Ex Ante Analysis," *Journal of the American Statistical Association*, 86, 603–610.

Dhrymes, P. J., Howrey, E. P., Hymans, S. H., Kmenta, J., Leamer, E. E., Quandt, R. E., Ramsey, J. B., Shapiro, H. T., and Zarnowitz, V. (1972), "Criteria for Evaluation of Econometric Models," *Annals of Economic and Social Measurement*, 1, 291–324.

Engel, C. (1994), "Can the Markov Switching Model Forecast Exchange Rates" *Journal of International Economics*, 36, 151–165.

Engle, R. F., and Kozicki, S. (1993), "Testing for Common Features," *Journal of Business & Economic Statistics*, 11, 369–395.

Fair, R. C., and Shiller, R. J. (1990), "Comparing Information in Forecasts From Econometric Models," *American Economic Review*, 80, 375–389.

Granger, C. W. J. (1969), "Prediction With a Generalized Cost of Error Function," *Operational Research Quarterly*, 20, 199–207.

Granger, C. W. J., and Newbold, P. (1977), *Forecasting Economic Time Series*, Orlando, FL: Academic Press.

Hamilton, J. D. (1989), "A New Approach to the Economic Analysis of Nonstationary Time Series and the Business Cycle," *Econometrica*, 57, 357–384.

Hannan, E. J. (1970), *Multiple Time Series*, New York: John Wiley.

Hogg, R. V., and Craig, A. T. (1978), *Introduction to Mathematical Statistics* (4th ed.), New York: MacMillan.

Howrey, E. P., Klein, L. R., and McCarthy, M. D. (1974), "Notes on Testing the Predictive Performance of Econometric Models," *International Economic Review*, 15, 366–383.

Kendall, M., and Stuart, A. (1979), *The Advanced Theory of Statistics* (Vol. 2, 4th ed.), New York: Oxford University Press.

Lehmann, E. L. (1975), *Nonparametrics: Statistical Methods Based on Ranks*, San Francisco: Holden-Day.

Leitch, G., and Tanner, J. E. (1991), "Econometric Forecast Evaluation: Profits Versus the Conventional Error Measures," *American Economic Review*, 81, 580–590.

Mariano, R. S., and Brown, B. W. (1983), "Prediction-Based Test for Misspecification in Nonlinear Simultaneous Systems," in *Studies in Econometrics, Time Series and Multivariate Statistics, Essays in Honor of T. W. Anderson*, eds. T. Amemiya, S. Karlin, and L. Goodman, New York: Academic Press, pp. 131–151.

Mark, N. (1995), "Exchange Rates and Fundamentals: Evidence on Long-Horizon Predictability," *American Economic Review*, 85, 201–218.

McCulloch, R., and Rossi, P. E. (1990), "Posterior, Predictive, and Utility-Based Approaches to Testing the Arbitrage Pricing Theory," *Journal of Financial Economics*, 28, 7–38.

Meese, R. A., and Rogoff, K. (1988), "Was it Real? The Exchange Rate-Interest Differential Relation Over the Modern Floating-Rate Period," *Journal of Finance*, 43, 933–948.

Mizrach, B. (1991), "Forecast Comparison in L_2," unpublished manuscript, Wharton School, University of Pennsylvania, Dept. of Finance.

Morgan, W. A. (1939–1940), "A Test for Significance of the Difference Between the Two Variances in a Sample From a Normal Bivariate Population," *Biometrika*, 31, 13–19.

Newey, W., and West, K. (1987), "A Simple, Positive Semi-Definite, Heteroskedasticity and Autocorrelation Consistent Covariance Matrix," *Econometrica*, 55, 703–708.

Priestley, M. B. (1981), *Spectral Analysis and Time Series*, New York: Academic Press.

Rudebusch, G. D. (1993), "The Uncertain Unit Root in Real GNP," *American Economic Review*, 83, 264–272.

Stock, J. H., and Watson, M. W. (1989), "Interpreting the Evidence on Money-Income Causality," *Journal of Econometrics*, 40, 161–181.

Toda, H. Y., and Phillips, P. C. B. (1993), "Vector Autoregression and Causality," *Econometrica*, 61, 1367–1393.

Vuong, Q. H. (1989), "Likelihood Ratio Tests for Model Selection and Nonnested Hypotheses," *Econometrica*, 57, 307–334.

Weiss, A. A. (1991), "Multi-step Estimation and Forecasting in Dynamic Models," *Journal of Econometrics*, 48, 135–149.

—— (1994), "Estimating Time Series Models Using the Relevant Cost Function," unpublished manuscript, University of Southern California, Dept. of
Economics.

Weiss, A. A., and Andersen, A. P. (1984), "Estimating Forecasting Models
Using the Relevant Forecast Evaluation Criterion," *Journal of the Royal
Statistical Society*, Ser. A, 137, 484–487.

West, K. D. (1994), "Asymptotic Inference About Predictive Ability," SSRI
Working Paper 9417, University of Wisconsin-Madison, Dept. of Economics.

West, K. D., Edison, H. J., and Cho, D. (1993), "A Utility-Based Comparison of
Some Models of Exchange Rate Volatility," *Journal of International Economics*, 35, 23–46.

Name Index